W9-BPK-405

SCHLIEMANN
OF TROY

SCHLIEMANN OF TROY

Treasure and Deceit

DAVID A. TRAILL

St. Martin's Press ❧ New York

SCHLIEMANN OF TROY: TREASURE AND DECEIT. Copyright © 1995 by David A. Traill. All rights reserved. Printed in the United States of America. No part of this book may be used or reproduced in any manner whatsoever without written permission except in the case of brief quotations embodied in critical articles or reviews. For information, address St. Martin's Press, 175 Fifth Avenue, New York, N.Y. 10010.

Library of Congress Cataloging-in-Publication Data

Traill, David A.
    Schliemann of Troy : treasure and deceit / by David A. Traill.
      p.   cm.
    Includes bibliographical references and index.
    ISBN 0-312-14042-8
    1. Schliemann, Heinrich, 1822–1890. 2. Archaeologists—Greece—
Biography. 3. Archaeologists—Germany—Biography. 4. Truthfulness
and falsehood. I. Title.
DF212.S4T724 1996
930.1'092—dc20
  [B]   95-40767
                                           CIP

First published in Great Britain by John Murray (Publishers) Ltd.

First U.S. Edition: December 1995
10 9 8 7 6 5 4 3 2 1

To
Vivienne, Laurie, Jonty and Vanessa
Alan and Amanda
Douglas, Catriona and Sarah

Contents

Illustrations

YUGOSLAVIA

ALBANIA

Thessaloniki

CORFU
(KERKYRA)

Larissa

I O N I A N

Prevesa

LEUKAS

A E G E

E U B O E A

Lamia

__Thermopylae__

Mt *Parnassos*   __Orchomenos__

__Delphi__

Levadia

CEPHALONIA   ITHACA

Thebes

Patras

Marathon

Salamis   *Athens*

Corinth

S E A

__Old Corinth__

Piraeus

ZAKYNTHOS   __Olympia__   __Mantinea__

__Mycenae__

Argos

Sounion

Tiryns

N

Tripolis   PELOPONNESE   *Nauplion*

Megalopolis

Sparta

Pylos

Bay of   *Kalamata*
Navarino

KYTHERA

M E D I T E R R A N

Chania

Ancient sites thus
__Delphi__

Greece and Western Turkey (for detail of boxed area see over)

TURKEY

Constantinople
(Istanbul)

SAMOTHRACE

Çanakkale (Dardanelles)
Ren Kioi (Erenkoy)

Troy
Ezine

Alexandria
Troas   Assos

TURKEY

LESBOS

CHIOS

Smyrna
(Izmir)

A
N

S
E

MYKONOS
DELOS
CYCLADES
PAROS
NAXOS

THERA
THERASSIA   DODECANESE   RHODES

E   A   N   S   E   A

Heraklion
Knossos
R   E   T   E

0   0
25
60   50
120   75
100
180   125
240   150
kilometres   miles

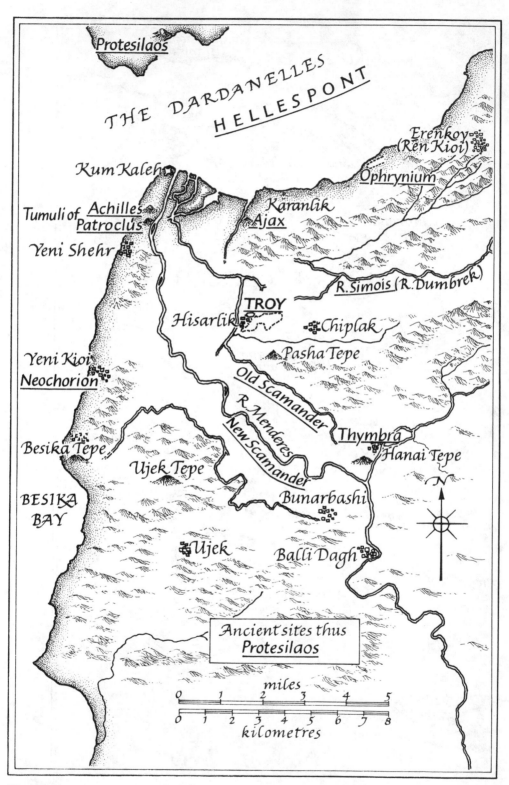

The Troad

Preface

More than a century after his death the career and character of Heinrich Schliemann continue to have important repercussions. The recent resurfacing in Moscow of 'Priam's Treasure' and other Trojan objects given to Germany by Schliemann and long presumed lost raises a complex array of legal problems about the restoration of art treasures and the spoils of war. But it also raises questions about how Schliemann came to possess these pieces in the first place. These questions have, in many cases, not been seriously asked before. This book provides some of the surprising answers.

After writing articles about Schliemann for more than a decade, principally for a scholarly audience, I decided a few years ago to bring my findings as well as my questions to a broader public. While studying Schliemann's letters to his British publisher, John Murray, at 50 Albemarle Street, where the firm's offices are still located in the building they occupied in Schliemann's day, I was asked if I would be interested in publishing my proposed biography with John Murray. I was delighted to accept the offer. The association has been a happy one and I am extremely grateful, in particular, to Grant McIntyre and Kate Chenevix Trench for their ready assistance, wise counsel and remarkable patience.

No one can go very far in studying Schliemann without delving into the vast Schliemann Archive in the Gennadius Library of the American School of Classical Studies, Athens. I am much indebted to the library's directors and staff over the past fifteen years for their courteous assistance in providing access to these papers. In particular, I am very grateful to the present director, David Jordan, for granting permission to publish a considerable number of passages from the letters and diaries, which appear here in print for the first time. I am grateful too to other institutions which kindly let me examine their archives and have granted permission to publish excerpts: the British Library, London; the Bodleian Library, Oxford; the Mitchell Library, Glasgow; the Deutsches Archäologisches Institut, Berlin. Over many years the Committee on Research of the University of California at Davis has supported my work on Schliemann with a series of research grants. Unfailingly generous and helpful on a wide variety of topics has been my friend and colleague, William M. Calder III, of the University of Illinois, Champaign-Urbana, whose encyclopaedic knowledge of the history of classical studies in the nineteenth century I have often tapped. Others to whom I am indebted include George Korres, Wilfried Bölke, Joachim Herrmann, Lesley Fitton, Donald Easton, David Gill, Mark Lehrer, Lynn Roller, Samuel Foulk, and my student assistant, Michael McArthur.

SCHLIEMANN
OF TROY

1

The Current Controversy

One of the great values of studying the history of archaeology is to realize that it is not a simple straightforward record of discovery; it is a record of discovery mixed with false assumptions and forgery and the refusal of established archaeologists to regard their work historically.

Glyn Daniel, *Towards a History of Archaeology*

T HE SUBJECT OF INNUMERABLE biographies, novels, encyclopaedia articles, plays and even an opera, Heinrich Schliemann is one of those nineteenth-century figures who packed so much into their lives that we are overwhelmed with admiration and a sense of our own inadequacy. Before the advent of aircraft made international travel fast and comparatively easy, Schliemann travelled to Saigon, Jerusalem, the Yosemite Valley, Tokyo, New Orleans, Havana, Calcutta, Tunis, Veracruz, the Niagara Falls, Hong Kong, Petra, Odessa, Luxor, San Francisco and Acapulco; the more obvious places like Paris, Rome and London he visited practically every year. He was a consummate businessman, who made several fortunes for himself: buying gold dust from the miners in Sacramento, dealing in commodities in St Petersburg, acquiring and renting prime property in Paris, investing in American and Cuban railways and Brazilian bonds, to name but a few of his activities. He could speak and write fluently in more than a dozen languages. He knew large sections of the Koran (in Arabic) by heart. But it is not for these achievements that he is world famous. His presence still looms over the discipline which he did so much to create. His life, filled with glamour and romance, is familiar to everyone with even a slight interest in archaeology.

When he was eight years old he was captivated by the stories of the Trojan War and resolved that one day he would excavate Troy. He devoted the early part of his life to commerce in order to earn enough money to be able to realize his childhood dream. At last, in his mid-forties he went to Paris to study

1

archaeology. On a trip to the plain of Troy in 1868 he reached, on the mound of Hisarlik, the historic decision that here, not at Bunarbashi (Pinarbashi), as most scholars then believed, was the site of Homer's Troy. Soon after this he set about proving his theory by the evidence of his spade – the first seeker of Troy to take this practical step. His theory received dramatic confirmation at the end of May 1873, when, with the help of his wife Sophia, he discovered a large treasure on the city wall, which he called 'Priam's Treasure'. In 1876 at Mycenae, again with the help of his wife, Schliemann excavated gold masks and masses of other jewellery from the mud of the Shaft Graves. In one of the graves he found a mummy wearing a gold mask, which he ripped off and, finding the remains of a human face underneath, telegraphed the King of Greece. 'I have gazed on the face of Agamemnon,' he said. The gold mask he called the 'Mask of Agamemnon' and it is still known by that name.

These highlights form part of the essential picture of Schliemann as he is known to archaeologists and the general public alike. Recent research, however, has shown that every statement in the preceding paragraph is false. How has so much misinformation about so important a figure gained such widespread acceptance? Much of it is attributable to Schliemann's own writings, though sometimes, as in the case of the telegram to King George, the fictionalizing tendencies of his biographers are to blame.[1] Part of the problem too, as Glyn Daniel suggests, is due to the lack of a serious interest among professional archaeologists in the history of their discipline.[2]

Schliemann's excavations at Troy and Mycenae in the last quarter of the nineteenth century brought him enduring fame. His astonishing discoveries at these and other Homeric sites seemed to many to confirm the historical reality of the Trojan War and to demonstrate that the world of heroes had indeed existed much as Homer described it. Schliemann claimed, rightly, to have opened up a whole new world for archaeology. The gold jewellery he unearthed at Mycenae bore eloquent testimony to a society of remarkable wealth, skill, and sophistication that had inhabited Greece a thousand years before Socrates. Before Schliemann, no one had dreamed of its existence. Unquestionably, these are great and lasting achievements.

Thanks to the sensational nature of his discoveries and his skill in self-advertisement, Schliemann quickly became a celebrity of worldwide renown. The general public was easily won over, but scholarly reaction was more sceptical. Some scholars saw the importance of his work and lent their enthusiastic support. A surprising number, however, were vociferous in their opposition. Some maintained, for instance, that the artefacts unearthed at Mycenae and Tiryns belonged to the Byzantine period. Others said that Schliemann was a charlatan who had salted his sites with purchased or manufactured pieces. Many of these criticisms were quickly and effectively discredited, so that in the last few years of his life Schliemann was an almost universally respected figure.

In the century since his death, the reliability of Schliemann's archaeological work has been confirmed both in its broad outlines and in a myriad of details by subsequent excavators at Mycenae, Tiryns and Troy, and, more generally, by the work of countless archaeologists at Bronze Age sites in Greece and throughout the Aegean. Consequently, Schliemann's reputation among archaeologists has tended to rise since his death. To the charge frequently brought by non-professionals that Schliemann excavated too much, too quickly, thereby destroying a great deal of valuable evidence, professionals reply that it is anachronistic to criticize Schliemann for not showing the painstaking care and circumspection that are expected of archaeologists today.

In the past twenty years, however, Schliemann has once again become a controversial figure. The famous excavator of Troy and Mycenae has been called a pathological liar. He has once again been accused of falsifying his excavation reports, of purchasing ancient artefacts and claiming to have found them in his own excavations, of salting his sites with pieces of gold jewellery, which were then 'excavated' in the presence of witnesses. It has been suggested that hundreds of objects which he excavated in Mycenae and which are now on display in the National Museum at Athens may be fakes. Among the pieces whose authenticity has been questioned is the famous 'Mask of Agamemnon' itself. Believed by most scholars to be two or three centuries too early to be that of the Homeric hero, is it rather some twenty-five centuries too late?

Most, though by no means all, of these charges have come from non-archaeologists. The reaction from archaeologists has been mixed. Many, particularly younger archaeologists, have welcomed the new evidence and have agreed that there is a need for a fundamental reassessment of Schliemann's work. For the most part, however, the archaeological establishment has been hostile to the new discoveries. A former President of the Archaeological Institute of America criticized recent research on Schliemann as 'psychological warfare' and a 'vendetta against Schliemann which threatens to obscure his archaeological achievements.'[3] Another prominent American archaeologist called the revelations 'a mean-spirited scholarly enterprise – particularly when aimed at one who can no longer defend himself.'[4] A leading expert in Mycenaean studies at the University of London, while conceding that Schliemann's virtues were tainted with 'baseness', has suggested that the scholars who have drawn attention to his shortcomings are even more reprehensible, for they exemplify 'baseness' unaccompanied 'by any redeeming virtues'![5]

What makes Schliemann and his work a century after his death such an emotional issue? At least part of the answer lies in the almost mythic nature of the persona created by Schliemann in his autobiography and elaborated by his biographers. Countless readers have been inspired by the story of his life. It is the quintessence of romanticism: how he had to put aside his childhood dream of excavating Troy in order to earn the means to accomplish it, and how after thirty years in commerce he was finally able to devote his energies to the task and triumphantly disprove the pedants who argued that Troy was a mere figment of Homer's imagination. In May 1886 a student of Worcester College, Oxford, wrote to Schliemann: 'There is no book outside of the Bible which has exercised so good an influence on my life as your own autobiography in *Ilios*. It shows an example of right and successful living which I make known as widely as possible among my own circle of friends.'[6]

Among more eminent readers of Schliemann's life, Gladstone and Freud were both profoundly affected by it. Freud considered Schliemann the man whose life he most envied.[7] In Germany Schliemann's autobiography was widely read, providing young people with a model of a man who, through determination and hard work, succeeded in achieving his childhood dream. Scholars have not been immune to the spell. Most of today's archaeologists heard or read about Schliemann's extraordinary life and achievements in their youth, for some account of his life has found a hallowed place in most introductory courses on classical archaeology over the past century. It is scarcely surprising if many should find the recent revelations unwelcome.

The central issue in the present controversy is Schliemann's own truthfulness. It is now conceded by almost everyone who has examined the evidence that Schliemann's autobiographical writings are tainted with falsehoods. Let us examine one of these in some detail. In his autobiographical introduction to *Ilios*, Schliemann relates the following incident:

Though my father was neither a scholar nor an archaeologist, he had a passion for ancient history. He often told me with warm enthusiasm of the tragic fate of Herculaneum and Pompeii, and seemed to consider him the luckiest of men who had the means and the time to visit the excavations which were then going on there. He also related to me with admiration the great deeds of the Homeric heroes and the events of the Trojan war, always finding in me a warm defender of the Trojan cause. With great grief I heard from him that Troy had been so completely destroyed that it had disappeared without leaving any traces of its existence. My joy may be imagined therefore, when, being nearly eight years old, I received from him, in 1829, as a Christmas gift, Dr. Georg Ludwig Jerrer's *Universal History*, with an engraving [see Pl. 1] representing Troy in flames, with its huge walls and the Scaean gate, from which Aeneas is escaping, carrying his father Anchises on his back and holding his son Ascanius by the hand; and I cried out, 'Father, you were mistaken: Jerrer must have seen Troy, otherwise he could not have represented it here.' 'My son,' he replied, 'that is merely a fanciful picture.' But to my question, whether ancient Troy had such huge walls as those depicted in the book, he answered in the affirmative. 'Father,' retorted I, 'if such walls once existed, they cannot possibly have been completely destroyed: vast ruins of them must remain, but they are hidden away beneath the dust of ages.' He maintained the contrary, whilst I remained firm in my opinion, and at last we both agreed that I should one day excavate Troy.[8]

A few pages later Schliemann adds:

. . . in the midst of the bustle of business I never forgot Troy, or the agreement I had made with my father and Minna [Heinrich's playmate] in 1830 to excavate it. I loved money indeed, but solely as the means of realizing this great idea of my life.[9]

This conversation with his father is among the best-known biographical 'facts' about Schliemann but is entirely fictitious. There is no mention anywhere of his childhood resolve until *after* the excavation of Troy. We have voluminous letters and diaries of Schliemann from all periods of his adult life, in which he discusses his most intimate concerns. To date no one has found a passage written prior to 1868 in which Schliemann gives an inkling of an interest in excavating Troy. In his prefaces to his American diary (1852) and *Ithaque le Péloponnèse et Troie* (1869) there is no hint of this childhood dream. On the contrary, in the preface to *Ithaque* he is concerned to show how by simply visiting the Homeric sites in 1868 he had fulfilled his lifetime dream: 'At last I was able to realize the dream of my whole life, and to visit at my leisure the scene of those events which had such an intense interest for me, and the country of the heroes whose adventures had delighted and comforted my childhood.'[10] In the same preface Schliemann recounts a different childhood incident: at the age of ten, he gave his father – once again it is a Christmas present – 'a badly-written Latin essay upon the principal events of the Trojan war and the adventures of Ulysses and Agamemnon.'[11] Later, when his fame rested on his achievements as an excavating archaeologist, a new childhood incident was devised to foreshadow these achievements. Hence the memorable story of his conversation with his father in *Ilios*.

By their very nature, of course, autobiographies tend to be self-serving. Only the naïve would expect them to be wholly candid. Moreover, in the nineteenth century the practice of embellishing the facts to give a satisfactory shape to a life seems to have been more widespread and presumably more acceptable than is the case today.[12] We should therefore avoid jumping to the conclusion that because he invented for his autobiography the kind of romantic stories that nineteenth-century readers loved and almost expected of their heroes, he was an unscrupulous liar. On the other hand, fiction should be treated as fiction. Why then do biographers of Schliemann present his childhood conversation with his father as biographical fact?[13] Clearly, if we want to penetrate the cocoon of myth woven by Schliemann and his biographers we need to adopt a more critical attitude to Schliemann's statements about himself than has hitherto been customary.

More disturbing than the fictitious episodes in Schliemann's autobiographical writings is his penchant for fraud. In 1852, when he was in Sacramento buying gold dust from the miners, his business arrangement with Davidson, a banker in San Francisco, broke down amid repeated charges that Schliemann was sending Davidson short-weight consignments of gold dust.[14] In 1859 Schliemann was sued for fraud in his business transactions in St Petersburg.[15] In 1869 he obtained both his American citizenship and his divorce from his Russian wife by bribing witnesses to sign sworn statements which he and they knew to be untrue.[16] As recently as the early 1980s, archaeologists maintained that Schliemann's archaeological work remained uncontaminated by this kind of behaviour.[17] But in 1975, as we shall see, a Greek archaeologist demonstrated that this optimistic view was untenable.[18] The question therefore is no longer *whether* but rather *to what extent* we should distrust Schliemann's archaeological reports.

Truthfulness is expected of all scholars and scientists. In archaeology it is of even greater importance than in most other fields. In the 'hard' sciences the findings of one research team are generally not accepted until they have been replicated in another laboratory. In archaeology, however, there is no second chance. The excavation of, say, a gold vase in a particular corner of a particular site cannot be replicated. Archaeology is therefore entirely dependent, to a degree that is not always appreciated by archaeologists themselves, on the truthfulness of excavators.

There are, of course, particularly nowadays, a number of external restraints. Archaeological digs are conducted by a team of trained specialists. Their collective knowledge of the excavation is a powerful constraint on the director to write an accurate account. Schliemann, however, often excavated with the help of only unskilled workmen and seems to have been free to alter the facts of the excavation in his published reports in ways that would be unthinkable today.

There are also constraints imposed by stratification. No one, for instance, could report finding a coin of Augustus in a Neolithic level without impugning his own credibility or the integrity of the strata excavated. Non-specialists, however, often assume that archaeologists have achieved a greater degree of precision in dating than is actually the case. In some societies, such as Athens of the fifth century BC, where change was comparatively rapid, pottery styles changed rapidly too. This has enabled archaeologists to date potsherds (pottery fragments) from that period with remarkable precision, often to a particular decade. In other societies, such as Troy in the Early Bronze Age, change came very slowly. Most of the pottery from the second earliest occupation level at Troy (Troy II) is virtually indistinguishable from corresponding pieces from immediately succeeding levels (Troy III, IV and V), though the earliest and latest of these occupation levels are separated by 700 years (see Appendix I). Obviously, the opportunity for an unscrupulous archaeologist to misreport his finds without being detected is greater at prehistoric sites, where change usually occurred slowly, than it would be at sites where change occurred rapidly.

I am not suggesting that Schliemann regularly misreported his finds. On the contrary, there is no doubt that for the most part Schliemann's archaeological reports are reliable. Later archaeologists have shown that the picture of sites presented by Schliemann's excavations is accurate. Hence the generally high esteem in which he is held by many, perhaps even most, classical archaeologists today. It is also true, on the other hand, that the vast majority of Schliemann's finds were mundane. What would have been the point in reporting that he found an unimpressive potsherd at location A rather than at location B? Common sense suggests that if Schliemann was going to misreport his finds, he would do so with the more impressive finds such as inscriptions and finds of metal, particularly those of gold and silver. Accordingly, we should beware of concluding that just because Schliemann's reporting of the pottery seems to be reliable, his reporting of the finds of gold and silver is equally trustworthy. With an individual like Schliemann, we need always to be on our guard. This is particularly true where his most spectacular finds are concerned.

Among the many previous biographers of Schliemann, Emil Ludwig and Ernst Meyer are the most important. Around 1925 Ludwig was invited by Schliemann's widow, Sophia, to write the first, and what must have been intended as the official, biography. One of the most popular writers of his day, he wrote best-selling biographies of Goethe (1920), Napoleon (1925) and Kaiser Wilhelm II (1926), which were translated into over twenty languages. By 1930 some two and a half million copies of his books had been sold. Sophia gave him access to her husband's papers, which are now kept in the Schliemann Archive of the Gennadius Library at the American School of Classical Studies in Athens. In addition, Ludwig scouted around for other documents. Although, exasperatingly, Ludwig does not cite his sources, his account is much more securely grounded on documentary evidence than its popular tone might suggest.

Ludwig saw Schliemann as the gifted amateur who proved the experts wrong.[19] In this regard Ludwig seems to have felt a special affinity for his subject. His historical studies of Napoleon and especially of Wilhelm II had provoked a hostile reaction from the academic establishment on the grounds that he was sometimes cavalier with facts. Thus it is not surprising that Schliemann's frequently tempestuous relations with the German academic establishment of his day met with Ludwig's sympathy. As in his other biographies, Ludwig's *Schliemann* emphasises psychological factors. Thus considerable space is given to Schliemann's disturbed childhood, his love affairs and the failure of his first marriage. There are numerous purple passages. Rather simplistically, Ludwig saw Schliemann's love for gold as a leitmotiv that unified his different careers, first as a merchant in St Petersburg, then as a banker buying gold dust in California, and lastly as an archaeologist excavating for ancient objects of gold. Despite the distortions that this view imposed, Ludwig's is a reasonably balanced account, in which Schliemann's obvious shortcomings are set beside his remarkable achievements.

With the rise of National Socialism in Germany, the attacks on Ludwig, who was Jewish, grew increasingly anti-semitic. In 1932 he became a Swiss citizen. In 1933 his books were burned in Germany. In 1931 the first edition of his *Schliemann* in English translation had been published in London and New York. Five years later Ernst Meyer's first collection of Schliemann's letters, *Briefe*, appeared in Germany. In the introduction he criticized Ludwig's biography on the grounds that Ludwig was incapable of understanding what was authentically German in Schliemann, a thinly veiled reference to Ludwig's Jewish origin.[20] Meyer made no secret of the fact that in selecting Schliemann's letters for publication he had been careful to omit what was contrary to the 'essential nature' of Schliemann.[21] In other words, the Schliemann that Meyer sought to present to the world was an authentic German hero stripped of the human flaws on which his Jewish biographer had chosen to dwell. Meyer was a member of the National Socialist party. In 1937 he was commissioned by the Mecklenburg gauleiter to begin work on a new biography of Schliemann with a study of the Schliemann papers in Athens.[22] The war inevitably interrupted Meyer's work. In the 1950s he brought out two further volumes of letters, and his biography of Schliemann, the most thorough to date, finally appeared in 1969, shortly after his death.

Though Meyer's knowledge of the primary sources was unrivalled, his work both as editor and biographer suffers from serious deficiencies.[23] His knowledge of English was inadequate for the task of editing letters in that language. Predictably, his picture of Schliemann is marred by a failure to examine his subject critically. When Meyer came across evidence that cast Schliemann in a negative light, his practice was to suppress it completely, bury it in a footnote, or gloss as a 'mistake' what was clearly a lie. Though his biography was little read outside Germany and never translated, Meyer's influence in developing the standard modern view of Schliemann has been considerable. In particular, the letters Meyer selected, edited and published have been fundamental to most subsequent research. His biography, naïve and hagiographical, remains a mine of useful information not easily obtained elsewhere.

On 6 January 1972, on the 150th anniversary of Schliemann's birth, an American classics professor, William M. Calder III, gave a commemorative lecture at the archaeologist's birthplace in Neubukow, Mecklenburg, which ushered in a new era in contemporary understanding of Schliemann.[24] Calder expressed dissatisfaction with the uncritical nature of most of the existing biographies. He pointed out that if a classicist were to undertake a biography of Cicero, he would certainly not take all of Cicero's statements about himself at face value, but would compare Cicero's claims with the testimony provided by other contemporary sources. The biographers of Schliemann, however, had uncritically accepted as fact even quite implausible episodes in Schliemann's autobiographical writings. As an example he cited the story of Schliemann's meeting with President Fillmore. The relevant diary entry, dated 21 February 1851, runs as follows:

In Baltimore I enjoyed a good oyster-breakfast, and on the 21st February. at 9 a.m. I started by rail to Washington, together with Mr Klaener, who had seen my name in the book at Barnum's Hotel, and called at my room in the morning at 4. On my arrival at Washington, I went immediately to the sessions of the House of Representatives and the House of Congress in the Capitol, a magnificent building on the top of a hill. With the most vivid interest and the sincerest delight, I heard the powerful speeches of Henry Clay, Senator of Kentucky, Hale of New Hampshire, Mason of Virginia, Douglas of Illinois, Davis of Massachusetts, etc. The chief topic of discussion was the late negro-riot at Boston. I left the Capitol at 4 o'clock, took my dinner (together with Mr Dean, whom I had previously met with on the railroad) at the ladies' table at the National-Hotel, and in the evening at 7 o'clock I drove to the President of the United States, to whom I made my introduction by stating that the great desire to see this beautiful country of the West, and to make the acquaintance of the great men who govern it had induced me to come over from Russia, and that I now deemed it my first and most agreeable duty to pay my respects to the President. He received me kindly, presented me to his wife, daughter, and father, and I had 1½ hours conversation with them.

The President is a very plain and friendly looking man of about 50; his name is Fillmore. His wife is about 46, a very noble and friendly looking lady; his daughter may be 17 years and is looking rather green. At 8¼ opened the 'levée' with the President, and there assembled more than 800 persons, from all parts of the Union, all eager to see and speak to the President. This latter introduced me to Mr Webster, Secretary of State; to Mr Clay, Senator of Kentucky, and to several others. The President's palace is a most magnificent mansion; there are no sentinels to watch and bar the doors; there exist no ceremonies to which the stranger has to submit to be presented to the first Magistrate. I staid there till 11 o'clock.[25]

Calder observed: 'A masterpiece. There are the accurate details: train-times, travelling companions, hotels, oysters. There is the inclusion of famous names: Webster, Clay, Douglas, and, of course, the Fillmores. There is the eye-witness appraisal: the noble site of the Capitol, Miss Fillmore's appearance. For any doubter there is what Sir Ronald Syme calls "the corroborative detail". Unlike Potsdam, the primitive and friendly Americans have no guards at their palaces.'[26]

Calder pointed, however, to the fundamental implausibility of Schliemann's account: can we really believe that the Fillmores would spend one and a half hours chatting to an unknown and uninvited foreign businessman immediately before welcoming eight hundred distinguished guests to a White House soirée? Congressional records indicate that on 21 February 1851, Senators Clay, Hale, Mason and Davis did indeed speak on the recent racial incident in Boston. However, Calder could find no newspaper report of a large reception that evening at the White House. There were, of course, many receptions across the country the following evening, 22 February (Washington's Birthday). Calder suggested that Schliemann probably read about one of them in a newspaper, turned it into a White House event and placed himself in the centre of it. Schliemann may well, of course, have heard the debate in the Senate on 21 February. However, his inclusion of Senator Douglas in the debate, who did not speak on the issue till the 22nd, suggests that this episode too is based on a newspaper report, perhaps one that conflated the two days' debate.

After drawing attention to many other instances of invented episodes in Schliemann's autobiographical writings, among them the account of how he obtained his American citizenship in 1850, Calder concluded: 'His auto-biography is not historical truth. It is a *Wunschbild*, a picture that he had created for himself and that he wished posterity to accept.'[27] Calder added: 'The mendacity of Schliemann is exceeded only by the gullibility of his biographers.'[28] His article marks the beginning of the new, sceptical view of Schliemann.

In 1978, when I was interested in learning more about Schliemann's connections with Sacramento in 1851–2 during the gold rush, a colleague drew my attention to Calder's article. I bore it in mind when I read Schliemann's intriguing description of the 1851 fire of San Francisco.

San Francisco, June 4th, 1851. A most horrible disaster has befallen this City! A conflagration greater than any of the preceding fires has reduced the whole city to ashes.

I arrived last night at 10½ o'clock and put up at the Union Hotel on the Plaza. I may have slept a quarter of an hour, when I was awoke by loud cries in the street: "fire, fire" and by the awful sounds of the alarm-bell. I sprung up in all haste and looking out of the window I saw that a frame building only 20 or 30 paces from the Union Hotel was on fire. I dressed in all haste and ran out of the house, but scarcely had I reached the end of Clay street when I saw already the Hôtel on fire from which I had just run out. Pushed on by a complete gale the fire spread with an appalling rapidity, sweeping away in a few minutes whole streets of frame buildings. Neither the iron houses nor the brick houses (which were hitherto considered as quite fireproof) could resist the fury of the element; the latter crumbled together with incredible rapidity, whilst the former got red-hot, then white-hot and fell together like card-houses. Particularly in the iron houses people considered themselves perfectly safe and they remained in them to the last extremity. As soon as the walls of the iron houses getting red-hot the goods inside began to smoke, the inhabitants wanted to get out, but usually it was already too late, for the locks and hinges of the doors having extended or partly melted by the heat, the doors were no more to be opened. Sometimes by burning their hands and arms people succeeded to open the doors and to get out, but finding themselves then surrounded by an ocean of flames they made but a few paces, staggered and fell, rose again and fell in order not to rise any more. It was tried in vain to arrest the progress of the fire by the blowing up of houses with gunpowder. Wishing to avoid all dangers I went up Montgommery street and ascended "Telegraph Hill" which is a mountain about 300 feet high close to the city. It was a frightful but sublime view, in fact the grandest spectacle I ever enjoyed. The fire continued to spread in all directions sweeping away the whole of Washington street, Kearny street, Montgommery street, California street, Sansome and many others, and except a few houses on Battery street, Bush street and on the Hillside, the whole beautiful city was burned down. The roaring of the storm, the cracking of the gunpowder, the cracking of the falling stone-walls, the cries of people and the wonderful spectacle of an immense city burning in a dark night all joined to make this catastrophe awful in the extreme. A report having spread out among the people that the fire had been caused by french incendiaries, the scorn of the enraged population fell upon the french and many a poor french chap was thrown headlong in the flames and consumed. I remained for the night on Telegraph hill and went at 6 in the morning down to the city. It was a horrible sight to see the smouldering ashes and ruins of

11

this a day before so flourishing city. Whilst I saw a great many germans, french-men, englishmen and other foreigners half in despair sitting and weeping on the ashes of their destroyed property, the americans never daunted, laughing and joking among themselves just as if nothing had happened, went boldly a-head to construct new houses and I saw them in many places at 6 o'clock in the morning busy to lay on the still hot ashes of the former buildings the foundations for the new ones. In the morning from 6 till 10 it is very hot in San Francisco; then all at once a strong gale springs up and from 10 a.m. off the cold increases till 3 o'clock in the morning so that it is impossible to walk here during the day after 10 or during the night without a very thick overcoat.[29]

There are some puzzling features about this account.[30] First, Schliemann had returned to Sacramento on 1 June from a week's trip to San Francisco (where he had been completely bored) and the Sonoma Valley. This return to San Francisco on 3 June is therefore rather surprising and, uncharacteristically, Schliemann gives no motive for it. The choice of hotel is also surprising, for earlier in his diary Schliemann tells us that he had stayed one night in the Union Hotel and then moved out because of the poor accommodation and high prices.

When I checked the local newspapers for an account of the fire, I discovered that there had been no fire on the night of 3–4 June. The fire described by Schliemann occurred on the night of 3–4 May. However, it was clearly not a simple mistake of writing 'June' for 'May', for the 4 June entry is preceded by two extended May entries, the first dated 14 May and the second, an undated entry in Spanish describing his trip to San Francisco and the Sonoma Valley (26–31 May). When I examined the original diary in Athens, I saw that the account of the fire filled exactly one leaf and that this leaf was not part of the original binding but had been subsequently glued in.

All of the essential facts in Schliemann's narrative occur in the Sacramento *Daily Union* reports of 6 and 7 May. It seems clear that Schliemann based his diary account on this source, imaginatively adapting it to a vivid first-person narrative. The wrong dating of the event seems to have been determined by the practical consideration that it was impossible to add a leaf after the 2 May entry, which ended in the middle of a page with the 14 May entry following immediately after.

Thus Calder's view of the unreliability of Schliemann's autobiographical statements had been confirmed. Did this mean that his archaeological reports were equally unreliable? Given the scholarly consensus that Schliemann's archaeological work had been validated by the findings of subsequent archaeologists, this seemed unlikely. Calder concluded that the 'disinterested recording of finds, their description, the drawings, need not be universally doubted.

Much can be controlled by the extant objects themselves. Rather, specific interpretation must be queried and often discarded.'

Shortly after this cautious view was published, G.S. Korres, Professor of Archaeology at the University of Athens, pointed out that a scholarly article of Schliemann's published in 1888 contained serious misrepresentation of fact. The article contained the texts of twelve modest inscriptions, which Schliemann claimed to have found in excavations in the garden of his house in Mouson Street, Athens, close to Syntagma Square. Korres, however, demonstrated that four of these inscriptions had been published between 1842 and 1871 and were known to have belonged to private collections in Athens. Schliemann must have acquired them from their owners in or before 1888. Korres called Schliemann's claims 'unconscionable' (*'contre toute conscience scientifique'*).[31]

These three studies, by Calder, Korres, and myself, together with a review article by W. Schindler,[32] all published in the 1970s, set the stage for the controversy over Schliemann which erupted in the following decade and still shows no sign of abating. Collectively, they made it clear that if we are to get at the truth of what Schliemann did, as opposed to what he would have us believe he did, we need to be sceptical. The controversy centres on just how far we are to take that scepticism when we consider the excavations themselves.

2

The Making of a Self-Made Man

'Talent means energy and persistence and nothing more.'
Schliemann (*Bw* I 121)

O N 6 JANUARY 1822 the twenty-nine-year-old Louise Schliemann gave
birth to her fifth child in Neubukow in the grand duchy of Mecklenburg-
Schwerin. Her husband, Ernst, aged forty-two, formerly a schoolteacher, now
a Lutheran minister, entered the boy's names in the parish register, underlining
the one by which he would be called: Johann Ludwig <u>Heinrich</u> Julius
Schliemann. The growing needs of his growing family prompted Ernst to seek
nomination for the well-endowed parish of Ankershagen. In the event, he was
successful and the family moved there in 1823.[1] In *Ilios* Schliemann gives a
charming picture of his childhood in the tiny village, emphasising the local
stories that fostered in him at a very early age a profound interest in what
might lie buried under the earth:

> Just behind our garden was a pond called 'das Silberschälchen', out of which a
> maiden was believed to rise each midnight, holding a silver bowl. There was also in
> the village a small hill surrounded by a ditch, probably a prehistoric burial place (or
> so-called Hünengrab), in which, as the legend ran, a robber knight in times of old
> had buried his beloved child in a golden cradle. Vast treasures were also said to be
> buried close to the ruins of a round tower in the garden of the proprietor of the
> village. My faith in the existence of these treasures was so great that, whenever I
> heard my father complain of his poverty, I always expressed my astonishment that
> he did not dig up the silver bowl or the golden cradle and so become rich.[2]

We are also told how his father awakened his interest in archaeological
excavation with his stories of Troy and the Homeric heroes and that, of his
playmates, only Minna Meincke and her sister Louise did not laugh at him
when he said that one day he would excavate Troy. Minna and young Heinrich
became close friends:

14

It was agreed between us that as soon as we were grown up we would marry, and then at once set to work to explore all the mysteries of Ankershagen; excavating the golden cradle, the silver basin, the vast treasures hidden by Henning, then Henning's sepulchre, and lastly Troy; nay, we could imagine nothing pleasanter than to spend all our lives in digging for the relics of the past.[3]

This idyllic picture that Schliemann's account conjures up disguises a far less attractive reality. Schliemann's father was a singularly unpleasant character. Egotistical, given to drink, and sexually promiscuous, he was spectacularly ill-suited to his profession. Domineering and coarse, he quarrelled openly and sometimes violently with his wife. Louise, an educated woman, who eased the pain of her failed marriage by playing the piano, was certainly a more positive influence on the young Heinrich. But her health had been seriously undermined by frequent pregnancies. Ernst enjoyed the good life and, despite his sizeable income, was constantly in debt. His irresponsible behaviour led to a series of catastrophes for the entire family.

In the autumn of 1829 Ernst took on a good-looking young woman, ostensibly to serve as a personal maid for Louise, though the household was already well supplied with servants. It soon became obvious that the young woman, Sophie Schwarz, was his mistress. The other servants talked and the affair became common knowledge in the village. In the spring of 1830, shortly after the beginning of her ninth pregnancy, Louise succeeded in dismissing Sophie from the household. Ernst was furious. Violent scenes ensued before the frightened eyes and ears of the children. The servants later reported that Louise had been beaten by her husband.[4] Ernst rented a room for Sophie in the nearby town of Waren and the affair continued. He became increasingly negligent of his pastoral duties. Meanwhile, Louise gave birth to her ninth child, Paul, in January 1831 and died two months later at the age of thirty-six. Ernst placed an advertisement in the *Mecklenburg-Schwerinschen Anzeigen*:

Yesterday was the unhappiest day of my life. Inexorable death snatched from me my loyal partner in life, wedded to me for almost seventeen years, and from my seven young children their loving mother, Louise Therese Sophie, née Bürger . . . Pierced with the deepest pain I stand, surrounded by my now motherless little ones, some of whom are not yet capable of understanding the dimension of their loss, and pray: May God reward the deceased with the enjoyment of the purest and calmest bliss for all the love and tender care she bestowed on me and my children, and may He not abandon me and my children but rather pour soothing balm on our deeply wounded hearts . . .[5]

15

The rhetorical skill with which the long, elaborate sentences have been woven together is quite remarkable. Far more remarkable, however, is the character of the individual who could publish these sentiments in such a context. Ernst must have been aware that his affair with Sophie was well known in the parish and had provoked widespread sympathy for Louise and contempt for himself.

Within a few months of the funeral Ernst installed Sophie Schwarz as his housekeeper. This was the last straw for his long-suffering parishioners. Two hundred of them came to his house, banging on pots and pans to show their disapproval. They threw things at the house and even broke the windows. The demonstration was repeated every Sunday for a month. The whole family was ostracized. Children were forbidden to play with the Schliemann family. Finally, the villagers lodged a formal protest with the authorities, asking for Ernst's removal from the parish. This started a lengthy legal process. Ernst's sophistication, wiliness and eloquence gave him considerable advantages over his largely uneducated accusers. The inquiries, appeals and counter-suits dragged on for ten years.[6] Eventually, thanks to the disappearance of the key witness, Sophie Schwarz, Ernst was cleared of the charges. He promptly demanded to be reinstated as pastor of Ankershagen. Since he had in the interim got into trouble with the law on more than one occasion and the whole parish was adamantly opposed to his reinstatement, a settlement was reached whereby he voluntarily relinquished his position in return for a cash payment.

Not surprisingly, in his autobiography Schliemann does not go into the lurid details that led to his family's humiliation. After referring to the tragic death of his mother he merely speaks of 'another misfortune, which resulted in all our acquaintances suddenly turning their backs upon us and refusing to have any further intercourse with us.'[7] In January 1832 Heinrich was sent off to live with his uncle Friedrich, who was also a minister, in Kalkhorst. Here life was considerably more normal. Friedrich employed a private tutor, Carl Andress, for his children, and young Heinrich benefited from his tuition as he prepared to attend the Gymnasium. Schliemann remained eternally grateful to Andress, who subsequently fell upon hard times, and Schliemann regularly sent him money at Christmas. In *Ilios* Schliemann summarized his education as follows:

The progress I made under this excellent philologist [Andress] was so great that, at Christmas 1832, I was able to present my father with a badly-written Latin essay upon the principal events of the Trojan war and the adventures of Ulysses and Agamemnon. At the age of eleven I went to the Gymnasium at Neu Strelitz, where I was placed in the third class. But just at that time a great disaster befell our family, and, being afraid that my father would no longer have the means of supporting me for a number of years, I left the Gymnasium after being in it only three months, and entered the *Realschule* of the same city, where I was placed in the second class. In the spring of 1835 I advanced to the first class, which I left in April 1836, at the age of fourteen, to become apprentice in the little grocer's shop of Ernest Ludwig Holtz, in the small town of Fürstenberg in Mecklenburg-Strelitz.[8]

The disaster that struck the Schliemann family in 1833 was Ernst's suspension without pay from his duties pending the outcome of the inquiry. Heinrich was sent to the less expensive, and less prestigious, *Realschule*, which did not prepare children for advancement to higher education. By modern standards, however, at least in English-speaking countries, the curriculum seems remarkably academic and very demanding for children of average ability. Schliemann's report card for his second year at *Realschule* includes three foreign languages: French ('satisfactory'), Latin ('unsatisfactory; translation cursory and pompous'), and English ('satisfactory'). For one who was later to show a unique aptitude for learning languages, Heinrich's school record in this area was surprisingly mediocre. Given his home background, one would not be surprised to find signs of juvenile delinquency, but his conduct was reported as 'good'.

Schliemann's apprenticeship at Fürstenberg led to what he later saw as one of the defining moments of his life:

I was employed in the little grocer's shop at Fürstenberg for five years and a half; for the first year by Mr. Holtz, and afterwards by the excellent Mr. Theodor Hückstaedt. My occupation consisted in retailing herrings, butter, potato-whiskey, milk, salt, coffee, sugar, oil, and candles; in grinding potatoes for the still, sweeping the shop, and the like employments. Our transactions were on such a small scale that our aggregate sales hardly amounted to 3000 thalers, or £450 annually; nay, we thought we had extraordinary luck when we sold two pounds' worth of groceries in a day. There I of course came in contact only with the lowest classes of society. I was engaged from five in the morning till eleven at night, and had not a moment's leisure for study. Moreover I rapidly forgot the little that I had learnt in childhood; but I did not lose the love of learning; indeed I never lost it, and, as long as I live, I shall never forget the evening when a drunken miller came into the shop. His name was Hermann Niederhoffer. He was the son of a protestant clergyman in Roebel (Mecklenburg), and had almost completed his studies at the Gymnasium of Neu Ruppin, when he was expelled on account of his bad conduct. Not knowing what to do with him, his father apprenticed him to the farmer Langermann in the village of Dambeck; and, as even there his conduct was not exemplary, he again apprenticed him for two years to the miller Dettmann at Güstrow. Dissatisfied with his lot, the young man gave himself up to drink, which, however, had not made him forget his Homer; for on the evening that he entered the shop he recited to us about a hundred lines of the poet, observing the rhythmic cadence of the verses. Although I did not understand a syllable, the melodious sound of the words made a deep impression upon me, and I wept bitter tears over my unhappy fate. Three times over did I get him to repeat to me those divine verses, rewarding his trouble with three glasses of whiskey, which I bought with the few pence that made up my whole fortune. From that moment I never ceased to pray God that by His grace I might yet have the happiness of learning Greek.[9]

The scene is virtually an archetype of Victorian literature: the young boy, whose soul is uplifted from the drudgery of the menial tasks he has been set by the shining vision of classical literature. It is the dominant theme of Thomas Hardy's *Jude the Obscure*, begun within ten years of the publication of *Ilios*.[10] One may wonder whether so idealized a scene ever happened. Probably we should regard it as part of the recasting of Schliemann's early life that was well underway by the late 1860s. Certainly, his letter of 27 March 1868 to his cousin Adolph, recalling their time together in 1832 and his admiration for Adolph's mastery of Greek and Latin, raises doubts: 'The way you read the hexameters of Homer produced in me – then a child of ten – such an enthusiasm, that 24 years later I put myself to the task of learning the language of the gods and heroes. It has ever since remained my favourite language.'[11]

One may well wonder why someone so adept at languages postponed for twenty-four years the happiness of learning 'the language of the gods and heroes.' Schliemann's own explanation is not convincing: 'Whatever the desire I had to learn Greek, I did not dare begin to study it until I had achieved a certain position of fortune, for I was afraid that the language would enchant me too much and would divert me from my commercial pursuits.'[12] By 1851 his own business was well enough established in St Petersburg for him to take a year and a half off to go to California. The 1851 autobiography, though it describes his apprenticeship in Fürstenberg, has no mention of this scene and nowhere in it or the 1851–2 diary is any interest shown in Greek, Homer or archaeology. It does not necessarily follow from this that the scene with the drunken miller's apprentice never happened, but if there really was such an incident, it clearly had considerably less emotional impact on Heinrich than we see represented in *Ilios*.[13]

There can be little doubt that in spite of the drudgery this apprenticeship had lasting beneficial effects on Heinrich. Hückstaedt was an educated and kindly man, who seems to have been conscientious about giving his young apprentice a thorough training in all aspects of the grocery business. Under his tutelage Schliemann also learned not to shirk hard work, a quality that distinguishes him from this point on and one he certainly did not learn from his father.[14] The five years of apprenticeship lasted until Easter 1841. As Heinrich had arranged to sail to America with a friend and the friend's father on 24 July, he seems to have agreed to work with Hückstaedt till the next quarter day, Whitsun. As it turned out, Ernst refused to allow Heinrich to go to America. Also, as he was moving a heavy cask one day, Heinrich felt a pain in his chest and spat blood. Shortly after this he decided to go to Rostock to take courses on book-keeping and English to improve his chances in a commercial career. Probably Hückstaedt, who must have seen the undeveloped potential in his apprentice, urged him to take this step.[15] His father meantime had abandoned Sophie Schwarz, married his maid Sophie Behnke and moved to Gehlsdorf, a village close to Rostock. But Heinrich decided that he could not live with his father and step-mother because of the violent quarrels that took place between them. In the spring of 1841, Schliemann later reported to his sisters, Sophie had to lock herself in the woodshed to avoid, as she said, being beaten to death by Ernst. She fled to Rostock and later brought the matter to court. Ernst was forced to swear before the court that he would treat his wife better or pay her alimony.

Heinrich's mother had left him a small bequest in her will. Ernst agreed to allow him to use this money to finance his training in book-keeping at Rostock but seems to have been unwilling to provide any support from his own resources. It was therefore in Heinrich's financial interests to complete his studies as quickly as possible. This he did:

> With the greatest zeal I began the enormous task of learning the Schwanbeck method of book-keeping. I worked from early morning till late in the evening and to the astonishment of the instructor and my fellow students, although I had to line nine books myself, on 10 September I finished the course, which others take a year to a year and a half to complete.[16]

About this point Schliemann's various accounts of his life diverge on a number of details, making it impossible to state the facts with certainty. More important perhaps than the details themselves is the clear evidence these discrepancies present of a cavalier attitude towards the truth. For instance the 1851 life omits all mention of his study of book-keeping in Rostock. This is not a casual omission, for Schliemann explains his dismissal from E.L. Deycke in Hamburg as due to his ignorance of this subject: 'My new employer, seeing that the work in the shop and in the store exceeded my forces, he wanted to employ me for book-keeping and other writings, but alas, I was entirely ignorant and hardly able to write my name, and so it happened that after a fortnight's service I was again dismissed.'[17] In his long letter to his sisters of 20 February 1842, however, in which he described his rapid completion of the course on book-keeping, he said that he left the job with Deycke because it provided no salary. In the same letter he related at great length how he travelled by coach from Rostock to Hamburg. According to his 1851 life, however, he walked directly from Fürstenberg to Hamburg, a journey that took him ten days! These discrepancies cannot be attributed to mistakes or memory lapses.

Whatever happened at Hamburg, it is clear that Heinrich did not find the kind of position he was hoping for. Dismayed by the grim prospects for employment, he finally decided, like thousands of other young Germans at this time, to seek better opportunities abroad. He sailed from Hamburg on board the ship *Dorothea* in late November 1841 bound for La Guayra, Colombia. His status on the ship depends on which version one chooses to believe. In 1842 he represented to his sisters that he had accepted a position in La Guayra and had been given free passage. According to the 1851 life he went as a paying passenger with no promise of a job in La Guayra; he had to sell his watch and some clothes to raise money for the fare.[18] According to *Ilios* he served as cabin-boy and there is no mention of paying a fare or of the prospect of a job when he reached his destination.[19] Again, these discrepancies are not due to memory lapses.

A few days after setting sail the *Dorothea* encountered a fierce storm and about midnight on 10 December ran aground off the island of Texel in the Netherlands. Thanks to the kindness of a number of people Heinrich was rescued, looked after and taken to Amsterdam. There his funds were soon exhausted and he ended up in hospital:

> I was seized by a violent fever, which was accompanied by unbearable toothache ... I was taken in a sledge to the hospital, where I passed the Christmas season in great pain. My two front teeth had broken off and on Christmas Eve their roots were extracted. The pain was so excruciating that I screamed.[20]

So at any rate he wrote to his sisters in February 1842. In *Ilios*, however, he is more candid: 'As my means of living were entirely exhausted, I feigned illness and was taken to hospital.'[21]

In Amsterdam Schliemann soon became aware of the overwhelming importance of a sound knowledge of several foreign languages, particularly if he wished to find a position as a clerk in one of the large trading companies. Almost immediately after leaving the hospital at the end of December he was interviewed for his first job with L. Hoyack and Co.[22] He told them he knew both the single-entry and double-entry systems of book-keeping and could write business letters in four modern languages and would soon have mastered his fifth, Dutch. This may well be true. But if they put his knowledge to the test, as he said they did, they would have found that he knew only three modern languages, English, French and German, and that his knowledge of the first two was far below the level required at a prestigious trading house. Moreover, Schliemann's handwriting at the beginning of 1842, while flowing and elegant, was very hard to read. His Dutch was obviously rudimentary. It seems most unlikely that Hoyack hired him as a clerk, though this is what Schliemann told his sisters in 1842. Much more likely is the version in *Ilios*. Here he states that his first job in Amsterdam was as an office-boy for F.C. Quien: 'my work consisted in stamping bills of exchange and getting them cashed in the town, and in carrying letters to and from the post-office.'[23] This is the kind of work that someone with only minimum knowledge of Dutch could do.

Schliemann at once set about acquiring the skills that he needed to win the position of clerk at one of the large trading houses. First and foremost, he had to become fluent in Dutch. He was immersed in the language. He heard and saw it all around him. It was not hard for him to understand, being closely related to his native Plattdeutsch (Low German). He was determined to master it and made steady progress every day. Next he had to improve his handwriting: 'First of all I took pains to learn to write legibly, and this I succeeded in doing after twenty lessons from the famous calligraphist Magnée of Brussels.'[24] His later handwriting is less elegant but decidedly more legible. He may also have had to learn the letter forms used in English and French handwriting, which differed considerably from those used in German at this time.

Next he devoted his energies to improving his knowledge of English and French. Presumably, his inadequate preparation in these languages had been noted and pointed out to him. His job as runner for F.C. Quien must have taken him to most of the leading financial institutions in Amsterdam. It would not have taken him long to find out which languages besides Dutch, English, French and German were most in demand in the trading houses. As Schliemann's fluency in about fifteen languages must seem to most readers even more astonishing than his achievements in archaeology, it is worth quoting his study methods in full:

I applied myself with extraordinary diligence to the study of English. Necessity taught me a method which greatly facilitates the study of the language. This method consists in reading a great deal aloud, without making a translation, taking a lesson every day, constantly writing essays upon subjects of interest, correcting these under the supervision of a teacher, learning them by heart, and repeating in the next lesson what was corrected on the previous day. My memory was bad, since from my childhood it had not been exercised upon any object; but I made use of every moment, and even stole time for study. In order to acquire a good pronunciation quickly, I went twice every Sunday to the English church, and repeated to myself in a low voice every word of the clergyman's sermon. I never went on my errands, even in the rain, without having my book in my hand and learning something by heart; and I never waited at the post-office without reading. By such methods I gradually strengthened my memory, and in three months' time found no difficulty in reciting from memory to my teacher, Mr. Taylor, in each day's lesson, word by word, twenty printed pages, after having read them over three times attentively. In this way I committed to memory the whole of Goldsmith's *Vicar of Wakefield* and Sir Walter Scott's *Ivanhoe*. From over-excitement I slept but little, and employed my sleepless hours at night in going over in my mind what I had read on the preceding evening. The memory being always much more concentrated at night than in the day-time, *I found these repetitions at night of paramount use*. Thus I succeeded in acquiring a thorough knowledge of the English language.

I then applied the same method to the study of French, the difficulties of which I overcame likewise in another six months. Of French authors I learned by heart the whole of Fénelon's *Aventures de Télémaque* and Bernardin de Saint Pierre's *Paul et Virginie*. This unremitting study had in the course of a single year strengthened my memory to such a degree, that the study of Dutch, Spanish, Italian and Portuguese appeared very easy, and it did not take me more than six weeks to write and speak each of these languages fluently.[25]

This is almost certainly a failsafe method of learning languages. The only difficulty the rest of us are likely to experience would probably be summoning the perseverance to follow it.

Early in 1844 he felt ready. He applied for a position with one of Europe's leading trading houses, B.H. Schröder & Co. This time he was successful. He began work as correspondent and book-keeper on 1 March. He quickly realized that though the firm did a considerable amount of business with Russia, there was no one who understood the language. Accordingly, he set to work to learn that language too. Six weeks later he wrote his first letter in Russian and was soon conversing fluently with Russian merchants when they came to Amsterdam for the indigo auctions.[26] In January 1846 the firm sent Schliemann to St Petersburg to act as their agent there: 'Here, as well as in Moscow, my exertions were in the first two months crowned with the fullest success, which far exceeded the most sanguine expectations of my employers and myself.'

Within a few months of his arrival in St Petersburg he established his own business as a wholesale dealer, though he continued to act as Schröder's agent for many years.[27] Friction soon developed with senior partners in the firm, who found that he had grown too self-assured and in his letters often adopted an arrogant tone.[28] But Schliemann had made himself indispensable for their Russian trade and both parties knew it. Relying on the expertise and contacts in the indigo trade that he had developed in Amsterdam, Schliemann built up his own business steadily by restricting himself initially to transactions in that commodity.

It was probably about the end of 1847 that he proposed indirectly to his childhood sweetheart Minna Meincke through C.E. Laué of Neustrelitz: 'But to my horror, I received a month later the heartrending answer that she was just married.' In 1848 he proposed to Sophie Hekker, a young St Petersburg woman of German extraction. Her father, who wanted a rich son-in-law, persuaded her, against her own wishes, to accept.[29] But Schliemann broke off the engagement when he saw how happily she was dancing with a young soldier.

In December 1847 Schliemann tried to persuade his father to send his youngest brother Paul to work for him in St Petersburg:

> There is plenty of room for Paul here; he will work throughout the day in my office, where he will attend to small tasks, such as writing up German, English, French and Dutch and later also Russian letters in the copy books, writing out freight charges, etc. . . . If it works out for him and he wants to stay permanently in St. Petersburg, I will marry him in five or six years to a little Russian, who has some money, and see to it that he always has a livelihood here.[30]

The genuine concern for his brother mixed with a preternatural desire to run his life for him is typical of Schliemann.[31] A letter to his father in 1855 provides an even more startling example:

> By today's post I have forwarded instructions for 500 Prussian Talers to be credited to your account, which sum I expect you to use in establishing yourself in the neighbourhood of Danzig [Gdansk] in a manner befitting the father of Heinrich Schliemann. In placing this sum at your disposal I must, however, stipulate that in future you keep a respectable man-servant and a respectable maid, and, above all, preserve a decent standard of cleanliness in your house, that your plates, dishes, cups, knives and forks always shine with cleanliness, that you have all the boards and floors scrubbed three times a week, and have at your table food that befits a person of your station in life.[32]

Heinrich also invited his brother Louis (whom he called Ludwig) to join him in St Petersburg but then thought better of it: 'I cannot take Ludwig because he is too taken with his own knowledge, of which he has little, and makes great demands without thinking that four years would pass before he learns Russian and therefore four years before he can be of use to me.'[33] In 1848 Louis decided to seek his fortune in America. He joined the gold rush to California in 1849 and after prospecting for gold himself he settled down to the much more profitable business of running a hotel and buying and selling real estate. In *Ilios* Schliemann states:

> Not having heard of my brother Louis Schliemann, who in the beginning of 1849 had emigrated to California, I went thither in the spring of 1850, and found that he was dead. Happening, therefore, to be in California when, on 4th July, 1850, it was made a State, and all those resident in the country became by that very fact natural-ized Americans, I joyfully embraced the opportunity of becoming a citizen of the United States.[34]

These two sentences contain a remarkable number of inaccuracies.[35] Heinrich had in fact received several letters from Louis after his arrival in California. He knew of his brother's death before he went to California.[36] He set out for America from St Petersburg on 10 December 1850 to see what could be recovered of his estate and did not reach California until 2 April 1851.[37] These distortions of the facts are due to Schliemann's need to conceal the fraudulent means by which he secured his American citizenship and divorce in 1869.

Schliemann's trip to America took him via Berlin, Amsterdam and London to Liverpool, from where he sailed on 28 December on the *Atlantic*. Unfortunately, the ship's engines became disabled during a storm in mid-ocean and the steamer had to limp back to Ireland under sail. He set sail from Liverpool again on 1 February and reached New York two weeks later. From there he went to Washington, where he attended a debate in the Senate, and, as we have seen, claimed to have had an interview with President Fillmore on 21 February. A week later he set sail from New York for Chagres, Panama, crossed the isthmus, and caught another steamer for San Francisco. As he sailed north towards Acapulco, he inserted a note in his diary that he had had an interview three days earlier with the Governor of Panama.[38]

In Sacramento Heinrich located his brother's grave and had a tombstone erected over it. The 4 June entry of his diary describes the fire of San Francisco. In September he opened a bank and started buying gold dust from the miners. This proved extremely profitable. Between October 1851 and April 1852 he shipped $1,350,000 worth of gold dust to the Rothschild agent in San Francisco, B. Davidson.[39] Exactly what precipitated his sudden departure from California in April 1852 is not entirely clear. It certainly was not the 'third attack of fever', which, according to his diary, kept him 'in almost continual ravery' from 17 to 28 March. His correspondence shows that throughout the period in question he was entirely *compos mentis* and working in Sacramento, not recuperating in San Jose, as he alleges in his diary, and suggests that he left because of an irretrievable breakdown in his business relationship with B. Davidson over the latter's repeated charges of short-weight consignments of gold dust.[40]

Before leaving California Schliemann renewed his proposal of marriage to Sophie Hekker in St Petersburg. No doubt suspecting that he would be turned down, he also proposed at the same time to Katerina Lyshin, the daughter of an advocate.[41] It so happened that the two young women were close friends. Naturally, each was very indignant to learn that her suitor had simultaneously proposed to her friend.

The trip back across Panama was particularly nightmarish for Schliemann and his fellow passengers. On the Atlantic side they had to wait two weeks for a steamer in the pouring rain, without shelter, plagued by mosquitoes, and reduced to eating iguanas raw for food.[42] On the way home he visited various relatives and friends in Mecklenburg. In Ankershagen he looked for his initials carved on the trees and window-panes of the parsonage, visited his mother's tomb and mused on the scenes of his youth, but there is no sign of any interest in the 'archaeological' aspects of Ankershagen, which, according to *Ilios*, had such a profound influence on his childhood. He reached St Petersburg on 4 August and married Katerina Lyshin in St Isaac's Cathedral on 7 October 1852. Later in 1852 he opened a branch office in Moscow.

The marriage produced three children, Serge (1855–1940), Natalia (1858–69) and Nadeshda (1861–?) but it was soon obvious that Katerina had little love for her husband. She seems to have despised his preoccupation with business and refused categorically to leave Russia with him, whether on a trip or, as he later proposed, to take up residence abroad.

The Crimean War (1853–6) created a great demand for indigo and other commodities such as saltpetre, brimstone and metals and Schliemann's business increased enormously in range and volume: 'I was able to realize large profits, and more than doubled my capital in a single year.'[43] In 1854 he learned Swedish and Polish, almost certainly for commercial reasons. When he began the study of modern Greek in 1855, it was probably for similar reasons.[44] There was in St Petersburg at this time a substantial community of Greeks, many of whom like Schliemann were engaged in international trade. The city of Rostov-on-Don, as Schliemann later observed, stood as a symbol of Greek trade and there were many Greeks living in the nearby seaport of Taganrog.[45]

Both were major ports and of particularly vital significance as trans-shipment centres in the Crimean War. Schliemann may well have thought it worthwhile learning Greek to solidify his relationships with this well-connected group. The modern Greek that he learned was not the 'demotic' version that prevails in Greece today but the *katharevousa*, the 'pure' or formal version, which, in its vocabulary and basic grammar, is not far removed from ancient Greek. So when Schliemann later turned to ancient Greek the step was not so great as it might at first appear.

One Greek friend who helped teach him the language was Theokletos Vimpos.[46] Through him Schliemann met Vimpos' mother and sister and formed a very positive view of Greek women and their fierce loyalty to their menfolk. Given his own unhappy marital situation, it would have been natural to wish that his wife was more like Vimpos' sister. The possibility of divorce and remarriage must have occurred to him. His preoccupation at this time with finding a suitable piece of property in which to invest is probably attributable to a desire to put his assets beyond the jurisdiction of Russian courts.

In March 1856 he told his father that he was interested in investing in property somewhere, perhaps in Germany: 'But before I buy, I would very much like to visit the countries of southern Europe, especially the homeland of my beloved Homer, particularly now that I can speak modern Greek as well as I do German. I would also like to see Italy, Spain, Portugal and Calcutta . . .'[47] This is the first sign – at least in his published letters – of an interest in visiting Greece. Significantly, it is connected with his love for Homer. But the desire to go to Greece is vague and unfocused. Moreover, it is closely linked in his mind with other warm spots. The mood in fact has much in common with that of today's northern European flipping through a travel brochure towards the end of another dreary winter. There is no sign here of a desire to excavate Troy or any other site. Now that he has the means and the time to fulfil his lifelong dream it does not even appear as an option to be discussed.

As the war drew to a close, Schliemann foresaw sharply decreased profits and even losses ahead. In March 1856, when the war ended, he thought of retiring from business at least for a year or two. In the summer and latter part of 1856, his correspondence shows a sense of disillusionment with business and a determination to immerse himself in cultural pursuits. His interest in ancient Greek and Latin dates from this period.[48] These new interests may reflect, as Schliemann later asserts, a long-postponed desire, though no trace of this desire has yet been found in his earlier letters or diaries. More probably, he found that though his hard-won wealth had procured him an *entrée* into the society of the Russian élite, he had not won their respect. While nobody could fail to be impressed by Schliemann's mastery of modern languages, undoubtedly many would have despised him as a *nouveau-riche párvenu*, sneering at his lack of a liberal education. When he boasted of his knowledge of thirteen modern languages, some, particularly those with a traditional classical education, would no doubt have pointed out the prevailing view that the hallmark of an educated man was not his knowledge of Portuguese and Polish but of Latin and ancient Greek.

In the large exercise book which he used for practising the languages he was learning, he again toyed with the idea of visiting Greece. In an entry dated 22 July 1856 he reflected, in modern Greek, on what his wealth meant to him:

> I can invite men of learning to my house and have around me a circle of friends and acquaintances at my call. I think that Greece will be of great interest to me and that I will stay there throughout this coming winter and then see the Pyramids of Egypt, the antiquities of Italy and everywhere stay for a few months so that I can study the languages, character and customs of the peoples.

Once again he is vague about his reasons for going to Greece. Once again Greece is closely linked with Italy and Egypt. This time however, Greece seems to be part of a programme of cultural self-improvement that includes literary salons and a leisurely Grand Tour. Here again there is no indication that a visit to Greece might be the fulfilment of a childhood dream, no sign of a specific interest in Homeric sites or even in archaeology, and no mention at all of Troy.

An interesting letter to his aunt Magdalena in Kalkhorst dated 31 December 1856 reveals Schliemann's change of attitude and indicates that he has started a kind of literary salon. After telling her that he now knows fifteen languages, including Latin and ancient Greek, he goes on:

> My terrific passion for languages, which torments me day and night, continually urges me to withdraw my fortune from the vicissitudes of trade and retire either into rural life or to a university town, like Bonn, for example, and surround myself there with scholars, dedicating myself entirely to scholarship. For years this passion has been in a bloody struggle with my two other passions, avarice and acquisitiveness, and as it succumbed in the unequal conflict, the latter two victorious passions have been daily adding to the turmoil of my business affairs . . . We have sought out for ourselves here a circle of friends whose inclinations for scholarship coincide with ours; they have a standing invitation to come to our house every Sunday.

In 1857 and 1858 Schliemann scaled down his activities primarily to making secured loans. This gave him time to study Greek literature. In November

1858 he set out on his Grand Tour: Sweden, Denmark, Germany, Italy, Egypt, Jerusalem, Petra, Syria, Smyrna, the Cyclades and Athens. Though a lively interest was shown in Roman and Greek ruins in Italy (Rome, Pompeii and Sicily), Petra, Syria (Baalbek) and Athens, the bulk of his time – more than three months – was spent in Egypt. Here he learned Arabic. The hundred or so pages of the diary devoted to Egypt are mainly written in that language. He spent less than two weeks in Greece. He took ill in Athens, when, as he later claimed, he was on the point of setting out for Ithaca, the home of Odysseus.[49] At this point he received disturbing letters from St Petersburg: one of his business associates, Stepan Solovieff, had gone into bankruptcy, maintaining that he did not owe Schliemann the substantial sum claimed and accusing Schliemann of fraud. Schliemann hurried back to Russia. As he passed the coast of the Troad (the plain of Troy) on 24 June 1859, he noted in his diary: 'In my mind's eye I saw the city, the citadel, the tents of the Achaeans and the priest Chryses, who, shamed and dishonoured by Agamemnon, prays to Apollo for vengeance.'[50] He spent less than a month preparing for the trial in St Petersburg and then resumed his Mediterranean tour. But he did not go back to visit the Homeric sites he had missed in Greece. Instead, Schliemann spent nearly two months in Spain. His main purpose was to find a good investment for his fortune.[51] He was thinking in terms of land and machinery that produced a commodity like olives, olive oil or oranges, for which there was a steady demand. But he combined this search with some fairly typical, if rather energetic, sightseeing.

When the lawsuit against Solovieff came before the Commercial Court in October 1859, Schliemann won the case but Solovieff appealed to the Senate. Schliemann was happy enough to resume his business operations. On his trip he had lost some of his enthusiasm for a life of leisure and in Italy had lamented: 'It is also too late to dedicate myself to a scholarly career.'[52] At the end of 1859 he made up his mind 'to continue my business affairs and never cease to have a trading house here'.[53] In the summer of 1861 the Senate found in Schliemann's favour, and about the same time he was appointed a judge of the Commercial Court.[54] By the end of 1861, however, he was once again disenchanted with business. He planned, however, to continue until January 1864, when he would become a merchant of the First Guild.[55] The outbreak of the American Civil War in 1861 prompted him to buy up large quantities of cotton. He also made significant profits trading in tea. Early in 1863, when Katerina and the children were absent, he used the nursery as a tea-tasting room.

In mid-April 1864 Schliemann went to Aachen, where he drank six glasses of the sulphurous water every day for five weeks. The treatment was probably taken to strengthen the body for the rigours of travel that lay ahead. From here he wrote to Schröder's in Hamburg, outlining his trip. Tunis was to be his first major destination.[56] He was going to dress up as an Arab and explore the interior and send a report to Schröder on the country's resources, the quality of its labour force and other aspects of its economy: 'From Tunis I intend to travel via Egypt, the East Indies, China, Japan, California and Mexico to Cuba and South America and then return to St Petersburg to take up business again in the event that circumstances have improved in the interim.'[57] And this, with the significant addition of India, is essentially what he did.[58] Particularly notable is his determination to return to business in St Petersburg. The idea of excavating Troy seems not to have occurred to him yet. This two-year trip around the world, of course, posed a problem when Schliemann came to write his autobiography in *Ilios*. Why, after all, now that he had made his fortune, had he not gone directly to Troy? It was hard to think of a good reason: 'But before devoting myself entirely to archaeology, and to the realization of the dream of my life, I wished to see a little more of the world.' This may make sense for the ordinary individual but not for one whose life has been driven by the need to make enough money to fulfil a childhood dream.

After Tunis Schliemann sailed to Egypt, where he broke out in spots, which at one point covered his whole body. He returned to Italy at the end of July and after several weeks of treatment at a spa near Bologna he was completely cured. He did some more sightseeing in Italy (Bologna, Florence, Naples, Pompeii, Capri, Paestum) but was troubled by deafness and pain in the ears, which, not surprisingly, he was unable to cure by sea-bathing off Naples. He returned to Paris and consulted a number of doctors there without success. He was referred to the Würzburg ear specialist, Dr von Troeltsch, who diagnosed 'narrowing of the auditory canal and excessive growth at the eardrum.'[59] The condition, technically known as exostosis, is aggravated by cold, particularly, as was pointed out repeatedly to Schliemann, as a result of bathing in cold water. After treatment in Würzburg, he felt much better and set out for Calcutta, stopping briefly at Alexandria, Cairo, Ceylon and Madras *en route*.

He stayed in India from 13 December 1864 to 26 January 1865. The trip combined business with pleasure. He saw fields of cotton and sugar-cane, discussed varieties of tea with an expert, and visited an indigo factory, mosques, and the Taj Mahal. His route took him from Calcutta to Delhi and then into the Himalayas to Mushoori, back to Delhi and on to Agra, Lucknow, Mirzapoor and Calcutta. Intermittent deafness returned in February in Singapore. He saw a doctor in Batavia (Jakarta), who operated on the right ear, apparently removing the bony growths that were constricting the auditory canal. This problem was to recur in one or other and occasionally both ears periodically throughout Schliemann's life.

After spending about a month on Java, he sailed to Saigon (25 March) and on to Canton, Hong Kong (4 April), Shanghai, Tientsin, Peking and the Great Wall. The remainder of the trip is summarized in *Ilios* as follows:

> I then went to Yokohama and Jeddo [Tokyo] in Japan, and thence crossed the Pacific Ocean in a small English vessel to San Francisco in California. Our passage lasted fifty days, which I employed in writing my first work, *La Chine et le Japon*. From San Francisco I went, by way of Nicaragua, to the Eastern United States, travelled through most of them, visited Havannah and the city of Mexico, and in the spring of 1866 settled down in Paris to study archaeology, henceforth with no other interruption than short trips to America.[60]

The last sentence of this summary is contradicted by the evidence of Schliemann's correspondence and diaries. He reached Paris before 14 January, hurried off to London and was back in Paris on 28 January 1866. After finding a publisher and looking for someone to help him edit his book – a friend suggested Alexandre Dumas[61] – he signed up on 1 February at the Collège de France and the Sorbonne. He enrolled in courses on French poetry of the sixteenth century, Arabic language and poetry, Greek philosophy, Greek literature (Sophocles' *Ajax*), Petrarch and his travels, comparative grammar, Egyptian philology and archaeology and modern French language and literature.[62] These choices show a pronounced interest in language and literature rather than archaeology. But Schliemann soon abandoned the lecture hall, and by 7 March he was once again in St Petersburg. He was in two minds about starting up his business activities there again. On 16 March he told J.H. Schröder of London that he would probably be resuming his import business, but on 30 March he told another correspondent that he would not. His relations with his wife had probably in the meantime taken a turn for the worse. He was now determined to start travelling again in July. He spoke of visiting Greece, Turkey, Egypt and Persia and even told his uncle that he would visit the ruins of Troy.[63] In the end he did not go so far south. In November he told Schröder of London that in July and August he had travelled to the Caspian Sea, the Sea of Azov and the Black Sea to assess the business prospects for Russia, only to conclude that they were grim; he had, accordingly, returned to Paris.[64] On the way, he visited a museum in Taganrog, where he saw skulls, swords, gold diadems, and wooden burial couches. On the hills behind the city there were signs of excavation everywhere, particularly at the highest point, where the palace of Mithridates was thought to be located.[65]

30

After wondering for years where he should invest his fortune he decided in 1866 on rental property in Paris. On 24 January he announced to J.H. Schröder that he had purchased four pieces of property: 5 Boulevard St Michel, 33 rue de l'Arcade, 6 and 8 rue de Calais, and 7, 9 and 17 rue des Blancs Moutons. The total cost was 1,736,400 francs.[66] About the same time he also purchased 6 Place St Michel. All were apartment buildings. Schliemann initially decided to take on the management of them himself but after a few months he entrusted this task to an agent. Exactly what prompted him to move such a large proportion of his wealth out of St Petersburg is not wholly clear. No doubt, as in most decisions of this magnitude, there were a number of contributing factors. The poor prospects for the Russian economy must have played a part. But probably it was the breakdown of his marriage and his fears of his wife's claims against him in the event of a divorce that influenced him most. He instructed his lawyer to ensure that he could no longer be considered a Russian subject.[67]

In an extraordinarily frank letter to a friend in St Petersburg, the Count von Fehleisen, Schliemann revealed the sorry state of his marriage:

> She contents herself with representing me to everyone as a terrible tyrant, a despot and a debauchee . . . After that [the first pregnancy] she resisted my approaches every night, screaming that I wanted to kill her, and I can tell you that since the summer of 1855, I have constantly had to commit thefts against the person of my wife and have had to steal my last two children from her in this way.[68]

Schliemann was nonetheless anxious for Katerina to join him in Paris. It was really the children he wanted to see. On 14 February he wrote to her: 'Every evening I go to the theatres or to scholarly lectures by the most famous professors in the world, like Touvé, Beulé, the Viscount de Rougé, etc. and I could now tell you stories for ten years without ever wearing you out.'[69] There is a touch of pathos in this letter or rather in what seems to lie behind it. He is clearly doing his best to make himself and his mode of life in Paris sound appealing. Given that his cultural activities were designed to meet with Katerina's approval, it seems likely that his sudden interest in cultural self-improvement in 1856 was also intended to please her. If so, then the crucial conversion from merchant to archaeologist that was effected between 1856 and 1870 may have found its original impetus in the impossible task of pleasing a woman who despised him. It is in this tragic irony, not in the trumpery of the 'childhood dream', that the real romance of Schliemann's life resides.

Katerina's response was unequivocal. She would not come to Paris. In April Schliemann tried another approach. He knew that Katerina liked Dresden. He proposed that they live there instead of in Paris. He invited her to join him there with the children to see if it might work out. If it did not, then he would not say another word about it. He rather spoiled the effect, however, by telling her not to say a word about the proposal to anyone. As she thought it over, he gave her something else to think about. If she would not live with him, he would pay her alimony of 6,100 silver roubles per year. A month later he reduced his offer of alimony to 4,800 silver roubles. Even with the lower sum there was no danger of Katerina and the children starving, but there would be a very substantial drop in their standard of living. Naturally, she talked over the Dresden proposal with her lawyer father. He seems to have told her to insist on a legal guarantee, not merely a notarized promise from Schliemann, that she would not be forced to move from Dresden to Paris or anywhere else against her wishes. Schliemann was enraged. In July he threatened her with an American divorce. The proposed alimony still stood at 4,800 silver roubles per year.[70]

In the meantime, Schliemann was enthusiastically attending the meetings of a number of learned societies. On 7 May he heard a lecture given at the Geography Society on a recent book by a Greek scholar, G. Nicolaides, *Topographie et plan stratégique de l'Iliade*.[71] This may well have been when Schliemann first learned that there was a scholarly debate over the site of Troy. Both Nicolaides and the lecturer, Victor Guérin, favoured Bunarbashi, dismissing the rival site, Hisarlik, with little more than a mention. Schliemann must have noticed the great interest taken in this matter by the learned geographers, and the reverence with which Homer's words were treated. The subject certainly seems to have intrigued him for he purchased a copy of Nicolaides' book.

Schliemann lost no time in taking steps towards obtaining his American divorce. In 1851 he had already filed the first stage of his application for American citizenship, in most states a prerequisite for divorce. Now that more than five years had elapsed, all he needed to do was to file a second declaration and he would immediately become an American citizen. He sailed from Liverpool on 18 September. In New York, however, he ran into a bureaucratic hitch. To be eligible for citizenship, he had to have been resident in the United States for the preceding five years and in that particular State for the preceding year. He and a witness had to swear that this was true. He was quite unprepared for this and so had to put aside his hope for American citizenship.

He then proceeded to visit some schools in New York. He seems to have been entertaining the possibility of having his children educated in America. He thought that schooling in Russia was inferior and throughout the summer of 1867 kept arguing that his children should be educated in France or

Germany. He had written to Katerina about the fine schools in Dresden. In New York he went about his study with his usual thoroughness, visiting classes, interviewing teachers and principals, and making notes even on such details as desk sizes and the specific arithmetical problems posed. His impressions were, in general, favourable. He also visited schools in Chicago, where he particularly appreciated the practice of educating boys and girls together.[72] He reported to his brother-in-law: 'I saw with astonishment how girls and boys of 12 and 13 years of age in the high schools translate Horace from the Latin and Sophocles from the Greek into English and German.' His brother-in-law wrote back that he did not believe him, though he phrased it more diplomatically.[73] For most of the trip, however, Schliemann was busy absorbing 'the most accurate information on the present prospects for the reconstruction of the southern states, the labour resources, the cultivation of sugar, rice and cotton.'[74] He travelled extensively throughout the midwest and south by rail. This enabled him also to check how well individual railway companies, in many of which he was a shareholder, were doing. He was interested in detailed information and visited the Bureau of Statistics in Washington. He also claims to have had a brief interview with President Andrew Johnson on 7 January 1868, but this almost certainly did not occur.[75]

He again visited Cuba on this trip. Here he was interested in the railways, in which he personally, as well as Schröder, were major investors. He also wanted to inform himself fully on other questions: 'the prospects for the island in general and for sugar production in particular in case political changes in the mother country might lead suddenly to the emancipation of slaves; also, the progress in the introduction of Chinese and Indian coolies. Only the latter, in my opinion, are capable of replacing the negro slaves.'[76]

On 3 January 1868 he saw Charles Dickens give a reading of *A Christmas Carol* in New York. He noted in his diary:

> He appeared to be about 50 years old but well fed and preserved. He had a book before him which he never used, because he knew it by heart, and, strange to say, he without looking on it, always turned the pages as he came to the end of one, so well he was acquainted with every word as it stood on the pages. He read *A Christmas Carrol* [sic] – a composition of gosts [sic] and humbug – but still by the manner he delivered it and by his gestures it pleased every one.[77]

On 5 January 1868, after a lengthy discussion of the prices of barrels of pork and other commodities, he made the following entry:

> Today is Christmas-eve in St. Petersburg and the watch in hand and adding to the N.Y. time 6 hours and 50 minutes, I always reckon what o'clock it is there and with

heart and soul I am continually with my little darlings, thinking how they are rejoicing at their Christmas-tree and shedding bitter tears that I cannot contribute to their cheerfulness by my presence. $100,000 I would give if I could spend this evening with them. Indeed much more philosophy and fortitude than I have are required to pass this day without being bathed in tears.

A week later he was sailing back to France, apparently quite unaware that he was about to embark on a new life.

3

From Grand Tour to Archaeological Survey

WHEN SCHLIEMANN RETURNED FROM America in late January 1868, he at once turned his energies to intellectual pursuits – philosophy, archaeology, ethnography. However, he missed his children acutely and felt a strong compulsion to effect a reconciliation with his wife and return to St Petersburg. But this would mean, as he explained to a friend, abandoning his studies, for in St Petersburg there were 'no resources for the mind.' He would have to resume business to have something to occupy himself, but 'I am disgusted with business and would certainly never have thought of returning to it were it not that it turns me crazy to live without my children. I cannot think yet without horror of leaving even for a time this beautiful Paris but there seems to be no other alternative. I am here totally absorbed by the studies of philosophy and other good things.'[1] He gave more specific information on his activities to another friend: 'Here in Paris I find that fanaticism is much more contagious even than yellow fever, because in all the courses that I am taking at the Sorbonne, the Collège de France, and at the Bibliothèque Impériale, as well as at the meetings of the learned societies of which I am a member – the Geographical and Ethnographical Societies and the Society for American and Oriental Archaeology – I am surrounded by fanatics for knowledge, who have made me a fanatic also.'[2]

On 4 April he wrote to his son Serge that he would be returning to St Petersburg. He outlined his route: Basel, Luzern, St Gotthard, Lugano, Milan, Venice, Rome, Naples, Palermo, Messina, Syracuse, Ithaca, Corfu, Dardanelles, the battlefield of Troy, Constantinople, Odessa, Kiev, Moscow.[3] The appearance of Ithaca and Troy in his itinerary is noteworthy. Since he hoped to arrive in St Petersburg by the end of May, however, it is clear that he must have been intending to visit the Homeric sites only as an interested tourist and not with a view to excavation. Shortly after this Schliemann's plans changed rather abruptly. He had been warned by a friend in St Petersburg that Solovieff's widow was planning to sue him on some other aspect of the Solovieff affair. The friend strongly advised against Schliemann's return to Russia in view of the disagreeable legal consequences he would have to face.[4] He decided that after Constantinople he would return to Paris via the Mediterranean.

After brief stops in Milan, Bologna and Florence, Schliemann arrived in Rome on 5 May equipped with a copy of John Murray's *Handbook of Rome and its Environs*.[5] He was a very diligent tourist. Over the next month he visited practically every church, art gallery, museum, monument and site in Rome that was recommended by the guidebook. For the most part, Schliemann's Rome diary, which he kept in Italian, is an annotated catalogue of the various attractions seen each day. Much of the detailed information he took from Murray's *Handbook*; some must also have come from the personal guides he employed to escort him around Rome and some from the custodians at individual sites. There are occasional personal touches, as when he remarks that he had to fire his first guide for coarseness and obscene language, but these are surprisingly few. He never once indicates, for instance, where he ate a meal.

Some of the galleries and museums he visited several times. This is scarcely surprising in the case of the Vatican Museums and the Galleria Borghese. His three visits to San Pietro in Montorio, however, suggest a more personal interest. That interest seems to have centered on Beatrice Cenci, who was buried there. A tragic sixteenth-century figure, she was famous for having killed her father, who had forced her to have incestuous relations with him. She was executed in 1599. Her name crops up several times in the Rome diary. Schliemann visited her prison in the Castel Sant' Angelo and ordered a copy of the painting of her in the Palazzo Barberini attributed to Guido. Her tragic story appealed to nineteenth-century sentiment; Murray's *Handbook* called the Barberini portrait one of the most celebrated paintings in Rome. It has recently been suggested, with some plausibility, that Schliemann may have felt a special sympathy for Beatrice, prompted by a perceived resemblance between her tyrannical father and Schliemann's own father.[6]

Schliemann also showed a remarkable interest in Cleopatra, singling out for special mention some five paintings and a statue of her. Among the three paintings of Cleopatra in the Palazzo Spada he was particularly impressed by Francesco Trevisano's version of the banquet scene at which Antony cast a pearl into Cleopatra's goblet, saying 'You only love me because I am rich.'[7] One can readily see psychological reasons why this painting might appeal to Schliemann. A rich man himself, he seems to have suspected that women were attracted to him for the same reason. This fear was perhaps a factor in the breakdown of his marriage with Katerina and was to evidence itself in almost comic fashion in his courting of his second wife, Sophia. Schliemann's preoccupation with Cleopatra was not just a Roman affair. Later on this trip he bought a coin of Antony and Cleopatra in Ithaca and inspected the Cleopatra coins in the museum in Athens. In 1888, he claimed to have found a marble bust of her while excavating for her palace in Alexandria. Probably, however, as we shall see, this bust was purchased earlier.[8]

The modern reader is also struck by the high regard Schliemann had for the paintings of Domenichino and Guido. They are the artists whose works he most frequently mentions as having particularly impressed him. Here too Schliemann was a mirror of contemporary taste. Murray's guide quotes, with apparent approval, the judgement of Poussin that Domenichino's *Communion of St Jerome* was the best painting in the world after Raphael's *Transfiguration*. A particular favourite of Schliemann's was Guido's *Aurora* on the ceiling of the Palazzo Rospigliosi, which he visited three times. Before leaving Rome he bought copies of Domenichino's *Hunt of Diana* and *Sibyl*, Guido's *Fortune* and Caravaggio's *Card-players* and ordered copies of Guido's *Aurora*, *Beatrice Cenci* and Desubleo's *Cleopatra*.[9] Remarkably, although he must have seen many paintings and sculptures on Homeric themes, he does not mention a single one. Also, he seems not to have bought any antiquities other than coins.

If Schliemann had not become a famous archaeologist, few readers of his Rome diary would infer that he was more interested in archaeology than in baroque painting. In his entry of 30 May Schliemann remarks: 'Then we visited the gallery in the Palazzo Rospigliosi, where the fresco of Aurora by Guido Reni on the ceiling of the first room is worth all the other paintings.' This kind of personal feeling, which occasionally flashes forth when he refers to the paintings, is lacking in the accounts of his visits to the Forum, the Palatine, the Colosseum, Ostia and other classical sites. It is tempting to give more prominence to the ancient sites than his visits to the art galleries, but we should not allow hindsight to distort the picture of Schliemann as he was in May 1868. Then he was a diligent tourist on the Grand Tour, distinguished not so much for an interest in archaeology as for the single-minded thoroughness with which he followed the recommendations of his guidebook.

This is not to say that seeds were not sown. On 7 May Schliemann noted that excavations were taking place 'everywhere' on the Palatine. On the following day, 'we then went up to the Palatine near the Villa Mills, where the Pope is having immense excavations done. Among many other things there I saw a set of steps which they have just excavated.' On 18 May he observed: 'I then visited the *Roman Emporium* on the bank of the Tiber, where they are now conducting large excavations and have already discovered more than 200 blocks of marble – verde antico, porto santo, etc. – of great value. Already they have uncovered two stairways or wharfs with rocks with holes for mooring ships. I saw there a block that they have begun to carve into eight columns. Now they are uncovering the large customs-house. Everything is covered with six metres of earth.' While I believe that these contacts with current excavations were eventually to prove of considerable importance in prodding Schliemann towards an archaeological career, it would be easy to exaggerate the impression they made on him at the time. Of some 22,000 words devoted to his visit to Rome this is all he wrote about the excavations he witnessed in progress. Before leaving for Naples, however, he had 'a long conversation with the very pleasant director of the excavations, Cavaliere Pietro Rosa, who is now making the plan of ancient Rome (his title is Conservator of the Palace of the Caesars). He recommends that I read Virgil VIII on the Palatine.'[10]

Schliemann's interests as a tourist in the Bay of Naples were decidedly more oriented to archaeology than they had been in Rome. To some extent, this reflects the fact that the main tourist attractions there are more emphatically archaeological than at Rome. He took trips to see the antiquities at Pompeii, Herculaneum, Cumae, Baiae, Pozzuoli, the Sibyl's grotto, Capri and Capua. He visited the National Museum in Naples, whose treasures were and are primarily antiquities from Pompeii, Herculaneum, and the environs of Naples, no less than seven times, usually for most of the day. He even attended lectures at the University of Naples on comparative literature, Greek literature (an exegesis of Pindar's ninth Pythian ode) and ancient and modern history. Of particular interest are his visits to Pompeii and Capri.

He spent most of three days in Pompeii. Of his first visit, on 8 June, he merely remarked: 'I remained until 3 o'clock in Pompeii, where the excavations proceed more energetically now that a railway line has been constructed to remove the rubbish.' Schliemann was to remember this solution to the problem of earth removal and introduced it to his excavations at Troy in 1890. His second visit, on 16 June, prompted a longer account:

> I set out this morning at six for Pompeii, where I remained till 4.30 p.m. traversing all the streets of the ancient city. They are now excavating very little and scarcely clear one house in two weeks. Pompeii was covered first with from 8 to 10 feet of pebbles or pumice, then with 8 to 10 feet of ashes, and then with boiling water, which turned the ash into a compact mass as hard as tufa; thus, by pouring liquid stucco in the hollow left by the bodies after they decayed and disappeared, Cavaliere Fiorelli has been able to restore in plaster casts four victims, two sliding-doors and a double door with a huge lock. Then I visited the school in which Giulio de Petra is the instructor (he is a Neapolitan). He has two students, Eduardo Brizio from Turin and Francesco Salvatore Dino (Neapolitan). It is not true that Pompeii was on the sea, because there are ruins of ancient houses in front of the Porta Marina, where the sea should have been. Of great interest in Pompeii are the

magnificent frescos painted with the utmost grace and *disinvoltura*; the houses, on whose outer walls are written in large letters the names of candidates running for public offices, a kind of poster; the narrow streets paved with broad flat stones of lava, with sidewalks on either side, and from time to time with large stones in the middle of the streets to allow people to cross from one side to the other, when it rained, without getting their feet wet. There is a comic theatre, a tragic theatre and an amphitheatre.[11] The latter could have held 12,000 spectators, the tragic theatre 5,000 and the other 1,500.

Fiorelli was the best field archaeologist of his day. He turned what had been little more than a search for art treasures at Pompeii into the first scientific study of an ancient town. He proceeded carefully to avoid destruction of important evidence. Schliemann met him at the National Museum in Naples on 10 May and obtained permission to visit certain restricted areas of the museum, including the *Raccolta pornografica* of obscene objects from Pompeii. However, he says nothing more about their encounter. Schliemann could have learned much from Fiorelli's techniques. His impatience with the speed of the excavations is characteristic.

In his enthusiasm for the Pompeian frescos he saw in the Naples museum, Schliemann becomes quite lyrical: 'These were obviously done with great speed but nonetheless with such elegance, *disinvoltura* and lightness that the artist's brush seems truly to have conquered nature itself. Everything appears to be alive; nothing is studied; everything is natural. If one compares with these masterpieces of antiquity the masterpieces of Raphael, the latter appear too artificial; there is no life in them, no *disinvoltura*, no spontaneity.' Art criticism of this kind did not come readily to Schliemann and no doubt he is here indebted to an Italian guidebook or guide.

On 19 June he sailed to Capri, where he climbed up the steps to Anacapri. 'Almost all the peasants I meet ask me for alms and if they are pretty, I ask for a kiss for every coin; but only boys agree to it.' He walked from Anacapri to the ruins of Tiberius' palace: 'Substantial ruins remain, among them two huge vaulted rooms which may have served for Tiberius' bestial behaviour. There is also a twisting corridor with mosaic paving which seems to lead down. Some English visitors, who have asked for permission to excavate it, think they will find some bedrooms along the way.' The owner of the hotel where he stayed overnight in Capri had nine children: 'Giuseppe 23, Filippo 12, Costanzo 7, Rosina 24, Giovannina 19, Mariuccia 18, Emilia 18, Amalia 7 and the beautiful twenty-year-old Teresina, with whom I fell in love; she is big and strong. I had a bad meal and drank three bottles of wine with the girls. In the evening I had 5 peasants come who danced the tarantella to the sound of the tambourine; I had to pay 5 francs. Then the girls danced and I danced along with them. We drank another 7 bottles of wine.' Then came the morning after: 'I feel ill today. The hotel-owner in Capri made me pay 31 francs, though I did not want to pay more than 8. The chamber-pot stank; all night I was attacked by flies, bugs, fleas, and mosquitos. Moreover, there was such filth there, the sea-water was so bad and everything so awful that I cannot think of it without disgust. I have terrible diarrhoea.'

After a brief stop in Sicily, where he climbed to the top of Mount Etna and was nearly blown over the rim into the crater by the strong winds, Schliemann reached Corfu on 6 July. From this point on, his travels are described in *Ithaque, le Péloponnèse et Troie* (hereafter *Ithaque*), which he wrote after he returned to Paris in September. Sometimes the published version of the trip differs significantly from the diary account.

Schliemann was now using as his guide Murray's *Handbook for Travellers in Greece* (1854). From it he learned that the ancients universally regarded Corfu as Homer's Scheria, where Odysseus was washed ashore naked near a river mouth and the next morning confronted Nausicaa and her companions playing ball on the beach, while the royal laundry dried on pebbles nearby.[12] Local tradition identified the river with the stream Cressida, some three miles south-west of the town of Corfu. Schliemann found that the stream was used for irrigation and had many channels running off from it, making it difficult to determine where the river actually met the sea.

> Despite this I wanted to see the spot where Nausicaa played ball with her companions and met Odysseus and since I could not jump across the channels I took off my clothes, keeping only my shirt and woollen undershirt and waded across. Often I was up to my middle in mud and water. Often I took a wrong turning and had to come back but finally my efforts were successful and I reached the mouth of the ancient river. Joyfully I imagined there Nausicaa's welcome of Odysseus. My state of undress caused me considerable embarrassment in front of the women who were busy pulling out the ripe flax from the ground, root and all, and throwing it over their heads to dry. In addition I had to suffer the taunts of the men who were engaged in digging a ditch.

This amusing episode well illustrates the problems presented by Schliemann's autobiographical writings. Though he does not explicitly draw a parallel between himself and Odysseus, it is hard to believe that he did not expect the reader to note that he also reached the river mouth in an embarrassing state of undress and that the women in the fields are modern counterparts to Nausicaa's companions. Is the whole incident therefore fiction? Perhaps. More probably, however, the scene has merely been touched up. The fieldworkers, male and female, seem real enough. No doubt Schliemann had to roll up his trousers to cross the stream. When he came to write up his diary, the literary possibilities of the scene suggested a more radical state of *déshabille*. In writing up this incident for publication in *Ithaque*, Schliemann included his state of undress but omitted his encounters with the fieldworkers. Perhaps he thought them too *risqué*.

Schliemann spent nine days (9–17 July) in Ithaca. Most of his stay was devoted to identifying the various parts of the island mentioned by Homer, such as the site of the main town and of Odysseus' palace, the sties where the loyal swineherd Eumaeus kept his master's pigs, and so on. Before concluding that this proves Schliemann's long-standing interest in Homeric geography, it is as well to recall that it is precisely these concerns that Murray's *Handbook* expects of its readers. The section on Ithaca provides an extraordinarily detailed discussion of the most likely locations of the various Homeric sites. The discussion includes quotations in Greek and runs to ten pages.

Schliemann found lodgings in Vathy, the principal town in Ithaca. On 10 July he climbed up to a cave in the hills on Mount Neion close to Vathy. This has traditionally been identified with the Cave of the Nymphs, where Odysseus, after being set down on the shore by the Phaeacians, hid the gifts he had received from them before setting out for Eumaeus' hut.[13] Though awkwardly located far above the shore, it nevertheless fits Homer's description in other respects, having stalactites and two entrances, one for mortals and one in the roof for gods.

From there he proceeded to what had long been identified as the Castle of Odysseus on the summit of Mount Aetos, the mountain that dominates the isthmus uniting the two halves of the island. At the head of the valley between Mount Neion and Mount Aetos he bought a vase and a Corinthian coin from a man who had apparently just found them in a tomb on the lower slopes of Mount Aetos. Though only about 385 metres high, Mount Aetos is very steep and awkward to climb. Schliemann noted grimly that it was scalable only by gods and goats. Near the summit he saw ruined walls, towers, and cisterns carved out of the rock. Only at the north end of the summit is there an expanse of flat ground large enough for a building of any size, and indeed occasional short stretches of walls are still to be seen there. Here then, Schliemann decided, as had others before him, was the site of Odysseus' palace. As he tried to conjure up this building in his mind, he came to another decision, one that unequivocally signals the beginning of his archaeological career.

I went up to the higher summit, from where three lines of walls can be distinguished. The upper part is almost flat and here no doubt was a large house.

There is a large cistern 20 feet in diameter and 10 feet deep. There are two small cisterns besides, 5 feet in diameter. Concerning the interior arrangement of the palace it is impossible to form any idea, but I will bring a spade with me to excavate.

Schliemann had heard lectures on archaeology in Paris, had seen professional archaeologists at work in Rome and Pompeii and amateurs digging at Tiberius' villa on Capri. He had bought antiquities dug from an ancient tomb and was now on the site of Odysseus' palace admiring a breathtaking view. The decision to try his own hand at excavation was, under the circumstances, a natural one. What appears to have been the immediate cause of this decision, a desire to determine the interior arrangement of Odysseus' palace, speaks well for Schliemann. At this critical point, on the threshold of his archaeological career, to characterize him as a goldseeker would be inadequate and unfair. It is the desire to find out more about how people once lived that distinguishes the archaeologist from the treasure-hunter. On this test, Schliemann's instincts place him clearly in the camp of the archaeologists.

From the summit of Mount Aetos the view was spectacular. Schliemann noted in his diary:

At the northern part of the castle two walls of large stones run down, which end in a kind of tower. For a long time I sat in the ruins of the palace reading the divine Odyssey, and, in particular, the recognition scene of Odysseus and Penelope, and wept profusely. There is a superb view from the summit. To the west is Cephalonia, to the north, the mountain Agoge with the island Asteris in the strait and Leucadia in the distance. To the east is Acarnania with the island Iatoko in the harbour of Phorcys. Besides, nowhere in the world is the sea so clear and the mountains so beautiful as in Greece.

On the following day Schliemann went south from Vathy to the plain of Marathia, where Murray's guide told him that various features mentioned by Homer – the cliff of Corax, the spring of Arethusa and the sties of Eumaeus – were to be found. On 12 July he rode to the north of the island looking for the Garden of Laertes, where Odysseus met his father. Murray's guide identified this with the site of the village of Leuce but Schliemann, citing local tradition, saw it in cultivated fields just south of the village of Ayios Ioannis. Here he sat down and read the recognition scene of Odysseus and Laertes in the twenty-fourth book of the *Odyssey*. Then he proceeded to the village of Leuce, where he had some wine and read Homer aloud to the crowd that had gathered around him. In *Ithaque*, though not in his diary, he adds that the villagers brought him 'a mass of ancient Greek coins, including some very rare pieces; all of them had been found in the excavations at the nearby site of the ancient

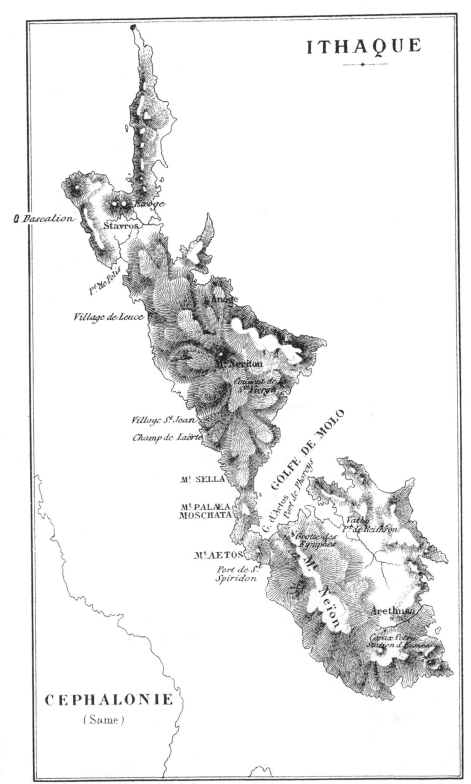

Fig. 1 Ithaca (from *Ithaque, le Péloponnèse et Troie*)

city of Polis. They wanted to give me them for nothing; but I insisted on paying twenty francs for them.'

Schliemann descended to the site of ancient Polis on the bay below the modern town of Stavros. Here he met a sailor who showed him the site of a collapsed cave on the bay, where a certain Dimitrios Loizos had excavated an ancient tomb. In it Loizos had found a spearhead, an Egyptian cantharos (goblet), a ring, ancient coins and a broken and much corroded sword. Schliemann bought all these finds from Loizos. Three days later he returned and bought more finds from Loizos, who was continuing to dig there.

The site of Loizos' cave was later excavated in 1930–2 by the British archaeologist Silvia Benton.[14] Among the finds she made were twelve bronze tripods of the ninth to eighth centuries BC. These three-footed stands constitute perhaps the most dramatic link with the Homeric poems that has as yet been established by modern archaeology. When Odysseus left the Phaeacians, he received among other gifts a tripod from Alcinous and each of twelve other nobles.[15] Since Loizos found a bronze tripod in 1873, the number of tripods found in that cave corresponds precisely to the number left by Odysseus in the Cave of the Nymphs.[16] Perhaps Homer was aware of a cult of the nymphs in Ithaca that featured thirteen tripods or perhaps the poet's work inspired such a cult.[17] Schliemann climbed up from the shore to Stavros and then on to the acropolis above the village. Here only broken walls were to be seen. After visiting some classical and Byzantine ruins, romantically called the 'School of Homer', he returned to Vathy by way of Anoge.

On 13 July he set out to excavate on the summit of Mount Aetos. He took with him a workman, a two-pronged fork and a pickaxe.

We went up the west slope, half by mule and the rest on foot. We began to dig in a part where the hardness of the ground and many old and young roots demonstrated that the place had not yet been excavated. We found pieces of bricks but nothing else. Looking everywhere for a likely spot I found a rock whose top, visible for only a short stretch, seemed to me to be worked and rounded. Taking the pickaxe and removing the earth from the rock I found that it formed a semi-circle. The other semi-circle was covered with earth. I instructed the workman to excavate there. We found the earth very hard and mixed with lime. After digging a little, the workman smashed a clay vessel and then a second and a third. Because of this, we dug with great care and succeeded in getting five or six vessels out whole, with only their handles broken. All the vessels are filled with ash and little bits of human bones. They are all of different shapes but painted. On one I was confident I could see human figures at first but once the vase was exposed to the air, the figures faded and darkened. The holes of the vessels are very small so that it almost appears that they were used to receive human remains. We found some in the shape of a saltcellar and a cup. All are made of clay. I also extracted bits of bronze wire with some threads wound around. Also a twisted (bent) corroded knife and bits of swords, one bronze, one iron. Also a clay idol or statue of a priestess. Unfortunately, we were too hasty and because of this we damaged many vessels. If we had loosened or cut the soil with a knife, we would perhaps have saved almost all the vessels . . . We also extracted from the hole eight or ten small bones and a boar's tusk.

The next day Schliemann returned with four workmen. He measured the flat area at the summit and the various cisterns but though he excavated all over the summit, he found only the outline of a small building on the eastern slope and bricks, mortar, and bones.

When he came to write up these two days of excavation in *Ithaque*, Schliemann glamorized his account in a number of ways. He increased the number of workmen from one to four. He transferred the discovery of the building from the second to the first day. Then he recast the account of the main find as follows:

While my workmen were busy with this excavation (i.e. of the building), I examined the entire site of the palace of Ulysses with the most rigorous attention; having found a large stone, one extremity of which seemed to describe a short curving line – perhaps the hundredth part of a circle – with my knife I removed the earth from the stone and I saw that it formed a semi-circle. Continuing to dig a little with the knife, I noticed that the circle was completed on the other side with small stones laid on top of one another, forming a kind of miniature wall. At first I wanted to dig out this circle with my knife, but it was impossible, for the earth, mixed with a white substance which I recognized to be the ash of calcified bones, was almost as hard as stone. I began to dig with the pickaxe, but scarcely had I gone more than ten centimetres when I broke a beautiful but very small vase, filled with human ash. I then continued to dig with the greatest care and I found about twenty vases, oddly shaped and completely different from one another. Some were lying down, others standing up but, unfortunately, because of the hardness of the soil and lack of proper implements, I broke most of them as I extracted them and I was able to bring out only five in good condition. The largest of them is only 11 cm high; the diameter of its opening is 1 cm. Another has an opening of only 6 millimetres. Two of the vases had rather attractive human figures painted on them when I took them from the ground. These painted figures vanished almost as soon as they were exposed to the sun, but I hope I can bring them back by rubbing them with alcohol and water. All these vases are filled with ashes of cremated human bodies.

Then Schliemann goes on to list the other objects found. These correspond closely to the objects listed in the diary. Returning to the vases, he confesses that he is unable to date them but considers them very early. He concludes: 'It is very possible that I have in my five little vases the bodies of Ulysses and Penelope or their offspring.'

It will be seen that the workman has disappeared from the account to allow all the limelight to fall on Schliemann, the vases now number 'about twenty', and the human ash in the five unbroken vases has become possibly that of Odysseus and Penelope. These small changes, clearly designed to make the modest find more exciting to his readers, remind us that though Schliemann's motives for excavating may have been laudable, his egotism and need to keep his public interested affect the veracity of his reports. One might argue, however, that the changes are of little consequence and that what matters is that Schliemann has stuck to the findspot and list of finds recorded in the diary. But should we believe the diary? There are grounds for scepticism. No one since Schliemann has found any evidence of burials on the summit of Mount Aetos. Also, it is a highly exposed and eroded site, which has not yielded to other archaeologists any complete or almost complete vases, though these have frequently been found at the saddle site (Ayios Georgios) below Mount Aetos and at Polis Bay. Before excavating, Schliemann had bought finds from both these sites. We should bear in mind the possibility that Schliemann found nothing of consequence at the summit but did not want to put that in his diary. He may have simply used his purchases and his imagination to create a dramatic find at what he believed to be the site of Odysseus' palace. The purchased items included a broken sword and a spearhead, which may be identical with the broken sword and knife of the 'find'.[18]

In *Ithaque* Schliemann rearranged the chronology of his trip. For instance, he made the two days of excavation on Mount Aetos *precede* his purchases at Polis Bay. Some incidents that appear in the book are not attested in the diary and must have simply been invented by Schliemann. Among these is his famous encounter with the dogs.

> On that day, wishing to approach the farmyard of a peasant at the south end of the island, I was furiously attacked by four large dogs, that were not frightened by the stones or threats I hurled at them. I cried out for help; but my guide had remained behind and it seems that there was nobody in the peasant's house. In this terrible predicament, I fortunately recalled what Ulysses had done in a similar danger (*Od.* 14.29–31): 'Suddenly the barking dogs saw Odysseus and ran up to him howling; but Odysseus prudently sat down and his stick fell from his hand.' So I followed the example of the wise king, bravely sitting down on the ground, and remaining immobile, and at once the four dogs, who seemed ready to devour me, formed a circle around me and continued barking but did not touch me.

Schliemann was rescued from this awkward position by his guide and the dogs' owner. It is clear, however, that the incident was invented by Schliemann. It was inspired by a passage in Murray's *Handbook*, where travellers in Ithaca encountering fierce dogs are advised to remember Odysseus' experience and to sit down and remain still.

From Ithaca Schliemann sailed to Patras and from there to Piraeus, crossing the isthmus at Corinth. On 20 July he took a room in the Grande Bretagne Hotel in Syntagma Square. The next few days he spent visiting the Acropolis and other sights in Athens with his old friend of St Petersburg days, Archbishop Vimpos. Among the residents of Athens he met were three with whom he was to have repeated contacts for the rest of his life: Achilles Postolaccas, the Conservator of the Numismatic Collection in Athens; Stephanos Koumanoudis, Professor of Latin and Roman Archaeology at the University of Athens; and Ernst Ziller, a German architect. On 24 August Postolaccas showed him a number of coins bearing the image of Cleopatra, but was unable to date the pots Schliemann had excavated on Mount Aetos. On 25 August Koumanoudis tried unsuccessfully to decipher the inscription from Polis Bay. On the same day, however, Ziller gave Schliemann 'important information about the Troad, where he uncovered the walls of the Pergamon [of Troy].'

Ziller had participated in the first real attempt to determine the site of ancient Troy by excavation. He assisted J. von Hahn in his excavations on Balli Dagh above Bunarbashi in 1864. Situated at the south end of the Troad, Bunarbashi was then the most widely supported contender for the site of Homeric Troy. The Balli Dagh above it was held to be the city's acropolis or 'Pergamon', as Homer called it. Although von Hahn had found no evidence that would date the site early enough to be Homer's Troy, he nonetheless remained convinced that this was the site that had inspired Homer.[19] Ziller seems to have shared von Hahn's convictions and communicated his enthusiasm to Schliemann. It was this meeting with Ziller, in the context of his growing interest in archaeology, that appears to have determined the course of the last twenty years of Schliemann's life. From this point on, Homeric archaeology was his major preoccupation.

Striking evidence of just how much this meeting fired Schliemann with enthusiasm for Troy is provided by the next entry in his diary, dated Nauplion 1 August.

> Since at the first ticket office of the French steamer they could not guarantee that I could disembark at the Dardanelles – because they arrive there at night and cannot disembark passengers – I decided to wait for the next Austrian steamer and so to make good use of the time, I wanted to see Mycenae and Argos. I bought powder for the bedbugs and mosquitos and quinine. I set off on 29 July for Piraeus.

A seasoned traveller, Schliemann was flexible enough to adjust his plans at a moment's notice, but it is clear that after his talk with Ziller his thoughts had turned first to Troy. He took an overnight boat from Piraeus to the isthmus and reached New Corinth early on the 30th. An earthquake had destroyed the town of Corinth in 1859. The Corinthians rebuilt their town a few miles east in a location more exposed to breezes and less subject to malaria. After breakfasting in a hotel he hired a horse and a guide and set off to climb Acrocorinth, pausing briefly to admire the ruins of the old city – the evocative columns of an archaic temple and a Roman amphitheatre – and bought six ancient vases from a peasant, which had been dug up in the adjacent fields. At the summit of Acrocorinth he saw ruined houses, mosques and the remains of the Turkish barracks. A number of villagers were digging deep pits at four different locations. They believed that before abandoning their garrison the Turks had buried fifteen large chests of money. They had been digging there for a year without success. Schliemann went down into the pits (two of them were about 17 metres deep) to look for signs of ancient walls but saw none. He remained at the summit for three hours, admiring the famous view over the Gulf of Corinth to Delphi, Mounts Parnassus and Cithaeron and the isthmus.

The next day, 31 July, Schliemann left for Mycenae with his guide. Two soldiers accompanied them for security against brigands.

We crossed barren stretches, then high mountains, and descended into the prosperous realm of Agamemnon. Of his capital, Mycenae, there remains the acropolis on a craggy hill in the foothills of two great mountains. All the walls are still extant. They are 400 metres in length. They are 15 to 35 ft in height and consist of great hewn stones 4 to 10 ft in length, 3 to 5 ft in thickness and 3 to 6 ft in breadth. The surface of the acropolis rises towards the centre and there are many terraces, also with cyclopean walls. There is a great gate with an entry-way 50 ft long and 30 ft broad, created by a wall parallel to the fortification wall. The gate is 10 ft high, 9½ ft broad. It is formed by 2 large stones, 6 ft broad and covered by another stone 15 ft long, 4 ft broad, and 6 ft 7 inches high in the centre. Above this stone there is a triangle, 12 ft long, 10 ft high, and 2 ft thick. On it there is a bas-relief of two lions, standing on their hind legs and having their fore-paws on a temple. Between them is a column with a capital comprising a series of four circles. I see in the gate the round holes in which the door hinges turned. There are three cisterns there. In one of them I saw a large snake. There is also a smaller gate on the opposite side of the acropolis. I saw everywhere many bricks and pieces of pots and therefore, assuredly, Agamemnon's palace was on the acropolis. Of the town there are no ruins apart from a few walls of cyclopean masonry and one large and two small underground chambers in the shape of a tholos [domed beehive]. The large underground chamber, which was apparently the treasury, is situated in the slope of a hill. The entrance is between two walls 30 ft high, made of stones 4 to 5 ft high and 2 to 3

48

ft broad. The dromos [entrance-way] is 27 ft broad. On top of the door is set a stone, 24 ft long and 18 ft broad. Above the doorway there is a triangular opening, in which there once were small pillars. The diameter of the first circular chamber is 47 ft 6 in. The height is 50 ft. The chamber is connected by a door with another room rudely cut into the hillside. It was full of small bats, square, but with a small vault. It is 23 ft square. The breadth of the large door is 20 to 22 ft. I see in it the holes for the door's hinges, and, in the same line, a row of round holes for bronze nails, whose points are still visible. Inside I see the nails in the stones everywhere and undoubtedly they used them to nail down the bronze plaques with which the entire large chamber of the treasury was fitted. On both sides of the main entrance shapes of bottles are carved into the wall.

Schliemann and his escort reached Mycenae about noon. Schliemann spent about four or five hours there, examining the famous Lion Gate, the Postern Gate, and the Treasury of Atreus and other features of the site. His diary account is rather disappointing, however, for it is almost entirely derived from Murray's *Handbook*. Of greater interest is his expanded account in *Ithaque*. There he puts forward an unusual interpretation of a passage in Pausanias that was to prove of monumental importance.

When Pausanias visited Mycenae in the second century AD, he saw underground treasuries and the tombs where Agamemnon and his suite were buried after they were assassinated by Aegisthus and Clytemnestra. The tombs of Aegisthus and Clytemnestra were said to be 'a little further from the wall, as they were not judged fit to be buried within, where Agamemnon lay and those who were murdered along with him.'[20] Pausanias' underground 'treasuries' seemed clearly to be what are now known as the 'tholos' or 'beehive' tombs. Reasoning that no king would be foolish enough to locate his treasury outside the city walls, most scholars in 1868 assumed that there must once have been an outer city wall that enclosed all these 'treasuries' and that it was to this wall that Pausanias was referring. On this interpretation, all the tombs in question would be located outside the citadel wall: those of Agamemnon and his followers within the supposed outer city wall and those of Aegisthus and Clytemnestra outside it. Schliemann, however, shows no awareness in *Ithaque* of the standard view and makes the common-sense interpretation that the wall referred to is the wall enclosing the citadel. This leads him to conclude that 'Pausanias saw all the mausoleums in the acropolis itself, and that only those of Aegisthus and Clytemnestra were buried outside the citadel walls.'[21]

Schliemann's interpretation of Pausanias' observations is probably explained by his ignorance of the scholarly arguments. Ironically, his simplistic common sense was to prove more fruitful than the scholarly view. There may have been another factor. In *Ithaque* Schliemann mentions that he saw an excavated trench which reached a depth of six metres. Just about the only place within the walls where anyone could have dug six metres without hitting the bedrock is on the site of what later proved to be the grave circle. Schliemann indicates that he tried without success to learn the purpose of the trench. It must be fairly obvious to the modern reader, as I suspect it was to Schliemann, that locals had been engaged in clandestine excavation. Schliemann may have even heard rumours in Argos or Nauplion that the grave-robbers had met with some success. If so, it is natural that he would not wish to signal this fact in *Ithaque* for fear that others might anticipate his plans to excavate the area more fully.

Schliemann also visited the large beehive tomb traditionally known, as he learned from Murray's *Handbook*, as the Treasury of Atreus or the Tomb of Agamemnon. He found the large interior chamber to be of conical shape, 16 metres in diameter and just over 16 metres high at the centre. He noted that 'in each of the stones there are two small holes with the remains of bronze nails and in the upper part of the dome entire nails are to be seen.'

There was a small side-chamber but it was pitch dark inside and Schliemann had forgotten to bring matches. In *Ithaque* he tells us that he asked the boy who had accompanied him from the village of Charvati (today Mycenae) to fetch some. The boy replied that there were none in the village.

> Convinced that even in the villages of the Peloponnese there are matches, I cried out that I would give him half a drachma (40 centimes) for three matches. The boy was completely dumbfounded by such generosity and could not at first believe it. Three times he asked me if I would really pay him fifty lepta if he fetched the matches; twice I gave him a simple response in the affirmative, but the third time I swore to him on the ashes of Agamemnon and Clytemnestra. Scarcely had I said the words when the child ran off at top speed for Charvati, more than two kilometres distant from the Treasury of Agamemnon, and soon returned, holding a bunch of brushwood in the one hand and about ten matches in the other. I asked him why he had brought three times as many matches as I had ordered; at first he gave evasive answers; but when pressed, he finally admitted that he had been afraid that some of the matches might be bad and that he had brought ten instead of three to ensure against any eventuality and to earn the promised reward whatever happened. At once he lit a large fire in the interior chamber, whose gleam frightened thousands of bats that had taken up their abode there and shrieked shrilly as they tried to escape. But blinded by the light from the flames, they could not find the door and flew back and forth endlessly across the ceiling, upsetting us considerably by flying into our faces and attaching themselves to our clothing.[22]

In 1877 a German scholar, who made an important early study of beehive tombs, C. Belger, questioned whether Schliemann had in fact seen any nails in the ceiling of the large chamber in 1868.[23] Neither he nor other friends had been able to see any in the summer of 1875 or early 1876. Belger's doubts were strengthened by Schliemann's claim in *Ithaque* that 'in the lintel and threshold of the main (=Lion) gate the holes for the bolts and the hinges and in the large paving stones the wheel-ruts of the chariots are to be clearly seen.'[24] Schliemann took this information straight from Murray's *Handbook*, which also remarks: 'two thirds of <the gate's> height, or perhaps more, was lately buried in the ruins; but the gateway has been cleared out and it is now to be seen complete.' This was presumably true when the *Handbook* was published in 1854. In 1875 when Belger visited the site, however, the threshold was buried under an estimated three metres of debris washed down by winter rains. By 1868, therefore, it would probably have been well and truly buried. The diary account makes no mention of the threshold.

Schliemann made his way to Argos, pausing briefly to examine the Argive Heraeum *en route*, and from Argos took a coach to Nauplion. The next two days were spent in seeing the sights of Nauplion, Argos, and Tiryns. One day he paid a boatman to row him across the bay to the marsh of Lerna, where Hercules killed the Hydra. Regarding lodgings, Murray's *Handbook* warned: 'Beware in Nauplion of dirt and vermin.' Schliemann commented grimly: 'Because the numerous bedbugs suck people's blood like leeches, they are here spared the expense of bloodletting.'[25] Schliemann sailed overnight from Nauplion to Athens, where he arrived on 4 August. The next evening he set sail for the Dardanelles.

Schliemann was in heaven, not because he was on his way to Troy, though he was no doubt excited about that, but because he relished the luxury of the French steamer's food and accommodation after his experiences in the Peloponnese. Since the French steamer did not disembark passengers at the Dardanelles, he had to continue to Constantinople and then retrace his steps on another steamer. The chronology of Schliemann's visit to the Troad given in *Ithaque* differs substantially from his diary record.[26] (See Appendix II)

In *Ithaque* Schliemann records that on arrival at the Dardanelles he promptly set out for Bunarbashi, which he reached in the evening. Homer indicates that just outside the walls of Troy there were two springs, one of cold water and the other of hot.[27] The presence of the requisite hot and cold springs was one of the factors cited in favour of Bunarbashi as the site of Troy. Schliemann immediately set out to investigate them.

> But these springs in no way correspond to Homer's description, for as the visitor goes downhill from Bunarbashi, he finds first of all, within the space of one square metre, *three springs*, of which one comes out of the ground and the other two from

51

the foot of a rock. A few metres further I found two more springs and within a space of 500 metres I counted a total of thirty-four. The Albanian who was accompanying me claimed that there were forty and that I had missed six. In support of his assertion he told me that this area was called Kirk Giös, which means 'forty eyes'. I held my pocket thermometer in each of the thirty-four springs, and I found each one to be 17.5°C.[28]

The next day Schliemann made another practical test of the site. In Book 22 of the *Iliad* Achilles chases Hector three times around the walls of Troy. So Schliemann decided to see how feasible it was to run around the Bunarbashi site. Near the Menderes river he came to a steep slope.

I left my guide with the horse at the top and I went down the precipice, which inclines at first at an angle of 45 degrees and then at an angle of about 65 degrees so that I was forced to go down on all fours. It took me almost fifteen minutes to get down and I came away convinced that no mortal, not even a goat, was ever able to run down a slope of 65 degrees and that Homer, always so precise in his topography, could not have wanted us to believe that Hector and Achilles ran down this impossible slope three times.

Next Schliemann made his way up to the Balli Dagh, the summit 3 kilometres south-east of Bunarbashi, which was widely held to be the acropolis of Troy. At Mycenae and Tiryns he had been struck by the large amount of pottery to be seen everywhere on the surface. On the way up to the Balli Dagh he noted a complete absence of pottery. On the plateau preceding the acropolis there were three tumuli, two of which were traditionally identified as the Tombs of Hector and Priam. On both the acropolis itself and the preceding plateau there were ruins of ancient buildings. Schliemann estimated that the plateau and acropolis could never have been inhabited by more than two thousand people, whereas the minimum population of Homeric Troy he reckoned to be about fifty thousand.

For all these reasons Schliemann was convinced that Bunarbashi-Balli Dagh could not be the site of Troy. Still, he considered it his duty to dig trial trenches 'in the disinterested goal of extirpating the absurd and erroneous dogma that Troy was situated on the heights of Bunarbashi.'[29]

The next two days, with the assistance of five workmen and his guide, he dug a series of trenches from the village of Bunarbashi up to the heights of Balli Dagh but nowhere found 'the least indication that the area had ever been inhabited by man.'[30] On the third day of excavation they dug at the summit, both on the acropolis itself and on the plateau leading up to it. They found plenty of pottery and evidence for different levels of occupation but

Schliemann was convinced that this insignificant town could not be Homer's Troy.[31]

On 14 August he set out across the plain of Troy with his workers and guide for the site of Hellenistic Ilium (also called Novum Ilium) and about 10 a.m. reached Hisarlik. Most ancient writers identified this site with that of Homeric Troy. Strabo, however, specified that the later Ilium was built on a different site from Homeric Ilium. Hence the protracted debate over the site of Homeric Ilium, which generated hundreds of books and articles in the eighteenth and nineteenth centuries.[32] By 1868, most scholars favoured the Bunarbashi-Balli Dagh site, though there was also substantial support for the view that Troy was wholly mythical and that it was folly to expect to find any physical remains of it. A small minority favoured Hisarlik. Among its champions were Charles Maclaren (1822 and 1863), Henry Owgam (1840), Gustav von Eckenbrecher (1843) and George Grote (1846). In *Ithaque* Schliemann indicated his allegiance to Hisarlik as follows:

> After having walked more than a half hour over this terrain, we arrived at a hill of some forty metres high, which has an almost perpendicular drop to the plain on the north side and is about 20 metres higher than the mountain-ridge, of which it forms the extremity. If it was possible to entertain doubts over the identity of Hissarlik with Novum Ilium, the form of this spur would make them disappear entirely, for it corresponds to the words of Strabo (13.1) 'continuous ridge.'
>
> The summit of this hill forms a continuous plateau about 233 metres square. By trenches dug in this hill the ingenious Frank Calvert has determined that it is in great part artificial and that it has been formed by the ruins and the debris of the successive temples and palaces over long centuries. By making a small dig on the east end of the summit he brought to light part of a large building, palace or temple, constructed of large hewn stones superimposed on one another without cement. What little of the building can be seen leaves no doubt that it was of great dimensions and that it was executed with consummate art. After having twice examined all the plain of Troy I fully share the conviction of this scholar, that the high plateau of Hisarlik is the site of ancient Troy and that the afore-mentioned hill is its Pergamon.[33]

Schliemann attributed the lack of hot and cold springs to the frequent earthquakes of the region. On the question of Achilles' pursuit of Hector around the walls he noted:

> The circumference of the site of Novum Ilium, five kilometers, is well indicated by the circuit walls, whose ruins can be seen in many places; the slopes which one has to cross in going around the city are so gentle that they can be traversed at running

speed without risk of falling. In running three times around the city Hector and Achilles thus covered fifteen kilometers.[34]

Schliemann left Hisarlik at about 3 p.m. and made his way north to the mound known as the Tomb of Ajax and then followed the coast westwards past the so-called Tombs of Patroclus and Achilles, to the headland of Sigeum, where he stayed the night at the village of Yenishehir. Here he dismissed his workmen, whom he had not asked to dig at Hisarlik, 'for without making trial trenches I had come away completely convinced that that spot is the site of ancient Troy.'[35] That night his host was about to kill a chicken for Schliemann's supper, 'but the poor creature seemed to suspect the dirty trick that they were going to play and it began to make such loud cries that I had compassion for it and I offered to pay its value if they set it free.'[36]

The next day Schliemann made his way back to Bunarbashi via Neochorion, Beshika-Tepe and Udjek-Tepe. On 16 August he returned to Hisarlik and then headed north-east up the valley of the Dumbrek to the ruins of Palaio Castro, identified with the ancient Ophrynium. He also studied the river system of the plain, paying particular attention to the formation of the river banks, and concluded that the theory that much of the lower part of the Troad had once been a bay that had been filled in by the accumulation of alluvium was simply erroneous.

On 17 August he went south from Bunarbashi to Alexandria Troas. Since it has some of the most impressive and extensive ruins in the Troad, it early became a contender for the site of Troy. But the city appears not to have been founded until the Hellenistic period and therefore is far too late for Homeric Troy. On the return trip his horse became so exhausted that he had to stop at the village of Udjek. Here he paid a man named Topal to get him a fresh horse and went to sleep. He was awakened about two in the morning with the news that his horse was ready. He soon realized that the horse was none other than the one he had been riding all day. He hurried as quickly as he could to Neochorion and wrote out a formal complaint about Topal and asked the mayor to take steps to have him imprisoned. He then hired a horse and a guide and set out across the Trojan plain to Renkoi and from there to the Dardanelles. Before leaving for Constantinople he saw 'the rich collection of vases and other curious objects that the ingenious and indefatigable archaeologist Frank Calvert has found in his many excavations.'[37]

The Calvert family, British in origin, played a leading role in the region throughout the nineteenth and early twentieth centuries. A number of them served as consuls for Britain, the US and other countries at the Dardanelles and at other sites in the Levant. The family owned a farm about four miles south-east of Hisarlik, managed by Frank Calvert's elder brother, Frederick. Frank (1828–1908) was the most scholarly of several brothers. He was interested in geology and archaeology and by 1868 had developed an unrivalled knowledge of the topography of the Troad. Generous and self-effacing to a fault, he was always ready to offer hospitality, provide practical information and act as guide. His house in the Dardanelles was a regular stopping-place for European visitors on the Grand Tour.

When he wrote up his visit to the Troad for publication Schliemann substantially altered the facts of his trip (see Appendix II). He expanded his survey and excavations at Bunarbashi from 1½ to over 4 days. Moreover, the diary stipulates only one workman on the afternoon of 11 August and only two workmen the next day. Thus he excavated for only two and a half man-days at Bunarbashi-Balli Dagh instead of the fifteen man-days claimed in *Ithaque*.

Unfortunately, the immediately preceding context of Schliemann's first visit to Hisarlik is lost. Though the diary itself is not missing a page at this point, the opening section of the entry for 10 August, in which Schliemann presumably recounted the morning's activities, is lacking. The entry appears to open in mid-sentence with Schliemann already in the vicinity of Hisarlik.

> . . . few ruins. The whole area is now cultivated with wheat and there are many oaks there. I saw only four columns there, half-buried in the earth. But the owner of the cafe in the nearby village, who is also the barber, guided me to other ruins. On a hill, which is almost 100 ft high, he showed me, covered with a great deal of soil, but recently partly excavated, a temple or palace of excellently worked cyclopean stones. From there I had a fine view over the plain of the Troad. Nearby lie many remains of fine columns. The barber speaks Arabic fairly well. We crossed a Turkish cemetery covered with pieces of bright marble columns and other sculptures.[38]

It is clear from Schliemann's 1870 diary that an Arabic-speaking barber owned a café in Chiplak, the village about a mile east of Hisarlik. Thus the hill commanding the fine view over the plain is clearly Hisarlik itself and the signs of recent excavation refer to Frank Calvert's preliminary excavation of the temple of Athena in 1865.[39] The four half-buried columns are those mentioned by numerous travellers and located about a mile south of Chiplak at a place now called Dikeli Tash.[40]

Perhaps the most striking feature of the passage is the casual nature of Schliemann's visit and his apparent unawareness that this site was Bunarbashi's main rival for the claim to be the site of Homeric Troy. When a few days later

Frank Calvert met Schliemann in the Dardanelles, it was Calvert's impression that Schliemann was unaware that Hisarlik was held by some scholars to be the site of Troy.[41] The diary entry here certainly bears out that impression.

Even before his exploratory excavations in 1865, Calvert had become convinced that Hisarlik was the site of Homeric Troy. In 1863 he had tried to interest the British Museum in helping to fund excavations there but the authorities refused to sanction even the modest sum of £100 that was recommended by the Keeper of Greek and Roman Antiquities, Charles Newton. Finally, in 1865, tired of trying to coax money from the British Museum and, after Hahn's negative results at Bunarbashi, even more convinced that Hisarlik must be the right site, Calvert made four small trenches on the eastern section of the mound, which he had in the meantime purchased. It was Calvert's excavations that Schliemann saw when he visited Hisarlik on 10 August. On 15 August, when Schliemann paid him a call at the Dardanelles, Calvert realized that this amateur archaeologist had the enthusiasm, drive and money to complete the task he had begun. He told Schliemann of his view that Hisarlik was the site of Troy. Though Schliemann had heard mention of this theory in Paris, he seems to have forgotten about it. Now, for the first time, he was forced to take it seriously. Calvert showed Schliemann his valuable collection of antiquities that he had excavated at various sites in the Troad, including Hisarlik. Among the finds from Hisarlik were pottery dating back to the sixth or seventh century BC and bas-relief sculpture from the Hellenistic temple.[42] Schliemann was impressed. He made up his mind there and then, or at least in the next day or two, that he would return next spring and begin excavations at Hisarlik. On 22 and 24 August he wrote from Constantinople to his father and sister Doris in Mecklenburg, announcing his plans: 'Next April I intend to lay bare the entire hill of Hissarlik, for I consider it certain that I will find there Pergamos, the citadel of Troy.'[43] But he could not bring himself, even in his diary, to reveal the full extent of his indebtedness to Calvert. In the closing section of his entry for 14 August, he included the following sentence: 'We crossed again the plain of ancient Troy, which I examined with great care, particularly the hill of Hasserlik [*sic*], where, in my opinion, Homer's Pergamos was located.' This comes as a complete surprise to the reader, for there is nothing preceding this entry to indicate his conversion to Hisarlik. These words were written after his meeting with Calvert on 15 August. The entry for the 16th reads:

> I made the acquaintance yesterday of Frank Calvert, the famous archaeologist, who shares my opinion that Homer's Troy is none other than Hasserlik. He advises me strongly to excavate there. He says that the hill is man-made. He showed me his

great collection of vases and other antiquities which he found in his excavations – among other things a bronze lion with Punic inscriptions signifying that it weighs a talent.

Schliemann has reduced Calvert's role to merely confirming his own view of the identity of Hisarlik with the site of Troy. In fact, as Calvert pointed out in 1874, 'When I first met the doctor, in August 1868, the subject of Hissarlik, as the probable site of Troy, was new to him.'⁴⁴ This process of minimizing Calvert's role in directing Schliemann's attention to Hisarlik was to continue, as we shall see.

When Schliemann reached Paris near the beginning of September, he threw himself immediately into the task of converting the account of his recent travels into a book. He read all the scholarly literature on Ithaca, Mycenae and Troy that he could get his hands on. He also wrote to Frank Calvert with a list of questions regarding Hisarlik. On 1 November he wrote to his son Serge:

> I work day and night on my archaeological work, for I hope with this book to make a small reputation as an author. I read about thirty pages of it to the Geographical and Archaeological Society here, of which I am a member, and I am happy to tell you that my composition was received with enthusiasm. If this work succeeds, I will continue to write books all my life, for I cannot imagine a more interesting career than that of an author of serious books. While writing, one is always so happy, so content, so collected, and when mingling with society, one has thousands and thousands of interesting things to talk about, which, being the products of long research and reflection, are pleasing to everyone. In fact the author is always sought out and is welcome everywhere, and although I am still only a novice, I have at least ten times more friends here than I would like ...

It would be easy to infer from this letter that Schliemann was more interested in becoming an author than an archaeologist. One of Schliemann's greatest gifts was his ability to become completely absorbed by what he was doing at the moment and to relish what others might regard as drudgery. Almost certainly, it was the attention of the intelligentsia that his newly acquired expertise on Homeric sites had brought him that appealed to him. His ability to speak knowledgeably on these topics had won him respect among members of the learned societies. This was what he had craved. Writing, he saw, would widen his reputation; so he plunged into the task with a will.

After his meeting with Calvert and avid reading in Paris, Schliemann was considerably more knowledgeable than he had been when he made the trip in July and August. As we have seen, in *Ithaque, le Péloponnèse et Troie* Schliemann altered the facts of his trip, making himself seem more knowledgeable, diligent and astute than he had actually been. It has recently been argued that 'he had to choose between recording his actual movements or the results of his research in Paris.'[45] Why? What was to prevent him from combining a truthful account of what he did and saw in July and August with a discussion of what he had learned about Homeric sites since then? Often he does in effect adopt this format. In Chapters 18 and 19 he interrupts the narrative of his visit to Hisarlik to give a list of learned arguments why Hisarlik should be seen as the site of Troy. Among them he mentions the ease of running around the site. He does not say that on his visit he personally ran around the site three times. On the other hand, in the interest of creating a livelier narrative, Schliemann did not shrink from recasting the facts of his trip. Thus at Bunarbashi we have accounts of how he took the temperature of the springs and attempted to run around the site. Another fictitious episode of the same kind is found in the Ithaca section.

Schliemann's study in Paris made it clear that there was a critical argument against Mount Aetos as the site of Odysseus' palace. When Telemachus returned from Pylos, Penelope's suitors lay in ambush for him on the island of Asteris. The only suitable candidate for Asteris is the small island of Dascalia in the strait between Cephalonia and Ithaca. However, Dascalia is located off Polis Bay, considerably to the north of Mount Aetos. It is therefore impractical for ambushing a ship sailing from the Peloponnese to Mount Aetos. Its location favours Polis Bay, not Mount Aetos, as the site of the palace. Schliemann felt he had to refute Dascalia's claim to be the Homeric Asteris. To do this he described in his book how some sailors had rowed him out to Dascalia and how, by autopsy, he had determined that it did not fit Homer's description of Asteris. The real Asteris, he speculated, located somewhere south of Mount Aetos, must have long since sunk beneath the waves. Schliemann's visit to Dascalia is no more real than his encounter with the savage dogs. It is contradicted by his diary account, which has been drastically altered in the book version to accommodate this addition.[46]

Schliemann finished work on *Ithaque* in late December. On 26 December he wrote to Frank Calvert thanking him for providing the information he requested about Hisarlik – 'of which I have largely made use for my work' – and requesting answers to some twenty more questions. This time the questions had to do with the practical business of planning an excavation: 'When is the best time to begin the work? . . . Can I get labourers enough, where and at what wages? . . . What sort of hat is best against the scorching sun?' and so on. He also indicated that he intended 'starting for St Petersburg on the 2nd January to see my family.'[47] This trip was to precipitate the final break-up of his marriage.

4

Divorce, Doctorate and Remarriage

THE YEAR 1869 WAS FILLED with perhaps the most momentous changes in Schliemann's life. In that year he published his first archaeological work, *Ithaque, le Péloponnèse et Troie*, in both French and German; acquired American citizenship in New York; was awarded a doctorate from the University of Rostock; divorced his Russian wife in Indianapolis; married Sophia Engastromenos in Athens; and in Paris learned of his daughter Natalia's death in St Petersburg. All of these events had profound and lasting reverberations.

As early as July 1867 Schliemann had threatened Katerina with an American divorce. He had gone to America in October of that year 'to pick up my U.S. citizenship papers,'[1] presumably with a view to initiating divorce proceedings. In the event, however, because of residence requirements, Schliemann was ineligible for US citizenship. Early in 1869 he made a last desperate attempt at reconciliation with Katerina. On 5 January (which was Christmas Eve 1868 in St Petersburg, for Russia was still operating on the Julian calendar), as he drew near to St Petersburg, Schliemann telegraphed that he would be arriving later that evening, laden 'with masses of gifts for the Christmas tree.' Forewarned, Katerina scooped up the children and left the house. Schliemann later reminded his wife of her callous behaviour on that occasion.

You had gone out precisely because you knew that your poor husband would come. I had gone to see you with the intention of staying with you at least a week and of restoring good harmony between us at any price; in fact, I swear in the name of God omnipotent, that I was then prepared to make all possible concessions and that I was ready to sacrifice even a million francs to restore domestic peace. But how did you act towards me!!! The hair bristles on my head with dismay and horror when I merely think of your infernal conduct. Not knowing how to torment me further, you reproached me cruelly for having [refused] to buy snuff in 1852 (and hence 16 years earlier), and for being unwilling in 1855 to buy a carriage! Having heard from me that in Paris I had formed a circle of friends as scholarly as they are charming, a circle such as even the Emperor of Russia would wish to have, having also heard from me that my drawing-room, my dining-room and my kitchen were

59

all loudly crying out for the mistress of the house, you dared to insinuate that I should take on a concubine. You even chose to push your effrontery further. You revealed to the police of St Petersburg, as an outrage against the Russian government, my referring, in my letters of 1868, in letters written to you, my wife, to the laws and to the whole mechanism of government, which employs religion only as a means to keep the ordinary people in the darkness of superstition and imbecility. You denounced me in order to put a stop on my passport and you would have succeeded in your plan if I had not taken the new passport immediately on arrival. Instead of eight days I managed to put up with living in your house for only four days and even during these four days I had to live like an intruding Tartar. Truly, your conduct towards me was such that I would never have been able to leave St Petersburg alive if I had tried to stay a day longer. You certainly did not hear from me a single bad word even when your terrible and execrable conduct had destroyed my heart and you will recall that when, in a fit of anger, I went out the door, I shouted that your monstrous behaviour would never debase my character, whose greatness you will see in all my actions, and after my DEATH you would bless the memory of your benefactor, whom you have only vilified during his life.[2]

Embittered by this experience, Schliemann now resolved on divorce. He left Paris and sailed to New York, where he put up at the Astor House Hotel on 27 March. His entry for 29 March reads as follows:

I got today my paper as citizen of the U.S. Since no divorce can be obtained in the State of New York except on acct. of adultery, whereas in Indiana even no previous residence is required I have decided on going on 31st inst to Indianapolis. Peter Cook, the lawyer, procures here divorce in a few weeks by false certificates and perjury; I will have nothing to do with such horrors. Messrs. [Mac] Killop Sprague and Co., 37 Park-row, Commercial Agency, gave me letter to Geo. E. Gordon, lawyer of Indianapolis.

I examined with lawyer Moore 7 Chamber Street the laws of Ohio, Indiana, Illinois etc in the law institute in Chamber street.[3]

This is one of the most remarkable passages in Schliemann's 1869 diary. Schliemann could only have obtained his citizenship papers by fraud. The law in effect in 1869 required two documents. The first, a record of the immigrant's intent to become a US citizen, Schliemann had filed in 1851. The second, which had to be dated at least five years later, affirmed that the immigrant had been residing in the United States for the preceding five years. Clearly, Schliemann, who had spent almost all of the preceding five years in Europe, did not qualify for citizenship. Yet on 29 March 1869, John Bolan of New York obligingly swore that Schliemann 'has resided within the United States for the continued term of five years, at least, next preceding the present time, and within the State of New York one year, at least, immediately preceding this application.'[4] Thanks to this perjured testimony Schliemann became a US citizen in 1869, two days after his arrival in New York. Schliemann's professed repugnance for the practice of obtaining divorce by 'false certificates and perjury' must therefore be taken with a considerable pinch of salt. But what is most revealing is not the fact that he obtained his citizenship by fraud but that he chose to suppress this fact in the one place where we might reasonably have expected candour – his diary. Instead we are confronted with a peculiar form of hypocrisy rendered all the more disturbing by the comparatively venial nature of the offence. Clearly, in composing his diary Schliemann was not writing an *aide-mémoire* for himself but rather trying to impress an audience.

This view of Schliemann's diary is confirmed by another statement in the entry of 29 March. As Schliemann must have learned from his consultations with the New York lawyers, Indiana's divorce law, although the most liberal in the United States, *did* have a residence requirement. Petitioners for divorce had to have been bona fide residents of Indiana for at least a year prior to filing their petitions. However, this requirement could easily be circumvented by false testimony. Schliemann's assertion that Indiana did not have a prior residence requirement does not mean that Schliemann was misinformed on the subject. Rather, it is an attempt to mislead future readers of the diary.

Schliemann reached Indianapolis on 1 April and went at once to the leading law firm, Hendricks, Hord and Hendricks. At their suggestion he also retained the services of another law firm, Seidensticker and Naltner. Notice of Schliemann's petition for divorce was published in the *Indiana Weekly State Journal* on 9, 16 and 23 April 1869. Legally, this was sufficient notification for out-of-state defendants in Indiana divorce cases at this time. In practice, the chance of Katerina learning in St Petersburg that she was about to be divorced in Indianapolis was miniscule.

A recent divorce case in Indiana, which had exploited the inadequacies of the Indiana divorce law, had led to heated public debate in April 1869. Schliemann summarized the case in a letter to a Greek friend in Paris:

> Some years ago a scoundrel married a lovely, rich girl whose tireless efforts substantially enlarged her husband's estate. The couple had many children (seven I believe), and gave the appearance of living in complete harmony. After 21 years of married life, the man fell in love with another young woman. He goes to another county of Indiana (I should explain that this state has 93 counties, each of which has courts entitled to grant divorces), and through false witnesses and perjured proofs he wins a divorce. Meanwhile his unhappy wife hasn't the slightest knowledge of the affair. After a divorce has been granted, nine days must always elapse

during which the divorce may be contested and invalidated. However, after this deadline, the divorce is valid even though the wife presents the most positive proofs that he won the divorce by perjuries and false witnesses. In spite of all this, the wife is forced to leave her husband's house immediately, and all her property along with the children belong to her husband.[5]

The Indianapolis *Journal* of 6 April declared that the 'adaptability of the infamous divorce act to evasive construction, and its utter worthlessness for serving the ends of justice, is too potent not to claim the attention of the Legislature.'[6] A special session of the state legislature had been convened to discuss the divorce law and other pressing issues. Schliemann's diary entry of 17 May contains the following:

> Since I was very much afraid the Senate's divorce-bill Nos. 316 and 317 would pass the Lower-House, I went there daily and remained there all the day. At last both bills were read on 11th inst. . . . Then the amendments were offered by the 24 democrats whom I had succeeded to get on my side through second hand; the first: to exclude pending suits was rejected; the 2d to strike out the word emergency could likewise not be sustained and by only one vote above the ⅔ of the votes it passed that the constitutional rule should not be suspended and that the bill 316 was to be read a third time. The following day, 13th May, to my greatest joy, 41 of the democratic members presented their resignations to the governor in order to avoid voting on the 15th amendment to the Constitution of the U.S. which gives to the coloured people the right of voting. By their resignation the House had no quorum and thus no more business could be transacted.[7]

Schliemann therefore was successful in preventing the passage of legislation that would have seriously damaged his prospects of winning a divorce in Indiana. His case came to trial on 30 June. He convinced the court that he 'for more than one year previous to the filing of his petition herein has been a resident of the State of Indiana.'[8] Schliemann does not explain in his diary or in his correspondence how he was able to prove this but clearly he must have produced false testimony to this effect. At the beginning of June he and Naltner spent a few days in Fort Wayne and it is very likely that they acquired the requisite testimony here.[9] As a further precaution, Schliemann had bought a house for $1,125 and signed a contract to buy a one-third share in a large starch factory for $12,000, thereby making himself appear a bona fide resident of Indiana.

On what grounds did Schliemann win his divorce? The law did not grant divorce to a petitioner simply because the defendant defaulted. Proper grounds had to be proved. The Indiana law, however, attracted large numbers of migratory divorces because among admissible grounds was 'any other cause for which the court shall deem it proper that a divorce should be granted.' In his letter of 11 July to Emile Egger Schliemann wrote that 'the court did not delay in granting me a divorce on the basis of my former wife's letters in which she refuses to live with me anywhere except in Russia.'[11] These letters were of course in Russian. Schliemann made English translations of them, which he presented to the court along with the originals.[12] The English translations contained sentences that must have been damaging to Katerina. In a letter dated 18 March 1868: 'You continually insist upon it & desire energetically that I follow you with our children to America and live there conjointly with you.' Again, in a letter dated 18 April 1868: 'The sole and only reason of all our disagreement is that you desire I should leave Russia and join you in America. But this I most decidedly decline and refuse to do . . .' Finally, in a letter dated 31 December 1868: 'You continue to torment me with your request to emigrate with our children to the U.S. in order to live there together with you . . . I therefore reiterate to you for the thousandth time that I oppose myself in the most decided way and in the most peremptory manner to live together with you in America or wherever it may be outside of Russia . . .' The references to America show that Schliemann doctored these translations, for in 1868 he was not residing in America nor had he any plan to do so. A later letter confirms that these translations were indeed doctored. In January 1870, when Schliemann learned that Katerina was trying to have the divorce annulled, he wrote urgently to Naltner to 'get the 3 Russian letters of my wife, with the translations, out of court and keep them for me. In my opinion, the translations of 2 letters are not very accurate; in Russian it always says that my wife will *never* follow me in foreign countries but there is nothing mentioned about America . . .'[13] What Schliemann does not tell Naltner is that the English translations were made by himself. They appear in his 1870 copybook written in Schliemann's own hand.[14]

The divorce was granted on 30 June 1869 in the Marion County Court of Common Pleas, Indianapolis. Schliemann waited two more weeks to obtain an official copy of the proceedings of the trial and three copies of the divorce decree. Then in mid-July he left Indianapolis for New York and from there set sail for France on 24 July.

Exactly when Schliemann decided to try to use his published books to earn a degree from the University of Rostock is unclear. The idea seems not yet to have occurred to him when he wrote to Serge on 1 November 1868. At that point he hoped that the book would earn him a 'small reputation as an author.' Perhaps it was his cousin Adolph who suggested the possibility to him after copies of *Ithaque, le Péloponnèse et Troie*, published early in 1869, had been sent to various members of his family in Mecklenburg. Adolph was Justizrat in Mecklenburg-Schwerin and had good connections with the University of Rostock. Unfortunately, most of Schliemann's letters for January and February 1869 are missing. By 12 March, the eve of Schliemann's departure for the United States, the process was well under way. Adolph had taken the matter in hand. He had given a copy of *Ithaque* to Professor L. Bachmann, who in turn had written back, praising the book. Adolph had then written to Heinrich in Paris, informing him of Bachmann's high opinion of his work. He seems also to have indicated that Heinrich should draw up a curriculum vitae and formally petition the Dean to be considered a candidate for the degree of Doctor of Philosophy. In lieu of the curriculum vitae, Heinrich submitted Greek and Latin versions of the autobiographical introduction to *Ithaque*. Much of this emerges from Schliemann's letter to Adolph:

> My heartiest thanks for the hard work you have done on my behalf. Prof. Bachmann's letter is most flattering. I send you herewith in a yellow envelope the introduction in ancient Greek and Latin, and a letter to the Dean. I had to write out the Greek twice over, because modern Greek comes more naturally to me; now, however, it is, I am convinced, *pure* ancient Greek, although not classical. I am pretty sure that it is free from error and would like the examination for the doctorate to focus only on this piece (besides my books), for here in France at least it is most unusual for anyone to write ancient Greek correctly. In fact among the professors of the four universities here there is only one who would be capable of doing so . . .[15]

By 12 April Adolph was able to report to Heinrich (now in Indianapolis) that the two scholars best qualified to judge, L. Bachmann and F.V. Fritzsche, had written favourable evaluations of his work. Some formalities still had to be gone through but success seemed assured. Incidental fees amounted to some 80 thaler and, in return for his services, Adolph asked for an additional 200 thaler to pay off his gambling debts. Heinrich sent only 200 thaler to cover both his graduation fees and Adolph's debts and sternly warned his cousin to stay away from cards and the bad company that led him astray.[16] The degree was duly awarded on 27 April 1869.[17]

In *Ilios* Schliemann describes how, after completing *Ithaque*, he applied for his doctorate as follows: 'Having sent a copy of this work together with a dissertation in ancient Greek, to the University of Rostock, that learned body honoured me with the diploma of Doctor of Philosophy.'[18] The degree was awarded, as the diploma specifies, for *Ithaque, le Péloponnèse et Troie*. Bachmann thought little of Schliemann's Greek: 'the faults in Greek idioms and sentence structure show that the writer has not completed a course on the syntax of this language and so does not know how to construct a fully self-contained sentence in ancient form.'[19] He concluded: 'it would have been better if the translation into Greek had never been submitted.' The Latin version he found quite satisfactory. Everyone agreed that *La Chine et le Japon* was a mere travelogue and could not seriously be considered.

Both Bachmann and Fritzsche were impressed by *Ithaque*, however. Fritzsche wrote: 'It is with astonishment that I have observed the wide-ranging knowledge of this autodidact. A man who could write this archaeological work can certainly be advanced to the doctorate. On the diploma this work should be expressly mentioned.'[20] Bachmann was of the same general opinion. Though he thought Schliemann's views on Troy misguided, he rightly considered the section on the topography of Ithaca a significant advance over the theories of Gell and others. What he did not know, however, was that Schliemann's work was largely based on Bowen's excellent study of Ithaca, which, in condensed form, was reproduced in the most widely used guidebook of the day, Murray's *Handbook for Travellers in Greece*.

Today, the significance of *Ithaque* rests primarily on the Troy and Mycenae sections. Schliemann's conviction that the heroic tombs of Mycenae were to be found within the city walls broke new ground in scholarly thinking about Mycenae. His own excavations were destined to demonstrate the accuracy of this unorthodox opinion. Similarly, his championing of the minority view that Hisarlik was the site of Troy led to the excavation of an immensely important site that is indeed now generally believed to be Troy.

There can be little doubt that Schliemann's account in *Ilios* was calculated to convey the impression that he had received his doctorate for a dissertation written in ancient Greek. Many readers were deceived. Schliemann exploited the ambiguity of the word 'dissertation', which in both English and German can mean simply 'essay' but in academic contexts denotes a scholarly thesis written for an advanced degree. His letter to Adolph of 12 March shows that he was anxious that the degree should be awarded for the Greek version of his *vita*. This did not happen. It is perfectly true that among the material judged by the Rostock examiners was an essay in ancient Greek. To call this essay a 'dissertation' was to choose to mislead.

Schliemann was not one to let the grass grow under his feet. Negotiations for his divorce, degree, and remarriage all went on simultaneously. The day before leaving France for America to start the divorce proceedings, he had written to Archbishop Theocletos Vimpos, whom he had first met in St Petersburg, asking for help in finding a suitable Greek wife. Vimpos had replied: 'Whoever seeks to choose a wife has before him a sack full of snakes, among which there is a single tortoise, and if he grasps and pulls out the tortoise, he is very lucky; but if he gets a snake, he is very unlucky.'[21] In a long letter dated 13 April 1869 Schliemann wrote back that he wanted to marry a Greek woman of the same angelic character as he had seen in Vimpos' mother and sister.[22] However, he inferred from Vimpos' gloomy assessment that such women were rare in Greece. Moreover, there was a major obstacle to any Greek marriage: Schliemann had already offered to marry his cousin, Sophie Bürger! He outlined to Vimpos how this had come about: 'I have a great need to have near me a heart that loves me. In great distress and despair over this I have often called on the ghost of my mother, who died thirty-seven years ago, begging her to help me. At that time I had a dream in which my mother told me to marry her brother's daughter, Sophie, in Mecklenburg. I have seen this girl only once, three years ago, and I enchanted her so much by recounting my travels and experiences that she later wrote me a love letter 10 pages long.' Sophie had become engaged to an architect but the marriage had been postponed. 'In my despair and particularly because of your letter and my mother's ghost and instructions, I wrote to Sophie, explaining every-thing to her and suggesting that she break off her engagement and marry me if she still had the same feelings for me as those expressed in her letter of three years earlier.'

As he reports them to Vimpos, Schliemann's feelings for Sophie at this point were confused. On the one hand, he believed that he could not be happy if he married her because she was a relative and a fellow German and, though she had the same lively nature as he and the same drive for knowledge, she had not had an opportunity to rise above her provincial background and hence 'she will always remain my pupil.' On the other hand, 'human nature is such that we always esteem and love those who are much more knowledgeable than we in those branches of learning for which we feel a great passion and for this reason I have great confidence that I would be very happy with her.' Finally, however, the age difference was decisive: 'But her age is very different from my own, because she is twenty whereas I have forty-seven years on my back.'

Meanwhile Vimpos had made progress in his role as matchmaker. In April Schliemann received from him photographs of potential Greek brides. Like cousin Adolph, Vimpos also requested, in return for his services, a sum of money to help pay off his creditors. On 26 April, Schliemann sent him 1000 francs and the following reaction to the photographs:

As an old traveller I am a good judge of faces and I can tell you immediately the character of the two girls from their pictures. As her name indicates, the parents of Polyxena Gusti are Italian, because Gusti is an Italian name, not Greek. She is of the right age to be my wife, but she is bossy, overbearing, domineering, irritable and vindictive. It seems to me that she acquired all these faults in her unenviable calling as a schoolmistress. But perhaps I am mistaken; perhaps, when I see her face to face, I will find in her a treasury of all the virtues. But Sophia Engastromenos is a splendid woman, easy to talk to, compassionate, kindly, and a good housewife, full of life and well brought up. But, unfortunately, she is far too young for a man of 47 years. I think I saw her in Athens. Perhaps she is the daughter of your relative, the agent.

I think that it would be better for me to marry a young widow of excellent character, who already knows what marriage means, because she would be less pleasure-loving and sensual. Girls believe that heaven and paradise rest on the fulfilment of their bodily desires. I too, my friend, was once pleasure-loving and sensual but my character has changed completely. I live now only in a metaphysical world and I care for nothing except scholarship. For this reason I want a wife at my side only for company. I repeat that my wife ought to have a great inclination for learning because otherwise she cannot love and respect me. Please see if you can find me a young widow with a Greek name and a soul inspired with a passion for learning.[23]

Overnight Schliemann changed his mind and the next day he wrote another letter to Vimpos:

With my letter of yesterday I sent you 1000 francs on Paris asking you to accept this remittance as a token of my love for you. My friend, I have fallen so much in love with Sophia Engastromenos that I swear to you that I will take no other wife. But please don't say anything about this to anyone, even to your sister, because I don't know yet if I am in a position to marry; first of all, because I am still not sure if I will get my divorce. Secondly, because of my domestic problems and my own indifference I have had no relations with a woman in six years. Long abstinence and self-restraint in many cases weaken sexual desire and the sex organs and I am afraid that I may now be incapable. But I wish to test this immediately after my arrival in Paris and if I am convinced that I am fit, then I will not hesitate to come to Athens and to talk with Sophia and to marry her if she consents. We must necessarily wait until that time, for if I am impotent <I shall not> marry. Yes, however great a woman's love for her husband is before marriage, she will always despise him if he is incapable of satisfying her physical needs. Naturally, I don't want a wife with a dowry. On the contrary, if I am found to be physically fit so that I can propose to Sophia in July, then I will buy her both underwear and stockings. But nevertheless, please answer the following questions:
1) What does Engastromenos do? What property does he have? How old is he and how many children does he have?
2) How many male and how many female children and what are the ages of each?
3) In particular, how old is Sophia?
4) What colour is Sophia's hair?

5) Where does the family itself live in Athens?

6) Does Sophia play the piano?

7) Does she speak foreign languages? Which?

8) Is she a good housekeeper?

9) Does she understand Homer and other ancient writers? Or is she completely ignorant of the language of our ancestors?

10) Would she consent to move to Paris and to accompany her husband on his travels in Italy and Egypt and elsewhere?

I warmly beg you to give me precise answers to all these questions, sending your letter to Paris . . .[24]

On the same day Schliemann tried to free himself of any obligation to Sophie Bürger by marrying her off to his step-brother Ernst:

In response to your last letter I have a great desire to marry you to our cousin Sophie Bürger of Boitzenburg. She is *very pretty*, blooming, good-natured and clever and I confess candidly that she is so full of perfections and virtues that I am quite in love with her and have made her proposals to marry her in July next. But in doing so, my heart had carried away my head and on mature reflection I find that I am far too old for her, for she is hardly 20, whereas I am 47. But she would make an excellent wife for you, for she is brought up in excellent circumstances and by nature economical and modest; she is not aware that economy and modesty are two mighty virtues. If you marry her, I give her a dowry of twenty thousand francs with the condition that she puts the money into your winehouse and besides I give you credit as heretofore. But all this is of course only to be done if, as I have reason to expect, she has accepted of my proposal. Besides, a dowry I only give if you marry my dearest Sophie and I don't give any thing at all if you marry another lady.[25]

After waiting anxiously to see how cousin Sophie would react to his proposal of marriage, Schliemann wrote again to Ernst:

With reference to my letter of 27th ult. I now inform you with immense joy that my dear cousin Sophie has not even deigned to answer my proposal. In fact she must have thought that I wanted to laugh at her, for, when three years ago she wrote me a hot love-letter of 10 pages, I replied with contempt, whilst now that I took that note up again, discussed it at great length, laughed at it a good deal, accused her of forgery, for she had sent to Elisa an envelope with false poststamps and marks to prove that she had written to me in June 1866 to Paris at a time when I myself had no idea yet of ever going to reside in the capital of France. Besides, I offended her by requesting she should at once dismiss her present bridegroom since he has not the money to support himself and far less to support a family; and after all that abuse I told her I would marry her as soon as I would be divorced. I

was much afraid that she had at once accepted my proposal but by merely returning a bill for 100 RT I had sent her and by not writing a word to me I now clearly
see that she is in great wrath against me. She is a clever, good looking, good hearted
girl and a good contriver in housekeeping. I was sure you would be happy with her,
the more so as she would have brought you a fine fortune. I could not have married
her for the sake of my descendency, for she is too near a relation to me. Thus had
she accepted my proposal and had you then not taken her off my hands, I would
have sent her at once 4000 RT to get rid of her.[26]

A few days after obtaining his divorce Schliemann wrote to Wirths, a business acquaintance in New York, about his plans for remarriage:

But now that I am free I feel a great desire to get a good, faithful loving creature as
a wife, for I feel exceedingly lonely in the world. I have withdrawn from the world
and am living here like an anchorite (but not like a saint), for this city being full of
female beauties I am very much afraid to fall here in love, which unfortunately can
and must not be, for sound reason forbids me to marry an American. But what do
you think if I go to fetch one from Athens (Greece). One who shares my enthusiasm for ancient greek literature and who has a great taste for philology and other
useful studies? I think there would be a great chance for me to be happy with such
a fanatic for sciences in which I am much advanced, so that she would always
remain my pupil. Thus she would esteem me and nothing makes a more lasting and
a stronger attachment than esteem.

Three such fanatics have been proposed to me in Athens and I have a great
desire to start on the 14th August or on the 18th Aug. from Marseilles for that
capital to go and see them. Please write me at once to Paris whether you and your
good Lady approve of my plan. Pray, consider that I am not any more young and
that consequently no young lady can fall in love with me.

On 6 September, shortly after his arrival in Athens, Schliemann sent Sophia
Engastromenos a gift with an accompanying letter:

Please accept this coral necklace in remembrance of me. I hope that it will please
you. But I draw to your attention that the ribbons are weak and that you should
exchange them for silk ones, because otherwise you risk tearing them and losing
the coral beads.

Please consult your excellent parents and write me if I may see you informally,
alone with them, not once but many times, because our agreement, to my mind,
was simply to get to know one another and to see if our personalities are compat-
ible. This is absolutely impossible in the company of many people.

Unfortunately, as it appears, marriages are always arranged quickly in Greece,
even after the first meeting, and for this reason half of all marriages are dissolved

within one year. My feelings revolt against such disastrous customs. Marriage is the most magnificent of all human institutions if the sole motives for it are respect, love, and virtue, but it (marriage) is the basest iron and the heaviest fetter if it is entered into for material advantage or sensual pleasure. Wealth contributes to marital happiness but does not in itself create it and the woman who marries me only for my money or to become a great lady in Paris, will be very sorry that she left Athens, because she would make both herself and me very unhappy. The woman who marries me should do so because of my worth as a man. I don't flatter myself foolishly. I am very well aware that a young and attractive girl cannot be in love with a man of 47 years [one word illegible] because of his attractive appearance. On account of the mere <passage of time> the man is not physically attractive. But I thought that a woman whose character completely harmonizes with my own and who has the same desire, the same enthusiasm for knowledge, could respect me, because we are all moulded in such a fashion that we always respect the one who is more capable than we are in the branches of knowledge we love most. Since such a woman would remain my pupil throughout her entire life I venture to hope that in time she would love me, first of all, because respect produces love, secondly, because I would try to be a good teacher and would devote every free amount of my life to helping my fanatic for knowledge in her philological and archaeological investigations.

In view of the foregoing I am not yet mad enough to throw myself blindly into a second marriage and, for this reason, if the fashion in Athens prevents me from seeing you frequently alone with your parents to get to know you fully, then I ask that we not think [three words illegible]. I further draw to your attention that fine clothing in no way increases your worth in my eyes and that I love you more in the ordinary clothes you always wear, the more so because in these clothes I see you in your natural state and not timid.

Please write your answer to this letter in your own hand and without the help of anyone, because I am a good judge of character and would notice immediately if someone else had helped you.[27]

Sophia's reply was brief.[28] She thanked Schliemann for his gift and indicated that her parents had given their consent to his frequent visits. She reassured him of her long-standing interest in studies. On 10 September Schliemann took Sophia, chaperoned by her mother, for an afternoon's cruise from Piraeus. The afternoon was not a success. Schliemann took the opportunity to question Sophia more closely about her motives for marriage. Her answers were unsatisfactory. Schliemann threatened to leave Athens. In desperation Sophia wrote to him on 15 September:

When I heard that you intended to leave on Thursday, a deep groan escaped my lips and such grief took hold of me that I could not control my tears. The kindness you have shown me <has encouraged me to cherish> the hope that the merciful providence of God was intending for me the supreme happiness of becoming your wife.

Yes, my esteemed Heinrich, there can be no greater happiness for me than if you decide to make me your wife. Because of this decision and action of yours, for the whole of my life I will be grateful to you and view you as my sole benefactor.

I swear to you, in the name of God on high, that my reverence for you will never fail and that I will regard your will as a divine command and for as long as Almighty God sees fit to keep me alive, I will be, with affection and justice, your most trustworthy and devoted wife. I swear too that the greatest of my <concerns> will be to make you truly happy.

I have not had the good fortune of getting a higher education and I acknowledge that I am much inferior to and unworthy of you and I imagine how much awkwardness and inconvenience you will have to endure before you can introduce your wife into Parisian society. Nonetheless, being aware of my failings and very eager to seem worthy of you, I will make every effort to come up to your desires. Besides, the desire which I have for learning, and which was transformed into enthusiasm the moment I had the good fortune to make your acquaintance and see in you such a fanatic for learning, gives me the confidence to assure you that your <best> student will do you, her teacher, honour and will learn with the greatest speed whatever subjects you wish to set for her.

With the greatest joy I would leave my homeland, the homeland of the gods and heroes, my revered parents, my beloved brothers and sisters, and my reverend uncle, to follow you to the end of the world; because I am completely confident that you would be for me father, mother, brother, sister, uncle and loving husband.

Nevertheless, I repeat, I assure you I will always have for you great reverence, boundless gratitude and the most humble respect for your will if you decide to take me as your wife. I will glorify God without end for the great happiness you confer on me.[29]

Despite the Homeric sentiments borrowed from Andromache's speech to Hector in *Iliad* 6, Schliemann's answer of 16 September was chilly:

I find it difficult to reply to your esteemed letter of yesterday, because I see in it the complete contradiction of the explanations you gave in answer to my question in the Piraeus why you have such a desire to move to Paris. You answered: 'Such is the will of my parents.' Thinking that I had misheard you I posed the same question in different words. I was exceedingly alarmed to hear from you the following explanation: 'Yes, we leave marriage plans and the choice of husband entirely up to the judgment of our parents because they are older and have great experience and know more about these things than we do. We blindly obey them.'

From these explanations of yours it was clear to me that you wished to take me as your husband not because of my worth as a man, but because you are a slave of your parents. Yes, your answer appeared to me to be so unworthy of an educated man that I could no longer speak to you and I decided to think no more about you. In your letter you revealed to me your reverence and love for me, promising me domestic happiness, the greatest of earthly blessings. But how can I trust your feelings when only six days earlier you showed me the greatest indifference. I know that the feelings which you expressed are, unfortunately, not produced on order. Moreover, the bad impression your explanations in the Piraeus made on me will not leave me. I sent you a ring in remembrance of the love for you I once had. I wanted to leave today with the French steamer for Messina and from there <to travel through> Italy but because of your letter I will wait until the day after tomorrow, Saturday, before departing with the Austrian steamer for Trieste and Switzerland because it is possible that up till that time God in his mercy may inspire in me other ideas.

From the overall tone of this letter one might conclude that Schliemann had abandoned his intention of marrying Sophia. Yet the final paragraph was clearly intended to be an invitation for further negotiation. Sophia took up the challenge immediately. Her reply is also dated 16 September.

With great <trepidation> I waited for your reply to my letter of 3/15 September to find out if your favourable behaviour towards me at our first meetings had possibly returned, since you set out our differences over the explanations I gave during our excursion to the Piraeus. But instead your esteemed letter of today's date has given me a new onset of grief.

Reading in it that you once felt love for me I call on God to restore in you that lost feeling. Learning from the same letter that you are leaving Athens next Saturday – and if you do, you take away my last hope – I have been thrown into deep despair. If I can ask nothing else of you, allow me at least to invite you to visit me in our house before your departure from Athens.

A week later, on 23 September 1869, they were married. Two days after that they sailed to Italy. After spending a week in Naples, a week in Rome, two days each in Florence, Venice and Munich, they returned to Paris in late October.[30] Since Schliemann was very anxious that Sophia should be able to converse fluently, like himself, with his international group of friends, Italian lessons began during the honeymoon in Italy and in Paris a French tutor was promptly engaged. Almost immediately after their arrival in Paris, Sophia began to feel homesick.[31] This seems to have developed into severe depression accompanied by headaches and nausea. Schliemann variously explained her illness as homesickness, failure to adjust to the colder climate of the north, and, finally, neuralgia brought on by a combination of these factors. In late November he promised to take Sophia back to Athens for a week and set her dancing for joy. When the time for the trip came, however, he postponed it till the spring.

Early in December Schliemann learned of the death of his eleven-year-old daughter, Natalia, in St Petersburg. Naturally, the event caused him deep grief and there is eloquent testimony to this in his correspondence. Two letters, however, also show rather more unusual reactions. In a letter to Serge written just after learning about Natalia, he explains her death as follows: 'God is now sending his punishment, for such crimes as your mother has committed against the father of her children – crimes such as these do *not* go unpunished.'[32] On Christmas Eve he wrote a solicitous letter to Katerina, strongly recommending a book on spiritualism as a source of comfort:

> I send you herewith a part of a book of the Spirits. You will receive the rest of it within three days, I cannot send you it all at once because this book is banned in Russia. In God's name, read it with the greatest attention, for if you do so, you will not weep any more over the death of our beloved <daughter>, you will not weep any more for we weep over only what we have lost; we do not weep if what we possess is still with us and becomes a hundred times more lovely, more sublime, and more glorious. Of our beloved Natasha all that has died is the fragile casing, which would have had to die sooner or later according to the law of nature. But the soul of Natasha *lives* and *is immortal*; it *is always with you and you will* <recover> *her presence by intuition.* According to the instruction that you will find in this book, you can put yourself *in communication with Natasha at any time* . . .

It is unclear whether Schliemann himself had found the book a comfort at this time and was therefore recommending it to Katerina. Since there is little other evidence in his writings of enthusiasm for spiritualism, it seems more likely, on the whole, that one of his acquaintances had given him the book and that now in passing it on to Katerina he was merely echoing the enthusiastic endorsements with which it had been given to him. Spiritualism was fashionable among the Parisian intelligentsia at this time. Though a pastor's son, Schliemann seems to have concerned himself little with spiritual matters even of a more orthodox kind. Perhaps most significant is the striking contrast between the transparently genuine solicitousness for his wife's emotional well-being and the brutal explanation for Natalia's death given to his fourteen-year-old son just over a week earlier.

5

Trial Trenches and Tribulations

S OPHIA'S HOMESICKNESS CONTINUED. She also suffered from migraines that would not leave her. By 21 January Heinrich had decided that they would leave for Greece in mid-February. By this time he was mixing socially with leading figures of the learned societies of Paris such as Charles-Ernest Beulé, the archaeologist at the Bibliothèque Nationale, Joseph-Ernest Renan, the philologist and historian of religion, and Emile Egger, Professor of Greek literature.

While Frank Calvert was trying to secure him a permit for Troy, Schliemann turned his attention to Mycenae. To Stephanos Koumanoudis, Secretary of the Greek Archaeological Society, he wrote: 'In accordance with the advice of my excellent friend, Mr Ernest Renan, I venture to ask you if I am sure of getting from the Greek government permission to make major excavations in the acropolis of Mycenae and under what terms.' Schliemann wished to know if he would have the right to keep the antiquities if he agreed not to take them out of Greece. He was convinced that he would have to dig 'at least 30 feet to reach the palace of Atreus and the tombs of the heroes, about whom Pausanias writes.' The shaft graves were indeed found at a depth of approximately 10 metres. The remarkable accuracy of Schliemann's estimations is striking. It may of course be mere coincidence. On the other hand, it may suggest that he had learned more from his visit to Mycenae in 1868 than he indicates in either *Ithaque* or his diary. Perhaps he had made inquiries among locals about the deep trench he had seen at Mycenae in 1868 and had learned that tombs had been discovered about this depth. On board the steamer *Niemen* bound for Piraeus, Schliemann wrote to Frank Calvert on 17 February, again sounding confident that excavations at Mycenae would be very productive: 'I have the fullest conviction that *great* things would be brought to light in that Acropolis.'[1] However, at this time Greece was very unsafe, with bands of brigands roaming the countryside. So Schliemann was pinning his hopes on the Troad and was eager to know if Calvert had been successful in obtaining a firman (permit) to excavate.

Shortly after his arrival in Athens things began to go badly for Schliemann. The Greek government refused permission to excavate at Mycenae and he learned that Frank Calvert had still not managed to obtain a firman for Hisarlik. Even more serious, however, was a disastrous breakdown in his relations with Sophia's parents. During the marriage negotiations, Schliemann, according to Sophia's mother, had promised Archbishop Vimpos that he would give either Sophia or her parents diamonds to the value of 150,000 francs (£6000). Sophia's parents were now accusing him of having reneged on this promise. Schliemann denied that any such commitment had been made. The details of the dispute emerge from a long letter Schliemann wrote to his father-in-law, dated Syra 5 March. Things came to a head on 25 February when, as Schliemann relates, Sophia announced 'in a loud voice in the presence of many witnesses that she no longer wished to live with such a man as I. I readily accepted the dissolution of our marriage that she had proclaimed in this manner and wished to depart forever. But moved by the many warm entreaties and tears of my mother-in-law, I forgave Sophia completely, but with the unalterable condition that we never return again to Athens and I swear a great oath that I will never contravene this sacred condition.'[2] The following day Schliemann left Athens for Syra and began a tour of 'the Cyclades and particularly the island of Santorini [Thera].'

With no companion other than his copy of Murray's *Handbook*, Schliemann hired his own personal caique and crew in Syra and set out. First stop was the island of Delos, sacred to Apollo. Uninhabited since the second century AD, its ruined buildings had not been buried by subsequent occupation; so although excavations had not yet begun there, much of the ancient city was visible to the visitor in 1870. Schliemann spent a day and a half on Delos. He climbed to the top of Mount Cynthos and wandered through the ruined buildings and twisted streets, trying to make sense of them with the help of his guidebook. As usual, in his own account of the visit, he incorporated a great deal of information provided by Murray.

Schliemann next visited Paros, where he hired a guide to show him the marble quarries, Naxos, and Thera (Santorini). Wherever he went he kept his eyes open for Greek inscriptions, which he carefully transcribed in his diary, and asked the villagers if they had any antiquities for sale. Thera was the high point of the trip. He stayed in the main town. His appreciation of the stunning view across the bay to Therasia, however, was marred by poor accommodation and bed-bugs. Next day, he hired a mule and headed south-west to the classical site of Thera high on the Mesavouna headland near Kamari. Here he assiduously copied inscriptions, several of which are still there today. From a nearby village he managed to buy an interesting dedicatory inscription:

'Dorocleides the son of Himeron to Hermes and Heracles. He spilled blood to win the victory in boxing and while still drawing his breath in hot gasps from his tough bout he stood up for the gruelling competition of the pancration. The same day saw Dorocleides twice an athletic victor.'[3]

The next day Schliemann wanted to cross the bay to Therasia. During the 1860s the deposits of pumice on Therasia had been extensively quarried to form a particularly high grade of cement for use in the construction of the Suez Canal, which opened in 1869. During the quarrying operations ancient ruins had come to light on the south coast. These ruins were first excavated in 1866 by two Therans, A. Alaphouzos (the owner) and P. Nomikos, and in the following spring by a French geologist, Ferdinand-André Fouqué, who had come to Thera to report on the 1866 eruption. In February 1868 a preliminary version of Fouqué's report, which also included an account of the prehistoric eruption as well as detailed notes on the excavation of the ancient house, was published in Paris. Fouqué rightly explained that Thera and Therasia were the remaining lower slopes of a large volcano, whose central cone had collapsed during a cataclysmic eruption, allowing the sea to rush in and form the caldera that separated them. Primarily on geological grounds, he dated this eruption, which had buried the ancient house under 20 metres of pumice, to *c.* 2000 BC. Schliemann had no doubt heard about the Therasia excavations in Paris or in Athens, though he does not seem to have been aware of Fouqué's explanation of how Thera and Therasia came to be separated. The older explanation, with which Schliemann concurs, was that they were separated in a violent earthquake, dated 205 BC, which had also swallowed up the central cone. Schliemann describes his visit from his arrival in the main village of Therasia as follows:

> Once in Manola I made the acquaintance of <the mayor>, who was kind enough to accompany me to the northern[4] extremity of the island, where the stone-age structures have been discovered under 64 feet of pumice. But unfortunately, the excavations have been covered over and now only a part of two small house-walls are to be seen – walls built on lava rock of irregularly shaped lava stones, joined together with yellow clay. The mayor told me that on another wall there are indications that the interior was covered with a coating of chalk. On seeing these walls, which vividly recall those of the houses bordering the Dead Sea, which are, rightly or wrongly, attributed to Sodom and Gomorrah, no-one would imagine a great antiquity for these buildings; and yet the coarse vases and, in particular, the stone implements found inside the houses leave no doubt of the enormous antiquity of these buildings.

Of particular interest is his analysis of the stratification that is clearly visible on the adjacent cliff.

The first stratum of pumice that covers the ruins is from 3 to 6 feet thick. Then comes a thin layer of from 4 to 5 inches broad of yellow pumice. If this stratum was built up by the accumulation of atmospheric dust then these buildings must be immensely ancient; but if the yellow stratum is also of volcanic origin, then the dwellings may date from an epoch as late as 2000 years B.C.; but the total absence of metal and the presence of stone instruments leave no doubt that the period is at least 2000 years B.C. Above the layer of yellow material is a stratum of 60 feet of pumice. The site is about 300 feet above sea-level.

Schliemann's reasoning is essentially archaeological. The lack of metal tools indicates the stone age and therefore a date of 2000 BC at the latest. His assessment of the geological layering, not surprisingly, lacks the professional sophistication of Fouqué. It does, however, seem to show a robust common sense, though this turns out to be illusory. Without further information one cannot conclude which hypothesis implies the earliest date for the buried buildings: a single eruption, producing three layers of deposits, three separate eruptions, or two eruptions separated by a long interval. It is clear, however, that there could be no more graphic lesson in the basic principle of stratigraphy that an occupation level must antedate the superimposed material.

It is curious that Schliemann's dating for the building coincides with Fouqué's. This may be chance or it may be that Fouqué had told Alaphazous his estimated date for the building and that Alaphazous passed this on to Schliemann when they met later that same day. Archaeologists now date the artefacts found at both Therasia and Acrotiri (Thera) to the Late Bronze Age. A number of scientific tests have recently shown surprising unanimity in pointing to *c.* 1630 BC for the date of the eruption. Many archaeologists, however, are reluctant to countenance so early a date for Late Bronze Age finds.[5]

Before leaving Thera Schliemann bought from Alaphazous some of the antiquities the Theran had found: a tiny vase of coarse workmanship, a quantity of carbonized barley, a piece of petrified cheese, two terracotta lamps, the fragments of an attractive vase, and part of a log that had formed the lintel over a doorway. From a goldsmith in Pyrgos he purchased an engraved gem, twenty coins, and a marble bust of Venus, all presumably classical pieces from the site of ancient Thera.

Shortly after his return to Athens Heinrich seems to have re-established fairly cordial relations with Sophia, though not with her parents. The couple went on day trips to Phyle and Marathon and on a longer excursion to Corinth and Delphi. On 3 April his permit to excavate at Mycenae had still not been approved. Schliemann wanted a contract that would allow him to retain half of the finds but Greek law had long insisted that all archaeological finds were the property of the state. Schliemann finally agreed to these terms and the permit was granted. Since excavations were not set to begin at Mycenae until 25 April, Schliemann decided to take a quick trip to Asia Minor: Constantinople, Troy, Smyrna, Ephesus, Magnesia, and Mytilene.[6] To his great annoyance Sophia refused to accompany him.[7]

It seems that *en route* to the Dardanelles, Schliemann decided to change his trip from a tour of Asia Minor to a preliminary excavation of Hisarlik. Perhaps the absence of Sophia was the decisive factor. He brought four workmen with him from the Dardanelles. Arriving at Hisarlik, he feasted his eyes on the view.

> The plain is covered with the beautiful green of spring and embroidered with millions of flowers. Numerous herds of sheep and cattle are to be seen, and also many horses and countless storks moving with slow measured steps. The view is further varied with the fine oaks to be seen here and there in the plain. Beyond the plain, at a distance of three miles, is the beautiful Hellespont, where ships are constantly to be seen. Beyond the Hellespont Samothrace can be distinguished with its fine mountains, among which Mt. Ida, which is covered with snow.

Without any official permit to excavate or even the consent of the owners, Schliemann began excavations on Hisarlik on 9 April 1870. In his published account of the dig he explained: 'Knowing in advance that the two Turkish owners would refuse to give me permission I did not ask them.'[8] He first excavated an oblong area at the highest point of the ridge and then, further west, two long narrow trenches intersecting to form a right angle (see Fig. 2).[9] The results were disappointing, particularly at the summit, where he had expected to find the principal building of Troy, whether the Palace of Priam or the Temple of Athena. After two days of excavation he 'lost all hope of finding the cyclopean walls of the temples and palace that Homer sings about in the Iliad.' He was surprised too, for, given the impressive ruins of Hellenistic Ilium to be seen in surrounding fields, he had expected to find beautiful buildings on what must have been the acropolis of that town. Instead, 'je ne trouve que de la camelote (I only find trash).'[10]

The trenches were more rewarding. Here he found pottery, nails, terracotta statuettes, rusted coins, bones, boars' tusks, and urns containing human ashes. The longer trench, running to the south-west edge of the ridge, gave some inkling of the complexity of the site. Here no less than five walls crossed the trench and another ran down its eastern edge. Moreover, walls superimposed on earlier ones provided clear evidence of different occupation levels. Near the south end he came across 'a wall 2 metres thick that blocks our way and also runs along the edge of our trench with a protrusion of 84 cm. This walling consists of very good stones of limestone, well hewn, 1 m long, 67 cm broad and from 34 to 50 cm thick, and it is immediately apparent that it has been built with great skill. These are clearly the walls of a palace or a temple, and up to the wall that traverses it, our trench is in a room of this building.' Schliemann later identified this walling as dating from the Greek period and saw in this section a Hellenic tower.[11] When he wrote up his 1870 dig for publication, however, he transferred this walling from the south-west edge of the ridge to the summit.

> At a depth of 5 metres we discovered on the 11 April a wall two metres thick formed of stones of limestone of great solidity and skilfully hewn; each of these stones is 1 m long, 67 cm broad and 43 [*sic*] to 50 cm thick. We followed this wall for a distance of 12 metres from west to east, where it turns north at a right angle. Since I discovered these walls at the highest point of the hill I am inclined to believe that these are the walls of the ancient temple of Ilian Minerva so often mentioned in the Iliad.

Comparing his diary and published accounts, it is clear that Schliemann hoped to find signs of an impressive building on the summit of the hill. Instead, he found them near the south-west edge of the ridge. It was a simple matter in writing up his report for publication to say that he found under the summit exactly the same kind of walling as he found elsewhere. Significantly, however, he did not invent new details, merely a new location for the walling. This may seem an innocuous change. It is in fact very serious. An archaeologist must report even the most mundane of facts with complete honesty or he forfeits his claim to credibility.

Some of the more interesting individual finds were also transferred from the trenches to the summit, among them the coins. In his diary account Schliemann mentions finding 'two copper coins ruined by rust' in the north–south trench on 13 April and 'a bad coin' on 16 April in the east–west trench. He reports finding no legible coins anywhere and no coins at all at the summit. On several occasions, however, he mentions buying coins at Troy and elsewhere in the Troad. For instance, on 11 April: 'I have just bought from a Turk two good copper coins of Ilium for 4 piasters'; and on 13 April: 'I have bought here enough coins of Ilium; I am delighted at this.'[12] According to the published account, however, he found under the summit a Trojan coin issued under Emperor Commodus (AD 180–92) with the inscription (in Greek) 'Hector of the Ilians' and a coin of Sigeum and in the trenches several legible coins of Ilium.[13] Conceivably, the coins he found, once properly cleaned, turned out to be legible. More probably, however, he simply substituted the purchased coins for the unsatisfactory ones he had excavated and distributed their findspots as he saw fit.

The kidnapping by brigands of a number of foreign visitors near Marathon on 11 April and their brutal murder ten days later caused an international scandal.[14] The incident dramatically illustrated how unsafe the Greek country-side was and Schliemann abandoned his plans to excavate at Mycenae and turned his attention back to Troy. He addressed the report of his excavations to the President of the Institute of France in the hope that it would be published in its *Mémoires*. He also urged Frank Calvert to try to buy the western half of Hisarlik for him.

> It would neither do for me to begin now to make excavations on your own part of that acropolis, for if I did so the two Turks would certainly not sell at any price. Whereas if we now for some weeks feign not to care about it I think the two Turks will be willing to sell their land when the order comes from Constantinople to prevent them taking out the stones, for when you visit the spot you will see that the land has literally been ruined by my diggings and that, as pasture, it has now hardly half its former value.
>
> Please buy the lot of land for me as cheap as you possibly can and pay in case of need even £100 / One Hundred Pounds for it. I send you the amount instantly on receipt of your notice that you make the purchase for me.[15]

In the meantime, Schliemann decided to return to Paris via Constantinople and the Danube, stopping at Schweizermühle in Saxony to see if the hydro-therapy practised there would cure Sophia of her chronic ill-health. To humour his wife, he took her sister Margo with them. It was a disastrous trip. Schliemann found Margo 'ignorant and insupportable.' Worse, the doctor at Schweizermühle recommended that Sophia return to Athens at once. Schliemann wrote to his brother Ernst on 19 May:

> The improvement that had shown itself in the first few days in my poor wife's condition has disappeared and to my horror I have to tell you that the doctor who has just examined her declares her incurable, for she is hysterical, she already has a beginning of spasms or of tubercolosis. He advises us to return with all speed to Athens and leave Sophia for some months with her parents, for he has a spark of hope that she can still be saved if I abstain from her for a long time – which is impossible if we live together. I will return therefore immediately from Athens via Constantinople to Paris.

Schliemann promptly acted on this advice and returned to Paris. However, an extraordinary letter, dated 1 June 1870, from Schliemann to Sophia, written apparently *en route* from Marseille to Athens, indicates that his reasons for not remaining with his wife were very different from those he gave his brother.[16] He saw in Sophia's persistent homesickness proof that she did not love him.

> But nonetheless I did not cease caring for you even for a moment, as ever a loving mother cared for her beloved child. To please you, I left all my important business in Paris and all my advantages there to run with you to your homeland. To please you, I sacrificed 4½ months there when each moment was very valuable to me. I thought that you would have immeasurable gratitude for me because of such a favour. But, on the contrary, as soon as we returned to your family, as if maddened by an evil demon, you became infuriated with me and before many witnesses you declared that you would no longer live with such a man as I. Yes, from 18 February not a single day has passed without your making me angry and without my cursing the day when, trusting in your false oaths, I decided to make you my wife.

At Schweizermühle, besides diagnosing her condition as hysterical and re-commending her return to Athens, the doctor

> affirms that you will be cured if you become pregnant, but how can I make you pregnant when you enrage me from morning till night. A man makes children in love not in anger. Besides, you are not the only one who is suffering; I too am suffering severely from the many unpleasantnesses you cause me every day. The constant anger which you cause me weakens me and shortens my life, a life which is very necessary both for my beloved children and for hundreds of beggars. In addition, what guarantee is there that the frightful resolve to end your own life would not return to you? We have many windows in our house in Paris and if you wish to commit suicide, how can I prevent such a scandalous act?
>
> Because of the aforesaid many weighty reasons it would be the worst of wrongs on my part if I were to continue to live with you. But night and day the idea torments me that perhaps you would be happy with a young husband and perhaps with a compatriot, who would consent to live with you in Athens, near your beloved mother. I am far from returning wrong for the many wrongs you have done me. I am far from preventing you from gaining your happiness on this earth. Not only do I give you back your freedom with the greatest joy, but I am also fully prepared to set up a suitable dowry for you in Athens and also to give your sister a dowry.
>
> Since your behaviour towards me has brought me to the extreme point of distress, I am also fully prepared to do all in my power to help you get a divorce with all speed. Although I have never done you any wrong – even in a dream – I will with pleasure sign that I am guilty of murder, piracy, adultery and any other crime.
>
> In any case, with this letter I swear a thousand oaths that I cannot and will not live any more with you, not even for a day. If I were to give myself a million francs a day, I am no longer capable of living even a day with you because you are killing me with your behaviour towards me. For this reason, please abandon any idea of

coming back with me. Rather than putting up with you beside me for one more day I would do a thousand times better if I committed suicide.

It would be easy to conclude that the marriage was over. Yet in just three weeks Schliemann wrote Sophia another long letter.[17] In it he acknowledged that he was partly to blame for her unhappiness in Paris, which he attributed to the excessive amount of studying he had forced on her and to his own mourning over the death of Natalia. He was eager to resume excavations at Troy and wanted Sophia to accompany him. He planned to leave Marseille for the Dardanelles on 2 July and Sophia was to join the ship at Piraeus when it stopped there late on 6 July. At this point Schliemann was still regarding Paris as his permanent home. He told Sophia of his plans to buy a plot of land between the Collège de France and the Sorbonne.[18] He also wrote to Frank Calvert, informing him that he would soon be resuming excavations and was holding out high hopes that he would find inscriptions.[19]

In July 1870 France and Germany appeared close to declaring war on each other. Schliemann disembarked at Piraeus and promptly postponed his plans for excavating at Hisarlik. The reason he gave for this to his correspondents was the poor state of Sophia's health, though, almost certainly, concern for his investments now that a war was looming must also have been a factor. On 13 July he wrote to Shröders in London, cancelling his purchase of French railway shares. The next day he and Sophia left Athens for Paris. On their way back France declared war on Germany. Interestingly, Schliemann's sympathies lay entirely with the French and he was confident that they would win. Since the doctors in Paris counselled sea-bathing for Sophia, the couple went off to Boulogne in August. Here they seemed to be happy together for a while. It was probably here that their first child, Andromache, was conceived.

After a brief trip across the Channel to York and Edinburgh, Heinrich and Sophia spent October with friends in Arcachon in western France and then returned to Athens in November. The unsettling effect of the war, the siege of Paris, where the starving inhabitants were forced to eat rats, his need for Sophia, and her refusal to live permanently away from Athens, as well as his plans to excavate at Troy and Mycenae – all these factors combined to convince Schliemann to abandon his dream of living among the intelligentsia of Paris. He resolved to build a house in Athens and make that his permanent home. In mid-December, impatient that Frank Calvert had failed to get a firman for his excavations or to buy the western half of Hisarlik for him, Schliemann set off to settle these matters himself.

En route he stopped at Ephesus and met J.T. Wood, who had been excavating there for seven years on behalf of the British Museum, and admired the extensive ruins, including the Temple of Diana, which was then coming to light. At Kum Kale in the Troad, he negotiated with the two Turkish owners of Hisarlik without success. Excavating their land in the spring without bothering to ask their permission had, of course, been inexcusable. Since, in addition, he had, by his own account, 'crushed them with insults,' when they had come to stop his excavations, and had ruined their land with his trenches, it is scarcely surprising that negotiations were difficult.[20] One owner refused Schliemann's offer of 1,000 francs (£40) for his portion, demanding instead 8,000 francs. The other owner was prepared to accept Schliemann's offer for his portion, but out of respect for his neighbour refused to sell unless the latter also agreed to do so.

Frustrated, but nonetheless convinced that he would eventually win them over, Schliemann proceeded to Constantinople to negotiate for the firman. He wrote to Sophia that he had immersed himself in learning Turkish. His diary certainly bears this out. Sixty-two pages are in that language, written, as it then was, in Arabic script.

6

Assault on Hisarlik

THE NEGOTIATIONS WITH THE owners of Hisarlik proved long and difficult. The Turks were no doubt wary of this brash businessman who had already illegally excavated at Hisarlik without firman in hand. In mid-January the Minister of Public Instruction, Safvet Pasha, requisitioned the western half of Hisarlik from the two Turkish owners. At this time Turkey, unlike Greece, had no law whereby the state could claim all antiquities found in Turkish soil. Legally, the landowner had all rights to whatever antiquities might be found on his property. To ensure that the new Imperial Museum in Constantinople would be a beneficiary of the excavations at Hisarlik, Safvet Pasha, not surprisingly, considered it imperative that the government own the site.

Schliemann was furious at this development. Availing himself of his US citizenship, he called on the American embassy for diplomatic support. After telling Safvet Pasha that he was not interested in excavating without the security of owning the land, he returned to Athens. At the end of January Paris surrendered to the German armies besieging it and Schliemann went off to see what damage his property had suffered in the Franco-Prussian war. At this point no one was allowed to enter Paris until a peace treaty had been drawn up and ratified. In a letter to his friend Gottschalk, Schliemann describes how he succeeded in overcoming this obstacle:

> Using the pass of the postmaster of Lagny – to whom I gave 5 fr. for the service – I managed to cross all the German lines; but not without difficulty, for three times I was on the point of being arrested because of my age, which was stated to be thirty on the pass, which did not seem to be altogether in accord with mine. But knowing the German's mania for empty titles, I managed to smooth over all obstacles by calling the lieutenants 'Monsieur le Général' and the ordinary soldiers 'Monsieur le Colonel'. With a fear impossible to describe I approached my house, 5 Boulevard St Michel, and my building, 6 Place St Michel, and when I saw intact everything that I had thought to find in ruins, my joy was immense and with tears in my eyes I gave as many kisses to my library as I would have given to a child raised from the dead.[1]

84

To his American friend Wirth, he wrote about his wife and his domestic plans:

I have left my dear wife at Athens for she expects shortly to get an Agamemnon or an Andromache or both together and she therefore cannot travel any more. I can tell you that this time I have hit the right one. But I feel inclined to think that I would have been as happy with any other Greek lady, for with the Greek wife the husband is her Heaven and the sole haven of her hope and she overwhelms him with love. In fact, the sole deficiency I find with the Greek wife is that she loves her conjugal companion too much.

We have decided to establish our principal domicile in Athens, for by Greek law all I find in my excavations is my own property but I dare not take it out of the country.[2]

Schliemann's immediate concern in Paris was to ensure that the payment of rent, temporarily suspended by law during the war, be resumed and that the arrears be made good. His hopes were dashed by the election on 26 March of the Paris Commune. Schliemann apparently left Paris on 5 April. The last letter in the copybook is dated 26 March. Thereafter sixteen pages have been excised from the copybook. No doubt these contained unflattering remarks about the new regime in Paris. Perhaps Schliemann thought it prudent to remove them before he left Paris in case he was searched and his writings were deemed incriminating.

Just before leaving Athens Schliemann had bought a site on the main street of the city between the royal palace and the university. He intended replacing the existing building there with a new house incorporating features he had seen and admired in American houses. He had written to American friends with plans and engaged the leading architect in Athens, Ernst Ziller. Once back in Greece, however, he decided to postpone the project indefinitely, indicating to Ziller that the revised estimate for the house was too expensive.[3] Probably, Schliemann was experiencing some financial difficulties. Though he was confident that the Commune of Paris could not last long, prospects for the prompt resumption of rent payments, Schliemann's chief source of income, must have looked rather bleak in May 1871. On top of that, expenditures for the planned excavation of Troy were bound to be high.

Shortly after reaching Athens Schliemann wrote to Frank Calvert:

I shall not be able to leave for Constantinople before the 22nd June and by what Mr John P. Brown, Secretary of the American Legation, writes me today I have not the slightest doubt that I shall at once come to terms with Safvet Pasha and be able to resume the excavations of Ancient Troy in the beginning of July and perhaps already end of June. I take Mrs Schliemann with me and we shall at once publish in Greek, French and German the description of our diggings, with which your name is so closely connected and for which we feel an immense enthusiasm.

On 7 May Sophia gave birth to a girl, who was promptly named Andromache. That Heinrich supposed that within six weeks of giving birth, Sophia would happily abandon the care of her baby to others and submit to the deprivations of living in a tent at Troy in the height of summer shows how little he knew his wife. When she refused to accompany him, he left in a rage and sent her a long, recriminating letter from Constantinople.[4]

... God heard my prayers for you. To my indescribable joy he restored you to full health with your pregnancy. Despite this, your misconduct towards me continued. But nevertheless I endured it steadfastly so that the child might not be harmed. Apart from this, I was convinced that after giving birth, your joy over the child, your restored health, and the progress you were making in your studies would finally open your eyes, would change your misconduct towards me and would make you submit to your husband and obey him, as you swore in your marriage vow, and you would learn that the other greatest gifts of Heaven are mean and worthless compared to domestic harmony and happiness.

The next day he addressed a formal proposal to Safvet Pasha:

I have already conducted some excavations at Hissarlik and I believe that I have found there the so-called Pergamus that formed part of the city of Troy; but the difficulties I encountered on the part of the proprietors of the land have fortunately been smoothed over by your Excellency's kindness, which has acquired it on your own account. I do not expect to find any treasure, Excellency. The period is too early to offer any hope of that, and my entire task will be restricted to archaeological verifications based on the writings of the poet Homer. If, however, I am fortunate enough to find any ancient objects of value that could be of interest to the Imperial Museum, I would be very happy to divide them, half for the Museum and the other half for me, in recompense for the funds expended by me at the site, and this equitable division will be made, by lot, in the presence of a representative of the said Museum, and I will be given the opportunity to export my half.

To Frank Calvert he explained what had happened:

To my utter despair I have met here on the part of Mr Goold and Safvet Pasha with new difficulties, which are all the more difficult as they are unexpected. For reasons only known to them and in spite of all their previous foul dealing they want me now to take out a firman in a regular way, which will require at least two months.[5]

After spending a few days in Athens Schliemann returned to Paris. Now that the Paris Commune had fallen he intended 'to assist my agent in coming to arrangements with my inmates regarding the house rents, which are now due for 12 months'.[6] The trip also included Berlin, where he met the leading German archaeologist, Ernst Curtius; and London, where he visited the British Museum. It was in London that he finally received his firman, as he wrote to Frank Calvert on 12 August:

> I received here today from the Amer. Legation of Constantinople my firman, perfectly in order; but since I have still to remove to my own house in Athens by 1/13 Sept. I can hardly hope to recommence the excavations before end Sept.[7]

When he got back to Athens in September, some disturbing news was waiting for him. He wrote at once to his Indianapolis lawyers:

> You remember that you obtained a divorce for me on the 30 June 1869 and until now my first wife has not in the least molested me on that ground. But now at once she files here a complaint against me for bigamy.

Schliemann suspected that Katerina was planning to challenge the divorce on the grounds that she had been given no prior notice of the suit, for it was on this issue in particular that Schliemann sought advice. Needless to say, such a lawsuit in Athens would have been extremely embarrassing for Schliemann. In December he wrote again to Hendricks:

> I am happy to inform you that my first wife merely intended to threaten me with a law-suit and that she has 3 weeks ago obtained in the Court of St Petersburg her divorce in *full form* so that even by the laws of Russia everything is now finished between us.

In fact, there was no threat of a lawsuit. It seems that the American divorce was invalid in Russia and that Katerina was initiating divorce proceedings of her own in St Petersburg. In a letter to her dated 6 January 1872, Schliemann pledged to give her his full co-operation in this matter.

More delays awaited Schliemann when he finally reached the Dardanelles on 27 September. The local governor held that the firman did not specify exactly where Schliemann was allowed to dig at Hisarlik. This delayed the excavations until 11 October. Regarding Sophia, Schliemann makes the following remarks in his published account of the 1871 excavations: 'My dear wife, an Athenian lady, who is an enthusiastic admirer of Homer, and knows almost the whole of the "Iliad" by heart, is present at the excavations from

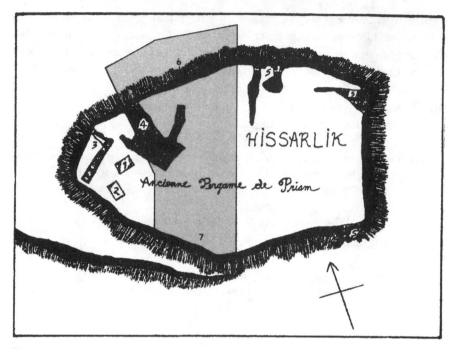

Fig. 2   Plan of excavations at Hisarlik 1870–1 (Scale 1:2500)

1. Schliemann's wooden house
2. Storehouse
3. Trenches excavated in 1870
4. 1871 excavations
5. Calvert's excavations
6-7. Broad trench through the mound, planned for 1872

morning to night.'[8] In fact, Sophia did not participate at all in the 1871 dig. Schliemann wrote letters to her dated 13 and 23 October, and 7, 14, 21 and 29 November, which demonstrate clearly that she remained in Athens throughout the season. The first of these indicates that there was once again a quarrel at Schliemann's departure. It begins: 'The pain that your conduct towards me caused me on the day of my departure was so heart-rending, so overwhelming that up till now I have been completely incapable of writing to you.'[9] The rest of this letter, however, and the other letters of this period are conciliatory and even at times effusively affectionate.

Schliemann's excavation plan was to dig from the northern edge of the plateau in towards and encompassing the area he had excavated at the summit in 1870. On the whole, however, it was a disappointing season. There were more than a few rainy days, particularly in the latter part of November, when the excavated earth turned to mud. There were also problems with the

workmen. Generally, Schliemann drew his workers from the Greek commu-
nities, many of whom came from outlying areas and took accommodation in
Chiplak, the nearest village, which was Turkish. The Greeks, being Christians,
would not work on Sundays; so Schliemann hired Turkish labourers for
Sunday work. The Turks did not appreciate being passed over on Monday
morning and stopped providing accommodation for the Greek workers. And
so on.

Schliemann's right-hand man was Nikolaos Zaphyros Yannakis, who was a
fount of local knowledge and acted as paymaster and Schliemann's personal
servant. Unfortunately, he lacked the capacity to command others and so
could not serve as a foreman. Schliemann was severely overworked, supervising about 70–80 workmen, receiving finds, and writing up reports. The
major finds of the season were three Greek inscriptions from the Greco-
Roman phase of Ilium. These, however, had no bearing on Homeric Troy.

Schliemann was disappointed to find that immediately below the Greco-
Roman material at the surface he was in what appeared to be the Stone Age.
Among the most frequent finds were little whorls with a hole in the middle,
usually of pottery but sometimes of stone. These were an enigma to
Schliemann. Archaeologists are still unsure of their purpose, though some
would probably have been used as spindle whorls and others perhaps as loom
weights. There were various knives, saws, and hammers, all of stone. But of
metal tools there was no sign.

Schliemann had expected a whole series of different occupation levels, par-
alleling the Hellenistic (after 325 BC), the classical (500–325 BC), and pre-classical periods of Greece. Little or nothing was known at this time about the
Stone, Bronze and Iron Ages in Mediterranean lands but the orthodox view,
based on experience in northern Europe, held that human society went
through these stages successively on the road to civilization. So as he dug
deeper, Schliemann would naturally have expected to encounter strata attributable to the Trojan Iron, Bronze and Stone Ages. Since the heroes in the
Homeric poems use almost exclusively bronze weapons, it was natural to look
for Homeric Troy at the Bronze Age level. Hence the bitter disappointment
at finding what seemed to be a Stone Age level immediately below the Greco-
Roman.

This was a serious setback. The chance discovery of the hand – and nothing
else – of a marble statue prompted Schliemann to philosophical reflection. He
realized that in his rapid digging he must have missed some works of art.

> But I am not digging to find works of art although I accept them with joy when I
> find them. I am digging only to enhance knowledge and I am doing it profoundly

in the stone age, profoundly in the darkness of time, in the strata of debris that must antedate Homer by thousands of years.

All the archaeologists that have visited the plain of Troy have decided the question of the site of the ancient city – and some have reached their decisions without even visiting the plain – but all have resolved the question theoretically. Many scholars even think, because of the miraculous element in the events described by Homer, that Troy never existed. But that is theory. No-one so far has ever taken the trouble to resolve this great question practically, as I am doing. And if by perseverance and at enormous expense I manage to prove that Troy never existed, I will be very happy if the scholarly world recognizes the merit in having resolved the question negatively.[10]

Here we see Schliemann at his best. Three weeks of excavations have led him to confront the unwelcome conclusion that Hisarlik was probably not occupied at the time of the Trojan War, though it was clearly occupied both earlier and later. Yet he is determined to press on, rightly aware that even negative findings are valuable, for they represent an advance in knowledge. Frederick Calvert and his wife tried to encourage Schliemann with the suggestion that the 'Stone Age' material might be fill (rubble) brought in from elsewhere in a later levelling of the surface of the mound.[11] Schliemann was grateful for their encouragement but remained unconvinced. He could see that the 'Stone Age' material was arranged in distinct strata and therefore could not be extraneous fill.

The stratification at Hisarlik is indeed unusual. The Calverts were right to suggest that efforts in the Greco-Roman period to level the mound had disturbed the regular succession of strata, though their theory about extraneous fill was wrong. In the levelling process the strata now called Troy VI, VII and VIII had been shaved off from the summit of the mound (see Fig. 3). This represents roughly the period 1900–325 BC, some sixteen hundred years of human habitation. Hence, in the centre of the mound, where Schliemann was excavating, Greco-Roman Ilium was sitting directly on top of Troy V, the last stage of the Early Bronze Age, not the Stone Age, as Schliemann was about to discover. Homeric Troy is now dated to the Late Bronze Age, *c.* thirteenth century BC. Traces of this settlement are to be found only away from the centre of the mound. Ironically, walls which Schliemann excavated in 1870 near the north-west edge of the mound were almost certainly those of a house in Troy VI.[12] Unfortunately for Schliemann, he judged these walls to be of Hellenistic date (after 325 BC) and lost interest in them.

As Schliemann dug deeper, bronze or copper finds began to appear.[13] On 8 November he found two copper brooches; the next day a copper knife, spearhead and needle; thereafter a small but steady flow of copper or bronze

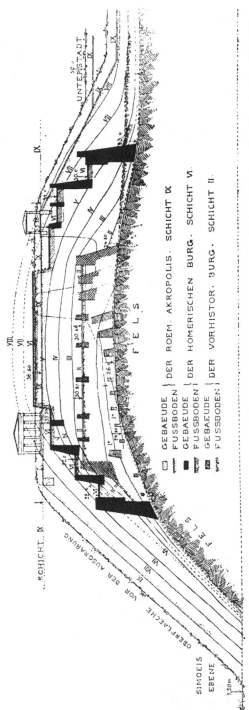

Fig. 3   Cross-section of Hisarlik showing how the remodelling in the Greco-Roman period (Troy IX) shaved off levels Troy VI, VII and VIII from the centre of the mound. (W. Dörpfeld, 1902)

tools or weapons. On 14 November, for instance, a battleaxe, a spearhead and several nails, all of copper. He also found terracotta pitchers, up to 1 metre high, filled with human bones. Heartened by these finds, Schliemann began to revise his views. He had found Bronze Age Troy after all! Surprisingly, the quality of the artefacts seemed to improve the deeper he got. Homeric Troy therefore must be at the bottom. As Schliemann's enthusiasm grew, the weather worsened. He closed the excavations on 24 November and went back to Athens, resolved to return in the spring and uncover the city of Priam.

Throughout, Schliemann kept a diary account of his excavations. He recorded the number of workmen he hired each day and summarized the day's progress and principal finds. About once a week he wrote a comprehensive report, in both German and Greek, to send to the *Augsburg Allgemeine Zeitung* and the Athens newspaper *Ephemeris ton Syzeteseon*.[14] These reports, slightly expanded, eventually became *Trojanische Alterthümer* or, in its English translation, *Troy and its Remains*. One of the reasons Schliemann had wanted Sophia to accompany him to Troy was to help him write the Greek reports. The sheer effort involved in writing out by hand rough and fair copies of these – in effect four preliminary drafts of his book – was enormous.

Back in Athens, after being forced to spend about twelve days in quarantine on Salamis, Schliemann worked on transcribing and interpreting the Greek inscriptions he had found. He sent the transcriptions to Ernst Curtius and they were published in 1872 in *Archäologische Zeitschrift*. Meanwhile, he explored the option of using a railway system to remove the vast quantities of material he would be digging out, but eventually decided against it. He also puzzled over the numerous pots with what he thought were owl faces on them. If he was right, then perhaps the Homeric epithet of Athena, *glaucopis*, should be translated 'owl-faced' rather than 'with gleaming eye', as most scholars believed. Since, however, many of these pots also exhibited female breasts, most scholars saw on them the face of a woman rather than an owl.

On 1 April 1872 he was back at Hisarlik. This time he brought two foremen with him, Theodorus Makrys and Spyros Demetriou, in addition to his paymaster, Nikolaos Yannakis. The French engineer, Adolphe Laurent, came and stayed for a month. His task was to draw up an accurate plan of the mound, including the trenches of 1870 and 1871. A third foreman, Georgios Photidos, who had worked as a miner in Australia, was soon added. Though Schliemann explicitly says in *Troy and its Remains* that Sophia was with him from the beginning of April, she did not in fact arrive until 24 May.[15]

Schliemann's plan for the 1872 season was to cut a huge north–south trench across the mound, reaching down to a floor 14 metres below the surface. This floor, and sometimes the whole trench itself, he referred to as the 'platform' in his reports. The trench was to be 79 metres broad and would encompass the 1871 excavations (see Fig. 2). The quantity of material that required shifting was prodigious – 78,000 cubic metres, Laurent reckoned.

As he began excavations at the north end of the mound Schliemann encountered what he took to be a buttress wall and behind that, a compacted jumble of debris.

> The debris is as hard as stone, and consists of the ruins of houses, among which I find axes of diorite, sling bullets of loadstone, a number of flint knives, innumerable handmills of lava, a great number of small idols of very fine marble, with or without the owl's head and woman's girdle, weights of clay in the form of pyramids and with a hole at the point, or made of stone and in the form of balls; lastly, a great many of those small terra-cotta whorls, which have already been so frequently spoken of in my previous reports.

The going was most difficult on the east side of the trench, where the stones were particularly numerous. To speed things up, Schliemann decided on 15 May to leave terraces on the east and west sides of the trench; their floors were 5 to 6 metres above the floor of the central part of the trench. On the east terrace he uncovered the remains of an impressive building.

> Just east of my excavations of last year, only 3 metres below the ground, a house, which must decidedly belong to the prehistoric period, is coming into view. Its surviving part is 17½ metres long, the walls are 190 cm thick and consist of hewn blocks of white limestone fitted together, which are so set that the walls have a smooth appearance. The walls go down only 6 metres deep . . .[16]

Unfortunately, Schliemann later removed this fine building to get to the ruins underneath. Blegen has suggested that this might have been the palace of the third stratum of Troy (Troy III *c.* 2200–2050 BC).[17] On 17 May, at a depth of 9 metres, or 3 metres below this house, Schliemann came upon perhaps his most exciting find to date: five gold ornaments – a pin, three simple rings of twisted wire, and a more sophisticated ear-ring (see Fig. 4).

In mid-May he received an important letter from Emile Burnouf, the Director of the French School at Athens, to whom he had written an enthusiastic letter about his excavations:

> You must keep these large vases, always with an indication of the stratum where you find them. That is of great importance for all the objects you discover, because on your return, when you put your collection in order, you must be able to arrange together everything found in the same stratum. Otherwise, no definite conclusion

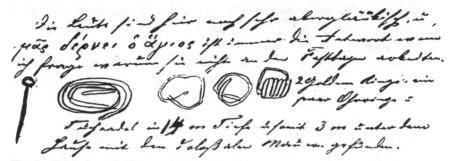

Fig. 4   Entry from Schliemann's 1872 diary mentioning the find of a gold pin and ear-rings with depth altered from 9 to 14 metres

could be drawn from your fine discoveries. . . . Only the position occupied by an object in the excavations can truly indicate its date.[18]

Up to this point Schliemann had been making drawings in his diary of the more interesting finds but without indicating the depth at which they had been found. From 15 May onwards all illustrations include an indication of the depth. Schliemann was always ready and eager to learn from others.

Among the many inconveniences of life at Hisarlik were the exotic and often dangerous fauna that they had to deal with – snakes, scorpions and sarantopodia ('forty-footers'), a kind of centipede whose bite was said to be fatal. These facts of life would not be likely to make field archaeology appealing to Sophia, who liked her comforts. On 7 June she 'found two "forty-footers" in her bed but succeeded in killing only one of them.'[19] On the same day 'Sophia began making an excavation with two workmen and enjoyed this role very much.'[20] Since Schliemann was employing 80–100 workmen at this point, Sophia's role here was modest. It is only reasonable to suppose, however, that her responsibilities grew as experience increased her self-confidence. Schliemann's diary says nothing more about her role in the excavations until her departure on 26 June.[21] Just before she left she copied out the Greek version of the lengthy 18 June report to take back to the Greek newspaper.

Schliemann was beginning to have second thoughts about the lowest stratum. The second level was yielding more impressive finds. Could it be Homeric Troy? His entry of 8 June reads: 'Unfortunately, nothing to be found in the lowest levels and I am beginning to be discouraged. . . . I am now beginning to believe that all the debris 8 to 10 metres deep derives from ancient Troy; only I don't know what to make of the splendid pottery in the lowest levels.'[22] Among the signs of higher civilization that he was encountering at the Troy II level were numerous bronze tools and weapons, moulds and crucibles and an extensive layer of a 'metal-like material', presumably the slag produced from smelting copper ore. Clearly, there were bronze workshops in the centre of Hisarlik at this time (Troy II is now dated roughly 2500–2200 BC).

On 12 June he stopped work on the south side of the mound and put Photidos in charge of excavations on Frank Calvert's land on the north side of the mound. Here the Greco-Roman Temple of Athena was located and Schliemann hoped that under its foundations he might find signs of a much earlier temple. Calvert had agreed to allow excavations on his land on condition that the finds be shared equally between Schliemann and himself. The next day Photidos' men came across what was definitely the find of the season, the Helios metope (see Fig. 5). This excellent piece of sculpture (2 m long × 86 cm high) had come from the Hellenistic temple of Athena. It is now considered to represent Helios, the sun god, driving his chariot across the sky. Schliemann, however, believed it represented Apollo, who also was wor-

Fig. 5   The Helios metope

shipped as a sun god. The piece posed two major problems: how was it to be divided equally between Schliemann and Calvert; and how was such a heavy block to be transported? To solve the second problem, Schliemann had a rather drastic solution: 'I would by all means advise to saw off from the marble of the Sungod a long piece to the right and left, so that on either side only one column remains, for it can lose *nothing* by that operation and it will gain that much that it can thus be loaded on one cart and transported to your house.' Calvert quickly urged him not to do this.

From the beginning Calvert had encouraged Schliemann to continue the excavations at Hisarlik that he himself had started. He had offered to help in any way he could. Schliemann drew freely on Calvert's generous offer. From 1 April to 31 August 1872 Schliemann wrote some forty letters to Frank Calvert. Almost all of them ask for some favour; many ask for several: have wheelbarrows repaired, forward outgoing and incoming mail, make financial arrangements for him, intervene on Schliemann's behalf with the Turkish authorities and so forth. Calvert seems to have performed these services willingly and gratis, though they must have consumed a great deal of his time. When the Helios metope was discovered, Schliemann had a clear obligation to return these favours with a generous arrangement over this valuable find. His correspondence shows no awareness of this obligation. He treats the matter as just another business transaction, in which the goal is to trick the other party into making all the concessions.

Schliemann offered to buy Calvert's share and asked him to name his price. After discussing the matter with his brother Frederick, Frank Calvert replied on 16 July:

> We think £500 would be given by an amateur for this beautiful marble. And we do not take our standard from what you write in the newspaper respecting it, but on its own merits. You will have expenses to move it, say £20, to London – therefore £480 would be its value here or £240 for my share; however if you give me £125 stg. I shall let you have it – that is for my part of the same.

On 18 July Schliemann offered Calvert less than a third of his asking price:

> I assure it by God and on my honour, the sculptured marble is not worth more than frs. 2000 [£80] and thus 1000 frs. [£40] for your share and that this is even the highest figure. I told it immediately to Mrs. Schliemann when it was brought to light. I assure you on my honour of my firm belief that *no* man will ever offer you even this. If you accept it, then please take £40 from the group [*sic*] you are going to get for me from Constantinople . . . I assure you I would never make the offer of £40 for the marble had I *not* found it myself.

Calvert responded the next day: 'You have very different ideas of the value of this marble to what I entertain. I think the *lowest* offer you ought to have made is not less than £50 at which price I shall alone be disposed to accept. If this suits you, make the arrangements accordingly.'

Sensing that the deal was within his grasp, Schliemann saw an opportunity to have Calvert solve the second problem for him. On 21 July he wrote: 'I cannot give you a penny more than £40 for the marble, but I will pay you £50 FOB the French steamer of 27/8 August, that is to say, you transport the block, *so as it is*, at your expense, to the steamer in the Dardanelles.' The deal was made on those terms. After a considerable correspondence over the details of transporting the block, which proved an exceptionally difficult undertaking, it was finally put on board the Greek ship *Taxiarches* at Karanlik, some 4 kilometres due north of Hisarlik on 2 August. The Turkish authorities detained the ship at Kum Kale but Frederick Calvert successfully intervened on Schliemann's behalf and the Helios metope was conveyed to Syra and thence to Athens.

Meanwhile, on 19 July, as work advanced on the north–south trench, Schliemann encountered a great wall blocking the trench towards the south end. It was 6 metres high and, to Schliemann's delight, built upon the bedrock at a depth of 4 metres. He took this to mean that it belonged to the earliest city, though this does not necessarily follow. His first impression was that the wall was part of a tower and this led him to some romantic fantasizing:

I believe that the Tower once stood on the western edge of the Acropolis, where its situation would be most interesting and imposing; for its top would have commanded, not only a view of the whole Plain of Troy, but of the sea with the islands of Tenedos, Imbros and Samothrace. There is not a more sublime view in the area of Troy than this, and I therefore presume that it is the 'Great Tower of Ilium' which Andromache ascended because 'she had heard that the Trojans were hard pressed and that the power of the Achaeans was great.'[23]

What Schliemann had found was a stretch of the fortification wall of Troy II at a point where sections from two different building phases diverged. The space between them created the impression of a tower or, as he later thought, a very broad wall with an oval depression on its top (see Fig. 8). In an effort to create a channel for the winter rains that might damage the 'tower', Schliemann sought to dig around it. He extended the trench along the wall to east and west but failed to find a corner. The 'tower' was now beginning to look more like a wall. He found four broad steps on it, which he thought might have led to an upper storey. On these steps, he tells us in the diary entry of

9 August, he found 'a huge mass of human bones'. In close association with them were a number of arrowheads, silver and copper nails, and terracotta plates and vessels. It seems very likely that Schliemann had come across some burials just outside the city wall – a standard location. In *Troy and its Remains* these finds are said to have come also from the oval depression or just outside the earlier course of the Troy II city wall but, oddly, the bones are no longer identified as human. The next day he divided with Frank Calvert the finds that had been made on his field and closed the excavations.

It would be quite irresponsible today, of course, for an archaeologist to attempt to excavate so large a trench, through so complex a sequence of strata, in only four months. Inevitably, Schliemann destroyed a great deal of valuable evidence. Architecture and findspots were inadequately recorded, even if judged not by today's exacting standards but by those of 1872. With more than a hundred workmen excavating at different parts of the mound without trained supervision, however, it would not be surprising if the findspot of a substantial number of the finds was inaccurately reported. Moreover, Schliemann was excavating a face that was slowly being advanced through the mound and at any given moment all levels were capable of yielding finds. Hence the potential for findspots being misreported was high. Given the difficult circumstances, Schliemann's reporting of the finds is substantially correct. However throughout the period Troy II–V (*c.* 2500–1800 BC), and even in some respects the whole period I–V (*c.* 3000–1800 BC), the pottery and other aspects of material culture changed remarkably little. So if an object actually discovered at a depth of 3 metres (Troy V) was mistakenly reported to Schliemann as 9 metres (Troy II) and so recorded in his diary and publications, there is usually no way for this error to be detected.

What can be detected are the occasional inconsistencies between the diary entries and Schliemann's publications, and sometimes between one publication and another. These arise, in particular, in connection with the moulds. These are of great significance in Early Bronze Age sites, for their presence attests to a certain level of metallurgical development. In 1872 Schliemann found a remarkable number of moulds for casting weapons and tools. Most of these he found at Troy II depths (8 to 10 metres) and there is little doubt that in this period the manufacture of bronze implements expanded rapidly in the Aegean and at Troy in particular. More surprising is his report of a mould found in Troy I (14 metres) (see Fig. 6). The diary, however, says that this particular mould was found on 17 April at a depth of 8 metres. Similarly, in *Troy and its Remains* the fragment of another mould, one for ten different implements, is attributed to Troy I (14 metres) but this mould was actually found on 25 March 1873 at a depth of 8 metres. In *Ilios* the same mould is attributed

Fig. 6   Mould for casting ornaments from Troy I (7½ cm long)

to Troy III (=II[24]) and its depth is given as 8½ metres. Finally, on the south side of the mound a mould for an ornament was found on 10 May 1872 (see Fig. 7). The diary entry gives no indication of the depth but other finds illustrated next to it are from the Greco-Roman stratum. However, in *TroyR* the mould is assigned to a depth of 2½ metres (Troy IV) and in *Ilios* to a depth of 4–5 metres (Troy III[25]).

·The 17 May find of a pin, three rings and an ear-ring, all of gold, at a depth of 9 metres, 3 metres below the ruins of the large building, Schliemann subsequently assigned to a depth of 14 metres, altering the diary entry (see Fig. 4), though this makes nonsense of the relationship between the find and the large house. Later he assigned it to 13 metres.[26] Surprisingly, there is no reference to this find in the summary reports of 23 May, 18 June or 13 July. It finally turns up in the report of 4 August, where we read:

> In the ashes of the same house, which has evidently been burnt, I also found, at a depth of 13 metres, a tolerably well preserved skeleton of a woman, of which I think I have collected nearly all the bones; the skull especially is in a good state of preservation, but has unfortunately been broken in our excavations; however, I can easily put it together again; the mouth is somewhat protruding, and shows astonishingly small teeth. By the side of the skeleton I found a finger-ring, three ear-rings, and a dress-pin of pure gold. The latter is perfectly simple, and has a round head; two of the ear-rings are of quite a primitive kind, and consist of simple gold wire 0.058 of an inch thick; as does also the third ear-ring, which, however, is much more finely wrought and ends in a leaf, which is formed of six gold wires of equal thickness, riveted together. The finger-ring is made of three gold wires of 0.115 of an

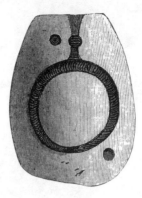

Fig. 7   Mould for casting ornaments attributed to Troy IV and Troy III (6¾ cm long)

inch thick. All of these objects bear evidence of having been exposed to great heat. The Trojan woman must, however, have also worn other ornaments, for by the side of the skeleton I collected several gold beads only 0.039 of an inch large, and also a very thin oval ring only a quarter of an inch in length.

The skeleton was actually found on 16 July at a depth of 9–10 metres in one of the 'Trojan houses' north of the 'tower'. The beads and oval ring are not mentioned in any regular diary entry. They first appear in the first draft of the 4 August report. What Schliemann has done is to combine two finds, separated by two months and some 50 metres, with a third, unrecorded, find to create a dramatic scenario – a Trojan woman trapped with her jewellery as her house collapsed in the fire that destroyed her city. Though this makes for lively reading, it is more Hollywood than archaeology. Worst of all, the find has been attributed to the lowest level of Troy when it is clear that both skeleton and jewellery rightly belong to Troy II.

Archaeologists, like the rest of us, make mistakes and later correct themselves. One might argue that this is what has happened here. But that does not seem to be the case. For instance, in none of the above cases does Schliemann acknowledge that he is correcting a mistake, not even in the case of the contradictions between published accounts. All the information is given as definitive. No conflict with earlier data is admitted. For someone trained in book-keeping, and meticulous and painstaking by nature, this can hardly be attributed to simple carelessness. It is clear, however, that Schliemann was careless with the truth. He had no qualms about adjusting the facts to suit preconceived theories.

Throughout the 1872 season Schliemann believed that Homeric Troy was to be found at the lowest level. The trouble was that although he was finding impressive pottery at this depth, there was little else to suggest the level of civilization presented in the Homeric poems. In June he began to wonder if perhaps the Troy II stratum, which was much richer in finds, might not be Homeric Troy. The discovery of the 'tower' built on the solid rock seems to have reassured him that he had been right after all. To confirm for readers of *Troy and its Remains* that he had indeed found Homeric Troy, he called his dubious 'tower' the 'Great Tower of Ilium' and evoked the picture of Andromache climbing it to view the fighting on the plain. He also combined the recently discovered skeleton with his earlier finds of gold jewellery, all from Troy II, and attributed this dramatic fiction to Troy I.

Schliemann did not massively distort his 1872 excavations. On the whole, details of findspots in *Troy and its Remains* correspond to those recorded in the diary. Though Schliemann enhanced the range of finds from Troy I with two moulds, most are attributed to Troy II or later. Though jewellery was added to the Troy I finds, not all found in 1872 was attributed to that level. In the 18 June report he tells us about the other 1872 find of jewellery of precious metals. At a depth of 9½ metres (Troy II) Schliemann had come across a large lump of wire he thought to be copper. Later the lump accidentally fell off his table and revealed itself to be a collection of jewellery: three bracelets, a gold ear-ring decorated with rows of tiny gold globules, and two bunches of ear-rings corroded together.[27]

In March 1872 John Brown, the American Chargé d'Affaires in Constantinople, wrote to Schliemann with the following advice: 'When you find any *small* objects, put them in your pocket . . . Money is the first question of the day in this. You must *not* find any big amount of gold or silver in your diggings.' Schliemann evidently took this advice. No finds of jewellery of precious metal are reported until after he has left Turkey. It looks too as if he became more cautious about even mentioning these finds in his diary. The oval ring and beads are not mentioned in any regular report, nor is the jewellery of the 18 June report.

Schliemann returned to Hisarlik for a few days in September with a surveyor, G. Siselas, and a photographer from the Dardanelles, E. Siebrecht. A plan of the excavations was drawn up and the trenches photographed from various angles. Back in Athens, he set to work. He had all the more interesting finds photographed and in some cases drawn too. These were to form the plates for the atlas of photographs that was to accompany his report. He then wrote brief explanatory notes on each object or group of objects. He also wrote out once again his periodic reports for both the 1871 and 1872 season, making a few changes here and there. It was at this point, for instance, that the jewellery found in the wire lump first made its appearance. He was now ready to look for a publisher and to prepare himself for a third and final season at Troy.

7

Priam's Treasure

O N 18 JANUARY SCHLIEMANN sent a proposal to the famous German publishing firm, Brockhaus of Leipzig, that they should publish his report
on his three years of excavation at Troy (1871–3) on commission. Schliemann
in effect assumed the costs of production so that the financial risks for
Brockhaus would be minimal. He outlined what he had done so far and how
he envisaged the work in its completed form.

> I have accordingly with today's steamer sent you the manuscript of 291 pages
> (including introduction) and would like it to be printed in Roman script in quarto.
> I have prepared 118 photographs of the objects found so far, but would like to add
> about 150 pages and 102 photographs of the excavations that I will resume on 1
> February for 5 months, so that the entire work would comprise at least 440 hand-
> written pages of this size and 220 photographs. On each photograph a precise
> indication of the scale (relative to actual size) and the depth at which each object
> was found are given. Furthermore, each object is numbered and has an accompa-
> nying annotation in the catalogue.

Brockhaus accepted Schliemann's proposal and the book was published early
in 1874, more or less as Schliemann envisaged it. Throughout 1873 he sent to
Brockhaus the periodic reports of the excavations in progress.

Meanwhile Frank Calvert wrote up a summary account of Schliemann's
excavations at Hisarlik, placing them in the larger context of the history of
excavations in the Troad. His account, which appeared in the *Levant Herald* of
3 February 1873, is admirably objective in tone, entirely free from the fanciful
romanticism that sometimes colours Schliemann's reports. He also brings out
much more clearly than Schliemann the essential similarity of all the strata
below the upper, historic levels.

> To a depth of 6 to 8 feet from the surface, Byzantine, Roman, and Greek relics are
> found, painted vases of the Archaic style being the oldest. Below this succeeds a
> continuous superposition of stratum on stratum of rubbish with remains of an

entirely different character. Innumerable flint flakes and saws, polished stone celts [axeheads] and hammers, corn-crushers and oblong handmills, staghorn and bone awls and ornaments, numerous polished and rough vases, wheel and hand made, thousands of terra cottas in the shape of cones, or of what are generally supposed to be spindle-whorls, or netweights, and also circular discs and large perforated cylinders. . . . Metals are scarce, consisting of a few celts, arrow-heads, and other small objects in bronze, and some trifling ornaments in gold and silver wire. Several moulds in stone, for casting implements, were also discovered. . . . It is an interesting feature that some of these houses have vitrified [glazed] floors; the carefully levelled and smooth surface of these floors prove that the vitrification was not the result of an accident. In one instance, a vitrified floor has been traced, in length about 20 feet. Fire appears to have been the general destroyer of these habitations . . .

What Schliemann saw as the 'Great Tower of Ilium' Calvert describes as follows:

Resting on the virgin soil, 60 or 70 feet above the level of the plain, and at a depth of 53 feet from the surface, is what appears to be a double wall, about 15 feet in height, the lines converging towards each other at an acute angle. The average breadth of the space enclosed between the two walls is 40 feet; the workmanship is inferior, the stones small and roughly put together . . .

Perhaps the most striking aspect of Calvert's article is his attempt to arrive at some kind of date for the prehistoric levels:

Judging from the ascertained fact that implements of chipped and polished flint knives, arrow heads, axes and hammers found together with bronze, gold, lead and even iron in the tomb at Ur, the capital of ancient Chaldea (B.C. 2,200–1800), it is to be inferred by analogy, that the stone implement bearing strata discovered by Mr. Schliemann are not referable to a later date. A further proof of the prehistorical nature of the primitive objects found at Hissarlik is the absence of any mention made by <Homer of> stones or flint articles; metals on the contrary are very common and worked by skilful artisans.

This reasoning leads Calvert to a conclusion that Schliemann could not have found palatable:

At Hissarlik we find incontestable proofs of the existence of a settlement at a very early date, several centuries prior to the Trojan War, as shown by the stone relics in the lower strata of excavations . . . A most important link, however, is missing between B.C. 1800 and 700, forming a gap of over a thousand years, including the

103

date of the Trojan War B.C. 1193–1184, no relics of an intervening epoch having yet been discovered between that indicated by the presence of prehistoric stone implements, etc., and by that of pottery of the Archaic style. . . . It is to be hoped that my energetic friend Mr. Schliemann, in his contemplated further researches, may be able to complete the missing link, in discovering the lost Homeric Troy, for if ever the world-famed city existed, the probability is that Hissarlik marks its site.

Calvert's approach to the problem of dating by turning to Near Eastern parallels shows greater sophistication than Schliemann at this time. His observation that the prehistoric levels (Troy I to V) were too early for Homeric Troy was, of course, anathema to Schliemann and found little support during his lifetime. Almost immediately after Schliemann's death, however, Calvert's view was adopted by Schliemann's colleague, Wilhelm Dörpfeld. By then the discovery of Mycenaean pottery in Troy VI had shown that this level must be close to the time of the Trojan War. By the 1890s Dörpfeld's redating of Homeric Troy to Troy VI was an acknowledgement of the obvious. It is truly remarkable that Calvert had a firm grasp of the truth some twenty years before developments in archaeology made the rejection of Schliemann's view inevitable. Given the enormous strides in archaeology since 1873, it is astonishing that Calvert's chronology corresponds closely to that of modern scholars and, in particular, that he identified with such accuracy the crucial missing period (1800–700 BC), whose remains were to be revealed only much later.[1]

Schliemann resumed excavations at Hisarlik early in 1873. The weather was grimmer than he had expected.

I returned here on the 31st of January with my wife, in order to continue the excavations, but we have been repeatedly interrupted by Greek church festivals, thunderstorms, and also by the excessive cold, so that I can scarcely reckon that I have had as yet more than eight good days' work. Last autumn, by the side of my two wooden houses, I had a house built for myself of stones from the old Trojan buildings, the walls of which were 2 feet thick, but I was compelled to let my foremen occupy it, for they were not sufficiently provided with clothes and wrappers, and would have perished through the great cold. My poor wife and I have therefore suffered very much, for the strong icy north wind blew with such violence through the chinks of our house-walls which were made of planks, that we were not even able to light our lamps of an evening; and although we had a fire in the hearth, yet the thermometer showed 4 degrees of cold (Réaumur=23° Fahrenheit), and the water standing near the hearth froze in solid masses. During the day we could to some degree bear the cold by working in the excavations, but of an evening we had nothing to keep us warm except our enthusiasm for the great work of discovering Troy.[2]

Once again, examination of the diary shows that the reality was rather different. Schliemann's decision not to sleep in the new stone house was made not for altruistic reasons but out of fear of dampness.[3] Sophia was spared the Arctic conditions. Very sensibly, she did not arrive until mid-April.[4]

Schliemann was anxious that the book on his excavations should appear as quickly as possible after the close of work in mid-June. As we have seen, the sections on the 1871 and 1872 excavations were already complete. To speed completion of the remaining reports, Schliemann brought from Athens the artist he had already employed for some of the plates, Polychronios Lempessis. Lempessis made quick sketches of the most interesting objects in Schliemann's diary and more formal drawings of them for the book of plates.

Early in the 1873 diary Schliemann comments on the Pasha's representative: 'To my satisfaction they have given me as overseer a Turk who is too courteous to look for a quarrel with me.' Clearly, Schliemann expected to be able to get around this man. Equally clearly, any Turkish overseer performing his duties to Schliemann's satisfaction was probably either venal or indolent.

Schliemann continued to work near the north-east corner on the site of what he still believed to be the Hellenistic temple of Athena. He hoped to find underneath it the remains of a much older temple, one that might conceivably be identified as the Temple of Athena that figures in the sixth book of the *Iliad*. He also began to excavate from the south-east corner of the mound, where Calvert had already dug, in a north-westerly direction to meet up with the continuation of the 'Tower'. This latter site, on Calvert land, proved very productive. He quickly found there three inscriptions, including a very long one dating to the third century BC and one honouring Gaius Caesar, the grandson of Augustus. One of these inscriptions seemed to indicate that the temple of Ilion (presumably that of Athena) in the Hellenistic period had been located near the south-east corner of the summit. From this point on, accordingly, Schliemann identified this as the site of the temple of Athena and saw the temple near the north slope as that of Apollo.[5] Schliemann sought to buy these inscriptions from Frank Calvert.

> The Greek vessel has come in which took last year the Apollo [Helios metope] and she is anchoring near Karanlik. I want to ship by her what trifles I have got *before* she proceeds to the Dardanelles and if possible tomorrow night, for on her return from the Dardanelles she will be closely watched by the authorities. I also want to ship by her the inscriptions if you agree to let me have your share of them at a small price.[6]

Schliemann offered Calvert 100 francs for his share in the inscriptions, assuring him that this was more than twice what he would get from the British

Museum. Calvert thought this too low: 'I am not a rich man, yet I will willingly give you 150 francs for your half share, for one of the inscriptions is historical and valuable.'[7] On 20 March Schliemann argued at great length that none of the inscriptions was of any historical value. He concluded: 'You offered me 150fr. for my share when you still thought the one inscription was historical; to settle the question I will give this amount for your share even now when it is certain that none of the inscriptions has any historical interest. But this is the very outside figure I can afford to give.'

Calvert had business to do in Constantinople and wanted the matter settled quickly. In his letter of 21 March he accepted the offer, though he thought it very little. In letting Schliemann take advantage of him once again, Calvert behaved with exasperating naïvety. Schliemann, on the other hand, deliberately lied to obtain the inscriptions. When he wrote them up in *Troy and its Remains*, he began his discussion of the long one as follows: 'This inscription, the great historical value of which cannot be denied . . .'[8]

Now that he had acquired the inscriptions, Schliemann felt free to send Calvert a stinging rebuttal of the article in the *Levant Herald*.[9] An even more vitriolic version of this attack is included in *Troy and its Remains*. Here Schliemann goes so far as to deny the existence of some of Calvert's trenches:

> Mr Calvert's excavations in the Pergamus were confined to two small cuttings which still exist, and he is wrong in saying that I have continued his excavations. As my plans of the Pergamus prove, my excavations of 1870, 1871, and up to the middle of June, 1872, were made exclusively on the Turkish portion of the Pergamus; and it was only in June that I began to excavate the site of the temple of Apollo upon Mr. Calvert's land, because a depression in the ground, 111½ feet long and 75½ feet broad, had betrayed the site to me. My friend's two small cuttings by no means gave any idea of the existence of such a temple.

Yet in the *Archaeological Journal* of 1865 Calvert had reported that he had come across 'a Temple of Minerva, consisting of marble columns, architraves, and portions of bas-reliefs, one of them being part of the figure of a gladiator' and in *Ithaque, le Péloponnèse et Troie* Schliemann had explicitly acknowledged that Calvert's excavation had revealed 'a large building, a palace or a temple.'[10] Moreover, the plan drawn in April 1872 (Fig. 2) clearly marks *four* trenches as Calvert's. Schliemann thought he could get away with saying that Calvert had made only two cuttings, because by 29 March 1873 his own trenches had obliterated two of Calvert's. A glance at the 1872 plan would have told him otherwise, but that had been left behind in Athens to be photographed.

Calvert heard some very upsetting news in Constantinople about the Helios metope. He wrote to Schliemann on 7 April:

At the Capital, I made the acquaintance of many antiquarian and professional people. Amongst others, some who have seen the bas relief found in my field, I mean that representing Apollo, now in your collection at Athens. They informed me the value you fixed on it was francs 150,000 but that was too high a figure, as francs 25,000 to 30,000 was its market value. This latter estimate however, is 10 to 12 times the amount you *swore* to me was the value, and I cannot believe you could have been aware at the time of its great worth.

A testy correspondence ensued. Calvert pressed Schliemann for half of the true value of the metope, while Schliemann argued that in business one cannot go back on a deal once it has been made. Calvert countered on 17 April:

You are mistaken, I think, in making the affair of the marble, a *commercial* transaction, for it is not one, the basis of our agreement being founded on mutual confidence as gentlemen. We both mistook the worth of the relic, in undervaluing it, I in estimating it at £450, and you at £80, but when you gave me your word of honour, that it was not worth more than the latter sum, as a gentleman, I accepted your statement, and closed for £50 (£40 for the marble and £10 for the damage done to the field) or rather £49, which was the sum I received.

Calvert had good legal grounds under both English and American law for his claim.[11] As partner in a joint venture with Schliemann, he was entitled to expect his partner to act in good faith. In other words, it was not a simple case of *caveat emptor* (or rather *caveat vendor*), as Schliemann maintained. Calvert sought legal advice and hinted that he might take Schliemann to court. In the end, however, he chose not to pursue the matter. On 25 April he wrote to Schliemann:

Do not suppose that I shall write to you further on the subject of the Apollo marble. I had hoped for an amicable agreement, but am disappointed. At the same time, for the sake of science, I assure you, I will not distract you in your work, nor bring an action against you before consulting a lawyer, and if he sees that justice is on my side, not until you have finished your labours, and returned to Athens.

Schliemann found two more inscriptions on Calvert land in April. He appears not to have paid Calvert for his share in either of them.

In March and April work was focused on excavating down to the level of the 'tower' a long trench extending from the tower to the south-east corner of the summit. Many interesting finds were made. In particular, the area in and around a building, which Schliemann at first thought might be the original temple of Athena but later decided must be a house, was particularly rich in finds. On 26 March he found a skull, on the 27th a gold ornament shaped like an arrowhead, on the 31st a human jaw and a bronze spearhead, and on 1 April a broken helmet. In the 4 April entry we read:

> The house was destroyed by a catastrophe, for we are finding many human skeletons; today, still another one – belonging to a strong man, whose skull I am having drawn. The house was certainly not left uninhabited after the destruction, for the rooms are generally found under calcined debris and red ash and then regularly accumulated layers of mussels, fishbones, bones, and other household remains; then there is once again burnt material followed by an unburnt layer and so on.[12]

In *Troy and its Remains* some of these finds have been creatively combined:

> By the side of the house, as well as in its larger apartments, I have found great quantities of human bones, but as yet only *two entire skeletons*, which must be those of *warriors*, for they were found at a depth of 7 meters (23 feet), with *copper helmets on their heads*. Beside one of the skeletons I found *a large lance*, a drawing of which I give . . . Unfortunately both helmets were broken; however, I hope to be able to put one of the two together when I return to Athens.

It will be seen that Schliemann has retreated from the 'many skeletons' of the diary account to two skeletons and many bones. Also, the one helmet has turned into two, with both allegedly found on the heads of the skeletons, though there is no hint of this in the diary. What Schliemann had found were in fact the remains of a teapot-shaped vessel in bronze. Its spout and one of the handle attachments he misidentified as the plume-holder for a helmet. Schliemann had no wish to find skeletons in burials at the Homeric level, for in Homer the dead are disposed of by cremation. Therefore, if skeletons turned up they had to be associated with the sacking of the city, when normal means of disposing of the dead were suspended. The diary evidence, however, suggests that he came across more skeletons, and therefore probably more burials, than he later cared to admit. Moreover, the bronze 'teapot' and weapon, if correctly associated, look like grave goods.

Close to the house he found what he took to be a sacrificial altar and near it a small piece of gold that he thought might be the setting for some object.[13] No mention of this gold piece appears in his published report. It too probably came from a grave.

Within a few days of Sophia's arrival in mid-April she was the object of what appears to have been a rape attempt. Schliemann wrote to his father-in-law on 29 April:

The scoundrel George Photidos, taking advantage of my absence, tried to rape Sophia. I wanted to take him and throw him in jail so that he would be condemned to 10 years emprisonment. But in view of the pleas of Sophia I have restricted myself to getting rid of him so that he may be hanged elsewhere. Sophia was ill for many days from the shock the scoundrel caused her.[14]

This excerpt constitutes the final paragraph of a letter which is primarily concerned with telling his father-in-law what to do with the accompanying thirty-three drawings of finds. Clearly, it would have been better to say nothing at all about the incident until both he and Sophia were back in Athens and Sophia's parents could see that their daughter was safe and well. Or if it was felt necessary to inform them at once, then common sense should have indicated that a separate letter be devoted to the matter, more details given and emphasis put on Sophia's recovery rather than on her many days of illness. Presumably, Schliemann is not exaggerating a less serious incident, in which Photidos made unwelcome advances, perhaps by stealing a kiss, for example. The 'many days' of illness would seem to rule that out. But what are we to make of the fact that when the nearby tumulus, Pasha Tepe, was excavated between 28 April and 1 May, Sophia was in charge of the workmen?[15] We are forced to conclude either that Schliemann sent his wife one mile from the main site, when she had barely recovered from the shock of attempted rape, to supervise a group of workmen she scarcely knew, or that the incident in question was far less serious than Schliemann suggests to his father-in-law. In either case, Schliemann's behaviour seems unconscionable.

Just about the time Schliemann's letter reached Athens, Sophia's father died. His death was sudden and unexpected. Sophia left Hisarlik on 7 May.[16] On that day Schliemann wrote to his friend Wirths about his shares in American railways. He began: 'I am writing you these lines whilst my poor wife is screaming and tearing her garments at my side, for we have just learned the sudden death of her excellent father.'[17] Letters between Hisarlik and Athens took about a week and the news of Sophia's father's death would almost certainly have been sent by telegram. The timing suggests that his death occurred just after he received Schliemann's letter concerning the attempted rape. Whether the shocking news was a factor in his death it is now impossible to say, but the coincidence is extraordinary.

Schliemann continued his excavations to the west of the 'tower'. In early April he uncovered a paved road running down from the mound to the plain, which he promptly concluded must lead to the Scaean Gate, close to which some of the most memorable scenes of the *Iliad* took place. At first Schliemann assumed that the Scaean Gate itself would be much lower down,

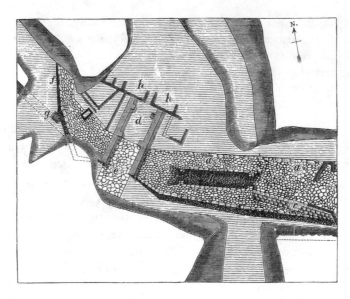

Fig. 8   Plan of 'Scaean Gate' area (Scale 1:750)

a. 'Great Tower of Ilium'
b. Oval depression
c. Steps
d. 'Scaean Gate'
e. Steep paved road leading to the Plain of Troy
f. City wall
g. Findspot of 'Priam's Treasure'
h. 'Palace of Priam'

close to the plain.[18] However, some twenty shafts were sunk at different locations away from the acropolis and in none of them was any sign of prehistoric
habitation found. Accordingly, when Schliemann uncovered a fine double
gate at the point where the road reached the city wall, he had no hesitation in
declaring that he had found the Scaean Gate. Here he found two bronze bars,
which he took to be bolts for the gates but which were in fact chisels.

By the end of April he was also excavating the area to the north of the gate.
He found a complex of two superimposed buildings. He quickly identified the
earlier structure with 'Priam's Palace'. He was hindered from determining its
full plan, however, by the more substantial remains of the later building that
covered much of it and by his own wooden house, which was situated directly
above its western end. A great many interesting vases were discovered here
and on 29 April the fragment of a copper sword and two knives.[19] On 9 May
he started widening the trench he opened in 1870 from the north-west edge
of the summit, continuing it eastwards. He also began excavating a new trench

110

from the western edge towards the 'Scaean Gate'. These two trenches converged at the city wall almost directly under Schliemann's wooden house. Here on 31 May Schliemann made one of the most famous finds in the history of archaeology. He describes it in *Troy and its Remains* as follows:

> In excavating this wall further and directly by the side of the palace of King Priam, I came upon a large copper article of the most remarkable form, which attracted my attention all the more as I thought I saw gold behind it. On the top of this copper article lay a stratum of red and calcined ruins, from 4¾ to 5¼ feet thick, as hard as stone, and above this again lay the above-mentioned wall of fortification (6 feet broad and 20 feet high) which was built of large stones and earth, and must have belonged to an early date after the destruction of Troy. In order to withdraw the treasure from the greed of my workmen, and to save it for archaeology, I had to be most expeditious, and although it was not yet time for breakfast, I immediately had '*païdos*' called . . . While the men were eating and resting, I cut out the Treasure with a large knife, which it was impossible to do without the very greatest exertion and the most fearful risk of my life, for the great fortification-wall, beneath which I had to dig, threatened every moment to fall down upon me. But the sight of so many objects, every one of which is of inestimable value to archaeology, made me foolhardy, and I never thought of any danger. It would, however, have been impossible for me to have removed the Treasure without the help of my dear wife, who stood by me ready to pack the things which I cut out in her shawl and to carry them away.

There follows a long, detailed list of impressive objects: a shield, cauldron, hasp or handle, and vase, all of copper; a bottle, cup and 'sauceboat', all of gold; an electrum (gold and silver alloy) cup; six talents, three large vases and two smaller ones with lids, all of silver; thirteen spearheads, fourteen battleaxes, seven daggers, one knife, a sword-fragment and a long, four-sided bar, all of copper; two diadems, a headband, sixty ear-rings, and 8,750 small gold ornaments, all of gold (see Plate 7).

Surprisingly, there is no regular diary entry recording this remarkable discovery. The earliest record of it is the first draft of Schliemann's 31 May report to his publishers:

> Behind the latter (wall), at a depth of 8 to 9 m, I exposed the Trojan circuit wall as it continues from the Scaean gate and found in one of the rooms of the house of Priam abutting on to this wall a copper container or utensil of the most remarkable shape, about 1 m long by ½ m broad, for two helmet-like bosses could be seen on it; there was also a bowl with a kind of large candlestick. This container was filled with silver and gold vases and cups, which I had to extract, conceal and send away in such haste in order to withdraw them from the greed of my workers, that I

neither know the number of the vessels nor am I in a position to describe their shape. I will, however, give a most detailed description of them from Athens, if the objects arrive safely, and append a photograph of each piece of the treasure to the atlas to this work. This much, however, I can already say, namely, that one of the cups is of very thick, solid gold, has two heavy handles and is in the shape of a champagne-glass with a rounded foot so that it can only be made to stand on its rim. It offers further evidence, if any were needed, that by *depas amphikypellon* Homer can only have understood this kind of cup and no other.

In the same vessel I further found a number of flat pieces of silver, which resemble battle-axes in shape and may be the Homeric talents; also a large quantity – I think more than two dozen – of spearheads, a key, many knives, etc.; in the intense conflagration which destroyed Troy many spearheads became soldered together on one side; the silver and even the gold vessels also bear the clearest marks of the frightful heat to which they were exposed. The wonderful copper vessel which contained all these treasures had unfortunately suffered so much from the fire, corrosion and the pressure of the superimposed house-walls that, unfortunately, it was possible to extract it from the hard debris only in pieces. I can at all events restore a part of it, but certainly not the entire thing. Directly next to this findspot a thick silver vase was found eight days ago, 18 cm high by 14 cm broad. There was also a copper helmet, which unfortunately broke in pieces, but the two pieces of its *phalos* (plume-holder), as well as a curved bar of copper, 15 cm long, fastened to it – I don't know how – which must have served some particular purpose, remained intact. I also found there the lower pieces of the *phalos* of another helmet. All these finds in the house of Priam, at a depth of 8 to 9 m, directly next to my wooden house are inducing me to have my house demolished and the large mound of earth between this excavation and the Scaean gate removed in order to bring as much as possible of the royal palace to light; it will, however, be very difficult, if not impossible, to make a plan of it without removing the post-Trojan house built on top, and I cannot make up my mind to do that.

There are significant discrepancies between the early draft report (31 May), a later draft (17 June), and the published account in *Troy and its Remains*. For instance, there is no mention of Sophia in the draft versions, whereas she plays a leading role in *Troy and its Remains*. As we have already seen, Sophia left on 7 May. From Schliemann's correspondence it is clear that she did not return.

There is no doubt about the location of the findspot. Three plans and an illustration in *Troy and its Remains* all clearly place it just outside the city wall about 15 metres west of the Scaean Gate (see Figs. 8 and 12).[20] Why then does the early draft place it *inside the wall* in a room of Priam's Palace? Easton argues that on the day of the discovery (31 May) Schliemann may 'have been uncertain where the wall's outer edge began.'[21] Perhaps so, but a few days later, when the wall was fully cleared, as it is in Fig. 12, there could be no doubt that the

Dr. Schliemann's House and Magazine

Plain of Troy and Hellespont

Upper House

Palace of Priam

Scaean Gate

Tower of Ilium

Fig. 9   Looking north up the great north–south trench with the ruins of Priam's Palace. Priam's Treasure was found almost directly beneath Schliemann's wooden house

113

findspot was *outside* the wall. Yet in the later draft (17 June) Schliemann states that he found the treasure 'on the 7th of this month, at a depth of 8½m, near the large circuit-wall running N.W. from the Scaean gate, in a narrow room of the royal palace enclosed by two walls.' Now there *is* just such a 'narrow room' immediately inside the wall from the true findspot. Even more interesting, it was directly under Schliemann's wooden house (demolished on 4 June) and not excavated until 6 or 7 June.[22]

It seems clear from the position of the findspot just outside the city wall that Schliemann had come upon a grave. However, he was more interested in finding within the unprepossessing ruins behind the Scaean Gate something that would convince the world that here had once been Priam's Palace. So in the early draft he reported that the impressive grave goods found outside the wall had actually been found in a room of the palace. Back in Athens, he decided to be more specific; so in the later draft he ascribed the find to the narrow room. Thanks to his training in book-keeping Schliemann was scrupulous over detail even when rewriting the truth. He altered the date of the find to 7 June, for it was not until that day that the narrow room was uncovered.

Later, when he consulted the plans, he saw that Laurent had clearly marked the findspot outside the wall. Deciding it was easier to alter his account than the plans, he changed the findspot to 'on the wall'. But he thought of a way of keeping the link with the palace:

> As I found all the above objects packed together on the great divine wall, it seems certain that they lay in a wooden chest, such as those which are mentioned in the *Iliad* (xxiv 228) as being in Priam's palace. This seems all the more certain as I found directly next to the objects a large copper key . . . Presumably, some member of Priam's family packed the treasure in the chest in great haste, carried it outside without having the time to remove the key, was overcome on the wall by the hand of the enemy or by the fire and had to abandon the chest, which was immediately buried 6 ft deep in the red ashes and debris of the nearby palace.

Brilliant! Implausible, of course, to the last degree – but who cares? The reader willingly suspends disbelief to savour the scene. Meanwhile, the connection between the treasure and the palace has been made. The sheer enthusiasm and vividness of the writing more than make up for the lack of logical cogency. This aspect of Schliemann's work scholars have usually attributed to a combination of naïvety, a vivid imagination and a fervent belief in Homer. I think that it can be more accurately attributed to a canny sense of what the public wanted to hear and an ability to satisfy that demand.

The *chef d'oeuvre* of 'Priam's Treasure' is the piece known because of its shape

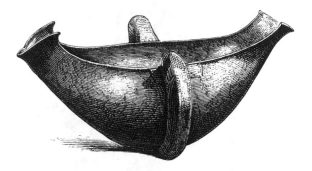

Fig. 10   Gold sauceboat (9 cm high)

as the gold sauceboat. Its shape was unique among all the vessels found at
Troy, whether of metal or pottery. Schliemann's statement in the early draft,
however, that it can only be made to stand on its rim is seriously inaccurate,
as a glance at the object shows. It is hard to believe that within a matter of a
day or two Schliemann could have so completely forgotten its shape. The
description fits, and was regularly applied by Schliemann, to the *depas
amphikypellon*, a tall double-handled clay pot, of which he had found many
examples (see Fig. 11). Schliemann's error would be more understandable if
we could suppose a considerable interval, at least two or three weeks, between
the last time he saw the piece and his composition of the draft of 31 May.

Remarkably, in this early draft, there is no mention of the jewellery. It makes
its first appearance in the later draft, written after Schliemann's return to
Athens. Since the jewellery was found in one of the large silver jugs, one might
argue that he did not actually discover the cache until after he reached Athens.
However, both small gold cups were allegedly found in the same silver jug at
the site. It is incredible, therefore, that Schliemann would not have thoroughly
examined the jug's interior before sending it off. Besides, even in the later draft
the jewellery was added as an afterthought. It is not described along with the
other items of the treasure but is tacked on after his account of the subsequent
excavations. Finally, there is Lempessis' drawing in the *Atlas* of fifty-six of the
gold ear-rings and a number of beads and other minor pieces (see Plate 8). All
the writing is in Schliemann's hand. It is obvious that the words 'Trésor de
Priam' were not part of the original design of the page; they were added only
as an afterthought. More important, the caption at the foot of the page originally read only 'This plate contains 56 gold earrings and other gold jewellery
in natural size' in German and French. Schliemann later added 'everything
from a depth of 8½ metres' to the German and 'everything belongs to the
Treasure of Priam discovered at 8½ metres depth' to the French, as careful

Fig. 11   *Depas amphikypellon* (28 cm high)

study of the alignment of the lines of the captions reveals. In other words, the jewellery was drawn by the artist and captioned by Schliemann before there was any thought of indicating that all these pieces came from Priam's Treasure.

There are two further important pieces of evidence relating to the discovery. The first comes from the pen of William C. Borlase, MP for East Cornwall and noted antiquarian, who in 1985 was guided around Schliemann's excavations at Hisarlik by Schliemann's trusted servant Nikolaos Zaphyros Yannakis. In an article highly critical of Schliemann published in *Fraser's Magazine* he pointed out the dramatic discrepancies between Schliemann's and Yannakis' accounts of the discovery (see pp. 178–9 below). Most notably, Yannakis attested that Sophia had not been present at the find. He also insisted that the treasure lay 'not "on" . . . but "*close to*" the outer side of the wall' and was 'contained in a little place built round with stones'. This information about Sophia and the findspot is correct. Yannakis' description of the findspot as 'a little place built around with stones' is supported by Laurent's plan (see Fig. 8); on Fig. 12 the spot can just be distinguished outside the wall at 'a'. The testimony of both Borlase and Yannakis finds dramatic confirmation in one of Schliemann's own letters to Charles Newton, Keeper of Greek and Roman Antiquities at the British Museum:

On account of her father's sudden death Mrs Schliemann left me in the beginning of May. The treasure was found end of May; but, since I am endeavouring to make

116

Samothrace
Imbros

Dr. Schliemann's Houses

Plain of Troy, seen through the great Trench

Later but Pre-Hellenic Buildings, partly over the Ruins of Priam's Palace

Hellespont
Plain of Troy

Scamander

Greek Tower (where the man stands)

a Place where the Treasure was found

Wall of Troy
Scaean Gate, and Paved Road to the Plain

Paved Road   TOWER OF ILIUM

Fig. 12   Looking west from the Scaean Gate after demolition of Schliemann's wooden house

an archaeologist of her, I wrote in my book that she had been present and assisted me in taking out the treasure. I merely did so to stimulate and encourage her for she has great capacities . . . If you wish now to visit my diggings at Troy I give you all my maps and plans by which you find every thing. You find also the labourers and servant who struck the treasure and assisted me to get it off.[23]

Yannakis stated that the 'key' was not found with Priam's Treasure but some 200 yards away. Given Schliemann's tendency to combine finds, this seems likely enough.[24] Yannakis remembered a large quantity of bronze pieces but was 'hazy' about the rest. In this respect he resembles Schliemann in the 31 May draft. The description of the copper objects at the beginning of this account makes archaeological sense. The details, though sketchy, have an air of authenticity. It is a different matter, however, with the gold and silver vessels. There is no attempt to describe them. Schliemann says he can give no details because he had to pack them away very quickly. Yet this applies just as much to the bronze objects. Why can he give convincing details about the copper objects but not about the gold and silver? The exception proves the rule. His attempt to describe the gold sauceboat is so inaccurate that it raises serious questions about when he last saw it.

We know a surprising amount about the events of 31 May. The treasure was discovered before nine-thirty in the morning.[25] Later that day the Turkish overseer, Amin, heard about the discovery from the workmen, as we learn from Schliemann's letter of 18 August 1873 to the secretary of the provincial governor at the Dardanelles:

> I managed to save the treasure because it was discovered while Amin Efendi was busy supervising another trench, and if you had seen the despair of the poor man when he later heard from the workers that I had found and removed a treasure, and if you had seen with what fury he burst into my room and demanded with loud cries, in the name of the Sultan, that I open immediately all my chests and all my cupboards, while my only response was to throw him out of the house – you would have taken pity on him.

About seven o'clock in the evening two German visitors arrived, Gustav von Eckenbrecher, an early proponent of the theory that Hisarlik was the site of Troy, and his artist son, Themistokles. The elder Eckenbrecher described his visit as follows:

> We left our horses below and climbed the steep slope over the debris and along narrow paths beside deep excavation trenches. At the top Schliemann came to meet us – a sunburnt, stocky figure of medium build. On his head, which was

shaved quite bald, was a straw-hat bound all around in Indian fashion with white muslin. His linen overcoat was covered with the dust of the excavations and his whole face even more so. He asked us if we spoke German. I told him my name and at once we were afforded a most hearty welcome. The larger of the small houses which he had built for himself was shown to us as our lodgings – for otherwise there would have been no accommodations to be found far and wide – but then he begged us to excuse him for he had pressing business to attend to and could no longer look after us for the present. It was, as we later learned, the evening on which he had to dispatch 'Priam's Treasure' to Athens, which had to be done with the greatest care. His wife, a young Athenian lady, his otherwise constant companion in his Trojan excavations, was not present; she had gone back to Athens.

The stone house where we were now staying, entirely surrounded by deep excavation trenches, consisted of a large room, adjoining which there was a kitchen and servants' quarters. For sleeping, Schliemann had assigned us his own very spacious bed . . . After we had fortified ourselves at the evening meal with fine bread and an authentically Asiatic roast of mutton tail and excellent Tenedos wine, Schliemann was once again free and we spent the rest of the beautiful spring evening sitting in front of the door of our house, talking of many things and recalling the events that happened here in remote antiquity. After sunset the sky and Hellespont gleamed in the glimmering twilight, the craggy peaks of Imbros and Samothrace were sharply distinguished on the horizon and even distant Athos was visible.

Before rejoining his guests Schliemann packed his finds in six baskets and a bag and at sunset sent a trusted workman, perhaps Yannakis, off with them to Frederick Calvert's farm. He had had them for about ten hours. The workman carried a letter for Calvert:

I am sorry to inform you that I am closely watched and expect that the turkish watchman who is angry at me, I do not know for what reason, will search my house tomorrow. I therefore take the liberty to deposit with you 6 baskets and a bag begging you will kindly *lock* them up and *not* allow by any means the turks to touch them. In order to use reciprocity I take great pleasure in presenting to your Lady my half share of all what has been found this year on your brother's field, except of course the inscriptions which I have paid to your brother and taken away. You remember that there is in the lot to be distributed the hand of Minerva of wonderful workmanship and worth a great deal of money. There are also 2 female heads of terracotta which are masterpieces of the last hellenic time.

The villagers betray me to the turk so that I cannot anymore take their horses. So, when I want to remove the baskets, pray, lend me for three hours in the night three horses. I shall gratefully acknowledge this service and pay you for each horse forty piastres; please do not refuse for I am quite in despair; having spent here more than 100,000 franks I cannot take away a little broken pottery.

119

Presumably, Amin, rebuffed, had gone off to seek authorization to search Schliemann's quarters. Under these circumstances, it would have been natural for Schliemann to dispatch from the site on the evening of 31 May not only what he had found that day but also any valuable pieces of whose existence Amin was unaware. Two considerations suggest that there would have been such pieces: first, Schliemann paid a bonus for any significant find brought by a workman and, second, the American Chargé d'Affaires in Constantinople had advised him to hide any finds of gold and silver from the Turkish authorities.[26] It is easy to see how these other pieces could readily have been combined in Schliemann's mind with whatever had actually been found on 31 May to form a single find.

There is therefore reason to suspect that some of the gold and silver vessels and the jewellery had been discovered several weeks earlier. At the end of March two of Schliemann's workers smuggled from the site a substantial horde of jewellery, including a pair of pendant ear-rings similar to those in Priam's Treasure.[27] The most reliable account of this find places the findspot near the eastern end of the great east–west trench.[28] Not far from here at the end of March Schliemann found a gold pendant for a necklace or ear-ring, which he identified as a gold arrowhead.[29] I suspect that he found many more gold pieces at this time and refrained from mentioning them in his diary, just as he had refrained from mentioning the gold beads and oval ring in the 1872 diary.[30]

Is there any hard evidence that Priam's Treasure has been assembled from earlier finds? The answer, rather surprisingly, is an unqualified 'Yes.' Plates 193 and 194 of the *Atlas* illustrate a total of twenty-seven objects attributed by Schliemann to Priam's Treasure, no less than eleven of which were found prior to 31 May 1873.

Ever since 1902, when Hubert Schmidt published the definitive catalogue of Schliemann's Trojan collection in Berlin, it has been known that some of the objects illustrated in the plates devoted to Priam's Treasure also appear on earlier plates. At that time the full implications of this were not understood. It is now clear that Plates 1–118 of the *Atlas* had been prepared and annotated before the beginning of the 1873 season. It follows therefore that any object appearing in these plates must have been found in 1871 or 1872.[31] Four flat axes and one chisel that appear among the objects of Priam's Treasure are also found in these earlier plates and must therefore have been found in 1871 or 1872.

In the course of the 1873 season, Lempessis was preparing drawings of the objects that would eventually become plates in the published work. Schliemann was numbering and annotating these objects as they were drawn.

It is clear from Schliemann's copybook that he had completed annotation of plates 118 to 170 by 14 May.[32] It follows therefore that any object appearing on these plates was found before that date. Schmidt identified a knife and dagger on plate 194 with drawings on plates 166 and 135 respectively.[33] The sword fragment on plate 194 appears to be the same as that on plate 163.[34]

It is clear that Priam's Treasure includes a core of pieces found on 31 May 1873 but that this core has been supplemented with items found earlier in that year and in previous years.

In the evening of 6 June Schliemann sent Spyros Demetriou, probably accompanied by Nikolaos Yannakis, to Frederick Calvert's farm. They took the three horses, loaded the six 'baskets' (probably more like hampers) and bag on them and set out for Karanlik (due north of Hisarlik), where Spyros got on board the waiting *Taxiarches* with the baskets and bag and accompanied his precious cargo back to Athens.[35] The next day Schliemann sent a telegram to his German publisher, Brockhaus: 'All danger has passed. So publish my article right away in *Augsburg Allgemeine Zeitung.*' The article was his specially written summary of the 1873 excavations up to the discovery of the 'small treasure' eight days before Priam's Treasure. It concluded with an assessment of the wealth of the finds at Hisarlik, which, given the dearth of finds in gold and silver up to that point, was surprisingly upbeat:

> The Pergamus is an exceedingly rich, or rather inexhaustible, horn of plenty of the most various, the most remarkable, and hitherto unparalleled, household and religious objects of the famous Trojan people and their successors. Quite apart from the monuments of undying glory that I have here brought to light, I have, with the antiquities I have found, uncovered a new world for archaeology.[36]

Clearly, Schliemann thought that this glowing account of the finds at Hisarlik would alert the suspicions of the Turkish officials. Now that all the most valuable finds had been safely smuggled out of Turkey, he felt free to publish it. It provided a suitable foretaste of what was to come. Schliemann's comments on the richness of Hisarlik make more sense if we suppose that he already had in his possession most of the gold and silver pieces comprised in Priam's Treasure.

On 10 June he sent a fair copy of his 31 May report on the treasure to Brockhaus.[37] Once back in Athens, he re-examined the treasure and telegraphed Brockhaus again on 27 June: 'Don't print my 31 May article for I will change it. Will add detailed description of the treasure.'[38] It was at this point that he wrote up the later draft version in his diary, which dated the discovery to 7 June and initially placed it 'near the city wall in a narrow room of the royal palace enclosed by two walls.' In the final version of this '17 June' report, which he sent to Brockhaus on 5 July, asking him to burn the 31 May version, the findspot was altered to the formulation we find in *Troy and its Remains* – 'on the city wall, directly next to Priam's house.'[39] He left it to the publisher's discretion whether to send a copy immediately to the *Augsburg Allgemeine Zeitung* or to wait until nearer the time when the book itself would appear.[40]

Knowing that once the account of the discovery of Priam's Treasure was printed he could expect the Turkish government to take legal steps to recover its half of the pieces, Schliemann started to make enquiries about his legal position. In a letter to P. Beaurain, his agent in Paris, he listed the gold and silver objects and expressed his fear that he might be sued:

> I will certainly be able to defend myself in the Greek courts by saying that I bought the treasure and that it was only for glory that I published that I had found it in the Palace of Priam. But still, I'm afraid, and so I beg you to tell me if there is a gold-smith's in Paris in which one could place absolute confidence, confidence such that I could entrust to him all the objects . . .[41]

Here about twelve words are no longer legible. The letter continues:

> . . . with an appearance of antiquity and naturally without affixing his stamp. But it is absolutely essential that he not betray me and that he do the work at a moderate price. Perhaps he could also reproduce the silver vases in galvanized copper, which he could blacken.
>
> In the course of your enquiries please speak of objects found in Norway and in God's name don't mention the word 'Troy'.

Though Schliemann does not state why he wanted these copies, the context suggests that he was contemplating passing off faked duplicates to the Turkish government for their share. Almost as shocking is the casual way he consid-ers defending himself by alleging that the pieces were purchased. He displays no sense of shame at resorting to this tactic. About a week later he wrote to Beaurain again. After enquiries in Athens he had become convinced that Greek courts were 'not competent to judge between two foreigners.'[42] Hence there was no reason to pursue the matter of having duplicates made and there is no evidence to suggest that he did.[43]

From July to December Schliemann worked on finishing off his book. A major task was the creation of more than 400 prints for each of the 218 plates – a total of about 100,000 prints – all to be made by hand by an Athenian pho-tographer.[44] After finishing the annotation of the last fifty plates, Schliemann personally translated the notes to all the plates into French. The main text itself was translated into French by Alexandros Rangabe.

Even before the beginning of the 1873 season Schliemann had started negotiations with the Greek government for permission to excavate Mycenae and Olympia. He wanted exemption, however, from the Greek law requiring that all his finds become the property of the state. He proposed that he should retain title to them until his death, at which time they would become the property of Greece. In return for the exemption, he promised to bequeath to Greece the sum of 200,000 francs to build a museum that would bear his name. However, the Prussian government had resumed the negotiations for permission to excavate at Olympia which they had begun as early as 1854 but had had to postpone because of war. In July Schliemann improved his proposal by throwing in all of his Trojan finds, including Priam's Treasure, as a gift to the Greek nation, but he was pessimistic about his chances of success. In the end, however, the Minister of Public Instruction, as Schliemann related to Charles Newton,

> gave the privilege of excavations in Olympia to the Prussian government and offered me only Mycenae and a decoration. But I rejected both with scorn and contempt, for I flatter myself that by the discovery of Troy I have a claim to the gratitude of the whole civilized world, particularly to that of Greece. Thus I am resolved upon breaking altogether with Greece and to excavate hence forward in Italy . . .[45]

Schliemann went on to offer the British Museum his entire Trojan collection, including Priam's Treasure, but asked Charles Newton to keep the matter confidential. He invited Newton to come to Athens to view the collection.

Meanwhile he had received a request from Déthier, the Director of the Imperial Museum in Constantinople, for a few examples of the owl-headed idols for his museum. Schliemann seized the opportunity. On 30 July he offered to dig at his own expense for three more months at Hisarlik with 100–150 men and to give all the proceeds to the Imperial Museum.[46] In return, the Turkish government had to acknowledge as his property what he had found up to that point. Clearly, this was an attempt to legitimize his possession of Priam's Treasure before its discovery was made public.

On 5 August his report on the discovery of Priam's Treasure was published in the *Augsburg Allgemeine Zeitung*. It caused a sensation. Abbreviated versions of the report appeared in leading newspapers all over the world. Naturally, criticism followed soon after. Many thought the attribution to Priam preposterous. But in general both scholars and the general public were impressed. Clearly, Schliemann's excavations had turned out to be much more important than they had expected.

Meanwhile Schliemann tried to interest the British Museum in buying his entire Trojan collection, including the Helios metope and Priam's Treasure, for £50,000 (roughly £3 million in today's terms).[47] In October he made the same offer to the Louvre.[48] Though he thought Schliemann's asking price too high, Charles Newton came to Athens in December to view the collection for himself. His suspicions were aroused when his enquiries produced the astonishing information that Sophia Schliemann had returned to Athens in early May and therefore could not have witnessed the discovery of Priam's Treasure. Newton must have asked Schliemann for a written statement as to why he had represented Sophia as present when she had in fact been in Athens. Hence the letter to Newton of 23 December in which Schliemann explained that he had represented his wife as present at the discovery as a way of stimulating her interest in archaeology.[49] In the same letter Schliemann asked for the private address of the Prime Minister, William Gladstone, who would have to approve the funds for the purchase of Schliemann's collection. On 28 December Schliemann sent Gladstone a complimentary copy of *Ithaque, le Péloponnèse et Troie*, assuring him that the Prime Minister's opinion that the Trojans spoke Greek 'has become an indisputable fact by my excavations.'[50]

8

Trial and Museum Tour

'. . . that remote antiquity which we, vaguely groping in
the twilight of an uncertified past, call prehistoric . . .'
C.T. Newton, January 1874

O N 28 JANUARY 1874 THERE appeared in the *Levant Herald* a remarkable
news item. A considerable cache of gold jewellery had apparently been
found in March 1873 by two of Schliemann's workmen, who had secretly
removed the treasure from the site. Some of the pieces had been melted down
and converted into modern jewellery for the fiancée of one of the workers.
Someone informed the Turkish authorities in December 1873. The workers
were arrested and part of the cache was recovered and taken to the museum
in Constantinople. The writer of the article in the *Levant Herald*, apparently
Frank Calvert, observed:

> Apart from the strong evidence which it affords as to the genuineness of the relics
> in Dr. Schliemann's possession, it possesses additional interest from the circum-
> stance that the discovery was made three months before that of the so-called
> 'Priam's treasure,' and that the two treasures were found, not in one place, but in
> two distinct spots, distant from each other about 150 yards. Considering, also, that
> a considerable amount of gold was found at a third spot, it is safe to assume that the
> ancient town – whatever may have been its name – possessed wealthy inhabitants.

This is the earliest account of the discovery of what has come to be known
as the 'Workmen's Treasure' or Treasure C. It differs significantly from
Schliemann's. The most striking discrepancy is in the findspot. Schliemann
indicates that the treasure was found just north of Priam's Palace and a little
west of the well on the west side of the great north–south trench. The difficulty is that Schliemann's reports do not indicate that he was excavating there
in March 1873. Calvert's article, on the other hand, does not precisely indicate

the findspot. However, he specifies that it was south of an ancient wall that was still not fully excavated and at a distance of 150 yards from the findspot of Priam's Treasure. If Calvert's measurement is correct, the findspot must have been located near the eastern end of the great east–west trench. Schliemann was actively digging here in March 1873 and, as we have seen, making valuable finds. When we recall that he reported finding a gold pendant and many funereal urns here in March 1873, it seems highly probable that many of the pieces attributed to Priam's Treasure were actually found here at this time but not recorded in Schliemann's diary. The Workmen's Treasure may be seen as a partial confirmation of this hypothesis.

The German edition of Schliemann's report on his excavations at Troy, *Trojanische Alterthümer*, appeared with its accompanying *Atlas* of photographs in late January 1874.[1] C.T. Newton's report in the February issue of the *Academy* provides an excellent sketch of the varied scholarly reactions Schliemann's discoveries had provoked.[2]

> First, it is confidently believed by those who regard the Trojan war as an historical event that these antiquities, found at a great depth under the Greek city of Ilium Novum, are actual remains of the Troy over which Priam ruled, which the Greeks sacked, and which Homer has immortalised. This, I need hardly add, is the opinion of Dr. Schliemann himself. Secondly, those who either reject entirely the story of the Trojan war, or think that there is no sure test by which the historical facts, possibly latent in the legend, can be detected and detached, still allow that there is a *prima facie* case for considering the Schliemann antiquities as prehistoric, and consequently antecedent to the earliest Greek antiquities as yet discovered. Thirdly, there are archaeologists, who, while admitting the truth of Dr. Schliemann's narrative and the genuineness of his antiquities, have maintained that they have no pretensions to the remote antiquity which he claims for them, and that they are probably the work of some barbarous race in Asia Minor, in comparatively recent and even Christian times. Lastly, some few persons have received Dr. Schliemann's narrative with scornful incredulity, and have insinuated that the gold and silver ornaments were fabricated at Athens, or that they were purchased by Dr. Schliemann in some other part of Asia Minor, and associated with the antiquities from Ilium Novum. In other words, they consider his story of the finding of a treasure as altogether apocryphal.

While scholarly opinion was divided as to the significance of Schliemann's discoveries, most published reactions were remarkably favourable, particularly in Britain. Almost all the reviewers, including the most critical, paid tribute to the great service Schliemann had done by conducting these massive excavations. Though archaeologists were already aware that excavation pursued as energetically as Schliemann's was bound to destroy a great deal of valuable evidence, none of the reviewers criticized him on these grounds. Moreover, the main battle of Troy was won. Though the supporters of Bunarbashi continued to fight a rearguard action, from this point on most scholars agreed with Schliemann that Hisarlik was the site of Troy.

But there were the inevitable reservations and criticisms. Few reviewers accepted Schliemann's contention that the 'palace' and 'treasure' he had found were Priam's. Many saw only a crude version of a woman's face on pots Schliemann called 'owl-headed'. The photographs in the *Atlas* were severely criticized, and rightly so. Though we can only praise Schliemann's decision to illustrate the site and finds through photographs rather than engravings – a progressive though by no means pioneering step in 1874 – the reviewers were fully justified in roundly condemning the quality of their execution. Most photographs were of poor quality, whether judged from an aesthetic or technical standpoint. The unfortunate outcome of these criticisms was that Schliemann never again used photographs to illustrate his finds.

Nobody likes criticism, but Schliemann seems to have been unusually sensitive to it. Any disagreement, however mildly expressed, almost always provoked from him a heated response. Max Müller, a strong supporter of Schliemann, ventured to criticize Schliemann's tendency to attribute to Homeric heroes the artefacts and buildings he found at Hisarlik: 'To look for the treasure of the Homeric Priamos at Hissarlik would be like looking for the treasure of the Nibelunge at Worms or for the bracelet of Helle in the Daradanelles.'[3] Schliemann retorted:

> The chief or king at the time of Troy's tragic end is called Priamos by Homer and by tradition, and for that reason I will call him by the same name, and shall continue to do so until Professor Max Müller proves to me that he had another name. In the same way I shall continue to call the last Trojan king's treasure Priam's treasure until the Professor proves that the Homeric Ilium's last monarch had a different name.[4]

The argument is typical of Schliemann's reasoning and reveals why he won a wide following but was distrusted by academics. His down-to-earth common sense at first seems irresistible but in fact begs fundamental questions. How, for instance, do we know that the treasure dates from the period of the Trojan War? Is there proof that it is a king's treasure rather than the grave goods of several wealthy individuals? Schliemann's argument is nothing more than rhetorical posturing.

Schliemann maintained that the 'owl-headed' pots proved that *glaucôpis*, the

Homeric epithet of Athena, meant 'owl-headed'. If so, Müller countered, then Hera *boôpis* should have been represented 'as a cow-headed monster'.[5] In late February Schliemann took up the challenge implicit in this observation and went off to Mycenae to prove that he was right. On his return he wrote to Max Müller:

> Having solicited from the Greek Ministry of Public Instruction the permission to make excavations at Mycenae and without waiting for an answer which I knew would be negative, I hurried to the Argolid and representing to the local authorities that I would get in a few days the permission to excavate and that I had now only come to make soundings in order to ascertain what the accumulation of rubbish amounts to in the different localities of Mycenae, I at once went to investigate its acropolis in 34 different places.[6]

He dug six shafts on the 'lowest terrace', that is, on or near the site of the grave circle that would be revealed in 1876, reaching the bedrock at depths ranging from 6 to 4.5 metres. Among other things he found 'a number of idols of which not less than 5 are Junos with a "polos" on the head and a number of little cows of terracotta. . . . Thus it is evident that Juno [Hera] was the patron deity of Mykene and that the cow was her *sacred animal*.' In fact, Schliemann's finds proved only that the Mycenaeans worshipped a female deity and that they were familiar with cows. He found no female idol with a cow's head.

Schliemann's 'soundings' lasted from 24 February to 1 March. He employed from three to twenty-six workmen. He discovered on the summit, where there was little depth of soil, the foundations of a large building, which later proved to be the royal palace. He also excavated the side-chamber of the Treasury of Atreus in search of a rich burial with little success. When the Ministry in Athens learned of Schliemann's activities, the local authorities were immediately informed that his digging must be stopped and his finds confiscated.[7] The local chief of police, Leonidas Leonardos, asked to see Schliemann's finds in Nauplion. He was shown a basket of potsherds.

> He took out two pieces, went out to show them to the Eparch [provincial governor] here, returned immediately and wrote a protocol that he gave me to sign, in which it was stated that sherds like those I had obtained by my excavations at Mycenae were to be found everywhere in Greece on the surface of the ground.[8]

Undeterred by governmental disapproval, Schliemann dug at the Argive Heraion (6 kilometres south-east of Mycenae) on 2 March with two workmen. He claims in his diary to have uncovered some of the paving of the old temple there. The workmen also showed him some Mycenaean chamber tombs in the vicinity. He bought a classical inscription in the nearby village of Phonika. Meanwhile, he was still trying to sell his Trojan collection to the Louvre.

Despite his unauthorized 'soundings', Schliemann received official permission to excavate at Mycenae in late March. But plans to commence were thwarted. Déthier, Director of the Imperial Museum in Constantinople, arrived in Athens. On behalf of the Turkish government he filed a lawsuit for its half share of Schliemann's Trojan finds. The court was asked to sequester the property in dispute. Schliemann sought to remove it from the jurisdiction of the court by putting it under the protection of a foreign embassy. The Americans were eager to oblige: 'Mr Constantinos and Mr Wait the consul called on me when the danger appeared greatest and offered me to put the U.S. seal on my collection in order to save it, but I thought this would render the case worse and did not consent to it.'[9] However, when Emile Burnouf, its Director, offered the sanctuary of the French School, pointing out that the collection would be on French soil, Schliemann accepted.[10] In early May, a crisis loomed. On 11 May Schliemann sent the French ambassador, de Gabriac, a note for the French Minister of Public Instruction, de Fourtou:[11]

> As Ambassador Gabriac has explained to you, my Trojan collection was in great danger and to save it, I made a donation of it to France. Gabriac had assured me that your acceptance would arrive on 7 May. Acceptance not having arrived by 11 May, I was forced, in order to save the collection, to make a solemn oath that it would never leave Athens, <and that I would build a museum to house it here.>[12] The donation is therefore rescinded.

The same day Burnouf sent Schliemann a terse letter asking him to remove the treasure as soon as possible from the French School. The next day, however, he sent a more conciliatory note.

> Your distress is no greater than my own. The extravagant behaviour of Madame Schliemann, to whom you yielded, when we were only asking for something extremely straightforward and reasonable, is the cause of all the trouble. Reflect on where we stand now, myself, M. de Gabriac, and even M. de Fourtou.
> I have won from M. de Gabriac the concession that he will not wire the French government until four o'clock this afternoon your decision of yesterday morning. So you still have time to go back on what has been done and to send him the ten sensible lines that we went over together.

Burnouf clearly wanted Schliemann to cancel his commitment to the Greek government. Equally clearly, Sophia did not. On 14 May Schliemann wrote another letter to Fourtou, which, though essentially the same as the 11 May letter, held out the prospect that he might yet change his mind:

> As a result of my discovery of the Homeric Ilium, I have become here the object of universal jealousy. It is accordingly very possible that in the not too distant future I will encounter obstacles which will disengage me from my commitment to Greece and that once free from all Turkish claims, I could reinstate the donation of the collection to the Louvre museums.

On 15 May the Greek court declared itself incompetent to decide on a case between two foreigners. There can be little doubt that Schliemann's agreement with the Greek government on 11 May played its part in securing this favourable verdict.

Infuriated, Déthier appealed the decision. On 19 May Schliemann described Déthier's mood to G.H. Boker, the US Ambassador to Turkey, and the rather wild rhetoric that was being bandied about:

> He threatens that if the <appeal court> reject also his demand, the whole Turkish fleet will come at once to the Piraeus, bombard it and take my Trojan collection by force. But would the American fleet interfere?

The appeal court found in favour of the Turks and an order was given to sequester Schliemann's Trojan collection. When the police came to Schliemann's house to enforce the order, however, the Trojan collection was not to be found.[13] Accordingly, Schliemann's house, including a bed valued at 5000 francs, the Helios metope and securities deposited in a bank in Athens, were placed under court order.[14] The court also appointed a committee of three experts to determine the value of the collection based on the photographs in the *Atlas* and to determine the sum Schliemann owed the Turkish museum in lieu of the antiquities themselves.

Meanwhile, Schliemann sought to ingratiate himself with the Greeks by undertaking, at his own expense, the demolition of the Venetian tower on the Acropolis, which spoiled the view of the Parthenon. He obtained ministerial approval for the project and had just started on the work when the Greek king, George I, intervened and stopped him.[15] A few days later Schliemann handed over the project to the Greek Archaeological Society, providing it with the necessary funds.

Though the Greek government and Germany had already signed a contract for the excavation of Olympia, Schliemann was still scheming to secure the excavation rights for himself. He wrote to François Lenormant, Professor of Archaeology at the Bibliothèque Nationale in Paris, on 2 July:

As soon as the Greek parliament reconvenes, I will try to snatch the Olympia excavations from Prussia and I think that I will succeed, for I am putting down 200,000 francs immediately and offering such advantageous terms for Greece that there won't be a single vote to confirm the misguided contract that the Greek government has concluded with Prussia.

There was every reason to expect that Olympia would be a very important site, as indeed it proved to be. No doubt there was speculation in archaeological circles in Athens about what the Germans might find. Some of that talk seems reflected in Schliemann's vision of his own excavations there:

> At Olympia I would find work enough for the remainder of my life. I would do the thing systematically and dig away the whole plain to the virgin soil. Immensely important prehistoric remains and whole forests of beautiful statues must be hidden there.[16]

His efforts to win Olympia, however, were unsuccessful.

During the summer recess of the law courts Schliemann went on trips to northern Greece and the Peloponnese. He set sail from the Piraeus for northern Greece on 23 July. On board he encountered, whether by accident or design, Agathonikos, the President of the Protodikaion (court of the first instance), who invited him to stay overnight with his father-in-law, the richest man in Lamia.[17] From there he rode south to Thermopylae, Gravia and Castri (Delphi). He commented on the disastrous effects of the earthquake of 1870, which had damaged Castri so severely that the decision had been made to move the inhabitants to a safer position, thereby allowing excavation of the ancient site. Once again he stayed at the monastery. Then he climbed Mount Parnassus, stopping at the Corycian cave *en route*. From Arachova he continued to the road junction where Oedipus killed his father, and took the road to Daulis. At Chaeroneia he described as 'pitiful' the ongoing excavations of Panagiotis Stamatakis, the Greek archaeologist who was later to supervise Schliemann's excavations at Mycenae.[18]

In Levadia he saw a very deep cave which he promptly identified with the site of the oracle of Trophonius. In Orchomenos he admired the tholos ('beehive') tomb known as the Treasury of Minyas and stayed overnight at the monastery. 'Many mosquitos,' he commented tersely in his diary and spent the night on the balcony under a mosquito net.[19] He would later excavate at both these sites. He returned to Athens about 5 August. After answering his mail and sending £200 to Sophia, who was staying at Ischia with her brother Spiro, he started on his trip to the Peloponnese on the 16th.

From Corinth he went to Stymphalia, and from there to the source of the Styx, the monastery of Megaspilion, Kalavryta, Olympia, Andritsaina, Bassae, the Falls of Neda, Kyparassia, and to the Bay of Navarino (Pylos), which he called the most beautiful bay in the world. Here he climed up to the 'Cave of Nestor' on the promontory of Coryphasion, where, it is said, Hermes hid the cattle he had stolen from Apollo. Here Schliemann noticed sherds similar to those he had found at Mycenae.[20] This can be regarded as the first inkling of awareness that Mycenaean influence extended far beyond the Argolid (plain of Argos). Then he headed west to Messene, Mistra and Sparta and returned to Athens via Tripolis, Argos and Corinth. After returning home he wrote up the highlights of his trip as a series of short articles.[21]

During Schliemann's tour of Greece a detailed exposé of his promise to give the Trojan collection now to Greece and now to France appeared in the *Athenaeum*.[22] Its author, S. Comnos, Director of the National Library in Athens, concluded by hinting that many of the Trojan pieces were probably forgeries. Though remarkably well informed, the article's sarcastic tone detracted from its effectiveness. More damaging were the revelations of Frank Calvert in two long letters published in the *Athenaeum* in November.[23] These were Calvert's response to Schliemann's fierce attack on him in *Troy and its Remains*.[24]

> Let me here point out that, whereas Dr. Schliemann has thought proper to represent me throughout his work as an adversary of his explorations and of the identity of Hissarlik with Troy, it was in truth I myself who first convinced him of that identity, and persuaded him to make the excavations which have yielded such interesting results . . . In 1868 Dr. Schliemann first visited the Troad. He asked me my opinion as to the true site of Troy, admitting that he had not as yet given any attention to that problem . . . In 1870 Dr. Schliemann commenced his excavations. A few insignificant walls were brought to light, which were at once pronounced by him to be the ruins of Priam's Palace. I examined these, and succeeded in convincing the Doctor that, inasmuch as they were built on the surface of the accumulated *debris* of the town, they must necessarily be referred to a much later period than the Heroic age.

Schliemann had also attempted to appropriate credit for the discovery of the large temple near the north-east corner of the site by denying that Calvert had excavated there. Calvert decisively refuted Schliemann on this point by referring to the Laurent plan of April 1872 (see Fig. 2). The general observations on Schliemann's character with which Calvert concluded his article, written, apparently, more in sorrow than in anger, were devastating:

Dr. Schliemann has taken occasion to express his surprise that, as proprietor of part of Hissarlik, I should against my material interest, have published my doubts as to the age and origin of the antiquities discovered by him. He seems unable to understand that in a question of this kind no personal considerations whatsoever ought to have any weight, and that it is simply childish to hope that they can be made to prevail against scientific truth. Whilst fully recognizing his enterprise, devotion, and energy in carrying out these excavations, I cannot but express the regret that Dr. Schliemann should have allowed the "enthusiasm," which, as he himself admits, "borders on fanaticism," to make it so paramount an object with him to discover the Troy described by Homer, as to induce him to suppress or pervert every fact brought to light that could not be reconciled with the Iliad.

Schliemann answered Calvert's article in March 1875.[25] On the question of who found the temple on the north side of the mound he adopted a rather peculiar position:

It is perfectly true that Mr. F. Calvert told me in August, 1868, that in one of the small ditches he had cut in his field at Hissarlik he had discovered a temple, but this discovery, in which I believed at the time, has been completely upset by the criticism of my pickaxe . . .

Schliemann argued that since *he* had not found even the foundations of a temple here, Calvert could not have done so either and suggested that Calvert should 'declare frankly his mistake' and withdraw his claim to be the discoverer. Schliemann does not deny, however, that there was once a temple here, for in *Troy and its Remains* he speaks of the 'Doric temple, which at one time stood on the north side, and in the depths of which I am working . . .'[26] On Calvert's role he remarks:

Not the least funny thing in Mr. Calvert's article is his assertion, that it was *he* who *first* indicated to me Hissarlik as the site of Troy, and that I had avowed him that I had previously not given any attention to the subject, . . . The Homeric topography has, of course, always been of paramount interest to me. I thoroughly studied and re-studied it, and read over and over again all what had been written on the subject, long before I saw Mr. Calvert. When I first visited the Troade [*sic*] in August, 1868, it had for years been settled in my mind that all the indications of the Iliad confirm the tradition of all antiquity, which identifies the site of the Greek Ilion with the place *ubi Troia fuit*. My work of 1868, *Ithaque, le Péloponnèse et Troie* (pp. 161, 162), shows that I sounded the ground on the heights of Bunarbashi in a thousand places, merely to obtain tangible *negative* proofs in favour of that identity.

133

As we have seen, *Ithaque* does indeed show what Schliemann claims but the diary makes clear that he excavated at Bunarbashi in the hope of obtaining positive results. In his response, which appeared in the *Guardian* of 11 August 1875, Calvert observed:

> After this, it is hardly astonishing to find Dr. Schliemann coolly calling upon me to disclaim in his favour the credit of the discovery of the temple of Apollo (supposed by me at the time to be that of Minerva), which I made in my own fields at Hissarlik, and which I recorded in the *Archaeological Journal* in 1865, several years before he ever visited Troy. In order to prove his case, and to account for his previous admission of my discovery and for his having duly recorded my excavations on the plan furnished by him to the Athens newspaper (which plan is reproduced, as I since learn, in the atlas accompanying the French edition of his work), Dr. Schliemann is now driven to say 'those two depressions were marked on said plan as excavations made by Mr. Calvert . . . as I was at the time on very friendly terms with him'! When Dr. Schliemann thus allows that he can accommodate scientific facts to personal feelings, it is, I submit, at least presumable that his facts may be similarly accommodated in a contrary direction, now that he is on terms with me that are *not* 'very friendly'.
>
> When I first met the doctor, in August 1868, the subject of Hissarlik, as the probable site of Troy, was new to him – whereas he had spent several days in making minute explorations on the site of Bounarbashi, the then all but universally reputed site of Troy: he had bestowed so cursory a glance at Hissarlik, that in writing from Paris after our first interview at the Dardanelles, on his way from the Troad, he had to make the most elementary inquiries regarding the topography of the latter site. For instance, on the 10th October, 1868, he asks – 'Where originates the Simois (Dumrek), and does it pass *Hasserlik* [*sic*] on the side towards Bounarbashi' (!) or on that towards the coast?' . . . In his letter to the *Guardian*, Dr. Schliemann further asserts that he had thoroughly studied and restudied the topography of Troy, and read over and over again all that had been written on the subject long before he saw me. I can prove that until I mentioned them to him, Dr. Schliemann knew nothing of Maclaren or Eckenbrecher, *the only two writers* who hit upon the theory that *Hissarlik was the site of Homer's Troy*. From me he took a note of their works, and writing from Paris (10th October, 1868) says – 'Eckenbrecher is here nowhere to be got, and the name does not even exist in the booksellers' catalogue . . . Charles Maclaren's *Plain of Troy* I have ordered' . . . Lastly, let me repeat from the same letter the following passage, which I had quoted in my communication to the *Athenaeum*, that Dr. Schliemann professes to answer, and which he would have done well to dispose of before pooh-poohing the statement that I was the first to suggest to him the idea of excavating at Hissarlik: – '*had anyone else proposed to me to dig away at my cost, I would not even have listened to him*.'[27]

134

Meantime the lawsuit dragged on. In April 1875, when it was over, Schliemann explained to a correspondent why in the winter of 1874–5 he tried to reach an out-of-court settlement: 'Had I left the matter to its legal course, it would have been finished four months ago by the payment of 10,000 francs. But being afraid that the Turks would never let me excavate again if the matter were not arranged amicably, I stopped the legal proceedings in the beginning of November last at the urgent request of the Turkish lawyers here.' This may well be an accurate assessment.

By February an agreement was beginning to take shape. Schliemann proposed to pay the Turks 20,000 francs for their half-share in Priam's Treasure and to provide them with another 30,000 francs from which they were to pay the wages of 150 labourers excavating at Troy for a period of four months under Schliemann's direction. All finds from these new excavations were to be the property of the Turkish government. The Turks, however, were not impressed with Schliemann's promises and in the end he had to pay them the full 50,000 francs without being given the right to excavate that he had sought. In return they agreed to relinquish all claims to Priam's Treasure.[28]

Meanwhile John Murray had brought out the English edition of Schliemann's book, *Troy and its Remains*. Instead of photographs, engravings had been made of the most significant objects, plans and views in the *Atlas* and these had been judiciously distributed throughout the book. The result was a much more convenient and attractive book than either the German or French editions. Schliemann was delighted: 'the volumes before me are beyond all praise.'[29]

Almost immediately after the lawsuit was settled, Schliemann left for France, apparently stopping briefly in Naples *en route* to find out which seemed the most promising sites in Italy for later investigation. Most of June and July Schliemann spent in England, dividing his time between London, where, owing to the great success of *Troy and its Remains*, he had become something of a celebrity, and Brighton, where Sophia preferred to relax with Andromache. On 24 June he gave a talk on Troy at the Society of Antiquaries. The summary given in the *Academy* shows that it was primarily a response to criticisms that had been made of his interpretation of his excavations.[30] He conceded that the plain of Troy was alluvial in origin and may once have been covered by water but maintained that in Homer's day it was much as it is today. He persisted in arguing that the pots with faces on them were 'owl-faced' and represented Athena *glaucôpis*. He dated the Troy II finds and therefore the Trojan War and the fall of Troy to about 2,000 years before Homer, or about 2,800 BC. Gladstone attended the meeting and expressed his admiration for Schliemann's zeal and industry. He agreed that Hisarlik was the probable site of Troy but argued that since the name of Dardanus, who ruled Troy six generations before Priam, appears in Egyptian inscriptions of the nineteenth dynasty, the fall of Troy could be no earlier than 1,500 BC. Gladstone's approval opened the doors of London society to Schliemann. At the end of June he wrote to a friend in Paris, explaining why he was forced to decline an invitation: 'I am received in London as if I had managed to climb up to the moon and had there resuscitated the Library of Alexandria from its cinders.'[31] He had dinner invitations till the end of July. In Paris, on the other hand, he met with a chilly reception at a session of the Société de Géographie. He said he would rather die than return there.

Naturally, he made use of his stay in London to acquire the luxury items that could not be found in Greece. He wrote to a friend asking for the names of the best hatter and bootmaker in London. He also enquired about the best obstetrician; Sophia was pregnant again. During the course of the lawsuit with the Turks (April 1874 to April 1875) she had suffered, according to Schliemann, no less than three miscarriages.[32] At the beginning of August she was left in Paris to rest with Andromache and her brother, while Schliemann set off on a tour of European museums.

Schliemann's conversations with the scholars who had seen his Trojan collection had taught him that much could be learned about the date and function of the strange objects he had found at Hisarlik by examining essentially similar objects that were to be found in the prehistoric collections of many European museums. He was of course already familiar with the contents of the Louvre and the British Museum. In the next four weeks Schliemann inspected the collections in Leyden, Copenhagen, Stockholm, Lübeck, Schwerin, Berlin, Danzig, Budapest, Vienna, Zurich, and Mainz. He used the opportunity to talk with the curators and other scholars and had an interview with Queen Sophie of the Netherlands in the Hague. He wrote up brief accounts of some of the collections, which appeared in the *Academy*.[33] The best arranged and most instructive of them was in Copenhagen, for Danish scholars were the current leaders in establishing systems of classification and chronology for prehistoric objects. Schliemann, however, having found some copper (or bronze) objects among the stone weapons and implements even in Troy I, rejected the standard view that there was a period in human development when the use of metal was unknown: 'there never was a time in which they were totally unacquainted with bronze.'[34] He was intrigued by the remarkably well-preserved 'Mound people': 'the skeletons of men, with part of their flesh, their hair, their beard, and with their splendidly preserved clothes, found in the very rudest kind of coffins, made of trunks of oak trees, which had been cut asunder and hollowed out by fire.'

136

Schliemann learned a great deal from these visits. In recognising the importance of comparative material, Schliemann was, if not ahead of his time, at least aligning himself with the most progressive thinkers among contemporary archaeologists. For most scholars, becoming acquainted with all the most important collections remained a remote and impractical ideal. It is in the astonishing energy, speed and thoroughness with which he turned this ideal into a reality that the essence of Schliemann's genius lies. His sharp eye for detail, his extraordinary memory, and his willingness to learn from others combined to make his trip an invaluable experience. His meeting in Berlin with Rudolf Virchow, the distinguished German physician, statesman and anthropologist, was also crucial. It marked the beginning of what was to be Schliemann's most lasting and important relationship. Though he had many acquaintances, Schliemann had few close friends. From 1879 up to his death, apart from one serious breach, Virchow was his closest friend.

Before setting out on his trip to the European museums, Schliemann asked Lord Stanhope, President of the Society of Antiquaries, to persuade the British government to apply for a firman to excavate at several sites in the Troad, including Hisarlik.[35] Once the firman was obtained, Schliemann would then conduct the excavations as the agent of the British government. Schliemann would be responsible for all the expenses. For his trouble Schliemann would be given one half of the finds assigned by the terms of the firman to the British government. Rather surprisingly, this ingenious arrangement was not taken up by the British authorities.

While visiting his sister Dorothea in Roebel, Schliemann learned of Frank Calvert's piece in the *Guardian*. He decided not to reply to it while still travelling. Later, however, when Friedrich Schlie, Director of the Schwerin Museum, who was planning a short account of Schliemann's life, wrote asking if Schliemann could add anything to the biographical details provided in the preface to *Ithaque, le Péloponnèse et Troie*, he responded with enthusiasm. He wrote of his childhood in Ankershagen and the stories and experiences that had awakened his interest in hidden treasure and excavation: the Ankershagen castle with its secret underground passageways, the little hill in a neighbouring village, which, when excavated, had produced barrels of beer thousands of years old, and the notorious local baron Henning, whose right foot kept emerging from his grave.

All these mysterious and frightening things made an indelible impression on my childish mind; even as an eight-year-old child I would have given my life to excavate Henning's grave or to bring the golden cradle up out of the hill and I went a thousand times to my father to ask him to undertake these excavations or at least to have the little pond emptied which lay behind our garden and was called 'the little silver basin'; in it, according to the story, there lay a silver basin. In addition there were Father's lectures on the discoveries in Herculaneum and Pompeii and his enthusiasm for Homer; he read Voss's translation of Homer frequently to us as little children and explained the story. His assurances that Troy had disappeared without trace always caused me the deepest sorrow, and, referring to the picture of Ilium in Jerrer's *History of the World*, which I received for Christmas 1829, I always insisted that those huge walls may have been buried but could not have been completely destroyed, and always assured him that some day I would bring it to light.[36]

These Ankershagen tales, which first appeared in 1875 and were later developed and incorporated into the autobiographical preface to *Ilios*, created the image of an individual obsessed since childhood with the idea of excavating Troy. So powerful was the image that it lasted virtually unchallenged for a century.[37] Without actually disproving Calvert's contention that in 1868 Schliemann was unaware that Hisarlik was a contender for the site of Troy, this image effectively rendered it ridiculous.

After his tour of the museums Schliemann was anxious to dig again. Obviously, because of his contretemps with the Turks, Troy was out of the question. Greece was also difficult, as he was not in favour with the current government. He decided to try his hand in Italy. Among the places he thought most likely to yield remains comparable in age to those of Troy were Albano (south of Rome, near Castel Gandolfo) and Motya (in Sicily). At Albano he had two goals: to ascertain whether, as reported, there really were signs of human occupation below the lava-beds of the last volcanic eruption; and to find the site of Alba Longa, the city ruled by Aeneas's son Ascanius and his descendants before the foundation of Rome. Fiorelli, the renowned excavator of Pompeii, had suggested that he try the vineyard of Carlo Meduzzi, where prehistoric pottery had allegedly been found. After negotiations with Meduzzi Schliemann obtained permission to dig in the field adjacent to the vineyard. For four days at the beginning of October he excavated with 'a large number of workmen' but found only virgin soil. Schliemann also questioned his workmen about the pottery finds. Three of them claimed knowledge of them; all swore that the pottery had been found in the soft earth *above* the volcanic deposit. Schliemann concluded that the claims that objects had been found *below* the lava-beds were spurious, prompted only by a desire to enhance their value. He found no trace of Alba Longa.[38]

He was equally unlucky at Motya, a few miles north of Marsala. It was thought to be one of the oldest sites in Sicily, being an early Phoenician colony. Schliemann excavated at various parts of the ancient city but the results were

138

disappointing.[39] He did find, however, the remains of several houses, including a large one, with chalk floors, arrowheads, coins and pottery. But since he found no pottery earlier than the fifth century BC, he was not impressed.

Though Schliemann clearly did have permission to conduct these trial excavations at Motya, he nevertheless ran foul of the archaeological authorities.[40] His excavations stopped abruptly on 25 October. For the next few weeks information about his activities is unusually scanty. In December he told Burnouf that after Motya he dug exploratory trenches at the Sicilian sites of Segesta, Taormina, Syracuse and then in mainland Italy at Arpinum, Capri, and Populonia. He found, however, that 'nowhere is there the slightest trace of the prehistoric period and even the accumulation of debris of the historic period is completely insignificant.'[41] To this list of sites should be added Paestum, for on 20 November he wrote to a friend: 'for four days I remained at Paestum doing exploratory excavations, for I thought that there was a prehistoric city underneath. But I was mistaken.'[42] Rather surprisingly, there is no record in his diary of any of these excavations after Motya. I see no reason, however, to suspect that they did not take place. Schliemann knew that there was little chance of publishing even brief notices of purely negative results and he may have decided only to keep notes if and when a site proved promising. His December letter to Burnouf reveals his disillusionment with excavation in Italy:

> The minister Bonghi is very anxious that I should undertake excavations at the vast cemeteries of Chiusi (Clusium), but I cannot bring myself to decide to do it, for there are no problems to solve and I would only be able to find there what every museum already possesses. I think that I should stay in the prehistoric period and continue the excavations in Asia Minor. As soon as Turkey is placated, I will bring into play every device I can to obtain a 'firman' and I think that I will succeed.

This passage reveals, or at least purports to reveal, that Schliemann's interest in excavating a site hinged on whether there was a particular problem to solve rather than its potential for producing works of art. This was a comparatively advanced view of the role of the archaeologist in 1875, which I suspect Schliemann had learned from Beulé or perhaps from Burnouf himself. To his credit, Schliemann did not merely give lip service to this ideal. More than most of his contemporaries, he aimed to solve problems and indeed often showed a surprising lack of aesthetic appreciation for great works of art, particularly if he had not found them himself.[43] But it is not true that there were no problems to solve at these sites. There were any number of unsolved archaeological problems at each of them. In what period did occupation of the site begin?

Were there signs of pre-Greek (or pre-Etruscan) occupation? What was the subsequent history of the site? Does the archaeological evidence confirm or contradict what we know about it from written sources? What Schliemann really meant, of course, was that there was no glamorous problem such as 'Where was Troy?' Also, he had developed unique expertise in prehistoric archaeology thanks to his experience at Troy and his tour of prehistoric collections. His lack of expertise in classical Greek and Etruscan archaeology must have been painfully apparent to him as he tried to make sense of what he found and as he talked with local experts. The decision to stick to what he knew was certainly sensible. No doubt he genuinely had a greater interest in sites that could be linked to the Homeric poems than in those where the interest was more strictly academic. He was certainly aware that this was the attitude of the general public. He knew that if he was to attain the lasting fame that he sought, it would not be for establishing the history of the early occupation of Populonia.

More surprising perhaps is Schliemann's conviction that he would be able to win a firman from the Turkish government. Schliemann assumed that he could always get his way by putting money in the right hands. Often of course this worked. But he had violated his last contract with the Turks and had fought a bruising year-long legal battle over Priam's Treasure. Even the most cynical observer might have predicted that Schliemann's chances of excavating Troy again were very slim indeed.

9

The Lions of Mycenae

MOST OF THE FIRST half of 1876 was spent in negotiating with the Turkish authorities for permission to resume excavations at Troy. At the end of April Schliemann left Constantinople for a few days to excavate at Cyzicus, an important Greco-Roman site in north-west Turkey about half-way between Constantinople and Troy, in order, as he explained to a friend, to do a favour for Rafet Bey, the son of Safvet Pasha, the Minister of Public Instruction. Since there could have been little or no expectation of coming across prehistoric levels here, this explanation is probably correct. Schliemann had maligned Safvet in *Troy and its Remains*. Regaining his favour was indispensable if he was to get his firman. Because of its comparative proximity to Constantinople Cyzicus had already been stripped of its statuary and hewn marble. Schliemann quickly decided that systematic excavation here was out of the question. After three days all that he found of note was a couple of inscriptions.

On 5 May he finally received his permit and started out for Troy. His first task was to build a series of huts to house the workmen and any scholars like Emile Burnouf who, he hoped, would assist him in the excavations. Schliemann was also eager to show distinguished visitors around the site and wanted to be able to offer them overnight accommodation. Among the celebrities he hoped to bring to the site was Gladstone. Early in 1876 the British Prime Minister had brought out a book on Homer, a copy of which he sent to Schliemann. On 8 May Schliemann wrote to Gladstone, praising the book in the most effusive terms:

Please accept my hearty thanks for the copy you sent me of your most valuable *Homeric Synchronism*, which Mrs. Schliemann and I have read and again read with wonder and admiration. This work, the masterpiece of the greatest scholar of all ages, will for ever remain classic and for ever be considered as the pearl of all that has been written or of all that will be written on Homer. I am really at a loss what amazes me more: the ingenuity of your researches or the great results you obtained by them. The arguments you put forward in this volume cannot be contradicted. Your conclusions cannot be shaken and the chronology of the Homeric poems and the Trojan war, between which the monuments at Hissarlik seemed to indicate an interval of 2000 years, are now proved to be separated by a very short period.

In the same letter he reminded Gladstone of his 'promise' to visit Hisarlik and asked him to fix a date, pointing out 'the intense sensation your visit will produce throughout the world.' Presumably, the blatant nature of this flattery was less obvious to Gladstone than it is to us. Gladstone's writings on Homer were voluminous but their effect on the progress of Homeric studies was negligible and today they are forgotten. Yet it would be rash to assume that Schliemann's flattery was wholly insincere. He spoke favourably of the book to other correspondents and henceforth adopted the more conventional dating for the Trojan War advocated by Gladstone, namely not earlier than 1500 BC. But as long as Schliemann persisted in identifying the Troy II level with the fall of Troy, he was inevitably going to encounter difficulties, for it was already obvious, as both Calvert and Lenormant had pointed out, that the Troy II pottery must be considerably earlier than 1500 BC.

Almost immediately, Schliemann clashed with the authorities. The governor of the Dardanelles, Ibrahim Pasha, was unimpressed with Schliemann's firman and would not allow the construction of huts at Hisarlik. He even prohibited Schliemann access to the site. Schliemann was confident, however, that these difficulties would soon be overcome and returned to Athens to send the necessary equipment to the Troad. Late in May his lobbying had failed to circumvent Ibrahim's obstructions. He decided to set up a formal meeting with Ibrahim Pasha to come to some arrangement. He wrote to Frank Calvert, now US consul in the Dardenelles, asking him to attend and protect his interests: 'After all what has happened between us, it is very painful to me indeed to be obliged to apply to you and to trouble you. But since you are U.S. consul, I can only look to you for protection.'

It seems that a deal was struck. Schliemann was allowed to build his huts and he agreed to pay for a second Turkish guard to supervise the excavations. The guard chosen by Ibrahim, however, Issed Effendi, did not please Schliemann, who complained that Issed's nickname 'the wild beast' was richly deserved. Nevertheless, he wired Burnouf: 'Everything arranged. Return to Troy today. Begin excavations immediately. Come soon as your Vichy treatment finished.' Once back at Troy, however, Schliemann was horrified to find that Ibrahim was throwing more obstacles in his path. Now there was a dispute over precisely what section of Hisarlik Schliemann had been given permission to excavate.

On 29 June Schliemann wrote an extraordinary letter. It was intended as a *reparation d'honneur* for Safvet Pasha, which Schliemann tried to have widely published. Presumably, this was an additional element in the agreement reached with Ibrahim. Schliemann said that his hostile remarks in the introduction to *Troy and its Remains* had been prompted by articles in a Constantinople paper, 'for, by an incomprehensible error, I thought that they had been written at his instigation. I regret profoundly this error and I beg a thousand pardons . . . I regret it all the more as His Excellency Safvet Pasha has from the beginning till the end been the benefactor of my Trojan discoveries.' The letter also indicated that because the difficulties caused by Ibrahim Pasha had rendered his firman inoperable, he was giving up and would not return as long as Ibrahim was governor of the Troad. Schliemann was determined to get his revenge. This scathing account of Ibrahim's obstructionist tactics he sent to Max Müller, who had it printed in *The Times*.

Back in Athens by 2 July, Schliemann lost no time in trying to secure permission to excavate in Greece. On 16 July he wrote to Max Müller: 'I have solicited here the permission to excavate the treasury of Minyas in Orchomenos, Tiryns, and Mycenae; without any doubt I shall at once get it and hope to begin the excavations in spite of the tremendous heat.'[1] A week later he wrote to Burnouf: 'I have permission to excavate Tiryns, Mycenae and Orchomenos and I have decided to begin excavating on Tuesday, 1 August at the first or second of these sites. Never fear, in these three sites I will find monuments of capital interest.'[2]

On 31 July Schliemann left Athens accompanied by Sophia and Professors Kastorches, Phinticles and Pappadakis, all of the University of Athens. Excavations began at Tiryns the next day and continued till 4 August. Schliemann's foreman here was none other than Spyros Demetriou, who had been one of his most trusted foremen at Troy and had played a leading role in smuggling Priam's Treasure out of Turkey. Some twenty shafts were dug, principally in the upper citadel but including three in the lower citadel and four outside the walls. In addition Schliemann dug two intersecting trenches near the highest point of the citadel. He found few stone constructions in his excavations in the citadel and concluded that most houses must have been made of mud brick. Among the finds he considered most significant were a number of terracotta figurines resembling those found earlier at Mycenae. Most of these represented either a cow or a female deity. The latter wore an elaborate headdress called a *polos* and often had her arms upraised, forming a crescent or, as Schliemann saw it, a cow's horns. He believed that all these figurines, cows and females alike, represented Hera, the sister and consort of Zeus. He noted that these figures were not found at a depth greater than 2.5 metres and therefore were of a comparatively late prehistoric period.

The permit to excavate at Mycenae had actually been awarded to the Greek

Archaeological Society rather than to Schliemann himself. But since Schliemann was eager to excavate and the Society was short of funds, the Society engaged him to carry out the excavations on its behalf but at his expense. It must have helped too that Schliemann was by far the most generous of the recent benefactors of the Society.[3] Panagiotis Stamatakis, an experienced young Greek archaeologist whose excavations at Chaeroneia he had thought 'pitiful', was to supervise his work on behalf of the Society. As an employee of the General Ephoria of Antiquities, Stamatakis was also to serve as the official representative of the Greek government. His reports on the excavations to the Society and the Ephoria form an invaluable supplement to Schliemann's accounts.[4]

Excavations began on 7 August. There were about 55 workmen, of whom 15 were directly employed by Schliemann at a rate of 2.5 drachmas a day while the rest worked for Spyros Demetriou. Schliemann paid Spyros at the rate of 1 drachma per cubic metre excavated by his men. There were three main areas of excavation. Schliemann's workmen dug at the Lion Gate, where the winter rains had buried the threshold and much of the gateway under a deep pile of debris, and at the tholos tomb traditionally known as the Treasury of Clytemnestra. Spyros's crew excavated within the Lion Gate on the site of what was to prove to be the grave circle, where the famous shaft graves were discovered.

For information on the day-to-day routine of the excavation, Stamatakis' long-neglected reports are much more revealing than Schliemann's. For instance, in his report of 16 August[5] to the Archaeological Society, we find:

> Mr. Schliemann visits the excavations from Charvati in the morning and evening, the rest of the day he stays in Charvati studying and writing so that all the work devolves on me, and there is too much for me to handle alone. I need two workmen or supervisors to help me in the supervision and in the reception and arrangement of the finds.

Elsewhere in the same report:

> The finds are classified by me according to type of material: metal, stone and pottery. This system has been accepted by Mr. Schliemann. We have come across no inscription or piece of sculpture so far. At a depth of 4 metres beside the wall of the acropolis there was uncovered the skeleton of a child, almost complete.

From these brief excerpts it is clear that at least in the early stages of the excavations Schliemann spent most of his time in the village and that the primary responsibility for running the excavation fell to Stamatakis. In *Mycenae* Schliemann gives no inkling of this. Yet his own diary silently confirms that this is true. His entries briefly summarize the day's progress and list the principal finds but he practically never seems to know where a given find comes from. More details on the conduct of the excavations are given in Stamatakis' report of 27 August to the General Ephoria:

> We receive the finds, cleaning and arranging them at the site, as a favour to Mr. Schliemann, so that when he comes to the site in the evening, he may find them set out in order and he can make his notes. We remain at the excavation from 6 a.m. till 6 p.m., supervising and gathering the finds. Mr. Schliemann, on the other hand, visits twice a day, in the morning and evening. When each day's finds have been viewed by Mr. Schliemann, we transfer them to our lodgings in Charvati, where we arrange them by type, putting numbered labels on them, on which is also recorded the depth at which they were found, and entering them in our daybook. Then we place each find in its proper place. This work of arranging and recording continues each day from 9 p.m. till 1 or 2 a.m., to the no small detriment of our health and for the convenience of Mr. Schliemann. Mr. Schliemann visits the objects arranged in our lodgings and studies them freely. We never impose the slightest obstacle. We enthusiastically assist him, often leaving our own work to facilitate his. Whenever he asked to take home one or more objects for further study, he has full freedom to do so. From the day when the painter he hired from Argos came to Charvati, Mr. Schliemann has continued to take freely from our lodgings all the objects he chooses to depict. We eagerly humour him in these matters, asking from him only the numbers of the objects taken and their return after they have been drawn.
>
> Mr. Schliemann has the practice of giving a bonus of 5 lepta to any workman who finds a significant antiquity. He has forced me willy-nilly to pay 2 or 3 dr every day on such bonuses. It is impossible for one, two or three overseers to gather all the smallest antiquities. With Mr. Schliemann's method, nothing can escape the workmen's eyes, when they are looking for a bonus. It is a small expense but the gain in antiquities is immense.

It was not long before Schliemann and Stamatakis quarrelled. When the entrance to the tholos tomb was discovered on 17 August, Stamatakis prohibited further work there on the grounds that he did not have sufficient personnel to supervise the workmen and collect and process the finds at so many different locations. Schliemann was furious. Four days later he suddenly increased the workmen from about forty to seventy and, without consulting Stamatakis, started excavating the area to the south of the grave circle. On 24 August, in direct contravention of Stamatakis' instructions, he resumed excavations at the tholos tomb. When this became known to Stamatakis, he told Schliemann that he could not supervise this work and consequently would not permit it. Stamatakis recounts the ensuing scene in his report of 27 August to the General Ephoria of Antiquities:

145

He replied in a hostile manner, as is his custom, that he was going to clean out the entrance to the underground chamber and that if I was not equal to the task, the Ministry would send more officials. I replied that the Ministry had granted permission for an excavation with 50–60 workmen, not with 90 workmen, and not with workmen paid by the cubic metre. He answered that he had permission to have as many excavations as he wished and under whatever terms he wished and that my only task was to receive the finds. I pointed out that my mission was not merely to receive the finds but also to have general supervision over all the work at Mycenae and to prevent any contravention of the law or of the Ministry's instructions. I added that since he had such an opinion of my mission, he should communicate this to the General Ephoria of Antiquities and if it approved the work undertaken, then that was fine. Otherwise, the sites being excavated would be reduced to one so that the collection of the finds could proceed in a proper manner and the workmen could be carefully supervised to prevent them from stealing objects, as it was rumoured a few days ago in Argos they were doing, and so that the finds could be properly recorded every day.

The following day at the excavations outside the underground chamber there appeared a line of walling of squared bricks and beside this another wall at a greater depth. In my absence, Schliemann instructed the workmen to destroy both these walls. When I got there later and learned this, I told the workmen not to destroy the walls before they had been carefully examined and if they appeared insignificant, then they would be destroyed, but if they were important, they should be preserved. While Mr. Schliemann was absent, the workmen followed my instructions. The next day, however, Saturday, Mr. Schliemann came to the site very early, bringing his wife along with him. He instructed the workmen to destroy the walls they had struck against. In case I should try, when I arrived later, to prevent further destruction, he left his wife in charge of the workmen as guardian of his instructions, while he proceeded to the acropolis. When I arrived a little later, I asked the workmen why they were destroying the walls when they were prohibited from doing so. Schliemann's wife answered that I had no right to give such instructions, that her husband was a scholar, that the walls were Roman and that it was appropriate to destroy them because they were impeding the workmen, that I had no idea about such matters, and that I ought not to trouble Mr. Schliemann with such instructions because he was easily provoked and might break off the excavations. I replied that Mr. Schliemann was not entirely free to do as he wished with the ancient objects, as he had done at Troy, and that he had been given a permit to conduct excavations at Mycenae in conformance with the law. Mr. Schliemann, from the very beginning of the excavations, has shown a tendency to destroy, against my wishes, everything Greek or Roman in order that only what he identifies as Pelasgian [prehistoric] houses and tombs remain and be preserved. Whenever potsherds of the Greek and Roman period are uncovered, he treats them with disgust. If in the course of the work they fall into his hands, he throws them away. We, however, collect everything – what he calls Pelasgian [prehistoric], and Greek and Roman pieces.

In the latter part of August the slabs that form the grave circle began to appear. Within the circle the workmen uncovered a number of slabs with bas-reliefs, which seemed to be tombstones. They formed two parallel lines, running from north to south. These tombstones (see Fig. 13) also sparked vigorous controversy, as Stamatakis reports:

> The sculpted tombstones he considers Pelasgian tombs and he has been anxious, from the day of their discovery, for us to remove them and bring them to Charvati. I, however, oppose their removal because the lower part of the slabs has not yet been uncovered that will allow us to see on what soil they are fixed and what relationship they have with the other similar slabs – some sculpted, some fallen, some forming rectangular cisterns, which Schliemann also considers to be Pelasgian tombs – or whether they have been placed there later, taken from buildings of an

Fig. 13   Tombstone above Shaft Grave V (1.33 m high × 1.06 m broad)

earlier period. He adduces security as an argument for their removal. However, from the day of their discovery a guard placed there for this purpose carefully guards them at night and on holidays. This justified resistance of mine Mr. Schliemann considers barbaric and uncivilized. I telegraphed the Ephoria on Saturday concerning his insistence that the slabs be removed.

I cannot remain in Mycenae if the excavations proceed as they have under Mr. Schliemann, because I bear great responsibility both in respect of the Ministry and the Ephoria. I request that the Ephoria ask the Ministry for my recall or my dismissal from the service.

Also in August the building to the north of the grave circle, now known as the granary, began to emerge. It was probably here that Schliemann 'very frequently' found, as early as 12 August, clay seals and sealings (seal impressions). Schliemann mistook them for door or wall ornaments. Their designs 'of impressed flowers or other ornamentation' are very similar, and in some cases identical, to those of the gold disks and buttons later found in the shaft graves (see Fig. 14).

It is fairly clear that the workmen hit on some Bronze Age tombs in August. For example, in his second report to *The Times*, dated 9 September, Schliemann reports finding a 'treasure' of bronze objects at a depth of 4 metres, consisting of 'five knives, two small wheels, two lances, two two-edged hatchets, hairpins, two vases, and remnants of four others, and of a tripod.' Such a large collection of bronze objects most probably came from a tomb. The diary allows us to date the discovery of this cache to 25 August. However, there is no mention in the diary of a bronze tripod until the 20 September entry. It appears virtually certain that Schliemann simply added this tripod to the cache of 25 August, for although the second report is dated 9 September, it was not in fact completed until 23 September, as Schliemann relates to Max Müller in his letter of 25 September:

> Enclosed I beg leave to send you my second article on Mykenae . . . I had written this article already two weeks ago, but happily did not send it at once because the excavations of last week have revealed so many things . . . so that I have had to alter a great deal . . .[6]

In the same letter, incidentally, Schliemann offered to send Max Müller a 'set of the usual Juno idols.' He regretted that he could send only a few 'for I am working here on national ground: all belongs to the nation and I am closely watched'. It follows therefore that Schliemann was either pocketing some of the finds himself or, more probably, rewarding the workmen for clandestinely bringing him finds that should have been handed over to Stamatakis or his assistants.

Fig. 14   Terracotta ornaments with designs similar to those on the gold disks
(actual size)

The discovery of a 'beautiful double sword of bronze with the nails of the
handle', recorded in the entry for 21 August, also suggests a burial. Since this is
one of the most impressive of the early finds, it is remarkable that there is no
mention of it in any of *The Times* reports. In *Mycenae* a sword answering this
description crops up in the 30 October report. There Schliemann associates it
with an alabaster sword pommel and says it was found in the large house south
of the grave circle which he identified as the royal palace.[7] In the corresponding diary entry (25 October) and *Times* report Schliemann refers to a large
alabaster 'doorknob' but makes no mention of any sword.[8] It seems that it was
only after the excavation of the shaft graves made clear that the 'doorknob' was
in fact a sword pommel that the idea occurred to Schliemann to associate it with
the sword he had found on 25 August and not yet mentioned in his reports.

Following the crisis on 27 August over the excavation of the tholos tomb,
the excavations were halted for three days (28, 29 and 30 August) and then
resumed on 31 August. From Stamatakis' next report to the General Ephoria
(17 September), it is apparent that the situation had not improved:

> The work proceeds in utter confusion. After the resumption of excavation, things
> went smoothly for three days. But after the arrival of Mr. Phinticles, the Vice-
> President of the Archaeological Society, the confusion returned. The workmen
> were suddenly increased from 80 to 130. The sites being excavated were increased
> from three to four, with a total of seven subgroups, so that the supervision and
> proper recording of the finds is exceedingly difficult. I have often spoken about
> this lack of order to Mr. Schliemann but he does not listen to me at all. Mr.
> Schliemann conducts the excavations as he wishes, paying no regard either to the
> law or to the instructions of the Ministry or to any official. Everywhere and at all
> times he prefers to look to his own advantage.

Schliemann's diary lends support to Stamatakis' claims about the sudden
increase in the number of workmen. There are no entries for 3 and 4

Fig. 15   Warrior vase (⅙ actual size)

September but for the 5th Schliemann records that he had 14 workmen, more than double the labour force he had on the 2nd. The same entry indicates that work had been begun in a field 'which borders on that which we first dug up and where all the tombs are'. The ruins of at least six 'Hellenic houses' had already been discovered. Thus it would appear that as early as 4 September Schliemann had begun excavating the area south of the grave circle. Digging deeper, the workmen uncovered the ruins of a Bronze Age house with several rooms. This is probably the complex now called the House of the Warrior Vase after the famous twelfth-century vase found there. This is one of the most interesting of all Mycenaean vases because it provides us with the best evidence for how warriors setting out from Mycenae for Troy might have looked if indeed the Trojan War ever took place (see Fig. 15). Fragments of this vase started to appear here on 19 September.

Schliemann reports excavating a number of tombs in September. On the 5th they uncovered a tomb containing potsherds and a coin, presumably to be dated after 600 BC. On 6 September the diary records: 'It is a very strange fact that all the tombs are full of potsherds among which some entire vases.' Schliemann's surprise that the tombs contained substantial amounts of

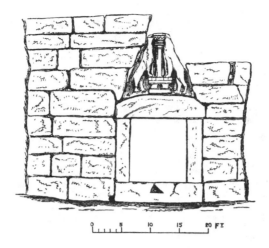

Fig. 16 Lion Gate, Mycenae

pottery is a striking reminder of just how inexperienced an excavator he was in 1876.

Schliemann had evidently managed to persuade Phinticles to countermand Stamatakis' ban on excavation at the Tomb of Clytemnestra, for on 8 September his diary reports that 'part of the dromos has been brought to light' and the day before a decorated piece of porphyry had been found, which must once have formed part of the decoration of the door frame of the tomb.[9] As usual, Schliemann shows no knowledge of the findspot.

The area immediately within the Lion Gate (see Fig. 16) had been put off limits by Stamatakis. He was afraid that the side walls might collapse and damage the gate itself and had requested that an engineer be sent to determine its structural soundness. Schliemann, however, kept trying to dig there whenever Stamatakis' back was turned. Stamatakis reports:

> Twice in my absence he started on this work and twice was prevented with considerable unpleasantness. He is rushing to finish the excavations. This is the source of the great confusion and the daily squabbles and differences with me.

On Wednesday 13 September there was another heated incident between the Schliemanns and Stamatakis:

> Last Wednesday at 10 a.m. a door-sill appeared in the course of the excavations and beside it a small column-base. As soon as it appeared, I told the workmen and the supervisor that the stone was not to be removed from its place until we had excavated down to its depth and its emplacement could be examined and recorded. At

151

3 o'clock Mr. Schliemann instructed the workmen, contrary to my view, to remove the door-sill before it was completely uncovered and to take it in the cart and throw it outside the wall. Seeing from a distance that it was being carried off, I hurried up and reproached the workmen for removing it when it was forbidden to do so. Mr. Schliemann, who happened to be there, began to insult me coarsely. Unable to control my temper, I replied with similar insults. Later his wife came up and began to abuse me in front of the workers, saying that I was illiterate and fit only to conduct animals and not archaeological excavations. She added that I had been sent simply to supervise and to receive the finds and that I had no right to make criticisms and to trouble her husband. She said that they had absolute permission from the Archaeological Society to conduct the excavations as they wanted. I made no reply to her intolerable abuse.

I request that the Ephoria send the above along with the enclosed daybook to the Council of the Athenian Archaeological Society, to which the permit to excavate at Mycenae (at Mr Schliemann's expense) was granted, and to request it to instruct Mr. Schliemann to stay within the law, to reduce the workmen to 80 and the sites being excavated to one, and to place the work on an orderly basis so that the supervision of the sites being excavated can be conducted in an appropriate fashion. The Council should also prohibit him from destroying later buildings without consultation with the ephor [supervisor], from crushing other objects in the removal of rubble and earth, and, in general, they should clarify the rights of excavation to which his permit entitles him. In addition, it should be made known to him what the duties of the ephor are. Otherwise, the Ephoria is requested to ask the Ministry for my recall from Mycenae.

Stamatakis' report of 17 September would have been sent on the weekly steamer from Nauplion to Piraeus, which sailed on the night of the 18–19. On the same steamer Sophia returned to Athens. A week later Heinrich wrote to her:

My dear Wife,

I have received your letter and 2 of your telegrams, from which I learn with admiration that you are endeavouring to the utmost to get our enemy replaced by a reasonable being. May Pallas Athena guide your steps and crown your praiseworthy efforts with success! The information that you are not coming today makes me quite ill, for I expected you for sure. At all events, I expect you now today week, for the work here is at a complete standstill without you. I hope Andromachidion is now perfectly well; but do *not* bring her here.

Our article on Tiryns having been published in the *Times* of 11th inst. under the heading 'the Birthplace of Hercules', I have *recomposed* yesterday our second article, for the excavations of last week have revealed so many things, which have forced me to change and remodel said dissertation entirely. For heaven's sake, do not publish a translation of the copy of it which you have taken with you, for, so as I had written it before, it contained *many false statements* . . . In writing the article yesterday I thought I had breakfasted when I had not got anything and thus I did not get anything all the day; but I have worked very hard.

I kiss you my darling and kiss our Andromachidion, remaining your affectionate husband.

H. Schliemann

Your article in the *Ephemeris* is much admired *all* over Greece and the Greek nation is proud to have a daughter who can write such articles.

From this letter it is clear that Sophia had gone back to Athens to have Stamatakis replaced. In this she was unsuccessful, though she did manage to persuade the Secretary of the Archaeological Society, S. Koumanoudis, to put pressure on Stamatakis to allow Schliemann more leeway. Within a week of her departure Heinrich already missed Sophia's assistance as supervisor of the workmen at the tholos tomb. No doubt he also missed her talent for humiliating Stamatakis in front of the workmen and thus undermining his authority. The letter also alludes to the substantial contribution Sophia made in keeping the Greek public informed about the progress of the excavations through her reports to the Greek press.

Stamatakis took advantage of Sophia's absence to make some headway at the Tomb of Clytemnestra. In the course of excavations here the stone benches of a later Greek theatre straddling the dromos (entrance-way) had been uncovered. Stamatakis wanted to conserve them but the dromos had to be cleared if the excavation of the tomb was to proceed. On 19 September, the day after Sophia's departure, he decided to try tunnelling underneath the benches. But even without Sophia to taunt him the hapless Stamatakis suffered further humiliation. The benches collapsed and fell into the dromos.

On the same day an exciting discovery was made within the grave circle. Just below the three sculpted tombstones a shaft had been cut out into the rock. This was to prove some 4 metres deep. Near the top the workmen found on 19 September a small bone button covered with gold leaf.

Schliemann completed his third and fourth reports to *The Times* on 8 October.[10] They review for the most part the work done in September. In the fourth report, published along with the third in *The Times* of 13 November, Schliemann expressed the view that the large building south of the grave circle was the royal palace.

Although there are no windows in the house, and although the scanty daylight through the doors must have been still diminished by the cyclopean circuit wall, which is only separated from the west side of the house by a 4 ft. broad corridor, yet this seems to have been the Royal Palace, because no building in a better style of architecture has been found yet in the acropolis. Certainly His Royal Majesty was not comfortably lodged in such a house, but comfort being unknown, it was unmissed. On the other hand, the objects discovered in this house prove that the family which occupied it had pretensions to luxury.

Among the finds attributed to the palace, Schliemann mentions some engraved gemstones and a six-sided mould used for casting jewellery and fragments of the 'warrior vase'. Sophia returned to Mycenae on 2 October.[11] The next day the workmen found a casserole and a large tripod, both of bronze, in a room of the so-called palace. Schliemann now began to wonder if the rooms of the palace were not in fact individual tombs. Also, he was finding 'many bones' there. It seems highly likely that the workmen had come upon a Bronze Age tomb.[12]

On 9 October Schliemann suddenly suspended the excavations and hurried off to Troy. He had been invited by the Turkish government to show Dom Pedro II, Emperor of Brazil, around the Troad. An extended account of this trip appeared in *The Times* of 6 November. The Emperor's party, which included the French count and diplomat Joseph Arthur de Gobineau, and a young German scholar, Dr Carl Henning, spent two days visiting Hisarlik, Bunarbashi and Tenedos.[13] Schliemann's account is filled with flattering references to the learning and sagacity of the Emperor, who was apparently convinced by the evidence of his eyes that Hisarlik must be the site of Troy. A rather different account was given by Gobineau in a letter to a friend.[14] He saw the trip as dominated by pedantic disputes between Schliemann and Henning, who took an instant dislike to one another. Gobineau made fun of both of them but reserved a special contempt for Schliemann, whom he considered an 'impudent charlatan, a liar and an imbecile'.

Excavations resumed at Mycenae on 25 October. In his sixth report to *The Times* Schliemann mentioned three engraved gems that had been found in the palace: the first with a long-horned cow's head, the second with two horses heraldically flanking two diminutive human figures, and the third representing a running stag with its head turned backwards. These gems have a surprising history in Schliemann's reports. The first does not appear in the diary; the second is mentioned in the entry of 19 September where, most unusually, it is marked with an asterisk; and the third is in the 26 October entry, where the context suggests that it may have been found near the Lion Gate. In *Mycenae*, however, Schliemann states that the first two gems were purchased from a villager in Chonika, a few miles south of Mycenae, and the third appears to be listed along with gems in chapter four.[15]

The diary entry for 25 October reads: 'The most interesting discovery made today is a large real tomb' just below one of the three tombstones above Shaft Grave V. Further details are given in the 30 October entry: 'These tombs are in a ditch which has been cut into the soft red rock, but I have not been able yet to find out how they were built, for I find in the ditch only 2 rows of large slabs of calcareous stone lying the one on the other. On these slabs I found bones of a human body; also part of the jaw with 3 mill teeth.' These slabs are too heavy and too high above the floor of Shaft Grave V (some 5 metres) to form its roof. The presence of a skeleton on the slabs and the discovery at this spot of a button covered in gold leaf (19 September) strongly suggest that there was a burial directly below the tombstone. Perhaps the sword pommel, also found on 25 October according to this diary but attributed in *Mycenae* to the 'palace' south of the grave circle, properly belongs to this burial.

On 29 October Dom Pedro and his train visited Mycenae. After a hurried look at the excavations, they all retired to the 'Treasury of Atreus', where they enjoyed a splendid lunch hosted by the mayor of Charvati and other local dignitaries. Dom Pedro and Gobineau were particularly impressed by the bas-reliefs on the tombstones. Gobineau's observations again reveal his strong dislike of Schliemann: 'I was delighted to see Mycenae again. The contemptible Schliemann is excavating there. He has found bas-reliefs, which, if genuine – I consider him capable of anything in the way of forgery – are of capital interest and will change opinions again on the origins of art. We had a charming dinner in the Tomb of Agamemnon, where the ground was strewn with olive branches.'[16] The visitors spent the night in Nauplion and returned the following morning to Charvati, where they were given breakfast at Stamatakis' house. Perhaps it was the importance attached to the tombstones by the imperial party that persuaded Stamatakis to order their removal to his house for safekeeping, for this seems to have happened on 30 October.[17]

Though the excavations were slowed by rain in November, paradoxically, the pace seemed to quicken. Valuable finds appeared with ever-increasing frequency, until at the end of the month the quantity and quality of the finds was breathtaking.

For the first two weeks of November, Schliemann had a photographer at the site, who took some 80 photographs, from which many of the engravings for *Mycenae* were subsequently made. The panoramic view of the excavations in the grave circle and the area south of it dates from this period (see Plates 13 and 16). The engraving in *Mycenae* is made from three separate photographs all taken from the same spot on the city wall west of Shaft Grave IV. Sophia stands facing the Tomb of Clytemnestra, whose excavation she supervised; Schliemann, in pith helmet, stands beside the parapet that encloses the circle and Stamatakis, wearing glasses and a close-fitting cap, sits on one of the fallen stones a little below him. This appears to be the only surviving photograph of Stamatakis. Stamatakis was omitted from the engraving, presumably at Schliemann's request. Since the photograph shows the two tombstones above Grave I (before the entrance to the grave circle), it must have been taken on or before 10 November, when, according to Schliemann's diary, they were removed to begin excavations there.[18]

On 8, 9 and 10 November, nine more buttons covered with gold leaf were found in Grave V, as well as 'a number of gold leafs and among them a very large one, on which were impressed a number of small circles and spiral ornaments. But all these objects are found separately and at distances of whole metres from each other.'[19] The 12 November entry reads: 'Wishing to terminate the excavations today in order to leave tomorrow morning, I pursued the excavations with the utmost vigour . . .'[20] He had excavated Grave I to a depth of 4.5 metres below the opening of the shaft without finding anything. 'Only towards evening I found there, on the bones of a corpse, quite a mass of large gold leafs with impressions of numerous circles and spiral lines; one of the leafs is of tremendous proportions and this seems to have covered the face of the deceased; but no, the body had evidently been burnt as all the bones and the gold leafs were enveloped in a mass of black ashes.'[21]

Given that Schliemann had not yet reached the bottom of any of the several shafts, which he rightly believed to be tombs, it is impossible to believe that he planned to depart the following day. This is mere dramatization after the fact. The leaf of 'tremendous proportions' is presumably the large gold diadem, whose maximum dimensions are 50 × 10 centimetres. Curious is Schliemann's description of the decoration of the gold leaf found in Grave I: 'impressions of gold circles and spirals'. Though this aptly describes a great deal of the repoussé work found in the shaft graves, it is inappropriate for the objects found in Grave I, which have circles but no spirals. However, at this stage Schliemann was attributing to Grave I four gold disks, which had in fact been found in Grave V. Two of these disks can be identified with some certainty; their ornamentation includes spirals.[22]

Rain on 14 November delayed the complete excavation of Grave I until the following day, when two more bodies were excavated. Remarkably, all three bodies were covered with exactly the same gold ornaments: a large diadem, eight rays, and five crosses, each formed of four leaves. Naturally, these finds caused great excitement. Stamatakis telegraphed his superiors in Athens and the nomarch (provincial governor) in Nauplion. Also on 15 November,

There were found in the tomb some bone-buttons with the same spiral ornamentation as on several gold buttons.[23] In the acropolis in 6 m depth, was also found a good deal of beautiful pottery, and quite a number of fragments of vases having on each side a protruding piece with 2 tubular holes for suspension.

The pottery with the tubular holes, which reminded Schliemann of pottery he encountered at Troy, was clearly not found in the tomb but rather elsewhere in the grave circle (or outside it). The depth at which it was found is 3 metres higher than the floor of Grave I. In the draft for his eighth report to *The Times* Schliemann reflects on the differences between Trojan and Mycenaean pottery: 'Whilst in Troy nearly all vases have three feet, tripods of terracotta never occur here among the handmade pottery and nearly all the vases have flat bottoms; vases with one or two tubular holes on either side, for suspension, occur here, but they are very rare.' In the published version of *The Times* report and also in *Mycenae* these reflections on the differences between Trojan and Mycenaean pottery have been omitted and terracotta tripods and the sherds with tubular holes on the sides have been added to the finds of Grave I. The importance of the links to the Trojan finds is clear from the way in which Schliemann refers to the pottery pieces in *Mycenae*.

... finally, many fragments of beautiful hand-made and of very ancient wheel-made pottery, among which was part of a vase with two tubular holes on either side for suspension with a string, like the vases in the lowest prehistoric city of Ilium. There are also fragments of terra-cotta tripods, of which I found such an enormous quantity at Troy, but which are less frequent at Mycenae, nearly all the vases having a flat bottom.

Meanwhile, Schliemann had begun digging down to the rock in most parts of the circle. The stelae (tombstones) above Grave III having been removed, Schliemann was expecting to find a very large shaft grave west of this point. But it was the mouth of Shaft Grave II that he uncovered first, on 16 November. On the same day a group of German visitors came to the site, among them the archaeologist Arthur Milchhöfer. After Schliemann's death he published his recollections of this visit. Particularly interesting are his remarks about Sophia and Stamatakis:[26]

His wife Sophia, a Greek, married to him for seven years, shared the hardships with him just as in Troy. A slight fever had already put her to bed and our acquaintance with her in Mycenae remained rather unusual – sort of ear to ear, as the thin partition wall no more than the illness hindered her from participating in our conversation with her sonorous voice . . . While Stamatakis . . . showed us visitors all the treasures with the greatest enthusiasm and affability, he treated Schliemann himself with such unconcealed distrust – practically ignoring him – that we could not help

Fig. 17   Ichnography of the grave circle, Mycenae, showing *(left to right)* Graves V, II and IV in the foreground and I and III behind

being embarrassed. I later got to know Stamatakis as a perhaps somewhat rigid but thoroughly honourable and a genuine individual. I also learned from him then the grounds for his behaviour, which were dictated by an over-punctilious conscientiousness.[27]

On 17 November the workmen discovered a cave under two overhanging rocks between Graves I and III. The upper part of this overhang and perhaps even part of the hollow itself appear just below the five figures in the centre of the grave circle in fig. 17.[28] Here the workmen found a number of 'Hera idols' and other objects including a curious bronze dagger with two blades. Schliemann continues:

As I considered one of the overhanging rocks particularly dangerous, I did all I could to keep my workmen back from it; however, as, in order to stimulate the workmen to be very attentive, I am in the habit of giving them a drink-penny for all objects, even the most trifling, which have any interest for science, and as so many small objects were found just below the dangerous rock, two of my workmen always returned to the spot. But seeing that the rock had a crack which widened, I literally dragged the two men from their perilous position, when all at once the rock fell with a thundering crash, and we were all three knocked down by its splinters, but none of us was injured.

It is a reasonable inference from the presence of the dagger, the many figurines and other unspecified finds that, as Schliemann himself suspected,[29] the hollow or 'cave' contained burials. The presence of numerous 'Hera idols' suggests that at least some of these burials are to be dated to Late Helladic III.

On 20 November an oval structure like a well-head emerged south-east of Grave II. The next day the huge mouth of Shaft Grave IV came into view. Since the 'well-head' turned out to be located in the middle of the opening, Schliemann immediately inferred that it was a sacrificial altar. On 21 November they reached the bottom of Grave II, where there was only a single burial. The grave goods, though modest compared with what was still to come, were impressive enough: a gold diadem and cup, both decorated with repoussé work, a bronze spearhead, two swords and two knives and a number of vases.

On 22 November there was no work because of rain. Rain hindered work on the 23rd too but in the evening they reached the floor of Grave III, which was excavated that evening and the following morning. The finds in this grave were stunning. Both in the sheer quantity of the gold objects it contained and in the quality of many of the pieces Grave III far surpassed what had been found in I and II. Here is how Schliemann describes it in his diary:

159

In this tomb were found the bones of three women, whom I recognize by the smallness of the teeth and the female ornaments. The bones of the three corpses, which were 1 m distant from each other, were really covered with masses of gold, particularly the head, on which rested a tremendous crown of large, splendidly ornamented leafs, and innumerable smaller and larger objects of gold, particularly round gold leafs, of which there certainly were 300, and smaller and larger pieces of gold, which had evidently been fastened to the rich clothes which had been burned with the dead. I particularly remarked with the woman the gold ornaments representing an altar with a bird on either side; also a number of smaller and larger gold vases . . .

The description of the finds in Grave III takes up forty-six pages of *Mycenae* and the objects occupy several display cases in the National Museum at Athens. Finally, Schliemann had uncovered signs of a civilization that seemed to match in grace and sophistication the world of the Homeric heroes. On 24 November, Schliemann wrote to Max Müller in Oxford:

There are in all 5 tombs, in the smallest of which I found yesterday the bones of a man and a woman covered by *at least* five kilograms of jewels of pure gold, with the most wonderful archaic, impressed ornaments; even the smallest leaf is covered with them.[30] To make only a superficial detailed description of this treasure would require more than a week. Today I emptied the tomb and still gathered there 6 kg. of beautifully ornamented gold leafs; also many earrings and ornaments representing an altar with 2 birds; one earring represents Hercules slaying the lion. There is no end to the variety of the ornaments. There were also found two sceptres with wonderfully chiselled crystal handles and many large bronze vessels and many gold vessels. I telegraphed today to the Times. I had hardly touched the second tomb[31] when I found a beautifully ornamented gold cup & 4 large bronze vessels. This tomb is the largest and will probably give most gold.

I have now the firmest conviction that these are the tombs which, as Pausanias, according to the accredited tradition, says, belong to Atreus, Agamemnon, Cassandra, Eurymedon etc. But how different is the civilisation which this treasure shows from that of Troy! I write you this in the midst of great turmoil.

On Saturday 25 November they continued excavating the fourth tomb. This proved to be even richer than Grave III. It contained five skeletons, all, as Schliemann supposed, of adult men.[32] After excavating two bodies on the 25th with their staggering array of grave goods, Stamatakis required the presence of the nomarch before proceeding further. The nomarch in turn insisted on more representation from Athens. Professor Phinticles arrived by steamer in Nauplion on the evening of the 27th. After being suspended for two days, the excavations resumed on the 28th. In his report to *The Times* about the excavation of the fourth tomb Schliemann points out that the initial stages are easy for him because they are done by the workmen.

But from that point – Mrs Schliemann and I – we have to do the work ourselves; the task is exceedingly difficult and painful, particularly in the present rainy weather, we cannot dig otherwise than on our knees and cutting with our knives the earth and stones away, so as not to injure or let escape any of the gold ornaments. Beginning the excavation of the lower strata of this tomb from the south side I at once struck five large bronze vessels, on one of which were exactly 100 very large and smaller buttons of bone covered with blades of gold, on which are engraved beautiful spiral ornaments or the symbolic sign of the holy fire; close to the same vessel I found a cowhead of bronze plated with silver and a gilded mouth, having on its front [brow] a golden sun and on its head two long golden horns. There can be no doubt that this head was intended to represent the goddess Hera, the patron deity of Mycenae. In further excavating from E. to W. I struck a heap of more than 20 bronze swords and many lances [spearheads]; most of the former had had wooden sheaths and handles inlaid with wood, of which plenty of remnants could be seen. Nearly all the handles showed gold casings and at the end of each of them was a large button [pommel] of wood or alabaster. On and around the swords and the wood could be seen a great deal of fine gold dust, which can leave no doubt that the handles and sheaths had been gilded. Some of the lances' shafts seemed to be well conserved, but they crumbled away when we touched them. I found there, at intervals of three feet, the bodies of three men, all of whom had the head turned to the E; the bones, particularly those of the legs, were of unusually large size. One of them had the head covered with a large heavy mask. We found in this tomb two more bodies with the head turned to the N. and the heads of both of them were covered with similar golden masks. All the three masks are made with a marvellous art and one thinks to see there all the hair of the eyebrows and the whimpers [eyelids]. Each mask shows so widely different a physiognomy from the other, and so altogether different from the ideal types of the statues of gods and heroes, but there cannot be the slightest doubt that every one of them faithfully represents the likeness of the deceased hero whose face it covered. Were it not so, all the masks would show the very same ideal type. One of the masks shows a small mouth, a long nose, large eyes and a large head; another a very large mouth, nose, and head and the third a small head, mouth and nose. The mask with the large mouth, nose and head is conserved with the greater part of the skull of the deceased.

The three masks of Shaft Grave IV were all found on the 28th. Schliemann's attempt to make them all sound very different from one another is misleading. Two are virtually identical.[33] The third is so different, however, that it seems to come from another culture.

Naturally, Schliemann was elated by the tremendous success. On 28 November he sent a telegram to King George of Greece:

With great joy I announce to Your Majesty that I have discovered the tombs which the tradition proclaimed by Pausanias indicates as the graves of Agamemnon, Cassandra, Eurymedon and their companions, all slain at a banquet by Clytemnestra and her lover Aegisthos.

I found in the tombs a huge treasure of archaeological objects of pure gold. This treasure alone is sufficient to fill a large museum, which will be the most brilliant in the world and which for all time to come will draw tens of thousands of visitors to Greece from every land. Since I am working merely out of a disinterested love for science, I ask nothing in return for this treasure, which with boundless enthusiasm I hand over untouched to Greece.

With God's help, Your Majesty, may these treasures constitute the cornerstone of unlimited national wealth.

There are no entries in Schliemann's diary after 28 November but the daily progress of the excavations can be followed from the reports in the Greek newspapers.[34] The fourth grave was fully cleared out on 29 November. The next day they turned their attention to the fifth tomb, where the mud that had long hindered complete excavation had now dried out. Schliemann's telegraphic report of the day's activities reads: 'Beginning today the excavation of the tomb of the sculptured tombstones, I found a gold breastplate and a gilt sword handle and a gold mask and many gold leaves and gigantic bones. All the masks portray the hero whose head they cover. The excavations continue.' The mask in question is the one popularly known as the Mask of Agamemnon, though Schliemann never seems to have thus identified it.[35] It is rather surprising that Schliemann did not point out that this was of much finer quality than the rest. Stamatakis did.[36] The middle burial was without mask, breastplate or other ornament. From this Schliemann inferred that an ancient tomb-robber had sunk a shaft that had hit upon this burial. In his haste to escape with the mask and the breastplate, the robber dropped the dozen gold covered buttons that were found above the tomb. The local newspaper, the *Argolis*, describes the rest of the excavations of 1 December as follows:

Pursuing their researches, Messrs. Schliemann, Stamatakis, and Phinticles were searching in the same part of the soil with knives. They found many gold buttons, a gold vessel, some small gold leaves, a small intact alabaster pot of the finest workmanship, on which there lay a small pot, and bronze cauldrons and swords. After this, however, they found a gold mask of a young man and a great leaf of gold, like a breastplate. But what was their surprise when under the mask and breastplate they found a human skeleton intact, still preserving a human appearance, although quite pale, as if with a tan complexion. It was a kind of mummy. The jawbone still preserves all its teeth, thirty-two in number. It looks as if it is asleep. The chest is broad and the breastplate is still preserved on top of it as if on skin. There were found with it one fine gold belt with gold tassels, and excellent gold-handled sword far surpassing all those found hitherto; also a fine dagger, one span in length, and (for the first time) pieces of wood more or less decayed. The sight of this alone astonished everyone. No longer was it a case of ashes and bones. It was a man from an earlier age in his entirety. Amazing! They considered moving the skeleton itself. But they saw that this was absolutely impossible and that if they as much as touched it, it would break up into what it was composed of – ashes. The best idea put forward was that these remains should be preserved undisturbed, untouched, in the spot in which they were found, as a revered and priceless ornament of ruined Mycenae – that they should be covered by a large, glass, dome-shaped cover and that a further roof should be set above that. May this excellent proposal be accomplished with all speed!

In a telegram to a Greek newspaper Schliemann said of the mummy: 'This corpse very much resembles the image which my imagination formed long ago of wide-ruling Agamemnon.'[37] Whether he was referring to the face of the mummy itself or the mask is unclear. Later the telegram became abbreviated in the popular (and scholarly) imagination to 'I have gazed on the face of Agamemnon.' Inevitably, the remark soon came to be applied not to the mask that was found on the mummy but to the best of them, the 'Mask of Agamemnon' of Grave IV.[38]

On 2 December the rest of the tomb was cleared out. In all, it produced about 2.4 kilograms of gold objects as well as numerous swords and other items. Attention was now focused on how the body was to be removed. Schliemann summoned a painter to make a drawing of the body before it disintegrated. A local chemist treated it with some kind of preservative. A slab was cut out in the soft rock below the body and the body carefully raised on to it. Schliemann sailed from Nauplion to Athens on the night of 4–5 December. Sophia had gone home a week earlier.[39] Thus she did not participate in the last few days of the excavations, missing both the mummy and the masks. Back in Athens, Schliemann prepared and sent off his final reports to *The Times* and negotiated for permission to photograph the finds for his book. He also enlisted the help of one of the leading French archaeologists, François Lenormant, to review his book manuscript and make helpful suggestions.[40]

Schliemann's excavation of Mycenae is undoubtedly his most brilliant achievement. It revealed a sophisticated civilization in Europe a thousand years earlier than that of classical Greece. It seemed plausible, at least at first, that he had indeed found the tombs of Agamemnon and his retinue; only later would it be determined that the tombs were about three hundred years too early. The richness and elegance of the finds and, above all, the testimony of Pausanias that Agamemnon and his followers were buried there, convinced even the stuffiest of pedants that Schliemann had indeed uncovered the world of the Homeric heroes. Schliemann's reports to *The Times* were picked up by newspapers all over the world. He was an international celebrity, his excavations at Mycenae a stunning success.

10

The Lion of London

SINCE THE DRAFT OF *Mycenae* had already been written in the form of the periodic reports to *The Times*, Schliemann spent January 1877 preparing the illustrations. His unfortunate experience with the photographs for the German edition of *Troy and its Remains* and the excellence of the engravings that Murray had produced for the English edition had convinced Schliemann to illustrate *Mycenae* with engravings. But first the objects had to be photographed. This entailed many visits to the National Bank in Athens, where the finds were being temporarily stored. A number of photographs had already been taken of the site itself, early in November, when the excavation of the shaft graves had hardly begun. Schliemann decided he needed another view, showing all five shaft graves. In January he sent an artist, D. Tounopoulos, to Mycenae to sketch an 'ichnography', or general view, of the grave circle (see Fig. 17). He was joined by Schliemann's engineer, V. Drosinos, who had to check the measurements for the plans. Drosinos noticed in one of the buildings south of the grave circle what appeared to be another shaft grave. As they cleared away the remaining earth, they came across yet another group of gold finds, including four splendid two-handled cups with dogs' heads on the handles biting the rim, a single-handled cup, and two signet rings. Had this gold once accompanied another shaft grave burial? Or was it simply a hoard of valuables? Scholars are still unsure.

In December 1876 Schliemann had written to his friend Wilhelm Rust: 'I will remain in London with my wife and child from March till August for I have to ensure that my book on Mycenae . . . will be published in exact conformance with my wishes with all 200 photographs.'[1] By the end of February the photographs were ready and Schliemann had written the manuscript of *Mycenae* and about half of the German translation. Before leaving for London in March he was thinking of ways to promote the forthcoming book. He sent his ideas to John Murray:

The idea has struck me that we will be able to sell five times more copies of the book on Mycenae if Mr. Gladstone writes the *preface* to it. I have no doubt he will do it in acknowledgement of the extraordinary services I have done in proving by my disinterested labours that his theories are correct . . . Persuade him both to speak on the 22nd. inst. in the Society of Antiquaries in Burlington House, before or after me, and to write the preface to our work.[2]

Schliemann arrived in London on 22 March. That same evening he gave a talk on his excavations at Mycenae to a crowded meeting of the Society of Antiquaries in Burlington House. Gladstone *did* attend and spoke in praise of Schliemann's achievements. Photographs were posted for the audience to examine. The talk was extremely well received and at its conclusion Schliemann was made an honorary member of the Society by acclamation. This was the first of many talks that Schliemann gave before learned societies in the spring and summer of 1877. He was also the honoured guest of the Grocers' and Salters' Companies. At their banquets he spoke of the pivotal role played in his life by the Ankershagen folktales of his youth and his experience first as an apprentice and later as a wholesale grocer.[3] The British Archaeological Association, the Royal Archaeological Institute, the Royal Institute of Architects and the Royal Historical Society all appointed him to honorary membership. Schliemann was the lion of London society.

Missing from the audience when Schliemann spoke to the Society of Antiquaries on 22 March, was Charles Newton. He had gone to Greece to examine the Mycenae finds on behalf of the British Museum. He had taken with him another British Museum scholar, the young Percy Gardner. Shortly after their arrival they were invited to join the party of Count Bernhard von Bülow, the German Chargé d'Affaires in Athens, who was about to take a trip to Olympia with Ernst Curtius and others to inspect the excavations which the Germans had been conducting there with spectacular success since October 1875. In a letter to Virchow in August 1876 Schliemann had complained: 'Since the beginning of the excavations at Olympia the German newspapers only mention my name disparagingly, print only libels against me, and have decided to refuse to publish my answers; so now I am writing only to the "Times" and occasionally to the "Academy". I am also writing my book on Mycenae, Tiryns, etc. in English, because in England I am respected and loved.'[4] Clearly, Schliemann began his excavations at Mycenae determined to regain the spotlight of the world's press. Equally clearly, Ernst Curtius was more than a little put out by the astonishing success of Schliemann's excavations at Mycenae. In his memoirs, von Bülow says of Curtius' behaviour on this trip:

He was not only a famous archaeologist but also a charming man, of excellent manners and stimulating conversation. There was only one thing I didn't like about him: his incessant, snide remarks about, and attacks on, Heinrich

Schliemann, who, after completing his successful excavations at Troy, was now beginning to get on the trail of the doomed House of Atreus and to bring to light their relics from the bowels of the earth. It pained me that an important and famous scholar like Curtius characterized a German idealist like Heinrich Schliemann, filled with a perhaps rather naive, but nonetheless devout, enthusiasm for scholarship and a fiery passion for the ancient world, as a bungler and swindler. One did not need to be a diplomat to see that his every word spoke of his jealousy of his successful rival.[5]

If jealousy played its part in shaping Curtius' negative view of Schliemann, so too must have the bitter memory of Schliemann's desperate attempts in 1874 to steal from him the permission to excavate Olympia.

On their way back to Athens Newton and Gardner visited Mycenae, where Stamatakis showed them around the site. Both scholars later spoke warmly of Stamatakis, emphasising that he had been present throughout the excavations and testified to the general accuracy of Schliemann's report in *The Times*.[6] After a close examination of the Mycenaean treasures in Athens both scholars expressed the opinion that most, if not all, the objects found in the shaft graves were to be dated before 700 BC. The view put forward by some scholars (notably Curtius) that some of the pieces might be of Byzantine date they held to be possible but improbable. More than one hundred years later, with our knowledge of the Mycenaean world immeasurably increased, the sensitivity and perceptiveness of these two scholars' judgements is striking. For instance, Gardner remarked of the signet rings: 'I do not believe that anyone looking at them by themselves would have imagined them to belong to a nascent, but rather to a declining or expiring art.' Thus Gardner seemed to sense that behind the glitter of the shaft graves lay a more highly developed civilization. He was proved right when Sir Arthur Evans uncovered Knossos at the turn of the century.

On his return to London Newton gave a series of lectures on the Mycenae finds to the Society of Antiquaries and the Royal Institution.[7] He pointed out that there were close parallels to the pottery and several of the gold objects Schliemann had found at Mycenae in a collection of finds in the British Museum. These finds had come from tombs in Ialysos in Rhodes. In one of the tombs an Egyptian scarab (beetle-shaped gem) with a cartouche of Amenophis III gave a fairly secure date of *c.* 1400 BC. A similar date for the Mycenae finds seemed likely. The link with the Ialysos finds and the datable Egyptian cartouche marks the first major step in the scholarly understanding of what Schliemann had found at Mycenae.

Though they did not mention them in their reports to the British press, Newton and Gardner had heard in Athens some disconcerting rumours about the Mycenaean treasures. Gardner recalls them in his obituary of Schliemann: 'Greeks smiled at his madness and made him the subject of daily scandal. Some declared that he first bought and buried the antiquities which he afterwards found.'[8] Later in his memoirs he records a somewhat different rumour: 'At the time both in Greece and in Germany the view prevailed that these wonderful works were mere forgeries, the production of some of the goldsmiths of Athens.'[9] Linked to these rumours was the general bewilderment of the archaeological community in Athens over Schliemann's abrupt termination of the excavations in December 1876, when the grave circle had not been fully explored.[10] Their surprise was fully justified, for when Stamatakis finished the excavation of the grave circle later in 1877, he uncovered Grave VI.[11] Given our heightened awareness of Schliemann's sometimes unscrupulous behaviour, these rumours deserve more serious consideration than they have so far received.

As we consider Schliemann's excavations today, we cannot help being struck by the parallels between Troy and Mycenae. At both sites there were few finds of precious metal until the last two weeks, when gold and silver suddenly appeared in great abundance. In Troy practically all the gold and silver was found amongst 'Priam's Treasure'. At Mycenae gold and silver finds were largely confined to the shaft graves; over ninety per cent of the gold was found in Graves III, IV and V between 23 November and 2 December. The discovery of a slightly older grave circle at Mycenae in the 1950s (Circle B) has confirmed that the finds in Graves, I, II and VI of Schliemann's grave circle (Grave Circle A) are what we would expect at the beginning of the Late Helladic period (see Appendix I). The tombs in Grave Circle B, however, in no way prepare us for the astonishing richness of Graves III, IV and V. This brings us to what is perhaps the most fundamental puzzle of the shaft graves. It was succinctly posed thirty years ago by one of the leading experts on Mycenaean art: 'How did the princes of the shaft graves get so rich?'[12] It has never been satisfactorily answered. Perhaps it would be useful to rephrase it more precisely: 'Why are Graves III, IV and V so rich?'

Many scholars comment on the extraordinary heterogeneity of the finds in the shaft graves. Emily Vermeule, a leading authority on Mycenaean art, listed them as follows: 'diadems and breast coverings, the gold face masks, the gold repoussé discs with ornaments both formal and pictorial, the cups and jugs in gold, silver, electrum, and bronze, inlaid or plain or studded with rosettes or made in the forms of the bull, lion, stag or shield, the long swords with engraved or modelled blades and hilts in a variety of materials, the daggers plain or inlaid, the knives, the gems and rings in gold, the seal-stones, the faience, alabaster, amethyst, amber, ostrich eggs, wood, cloth, ivory . . .'[13]

More troubling than the range of goods are the extraordinary discrepancies in style and quality within a single type of item and often within a single grave. For instance, in Graves IV and V five gold masks were found. Stylistically, these fall into three distinct groups.[14] The first comprises the two virtually identical masks from Grave IV.[15] These masks share the following features: no beard or moustache, continuous *engraved* eyebrows forming a single arch, eyes closed with eyelids meeting mid-eye and lashes indicated, ears entirely within the framework of the mask, no indication of cheeks, chin or nostrils. The second group comprises only the so-called 'Mask of Agamemnon' from Grave V. Stylistically, it looks like a much improved version of the masks in the first group. Its features include: ear-to-ear beard, handlebar moustache, imperial (short tuft of hair below the centre of lower lip), eyebrows forming two arches with individual hairs *cut out* rather than simply engraved, eyes oddly depicted as both open and closed, eyelids meeting mid-eye with no indication of lashes, ears partially cut out like flaps, cheeks, chin, and nostrils all indicated. It is by far the most skilfully worked of the masks and it appeals to a modern sense of aesthetics. The face has a calm, noble dignity, worthy of a king. While the masks in the first and second groups are flat, those in the third group, which includes one mask from each of Graves IV and V, are rounded – virtually three-dimensional. They are much heavier than the other masks – more than twice as heavy as the 'Agamemnon' mask and four to five times the weight of the masks in the first group. One has round, open eyes, a smile, and what has been interpreted as either a pencil-thin moustache or crinkling cheeks. The other has almond-shaped, open eyes, no moustache and no smile. The podgy faces are no one's idea of what kings should look like. At least one scholar has thought that the mask with the 'moustache' may depict a woman.[16] A competent art critic, given only the information that these five masks were prehistoric, might well deduce that the 'Agamemnon' mask came from the same culture as the masks of the first category but was at least a century later, while the other two masks came from an entirely different culture. Pottery and other evidence, however, suggest that the burials from which all five masks came represent no more than two generations of the same ruling family at Mycenae.[17]

There are other disturbing facts related to the distribution of the finds. For instance, no less than 701 elaborately decorated disks were found in Grave III but none elsewhere. Hundreds of gold-covered buttons were found in Graves IV and V but none, apparently, in Grave III. Large numbers of ornaments in the form of animals ('cutouts') in gold leaf were found in Graves III and IV but none in V.[18] It is also puzzling that so many gold disks were found in a tomb with only three bodies. There are more than enough disks to cover all three bodies completely. How were they used? Holes in some of them suggest that they were sewn to the (long since vanished) clothing in which the deceased were dressed. But if this was their function, why are there far more than would be needed to cover all three bodies? Why do four out of five disks have no such holes? Were they also attached to the dead people's clothing? If so, how?[19] Archaeologists continue to wrestle with these problems.

The astonishing richness of the shaft graves and the discrepancies of style that their contents display have defied the best efforts of archaeologists and art historians to account for them. A few years ago I suggested that Schliemann may have supplemented the genuine finds of these graves with other items. These could have been authentic finds made elsewhere on or near the site, and kept hidden from Stamatakis; authentic finds made by local villagers during clandestine excavation of some of the hundreds of tholos and chamber tombs in the Argolid and purchased by Schliemann; or faked duplicates of genuine finds.

There are clear indications in the diary that Schliemann came across many more tombs than the five shaft graves. For instance, about 3 metres above the mouth of Grave III on the sloping rock, he found 'many human bodies' together with obsidian knives and five vases.[20] Under the House of the Warrior Vase the British excavators found sixteen graves in 1950. All of them were empty or nearly so.[21] It seems likely that Schliemann's workmen came across these tombs, for in his 3 October diary entry, he mentions finding in this house a large bronze tripod, a small 'casserole', lots of fine potsherds and many bones. He concluded that all the rooms of the house were in fact tombs. Several of these graves, while modest compared to the shaft graves, may well have contained gold pieces.

In addition there is suggestive evidence that there were burials just below some of the grave stelae. Just below the stele above Grave V, for instance, Schliemann reports '2 rows of large slabs of calcareous stone lying the one on the other. On these slabs I found bones of a human body.'[22] Scattered in the vicinity he found a dozen gold buttons, gold leaf and other grave goods. Similar slabs, though apparently no bodies, were found above Graves I, III and IV.[23] Again, though Schliemann's own excavations south of the grave circle did not uncover the 'Golden Treasure', he did excavate very close to it. From the description of the findspot, the treasure appears to have been found in an unexcavated part of a shaft grave that had been partially excavated by Schliemann's workmen.[24] Finally, the finds recorded for 21 and 25 August, 6 September and 25 October suggest that graves of unspecified location were excavated on these dates, while those for 26 October suggest a grave near the Lion Gate, perhaps of Late Helladic III date.[25]

We know that Schliemann had a policy of giving a bonus to any workman who brought him a find. Stamatakis felt himself obliged to adopt the same policy. We know, however, that Schliemann continued to receive pieces illegally, for he admitted as much to Max Müller. It would appear then that Schliemann let it be known to the workmen, perhaps through his foreman, Spyros Demetriou, that he would pay a higher price for the finds than Stamatakis provided they were successfully kept hidden from his Greek colleague. It is quite likely, therefore, that any gold or silver pieces found in the excavations would be handed over to Schliemann. The few valuable pieces recorded in the diary before the discovery of the shaft graves may be those actually spotted by Stamatakis or his assistant.

On 2 November Schliemann took seven men and excavated at several locations outside the citadel: at a 'cyclopean building' (probably the tholos tomb now known as Kato Phournos), on the ridge to the west of the site, and somewhere north-west of the Lion Gate.[26] It is unclear whether he had permission to do this.[27] Though Schliemann reports that these diggings were unproductive except at the third location, where large quantities of sherds were found, it is possible that some valuable finds were made. It is also possible that Schliemann sponsored or encouraged clandestine excavations at other tombs in the area, such as, for instance, the chamber tombs he had been shown near the Argive Heraeum in 1874. There were also dozens of tholos tombs in the Argolid, including one near the Argive Heraeum, discovered in 1872 but not officially excavated until 1878.[28] Tholos and chamber tombs near Dendra (about four miles south of Mycenae) have yielded some of the richest burials outside of the shaft graves at Mycenae.

As to the third explanation for the richness and variety of the shaft graves, that Schliemann included fakes, we have seen how upset he was that the success of the excavations at Olympia had stolen the limelight from him. In 1873 he also seriously explored the possibility of having some of the gold and silver pieces from Priam's Treasure duplicated for illicit purposes. Given these circumstances, it is not unreasonable to suppose that Schliemann would have taken pains to ensure that the tombs he found would be richly furnished. There are grounds for suspicion. Just as Priam's Treasure is a hoard of unparalleled richness for the Aegean Early Bronze Age, so too Graves III, IV and V have no parallel for wealth among tombs of the Late Bronze Age. There are more than eight hundred Mycenaean sites in Greece.[29] Not one has yielded a tomb with even one tenth of the gold found in Grave IV.

One of the striking features of the Graves III, IV and V is the number of duplicates they contain. For instance, though there are 701 gold disks in Grave III, they are ornamented with only fourteen different patterns, there being roughly fifty examples of each pattern. Similarly, there are multiple copies of most of the gold cutouts in Graves III and IV. While there is nothing inherently suspicious about the occurrence of duplicates *per se*, since even in the Bronze Age goldsmiths used moulds for mass production, the fact is that nowhere else do duplicates occur in such numbers. Only 128, or one fifth, of the gold disks have attachment holes. There are, however, several examples of each design with these holes. If these disks had come into Schliemann's hands before the opening of Grave III, it would have been a comparatively easy task for a goldsmith to make many more copies of each design. Not seeing any significance in the holes, he may have failed to reproduce them in the copies.

While suspicion naturally focuses on those objects that occur in multiple copies, a few unique objects are also questionable. For instance, the Mask of Agamemnon is the only mask to show facial hair. Moreover, there is no parallel in either Minoan or Mycenaean art for either a handlebar moustache or imperial.[30] One might therefore be tempted to suspect that it is a modern fake. On the other hand, the beard from ear to ear is found on the warrior-vase warriors and also on the inlaid heads on a silver cup found in a chamber tomb at Mycenae. Also, the hair below the chin is brushed down as if to form a typical Mycenaean V-shaped (goat's) beard. There are therefore excellent reasons for assuming the mask's authenticity. Careful scrutiny of the mask shows that originally the moustache was made to turn down at the ends of the mouth.[31] The upturning 'handlebars' were added only later. Whether that 'later' was in the Mycenaean period or in the time of Schliemann is difficult but perhaps not impossible to determine. Conceivably, the mask itself may be an authentically Mycenaean piece, to which Schliemann had the 'handlebars' and, presumably, the imperial added to give it a more authoritative appearance. Whenever it was done, the addition was rather crudely effected.

If Schliemann used authentic finds, either from the site or elsewhere, to enhance the shaft grave finds, proving this today would be extremely difficult. On the other hand, if there are any modern fakes, they can be easily detected by a simple microscopic examination that would not harm the objects. Unfortunately, the Greek authorities have so far refused permission for such an examination.[32]

The key to dating archaeological finds, as is well known, lies in the pottery. Ceramic evidence dates all the shaft graves of Circles A and B within the period from Middle Helladic III to the beginning of Late Helladic II, or roughly 1600–1480 BC.[33] Now if it can be shown that Schliemann's shaft graves contain artefacts that must be dated significantly later than Late Helladic I (or in the case of Grave I, later than LH IIA), then it follows that these graves are not a 'sealed deposit' and some new hypothesis must be adduced to account for the facts. If we ask the question 'Are there any objects

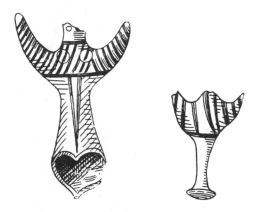

Fig. 18   Terracotta idols from Shaft Grave I (Approximately ½ actual size)

that Schliemann claims to have found in the shaft graves, which we now know are too late?' the answer is an unequivocal 'yes.' The two figurines of Shaft Grave I (see Fig. 18) are of a type that is not earlier than Late Helladic III B. All scholars are agreed that they cannot belong to the Late Helladic I/IIA burials in this tomb. Why then did Schliemann report finding them there? There are several ways of approaching this problem.[34] One can assume either that Schliemann made an innocent mistake; or that he deliberately reported finding them there when he did not; or that he actually found them there and so reported them, though he knew they did not belong. In favour of the first approach are the following considerations: the excavators reached the first body in Shaft Grave 1 on 12 November; it rained all day on the 14th; it was not until the 16th during the final clearing of the tomb that the figurines were found. Clearly, the figurines might have been washed down from a higher stratum into the partially opened tomb on the 14th.

In favour of the second approach is the fact that it had been one of Schliemann's principal disappointments that he had not found any figurines in the earlier prehistoric strata, where the pottery seemed to be closer to that of Troy II. As we have seen, he was fully aware that these figurines were typical of the later prehistoric period.[35] According to the third view, he may well have realized that the figurines had been washed down into the tomb but have chosen to ignore this explanation, since chance had provided what had long been sought. In *Mycenae* he attaches special significance to them: 'The most important objects found in this tomb are no doubt the two two-horned Hera-idols . . .'[36]

Whatever the case with the figurines, Schliemann certainly seems to have added to the contents of Shaft Grave I fragments of handmade pottery that he considered reminiscent of Trojan pottery. The attribution of the figurines and the 'Trojan' pottery to Grave I looks like an attempt to establish links between the shaft graves and Troy II.[37]

This is not the place to embark on a detailed critique of the shaft grave finds, but there are a few that pose problems. Specialists have accepted all the items of the shaft graves, with the exception of the two figurines, as authentic finds of the Late Helladic I period (1550–1500 BC). There are a number of other pieces that are at least questionable. For instance, the long-stemmed gold and silver vases, whose shapes are surprising for the period but which would be quite at home in LH III (1400–1050 BC): 'Nestor's Cup' (Grave IV), the gold (Grave IV) and silver (Grave III) cups with repoussé rosettes, and the cup with running lions (Grave V). The doves on the handles of 'Nestor's cup' irresistibly reminded Schliemann of the splendid cup Nestor brought to Troy, for Homer tells us that it had four handles, on each of which pecked two golden doves (*Iliad* 11. 634–35). It is precisely this feature, however, that makes the cup a very unlikely candidate for a Late Helladic I grave. If this cup had come from an unknown context, scholars would have had little hesitation in assigning it, on grounds of both its overall shape and the sculptured doves, to Late Helladic IIIC (1180–1060 BC).[38]

To some extent, the startling discrepancies in style and sophistication between different objects in the same shaft grave can be attributed to the fact that while many of the pieces are the work of local craftsmen, some of the finest objects are undoubtedly Cretan imports or were made by Cretan craftsmen working on the mainland. By 1550 BC Crete had developed a long tradition of excellence in many crafts – gem-making, for instance – that were virtually unpractised on the mainland. Thus, it is generally agreed that the showy but rather crude gold crosses from Grave III are local work, while the exquisite gold signet rings and seals from the same grave are probably Cretan. It is not always the case, however, that whatever is crude is local and whatever is sophisticated is Cretan. An excellent case in point is provided by the six inlaid daggers of Graves IV and V. These are among the most technologically and artistically sophisticated objects of the shaft graves. Many experts believe that they must be the work of Cretan craftsmen.[39] No comparable inlay work, however, has been found in Crete, whereas the mainland has produced half a dozen more inlaid daggers and a number of vessels of precious metals similarly decorated with inlay work.[40] Nothing comparable, however, was found in Grave Circle B and apart from the pieces in Graves IV and V all metal inlay of this kind comes from Late Helladic II or III contexts. The exquisite portrayals of the lion hunt and the Nile scene on the daggers from Graves IV and V are, stylistically, the most advanced examples that have been found. It is surprising that they are among the earliest – particularly if, as seems increasingly likely, this technique of inlaying was developed on the mainland rather than on Crete.

Schliemann stayed in London until early summer. He kept hard at work with John Murray, supervising the production of his book. He also opened negotiations with other publishers for the German, French and American editions and studied and discussed with Newton the Ialysos finds in the British Museum. When Sophia arrived, a special session of the Royal Archaeological Institute was arranged in her honour, as she had also been made an honorary member of the Institute but had been unable to attend the earlier session in May, at which the diplomas had been presented to Heinrich. She gave a short speech on the culture of the ancient Greeks and on her contribution to the excavations at Troy and Mycenae. Unfortunately, her speech adds nothing to what Schliemann had already written about her and indeed part of it is taken almost verbatim from one of the reports to *The Times*.[41]

As Schliemann was correcting the proofs of the English and German editions of *Mycenae* in Boulogne, the July issue of *Fraser's Magazine* brought an unwelcome surprise. It contained an article by the artist-journalist, William Simpson, famous for his drawings of the Crimean War. Simpson, who had visited Hisarlik in April, congratulated Schliemann on his important discoveries and was inclined to accept the view that Hisarlik was Troy. However, he deplored the readiness with which Schliemann identified, without any plausible evidence, a city gate as the 'Scaean Gate' and an unimpressive mud building as 'Priam's Palace'. The building was so small, he suggested, that it would be better termed Priam's pigsty. He further pointed out that since Priam's Palace sat athwart the Scaean Gate, blocking the entrance to the city, the gate and palace could not be contemporary (see Fig. 8).

Schliemann was furious. A long letter of rebuttal appeared in *The Times* of 16 August. He argued, correctly, that the building he identified as Priam's Palace was not the mud building sitting across the gate but rather the older stone building to the north-west of the gate on which the mud building was partially superimposed. What Schliemann did not acknowledge, however, was that the general plan in *Troy and its Remains* (see Plan I, Appendix V and Fig. 8) both clearly identify the mud building across the gate as Priam's Palace.

The honours that were showered on Schliemann in the spring and summer of 1877 indicate that his reputation in Britain had reached its peak. To show his gratitude, he announced in the letter of 16 August to *The Times*, that he would bring his Trojan collection, including Priam's Treasure, to London and exhibit it at the South Kensington (now the Victoria and Albert) Museum. It is not too fanciful, however, to see in Simpson's article the beginning of a decline in the esteem in which he was held by the British public.

There was another important development in July, this time a fortunate one for Schliemann. Near Spata in Attica a villager discovered a dark hole that had mysteriously opened up in a small hill. It turned out to be a chamber tomb, which held objects and pottery similar to those found at Mycenae. A short report appeared in *The Times* of 10 August. Schliemann, who had already decided to return to Athens to pack up the Trojan collection for dispatch to London, saw an opportunity of including an account of this discovery in his book. The speed with which he acted is amazing. He left Marseille on 22 September and a week later sent off the English and German versions of his report on the Spata finds to Murray and Brockhaus. To Murray he wrote: 'It has cost superhuman efforts to visit the distant Spatha, to examine all the antiquities and the locality and to write a long dissertation on them in two languages – and all that in two days with continual interruptions.'[42]

Philip Smith, who had edited *Troy and its Remains*, was also engaged to edit *Mycenae*. For this he was to receive £200.[43] In August, since Schliemann had still not managed to extract a preface from Gladstone, he promised Smith an extra £50 if he got Gladstone to do it. By the end of August, however, when the text of the English edition was already printed, Gladstone had still not agreed to write the preface. Schliemann wrote to Murray: 'Write at once to <Gladstone>, begging him warmly to write us a preface, however short; reminding him that, merely to show my gratitude to him I bring the whole Trojan collection to London.'[44] Finally, the reluctant Gladstone was won over. Schliemann wrote to him from Paris: 'Your consent to write a Preface to my book is the most brilliant reward to which my ambition could possibly aspire; it is the most energetic stimulus in my explorations for the remainder of my life.'[45] When the preface was finished in November, Schliemann wrote: 'I thank you most cordially for your Preface which is the Masterpiece of the greatest scholar of all ages and which will be read by the present and all future generations with the warmest admiration.'[46] After sending Gladstone a small box of Trojan antiquities, Schliemann informed him that the book was ready, that he had taken the liberty of dedicating it to him, and that he would be receiving a copy the next day.[47] The book was officially published in its British, American and German editions on 7 December but bore the imprint 1878.[48]

Coinciding with the publication of *Mycenae* there came more dramatic news from Greece: Stamatakis had discovered a sixth shaft grave. Located north of Grave I, it contained, according to the earliest reports, a large cache of grave goods in gold and bronze, and two skeletons.[49] This, Schliemann must have thought, would vindicate his claims and silence the critics.

1. Aeneas escaping from Troy. This engraving, according to Schliemann, inspired his childhood dream of excavating Troy

2. Ankershagen today, showing the parsonage where Schliemann lived from 1823–31 and the church where his father preached

3. The school in Neustrelitz *c.* 1853 where from 1833 and 1836 Schliemann successively attended the Gymnasium and the Realschule

4. Schliemann as a young merchant in St Petersburg, 1861

5. B. H. Schröder (1807–89), Schliemann's employer in Amsterdam

6. Schliemann in Eastern costume *c.* 1858

7. 'Priam's Treasure', attributed to 1873. Several of the pieces here were in fact found in 1871 or 1872

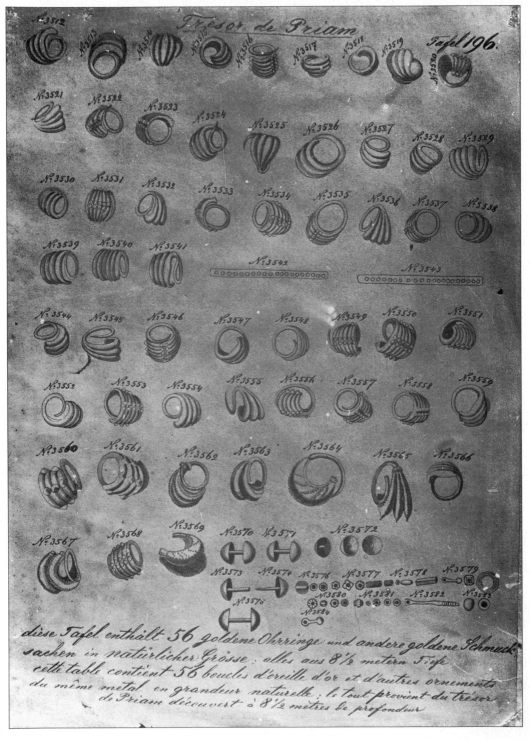

8. Drawings of gold rings and ear-rings found in 1873 and, as the heading and caption show, only later attributed to Priam's Treasure

9. Spyros Demetriou at the
Tomb of Clytemnestra, 1876

10. Sophia Schliemann at the Tomb of Clytemnestra, 1876 (engraving from *Mycenae*)

11. Rudolf Virchow (1821–1902), friend and adviser to Schliemann

12. Wilhelm Dörpfeld (1853–1940), Schliemann's collaborator and successor at Troy

13. Grave circle, Mycenae. Left-hand side of a photographic panorama of the excavation taken for the engravings in *Mycenae*

14. Detail of above showing Schliemann with two workmen, one standing in Shaft Grave I

15. 'Nestor's cup' found in Shaft Grave IV

16. Right-hand photograph of panorama of grave circle, Mycenae

17. Detail of above showing Schliemann with Panagiotis Stamatakis in foreground

18. Gold masks from Shaft Graves IV and V with the 'Mask of Agamemnon' in the centre

19. Iliou Melathron, Schliemann's house in Athens

20. Sophia Schliemann (*undated*)

21. Sophia with Andromache (*left*) and
Agamemnon, 1880

22. Schliemann speaking to the Society of Antiquaries at Burlington House, March 1877

23. Excavation buildings on Hisarlik, 1890, dubbed 'Schliemannopolis' by visitors

24. Hisarlik Conference II, 1890 (*left to right*) Rudolf Virchow, Wilhelm Grempler, Ghalil Edhem, Schliemann, Wilhelm Dörpfeld, Edith Calvert, Charles Babin, Mme Babin, Friedrich von Duhn, Karl Humann; (*seated*) Frank Calvert, Osman Hamdy Bey, Charles Waldstein

25. Schliemann's Cleopatra

26. One of Schliemann's
'owl-headed' vases from Troy

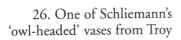

27. Priam's Treasure on display in Berlin's Ethnographic Museum, prior to the Second World War

28. The Grand Hotel, Naples, where Schliemann died

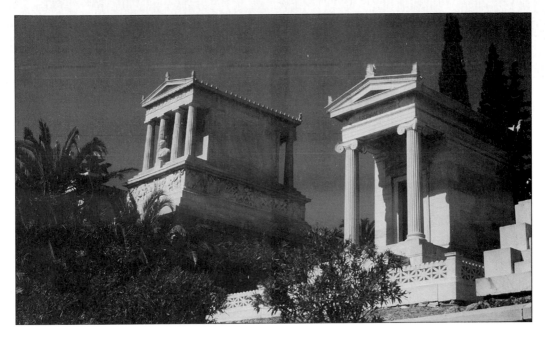

29. The Schliemann mausoleum in Athens (*left*)

30. Detail of north frieze on Schliemann's tomb, showing Heinrich and Sophia at an excavation with workers

31. Detail of south frieze showing the fighting over the body of Patroclus

32. Troy today

11

Ithaca, Troy and Reconciliation with Germany

THE REVIEWERS LOST NO time. The first reviews of *Mycenae* appeared a week after publication. In general, they were favourable. Almost everyone agreed that the finds were of great importance, even if few were prepared to see in the shaft graves the tombs of Agamemnon and his followers. There was great uncertainty as to the date that should be assigned to them. C.T. Newton, largely on the basis of Egyptian evidence, which pointed to a date of about 1400 BC, conservatively suggested the eleventh century BC as an approximate date.[1] He argued cogently that what the ancient traveller Pausanias and Schliemann called 'treasuries' were in fact tombs and suggested that they might represent an older period than that of the shaft graves.[2]

A.S. Murray, however, Newton's colleague at the British Museum, was reluctant to date the pottery earlier than the sixth century BC. Murray also pointed to a number of parallels between the finds at Mycenae and the Late Bronze Age finds at Hallstatt in Austria, concluding rather snidely: 'From all this one would be inclined to say that some Germanic tribe must have strayed to Mycenae, and on that theory it will seem no less than a whim of Fortune that their discoverer should be one of their own nationality.'[3] Newton dealt with these disparaging rumours directly: 'It was even insinuated that they had been brought from other localities and dexterously inserted in the soil of Mycenae by their discoverer; that he had, to use an American expression, "salted" his tombs. These doubts and insinuations would hardly be worth noticing here were it not that more than one distinguished archaeologist helped to give them currency, misled, as they have since frankly acknowledged, by first impressions.'[4]

A.H. Sayce, later Professor of Assyriology at Oxford, emphasized the similarities between the figures on the signet ring found south of the grave circle and those on Babylonian gems of the early period and on this basis suggested the thirteenth century BC as a date for the Mycenaean finds. He thought that Phoenician traders may have brought these Assyro-Babylonian influences to Greece. He dissented from Newton in dating the tholos tombs later than the shaft graves.[5]

About the German reviews Schliemann wrote to an English friend: 'I am happy to say that *all* the German critics speak very favourably of my book and highly appreciate it. I thought I should not live to see myself appreciated in Germany, because for years I have been ill-treated there. My former greatest enemy, the Deutsches Literaturblatt of Leipzig is now loudest in its praises.'[6] To Gladstone he wrote: 'My *Mycenae* has been everywhere well received and has probably had a larger sale than any archaeological work ever published. Messrs Scribner, Armstrong & Co., my New York publishers, write me: "Your *Mycenae* has met with the most flattering reception both by the press and public, and it is, and bids fair to remain, the leading publication of the year."'[7]

In the February issue of *Fraser's Magazine* there appeared an article by William C. Borlase, recounting his visit to Troy in 1875.[8] Borlase, who had employed Schliemann's servant Nikolaos Zaphyros Yannakis as his guide, was highly critical of Schliemann. He agreed with Simpson's observation that the building Schliemann identified as Priam's Palace absurdly sat across the Scaean Gate. Most damaging, however, was the following passage:

About twenty yards N. W. of the Scaean gate is the point where the so-called treasure of Priam was found, but the details of that discovery, as related by Nicholas Zaphyros, were so utterly different to Herr Schliemann's own account, that I find any attempt to reconcile them out of the question. To take an instance of discrepancy, in which I am able to verify the truth of Nicholas's account, Herr Schliemann states that, upon making the discovery, he sent all his workmen to dinner, and dug out the articles himself, adding, 'It would have been impossible for me to have removed the treasure without the help of my dear wife, who stood by me ready to pack the things which I cut out in her shawl, and carry them away.' Nicholas, on the other hand, told me that he had assisted in digging out the things, and in taking them to the house. On my asking what part Madame Schliemann took, he replied, '*She* was not here; she was at Athens at the time;' and on subsequent inquiry this was confirmed at the Dardanelles. I should still have thought there must have been some mistake, were it not that I know on the best authority that Herr Schliemann has himself owned in conversation with a gentleman holding a high and responsible position in European archaeological circles, and who permits me, if necessary, to use his name, that his wife was not really there, but that he brought in her name to give her a zest for archaeology. This little piece of embellishment is in every way unlucky, since Madame Schliemann was held to be a most important witness of the great discovery – In fact, her presence was the only corroboration of it until Nicholas Zaphyros affirmed to me that *he was there*. He, Nicholas, remembered that there was a large quantity of bronze articles, but his memory was hazy as to the rest of the treasure. He persisted in stating that it lay not 'on,' as stated by Herr Schliemann, but *close to* the outer side of the wall; that there were no signs whatever of its having been compacted into a chest, but, on the contrary, that it was contained in a little place built round with stones, and having flat stones to cover it; and lastly, that the key, reported as found 'close by the side of the articles,' came from the stratum of the time of Lysimachus (to which it much more properly belongs), at a distance of some 200 yards from the spot. The man's statements on these points were direct and graphic, and I think it is right to record them.

The accuracy of Borlase's account is attested by his quotation of the exact phrase ('a zest for archaeology') used by Schliemann in his letter of December 1873 to Newton, the distinguished archaeologist referred to. Also in that letter Schliemann had declared that Nikolaos had helped him remove the treasure and that Sophia had returned to Athens before the treasure was discovered. When Borlase's article reached Schliemann in Athens, he promptly wrote to Max Müller asking him 'to send a short general answer to my libellers *without* referring specially to the article in Frasers and without even mentioning its author's name . . . that I obtained a new firman for Hissarlik and shall resume the excavations there as soon as there is any safety for my life.'[9] Schliemann blamed Calvert for these difficulties: 'I have in the Troad a foul fiend by the name of Frank Calvert, who has given the text as well to the libel of Mr. Gallenga as to that of Wm. Simpson in Frasers Mag. of July last and to the libel now before us. That Calvert has been libelling me for years; I answered him in the *Guardian* three times showing by my last answer that he is of bad faith and a liar.' Schliemann went on to assure Müller that 'Nicolas never came into the trenches and never saw the treasure or the key of copper that was found with it' and that 'Mrs Schliemann of course was present and assisted me; she never left me'. Müller responded with a note to *The Times*, in which he announced that Schliemann had a new firman and intended to resume excavations at Troy, where his first concern would be to disprove his critics by laying open the area just north of the gate.[10]

Schliemann was correct in supposing that Calvert was the source of much of this damaging information. Though he would soon start interacting and corresponding with Schliemann in an apparently friendly manner, Calvert had clearly had his eyes opened by the treatment he had received over the Helios metope. In July 1878 he wrote to Simpson:

I do not leave an opportunity escape to open people's eyes to the humbug of Schliemann. A Minister and an Ambassador frankly gave me their opinion (when I accompanied them to Hissarlik) of S. One said he was a charlatan, the other, an impostor. I do not give names, not knowing whether I am at liberty to do so. Gallenga, the Times correspondent I had here with me three days – he was well indoctrinated – was furious at S., who he called the greatest impostor of the day. An article was written to the Times in that sense. To my disappointment and I expect to that of the correspondent all the truths were eliminated from the letter and quite a different version given of the Dr.[11]

In the same letter Calvert characterized Schliemann as 'fawning or biting venomously to suit his purpose.'

Early in April Gladstone must have been surprised to receive the following letter from Paris:

On the 16th March Mrs Schliemann was delivered here of a son, who is going to be baptized according to the Greek rite, and my wife joins me in warmly begging you to do me the great honour to be his godfather. You need, of course, not be present at his baptism, we get a person to represent you, only, pray write me at once what name you choose to give him. If you have no objection, I would beg you to give him an Homeric name, his sister having a Trojan one (Andromache).

Mrs Schliemann is still very ill; as soon as she is better, I shall continue the excavations at Troy or Mycenae.

Gladstone politely but firmly refused to be the child's godfather or to choose his name. Schliemann called the boy Agamemnon to commemorate his excavations at Mycenae.

A few days later Gladstone received a copy of the German edition of *Mycenae* with apologies from Schliemann that it was not dedicated to him:

Having found the treasure in Greece, I was obliged to dedicate the German account of the discovery to the greek king, for his friendship is important to me . . . The German book I translated myself from the English, the French is also a translation of the English. Mr Hachette . . . got it translated by Prof. Girordin, who, however, misunderstood the text in a thousand places and particularly your glorious preface . . . You have no idea how difficult you are to translate . . . In ancient Greek your phrases can be rendered with perfectly the same beauty which they have in English but in no modern language.

One wonders too what Gladstone made of Schliemann's remarks about Emile Burnouf, who was about to review the book:

My friend Burnouf is undoubtedly the greatest scholar in France and if he were not always carried away by the mania to show that the legend of Christ is merely derived from the holy fire kindled by friction from the 卐 and the 12 apostles are nothing else than the 12 months in the year, he would long since be president of the French Academy.

Relations between Heinrich and Sophia seem to have been difficult at this time. To ensure the best medical attention for his wife during her pregnancy, Schliemann brought her to Paris, where she remained until the child was born in March 1878. Between 22 August 1877 and his son's birth, however, Schliemann spent only twenty-seven days in Paris. In May Schliemann took Sophia and the children back to Athens. The birth of a second child had made it all the more necessary for his new house in Athens to be completed. Schliemann approached this task with his usual energy and passion for detail. Throughout 1878 and 1879, he was constantly receiving brochures from companies all over Europe and ordering furnishings and fitments for the house. Meanwhile he placed his family in a hotel in Kephissia and returned to Paris in June, from where he sent the following instructions to his agent Dendopoulos:

> If my wife and children continue to live in the hotel in Kephissia, you are author-ised to pay her 560 francs a week and *no more*. But the moment she leaves the hotel in Kephissia to stay in a private house, whether in the same village or at Athens . . . then you will pay her per week only: f. 210 for lodging and food, f. 70 for clothing, f. 70 for extras – a total of f. 350 per week . . . Please write me every week how my wife and children are doing, but no more telegrams. Tell me how they are lodged and how many of the Kastromenoses are with them . . .[12]

Further signs of domestic tension are clear from two letters in July. To Sophia's brother he wrote, 'She is always angry with me'; and to Dendopoulos:

> Tell Batieia [Sophia], I swear a great oath on the lives of our children . . . that I did not give the maid Clytaemnestra a dress, or any other item of women's clothing . . . On the day of my departure from Athens, seeing her coughing and utterly without warm clothes I gave her one of my coats, the old black frock-coat . . .[13]

In the summer of 1878 various bizarre theories started appearing to explain the surprising wealth of the shaft graves. Though most scholars had accepted a date around 1000 BC or earlier, a number were reluctant to put it so early. One suggested that the treasure was the share of the Persian booty acquired by the Mycenaeans after the Battle of Plataea (480 BC) and hidden in the tombs eleven years later when Mycenae was besieged by Argos (468 BC).[14] It is easy to laugh at such theories now that the facts of Mycenaean and Minoan civilization have become well established. It is important to remember, however, that it was not at all obvious in the 1870s that the Archaic period of Greece had been preceded by a civilization that was both wealthier and in some ways more advanced.

Another scholar suggested that the shaft grave finds were to be dated to the third or fourth century AD, having been brought to Mycenae by marauding Goths: 'the gold masks may have been taken from some Scythian graves, such having been found in Kertch. The gold cups, with arcades of round and ogival arches, and the gold signet rings, may have been loot from Byzantium.'[15] While this theory has long since been discredited, the question of the 'northern' appearance of some of the shaft grave objects is still discussed, though the northern migrations that may have given rise to these influences are now dated to the beginning of the second millennium BC.

Stamatakis continued excavations at Mycenae, where his attention shifted to the 'Treasury of Atreus'. The discovery of human bones together with gold ornaments similar to those discovered in the shaft graves seemed to establish that these 'treasuries' were in fact tombs, as many scholars had urged all along. This was confirmed by further finds of gold jewellery in another 'treasury' or tholos tomb near the Argive Heraeum, the sanctuary of Hera south of Mycenae.[16] Having already excavated the tholos tomb at Spata, Stamatakis was now in a position to make a real contribution, largely unacknowledged then or since, to the understanding of the chronology of the Mycenaean world. Seeing similarities between the finds of the tholos tombs on the one hand and those from *outside* the grave circle at Mycenae on the other, he reached the important and essentially correct conclusion that all these finds were contemporary with one another and later than those of the shaft graves.[17]

By 30 July Schliemann was in Constantinople negotiating for his permit. His chief support, as he later gratefully acknowledged by dedicating *Ilios* to him, came from the British Ambassador, Sir Austen Layard, the excavator of Nimrud. About 7 August, Calvert informed Simpson, Schliemann turned up at the Dardanelles

with a firman for Hissarlik. He demanded the authorities for a bodyguard of 50 men, which request was refused. Next day he left for Athens to return here shortly to commence operations. Priam's Palace, that damning piece of evidence, will form, I suppose, the first object to be destroyed by his pick. I was told that Dr. S. has consented to give up everything he finds in the projected excavations to the Turkish govt. This information may be incorrect. If it be true he is up to some dodge.[18]

Schliemann did not return from Athens immediately. Instead, he went off to Ithaca, where he excavated at various sites. After carefully examining and reflecting upon the topography of the Polis Bay area, Schliemann concluded that Odysseus' capital could not have been located there. Nevertheless, in the interests of science he sank many shafts but found nothing earlier than the sixth century BC. Here again, as at Bunarbashi in 1868, it looks like a case of being wise after the event. At the St George site on the saddle of Mount Aetos, he found impressive polygonal walls but only classical pottery. At the summit of Aetos there were traces of what he considered 'chambers of the large cyclopean mansion, which is said to have stood there and is commonly called "the castle of Ulysses".'[19] Just below the summit, within an enclosing circuit wall, there was space, he reckoned, for 2000 houses. Here he found the reasonably well-preserved ruins of 190 houses. He dug here with thirty workmen for two weeks, with little success. The highly exposed nature of the site had caused severe erosion. The fragments of pottery that turned up did not resemble Mycenaean ware but rather that of Troy I and II.

Near the south-east tip of the island is a white cliff, traditionally identified with Homer's Korax (Raven Rock), with a spring below it – Homer's Arethusa, where Eumaeus watered his pigs. In the rocky plain above the cliff Schliemann excavated what seemed to him to be stables, 'which must have given to Homer the idea for the twelve pig sties built by the divine swineherd Eumaeus.'[20]

At Hisarlik Schliemann had already built accommodation for the overseers, his workmen, and himself and a storeroom for the finds on the north-west slope. He was to assume all expenses, which amounted to £500 a month. Two thirds of the finds were to go to the Imperial Museum in Constantinople and one third to Schliemann. The key to the storeroom was to be kept by the Turkish overseer. Since the Turko-Russian war had just finished and the countryside was still unsafe, Schliemann hired ten gendarmes for protection. Excavations began on 30 September.

> My endeavours were principally directed to the excavation of the large mansion to the west and north-west of the gate, and to that of the gate itself, which, contrary to what my severe critics repeatedly pretended, was not barred by a solid wall of masonry, but merely by a huge mass of wood ashes. The latter was carefully examined by Capt. Beamish, Lieut. H.C. Sayce and other officers of HMS *Pallas*, all of whom would be happy to undertake my defence should the attacks be renewed.[21]

It is noticeable how much more circumspect Schliemann has become – no more 'Priam's Palace' and 'Scaean Gate'. But the old fire has not gone. Clearly smarting from Simpson's jibe about 'Priam's pigsty', Schliemann lost no time, as Calvert had predicted, in removing the mud building sitting across the gates. Whatever the officers of HMS *Pallas* saw, both *Troy and its Remains* and *Ilios* clearly show a solid mud building blocking the gate.[22]

> The large mansion I identified with that of ancient Troy's last chief or king, because I had found in my former excavations in it or close to it a large treasure and a great deal of beautiful pottery; but now I maintain that identity with still more powerful reasons than before, having again discovered in it or close to it three small and one large treasure of gold ornaments.

For Schliemann it was the presence of significant 'treasures' that stamped the building as the palace. This explains why in June 1873, when he had to change the findspot of Priam's Treasure or have the entire city plan redrawn, he could not bring himself to say that the treasure had been found just outside the city wall, as the plan unmistakably shows, for then the treasure could not plausibly validate the building as a palace. Instead, he fudged. By saying that he found the treasure 'on' the wall, the treasure could still be associated with the palace and 'on' was sufficiently vague that the plan did not need to be redrawn.

The four treasures found in 1878 were all substantial, comprising fifty earrings, numerous small beads, bracelets, pins, etc., all of gold. Many of the pieces, particularly the ear-rings and the beads, were similar, and often identical, to earlier finds. The main difference was the prominence now of pieces with spiral designs that recalled Mycenaean finds. While this very fact might seem to invite suspicion, there is no good reason for suspecting any of these pieces, as similar finds have been made at these levels by other archaeologists either at Hisarlik or at other Anatolian sites.

More suspicious perhaps is the timing of their discovery. On 9 November Schliemann, mortified that none of the four reports he had sent to *The Times* had been published, wrote to John Murray, asking him to forward to the editor of *The Times* a letter enclosed which requested that the four reports be returned. Three days later Schliemann wrote again to Murray: 'I trust that the three treasures I discovered yesterday, and of which I send today a detailed account to Prof. Chenery of The Times will induce him to publish all my letters from Troy, and I therefore beg you today by telegraph to destroy enclosure for said gentleman.'[23] Once again, most of the season's valuable finds were made in the last two weeks of excavation, three of the four treasures being found on 11 November.

On the houses on the east side of the great north–south trench Schliemann uncovered vitrified floors. Dr Edward Moss of HMS *Research* attributed the vitrification to the action of intense heat on the clay, the straw in the clay supplying the silica. Schliemann made much of this discovery in 1878. Ironically, when Frank Calvert had commented on the vitrified floors that had been uncovered in his earlier excavations Schliemann had vehemently denied their existence.[24] Another interesting find this year comprised two elaborate hairpins (*Ilios*, nos. 834 and 849). In his first report to *The Times* (27 November 1878) Schiemann attributed them to a level later than Homeric Troy, partly because the pottery with which they were associated belonged to a later period. In his later reports, however, no mention is made of the pottery and the pins are confidently assigned to Troy II.[25] Finally, what most astonished Schliemann in this season's excavations was the discovery of 'billions' of sea-shells at prehistoric occupation levels.

Schliemann wrestled with the Turkish authorities over the time, place and manner of the division of the finds. He wanted it to be done at Hisarlik rather than at Constantinople, on 20 rather than 27 November and with Kadry Bey representing the Turkish government rather than another official. Kadry Bey was the Turkish overseer of the excavations, whose salary was paid by Schliemann. Finally, after several letters to Sir Austen Layard, he got his way. Schliemann took a selection of his share promptly to London to exhibit in the South Kensington Museum alongside his earlier finds.[26] The Turkish share of the 1878 finds is on display in the Archaeological Museum in Istanbul along with other finds from Troy.

Schliemann stayed only a couple of days in London. On his way back to Athens he stopped in Paris to give a talk at the Académie des Inscriptions et Belles Lettres to coincide with the belated appearance of the French edition of his book on Mycenae. From there he wrote to John Murray, sketching the outline for his new book on Troy. He suggested as a title, *Ithaca and Troy*.[27]

In January 1879 A.S. Murray of the British Museum, in an article in *The Nineteenth Century*, renewed his attack on Schliemann's interpretation of the finds at Mycenae. Schliemann's reaction was characteristic. He wrote at once to John Murray: 'That foul fiend was a year ago crushed by Lindenschmit of Mainz but he has revived and must now be morally killed.' He asked Murray to send copies of the article at once to Sayce, Lenormant, Burnouf and Lindenschmit. Schliemann wanted Murray to have Lenormant's response printed in the *Athenaeum* and Lindenschmit's and Burnouf's ('translated as cheaply as possible') in the *Builder*. Schliemann himself would tell Sayce and Schels where to send theirs. Like a general deploying his troops, Schliemann drew up his scholars to do battle for him. He knew that some of them at least would carry out his orders. They were being paid for their services.[28] Also in January Schliemann received a letter that marked a significant turning-point in his life. It came from Dr Rudolf Virchow.

After meeting Virchow briefly in 1875 Schliemann had invited him in August 1876 to drop everything and 'in the interests of science' come and join him at Mycenae. Virchow had not done so and had sent his apologies only six months later. He had been very busy. While Schliemann had been digging at Mycenae, Virchow had been attending learned conferences at Jena, Budapest, Brussels and Hamburg, teaching pathology in the medical faculty of the University of Berlin, where he had recently been made Dean, and serving as a city councillor for Berlin and as a member of the Prussian parliament. In addition he was President of the Berlin Anthropological Society and the editor of two scholarly journals. Partly to make amends for the late apology, but no doubt principally out of genuine regard for his achievements, Virchow saw to it that Schliemann was appointed an honorary member of the German Anthropological Society, in September 1877.[29] This was more than just another feather in Schliemann's cap. It provided him with an entrée into the German intellectual establishment.

Schliemann had decided that it would lend credibility to his excavations if he could persuade some well-known figures to participate. Accordingly, over the winter he had invited Burnouf, Lenormant and Sayce to join him at Troy when his excavations resumed there in the spring of 1879, offering them travelling expenses, food and lodging, as well as a generous salary.[30] Only Burnouf accepted, for Sayce had teaching duties and Lenormant did not want to leave Paris. In November 1878 Schliemann had informed Virchow briefly of the results of the 1878 season, offering to send him samples of the vitrified flooring. He indicated that excavation would resume on 1 March 1879 but did not ask Virchow to join him.[31] He must have been pleasantly surprised therefore to receive Virchow's letter in January, gratefully accepting the offer of samples and politely asking if it would be all right if he came to Troy in the spring.[32] Schliemann responded with enthusiasm and insisted on paying Virchow's travel expenses.[33]

Thus began the most important friendship of Schliemann's life. Schliemann and Virchow came from similar backgrounds and were the same age, Virchow being just three months older. His home state, Pomerania, was adjacent to Mecklenburg. Both states were often looked down on by other Germans for their backwardness. Virchow did not come from a privileged background. Since his father was just a small farmer, he received his tertiary education at an institute specifically set up to provide free medical training to talented children of the poor. He was a compulsive worker. In his final year at school he wrote an essay entitled: 'A Life Full of Effort and Work is not a Burden but a Blessing'. Like Schliemann, Virchow suffered at the hands of the German establishment, in his case for his liberal political views.[34] By 1879 he was an experienced archaeologist, having conducted excavations at several pre-historic sites in north-eastern Germany from 1867 onwards. It was his dis-covery of urns with human faces that brought about their first meeting in Berlin in August 1875. The sudden surge in correspondence from January 1879 onwards marks a change in their relationship. Only four letters were exchanged in the period 1876–8, but eighty in 1879 alone, and 114 in 1880.

In his series of articles 'Memories of Schliemann' in *Gartenlaube* Virchow provides us with an excellent picture of both men and of the atmosphere of the 1879 excavations from the day in early April when he and Burnouf arrived:

We had both landed at the Dardanelles on the same day, although coming from quite different directions. Schliemann greeted us: 'Now you do as you please; at my place it's a republic.' He really meant it; so each was able to carry out the tasks he had set himself. M. Burnouf pursued his astronomical and geodetic studies, sketched plans, and ascertained the arrangement of the ancient houses. I did my researches on the geology of the Troad and particularly on the development of the Trojan plain, on the river-courses, springs, people, animals, and plants. Only at the excavations and at the evening meal did we all meet together. But Schliemann's stamina easily outstripped ours. By seven in the morning, when we both emerged from our wooden cabin, Schliemann had already a good part of his day's work behind him. Before sunrise he had ridden to the Hellespont (¾ hour away), to take his daily bathe in the sea. After his return he had had his breakfast, overseen the roll-call of the workmen, made the arrangements for the day's excavations, and when we were climbing up the hill, we found him positioned at a vantage-point, keeping watch on all sides and determining the course of the work with new instructions. Then we dispersed as each saw fit, and ate at whatever time suited, and only on days when, usually in the afternoon, some more remote spot was to be investigated, did we get together and ride out as a group.

There was only one circumstance in which Schliemann freed himself from supervising his workers and it is of particular importance for our assessment of him. It was not long before it was known throughout the nearer part of the Troad that a 'great Hakim' (doctor) was staying at Hissarlik. Schliemann himself had contributed not a little to spreading this news. He was tireless in caring for the sick. Normally, he treated them himself, insofar as his supplies permitted and his own experience offered him definite guidance, but as I was now at hand, he brought the sick to me and acted as my interpreter and medical orderly. Every day there were more invalids but he never failed to provide this service. Even on our short trips he curbed that otherwise virtually uncontrollable impatience of his. I will never forget how, quite late at night, when we were on our way back home from a long ride, he went with me into the huts of the neighbouring villagers and patiently held the lamp, while I completed my examinations and saw to the necessary treatment. There was no proper doctor closer than about ten hours away . . .[35]

Virchow then goes on to describe the difficulties he had in developing a collection of flora of the Troad.

> It took no little effort to bring all these plants home in tolerable condition and even more to put them in order and dry them. I often stayed up late at night working at this, and the guards, who stood around our hut, were astonished to see a light so late at my little window. Schliemann learned about this from the guards and though he strongly advised against working late at night, he began to place more and more importance on the systematic study of the flora of the region, which at that time was little known. He wanted to include an overview of the subject in the new edition of 'Ilios' and when he was later involved in writing this work he continuously pressed me for the list. I informed him that this was not so easy and that Professor Ascherson, to whom I had given the entire collection after my return, needed time to determine his findings, particularly since there were a couple of new species. But even the news that one of these was to be named after him and the other after me did not moderate his impatience. On the contrary, on 29 October 1879 he wrote to me: 'Both the unknown plants must be named after you, the scholarly researcher. To call them after someone who had nothing to do with them and understands nothing about them would be a parody, of which you are not capable.' This however did not deter Mr. Ascherson from establishing a *Fritillaria Schliemanni* and from fixing on an *Astragulus Virchowii* for me.

Virchow attributed their friendship to the bond that developed in 1879 during a strenuous trip on horseback up Mount Ida and its environs.

> One day we had arrived at Assos on a ride we took together through the Troad. The hill on which the famous bastion was built is an old volcano, the coast before it was chockfull of huge blocks of stones. Nonetheless we had to swim. But it was a dangerous undertaking. We could easily break our legs and there was no prospect that we would get into open water. He showed me what to do. He laid himself down headfirst on the stone and gradually pushed himself forward until at least his body was covered with water. That did not happen, however, until a few hundred metres from the shore. Several hours later, about midnight, we boarded a small felucca to return by sea along the entire Trojan coast to the Hellespont. Our trip began in the face of contrary winds and our captain (Reis) had to tack between the island Mytilene [Lesbos] and the mainland. Everyone was seasick; I was in bad shape; Schliemann was lying quite still beside me in the bilge. When dawn came and we were flying along the coast from Alexandria Troas with a favourable breeze, he finally got up and showed how he was soaked through on his right side. He had been lying in bilge-water but had not wanted to disturb me. Before noon we came to Karanlik Limani, a bay on the Hellespont, and Schliemann's first desire was for another bathe. He wanted me to accompany him and I complied. I have to confess

that it was refreshing to plunge into the crystal-clear waters of the bay. But scarcely had we put our clothes on again, when he became restless. We had been away from Hissarlik almost eight days and the excavations had proceeded in the meantime. What could have happened there while we were gone! Schliemann started to move so fast that at first I could not keep up with him. Then I made a big effort and over-took him. It became a marathon and we didn't stop until we stood on top of the mound again.

From these days dates the personal, I might almost say physical, regard that Schliemann held for me. In the days before Assos we had been on a riding trip, in which we had at times been up to fourteen hours in the saddle. He said to me one day: 'I would not have believed it of you. You are the first German professor to have done anything like that here.'[36]

The 1879 season at Hisarlik itself was rather disappointing. A great deal of earth was removed, particularly in the north-east sector, and some progress was made in determining the course of the circuit wall. Schliemann's 'Great Tower of Ilium' to the east of the Scaean Gate was shown to be merely two different stages of the circuit wall. Two 'treasures' were found, both 'in the presence of Virchow and Burnouf', the first on 10 April in the north-central part of the mound, and the second, also in April, on the circuit wall, a little east of Priam's Palace.[37] Schliemann attributed both these finds to the 'Trojan' (i.e. Homeric) stratum, Troy II. An impressive basket pendant ear-ring in the first treasure, however, was only spotted by Virchow in a barrow of debris as it was being wheeled away; so that piece at least should be regarded as an unstratified find. The other items in this small treasure, three small orna-mented, gold discs rather like those from Grave III at Mycenae, were found at a depth probably too shallow for Troy II.[38] The second treasure, the actual discovery of which was in all likelihood not witnessed by either Burnouf or Virchow, was found at a deeper level.[39] Considerably larger, it comprised three more basket ear-rings, two with pendants, one without, a number of shell ear-rings, and a small silver 'frying-pan' like the bronze 'shield' 'frying-pan' of Priam's Treasure.

The main focus of the work in 1879, however, was on the plain itself – its geological history and the tumuli scattered about it. Strabo reports that the plain had been an inlet of the sea at the time of the Trojan War and that since then it had been filled in by silt brought down by the river. Schliemann was eager to disprove this statement, for it was one of the chief arguments against the Troy-Hisarlik theory. If the sea had come up to the walls of Troy, how could the Greeks and Trojans have ranged back and forth on the plain between the city and the sea, as Homer tells us? Schliemann, Burnouf and Virchow sank shafts in different parts of the plain and the general conclusion reached was that there had once been an inland lake in the northern part of the plain and that the Menderes (Homer's Scamander) had flowed much closer to Hisarlik. Thanks to a series of core samples taken in 1977 we now know that in prehistoric times the plain was covered by an extensive arm of the sea, which reached up to Hisarlik in the Troy VI period and considerably further upstream in Troy II, but which by Strabo's own time (*c.* 60 BC–AD 21) had been reduced to a very small bay at the river mouth.[40] Strabo therefore was correct and the findings of Schliemann, Virchow and Burnouf, based as they were on inadequate samples, were in error. Virchow, however, soon began to suspect the truth.

Schliemann excavated in 1879 six of the tumuli, the so-called 'Heroic Tombs', located in different parts of the Trojan plain. Four of these yielded nothing except a few animal bones and, in one case, some Roman tiles.[41] At Ujek Tepe, about 4½ miles south-west of Hisarlik and by far the largest tumulus on the plain, he sank a vertical shaft from the summit and started a horizontal tunnel to meet it from the north side. At the bottom of the shaft he found a tower-like, square structure of stone, thought by Burnouf and himself to be older than the mound itself, which from pottery they dated to the later Roman period. Schliemann identified the mound with that raised by Caracalla for his favourite, Festus, whom he allegedly killed for the pleasure of holding in his honour games that would rival those given by Achilles for Patroclus. Perhaps the most significant tomb, however, was Beshika Tepe, located close to Beshika Bay. Here Schliemann found burnished pottery that seemed to be contemporary with the earliest levels at Troy (I and II).[42]

After Virchow left Troy at the end of April he stopped in Athens, where he was hospitably received by Sophia. Since Agamemnon was still a baby, she had not participated in the excavations in either 1878 or 1879. Virchow found her charming. Complying with Schliemann's request, he gave her a medical examination and reported to Schliemann that she was in good health, though perhaps a little overwrought. He attributed this partly to Schliemann's absence and urged him to see more of her and, perhaps by cultivating society a bit more, to ensure that she had more fun in her life. He prescribed drinking Kissingen water for a month and an hour's walk every day.[43] Since Kissingen water was not to be had in Athens, Schliemann decided that both he and Sophia would go to Bad Kissingen in Bavaria later in the summer and both of them would take the cure.

At the beginning of June a young American architecture student named Francis Bacon arrived at Hisarlik. He and some friends were cruising the Aegean by yacht and were on their way to Assos, where they would later conduct excavations (1881–3). Bacon was also destined to marry Frank

Calvert's niece and it is through this connection that some of Calvert's collection of antiquities are today housed in Worcester, Massachusetts. Bacon found the excavations

> mighty interesting . . . There were quantities of immense jars used, perhaps, for storing wine and grain. These were left just as found, propped up by the earth around them. They were as tall as I am. I loafed around there all day! Went to a fine spring under the hill, sat in the shade of a fig tree, and ate my lunch out of a New York *Herald*. In the afternoon Dr. Schliemann came riding up. He spoke to me, and I asked him some questions about some architectural fragments. He was very pleasant, made me come into his room, had the servant bring coffee, etc., and showed me what he had found lately. He was just giving up the work for the summer and was going to Athens the next day. He took me all over the excavations, and was very enthusiastic. He swears by Homer![44]

Back in Athens a few days later Schliemann reminded Virchow of his promise to recommend a well-educated young German woman who could serve as both a governess for Andromache and a companion for Sophia. A considerable amount of correspondence was devoted to this topic in June and July, as Schliemann travelled to Paris and on to Bad Kissingen. Virchow reported that he had found a young woman, Fräulein Mellien, who appeared suitable, and despite his reluctance to become entangled in a situation where he would feel responsibilites to both parties, he found himself interviewing her and generally acting as middleman in the complicated process of negotiating her duties and salary.[45] Even her name had to be negotiated. Schliemann insisted on a Homeric name but Fräulein Mellien refused to be called Hecuba. Eventually, the name Briseis was settled upon.[46] Since, however, the young woman had made it clear that she would not be Agamemnon's nursemaid, Schliemann soon turned to Virchow for help in finding a suitable young Swiss 'bonne'.[47] Amazingly, Virchow and his wife again allowed themselves to become involved. This time they did not find anyone suitable. Schliemann hired an English woman instead.[48]

Once Virchow began expressing doubts about the geological formation of the Troad, Schliemann, whose views on the matter had already been dogmatically stated in *The Times*, became alarmed that his colleague might publish a contradictory interpretation. He insisted that they both go back to the Troad in October and make deeper borings to settle the matter and if Virchow could not go himself, he should send a competent geologist in his stead. He asked Virchow to write at once to the German ambassador in Constantinople to get a firman for this project. Schliemann himself fired off a number of letters to various people, including the long-suffering Layard, to secure permission and acquire the necessary equipment. After meeting Virchow in London in September, however, he seems to have been persuaded that further borings would be unlikely to settle the matter. When Virchow eventually expressed his views in *Ilios*, to which he contributed two appendices, he directly contradicted Schliemann by stating that in prehistoric times the plain had been covered by a branch of the sea.[49]

Hanai Tepe, the mound near the Calvert farm about four miles south of Hisarlik, was being excavated by Frank Calvert, who had cut a trench diagonally through the middle. Schliemann paid the wages of Calvert's workmen on condition that he received an equal share of the finds. These finds included quite a few skeletons but neither gold objects nor anything of any artistic value. Schliemann told Calvert that he was sending his half-share to Virchow for the Berlin Museum and persuaded Calvert do the same.[50] To reward Calvert for his generosity Schliemann urged Virchow to 'get a little medal for him, for that sort of finery really means something to him and he can always be useful.'[51] Virchow did his best, but since Calvert was not a German citizen, there were many bureaucratic obstacles. Schliemann doggedly pursued the matter, repeatedly reminding Virchow of the need of a medal for Calvert. On the one hand, it is agreeable to see Schliemann fighting on behalf of Calvert. On the other, one wonders at Virchow's patience.

The cure at Bad Kissingen seemed to do Sophia some good, though Schliemann found it debilitating and was unable to get as much work done on his book as he had hoped. On 22 July, Bismarck, who was also at Kissingen, invited Schliemann to dinner. They discussed the excavations at both Troy and Mycenae and afterwards Schliemann sent him a complimentary copy of *Mycènes*.[52] The Chancellor observed that the sheer size of the great *pithoi* (pitchers) that had been found suggested a fairly high degree of civilization, as vessels of that size were not easy either to create or to fire. Schliemann was careful to immortalize his remarks in *Ilios*.[53]

Throughout 1878 and 1879 Schliemann had been trying to have himself appointed as unpaid American consul in Athens. To this end he coaxed his acquaintances, John M. Francis, the former US Minister to Greece, and Kate Field, a publicist for Bell Telephones, to make representations on his behalf. In return for the expected honour he promised he 'would of course amply reward the Smithsonian Hall in Washington by gifts of antiquities.'[54] On 29 August 1879 he wrote enthusiastically to John Murray about prospective sales in America: 'If they make me Consul, as appears most likely, the sale there will be immense.' Ironically, by this time the US government had already decided not to give him the appointment.

By early September, just before showing Virchow around his Trojan collection in London, Schliemann had reached a fateful decision – to bequeath the entire collection to Germany.[55] He wrote to his lawyer in Paris and altered his will accordingly. On the same day he wrote to Virchow: 'You have reconciled me with Germany. As a result Germany receives a considerable bequest in my will, which I am rewriting today. No one but Virchow could have brought this about!'[56] Virchow, however, denies having influenced this decision: 'I never gave him a speech about his duty to remember his fatherland and I never asked him to remove his Trojan collection from England and bring it to Germany. Only when he himself had such thoughts and he revealed them in my presence, mainly in the form of an observation, he found in me, of course, a joyful echo. I was the more ready to give open expression to it knowing that Frau Schliemann had long been influencing her husband in this direction.'

What then brought about this sudden reconciliation with Germany? Though Schliemann's effusive remarks to Virchow are clearly designed to flatter and are therefore suspect, it seems clear nonetheless that Virchow's friendship played a significant and probably decisive role. Virchow later recalled an incident during their trip to Mount Ida in 1879.

> One morning, when, separated from our companions, we were riding along through the foothills of Mt Ida, surrounded by burgeoning springtime and the song of the nightingale, he broke the silence with the question whether he should not will his collections to Germany: Germany was the country where Homer was most widely and deeply appreciated and nowhere would his collection do more good than in Berlin. I merely expressed my agreement, but I had the pleasure of not taking my leave of him before having obtained from him the positive agreement that after his death the collection was to come here (to Berlin).[57]

During his stay at Hisarlik Virchow would evoke memories of Schliemann's childhood by throwing in words or expressions in their shared native *Plattdeutsch* that Schliemann had not heard for decades.[58] Undoubtedly, too, his dinner with Bismarck must have made Schliemann realize that he was now a respected figure in his own country, where once scholars had laughed at him. Perhaps Bismarck had even hinted that if he gave his finds to a German museum, his country would find a suitable way to show its gratitude.

In August Schliemann planned an elaborate dinner to honour Virchow on his visit to London. He wrote to John Murray:

> I intend to give on about the 18th Sept. a banquet in honour of Virchow at Lanam's Hotel, to which you yourself, your son and Mr Cooke are warmly invited. Mr Fergusson and Prof. Chenery of the Times also promised to come. But, pray, make

me a list of all the other personages whom I should invite, for I think that no man thinks himself too high to meet Virchow. Thus, pray, consider whether I could invite Lord Salisbury, Mr. Gladstone, the Archbishop of Canterbury, Sir Alcock, Mr Reed, Dr. John Percy, Prof. Max Müller, Mr Newton . . . because by all these excellent men I have been invited before.[59]

When Virchow learned of these plans, he was horrified and begged Schliemann to cancel them, threatening not to come if they were not changed. He did not mind meeting Schliemann's friends, he said, and in fact would welcome doing so, but not with himself as the focus of attention: 'The more I am in the background, the better.'[60]

On 20 September, during Virchow's visit to London, Schliemann received urgent news from Sophia, who was holidaying with the children in Boulogne: Agamemnon was dangerously ill. Schliemann took a night ferry over, saw his son and, presumably, the French doctor, and promptly telegraphed Virchow: 'Acute cholerine, thirst, diarrhoea, vomiting, feverish. Mixture chalk with laudanum. Poultices. You can save our son. We expect you impatiently tomorrow.' Virchow stopped at Boulogne on the 22nd on his way to Brussels and, as Schliemann wrote to Virchow's wife, 'rescued little Agamemnon; without him the boy would have died.'[61]

Three days later Schliemann was back in London, consulting the famous goldsmith and jeweller Carlo Giuliano about the techniques used in making some of the more elaborate pieces of Trojan jewellery. He bought a fine necklace and bracelet from him and sent them as a birthday present to Virchow's daughter, Adèle. No doubt, Schliemann intended this very expensive gift as a token of his gratitude to Virchow. But Virchow was annoyed at this lack of tact that inevitably put his own present in the shade: 'You have robbed me of the priority of a father's idea more than Jacob robbed his brother Esau of the priority of their father's blessing . . . The things that you sent naturally far surpassed mine, but that is the very point that puts you in the wrong. I beg you most emphatically to give up this practice so that I can still continue to deal with you as a friend – giving that up would cost me a great deal.'[62] In his reply to this letter Schliemann ignored the issue completely and acted as if nothing had happened. For her birthday the following year, he sent Adèle a cheque for 1000 marks. Virchow reprimanded Schliemann again and sent the cheque back.[63]

Back in Athens in October Schliemann heard some important news. When Sayce had visited Hisarlik in the summer with Frank Calvert, they had both concluded after a close examination of the excavations that the stratum of the 'burnt city', which had produced the most valuable finds, including Priam's

Treasure, was not the second occupation level (or 'city' as they called it) but rather the third. Both Sayce and Calvert communicated this to Schliemann by letter and Sayce published his views in the *Athenaeum*.[64]

Schliemann immediately adopted this finding, for he had observed a significant difference between the earlier and later pottery of Troy I. In *Ilios* he divided the former Troy I level in two, calling only the lower section Troy I and the upper section Troy II. The burnt layer, formerly designated Troy II, now became Troy III, former Troy III became Troy IV and so on. Since in all his later publications he attributed the burnt layer to Troy II and restored their former labels to all the levels above that, I shall ignore the confusing and anomalous terminology of *Ilios* and continue to designate the burnt layer Troy II.[65] Schliemann never changed his mind about which stratum was the 'Homeric' one. He merely changed the label with which he designated the stratum.

As he reflected on his plan to will his Trojan collection to Germany, the thought seems to have occurred to Schliemann that he was throwing away a valuable bargaining chip. Why not give it to Germany *in his lifetime* and make sure that he got something in return? Some such reasoning seems to lie behind his letter of 11 December to Virchow:

> In strictest confidence I want you to know that I intend to donate my Trojan collection to the Berlin Museum just a year or two after the publication of my book on condition that the rooms where it is exhibited be attractive and suitable and forever bear my name – terms that must be guaranteed by an act of the German parliament. This must remain strictly confidential for it would do me considerable damage in England.[66]

Virchow replied on 27 December: 'I have communicated to [Museum] Director Schöne your secret regarding earlier donation of the collection; he has to know. As we are going to build a new Anthropological and Ethnographical Museum, your wish to have special rooms for the collection is perfectly feasible.'[67]

12

Ilios, *Orchomenos and German Honours*

IN THE SUMMER OF 1879 Schliemann had sent John Murray a description of his proposed book, which he intended to be a comprehensive account of all his excavations at Troy and 'altogether scientific and not any more in the form of a journal like *Troy and its Remains*.'[1] It was already beginning to take shape in his mind: an introduction by Virchow, who would also do sections on the flora and mineralogy; the topography (with the assistance of Burnouf); the history of Ilion; then the results of the excavations. He planned to begin work on the book in August 1879 and expected it to be ready for publication in November 1880. Most of 1880 was spent in writing, revising, editing and proof-reading his new book.

He decided to ask Sayce to serve as editor rather than Philip Smith, the editor of *Troy* and *Mycenae*, and wrote to him on 11 August 1879: 'Would you against a fair remuneration assist me in editing it? Your name must not appear on the title page as editor, but all the observations you may make shall be put to your credit.'[2] By the end of December Schliemann had decided on the title – *Ilios*. Before the first galley proofs began to appear in February 1880 Schliemann sent Sayce a cheque for £100 together with an explanation of what was expected of him:

> Grammatical blunders you will find but a few. But you will find many passages which ought to be transferred to other places. You will find others which must be given in footnotes. You will see where I have used certain authors too much, others too little. You may find certain passages, which must be struck out as unworthy of such a book. Now you have carte-blanche to do as you please; my only request is to put a book out such as may be worthy of Troy.[3]

Burnouf and Virchow were also to help in the editorial process. Philip Smith was hired to do the more routine editing. On 30 September 1879 Smith assured Schliemann that he understood his position: 'I have no desire in any way to be regarded as *Editor* of the work, but as was understood in the case of *Mycenae*, merely as assisting you in the preparation of the work for press. You may rely on me not to speak of my cooperation with you in any other light than this, nor to speak of it unnecessarily at all.'[4] While the insistence on anonymity was a little unusual, there was nothing improper in these arrangements. Nor should it be thought that any of these editors was in any sense a 'ghost-writer' for Schliemann.

In late December 1879 Schliemann dispatched the first 570 pages of his manuscript to John Murray to be edited by Smith and sent to the printers. Copies of the galley proofs were then to be sent directly to Virchow, Burnouf and Sayce who would return them to Schliemann with their comments, corrections and additions. He would consider their suggestions and send back his composite version to Smith for final editing. In March 1880 Schliemann confided to John Murray his assessments of his collaborators. 'Burnouf is a zero as a reviser; he has not changed a word, nor suggested an idea. Virchow is precious for the ideas he submits and the changes he suggests. But the most precious of all is Sayce, who desires to make the book in the highest degree worthy of its author and the great subject it treats and who therefore makes ten times more corrections than Ph. Smith.'[5] It is fascinating to watch this process in operation. The discussion of the introductory autobiography is particularly revealing.

The introduction to *Ilios* was designed to show 'how the work of my later life has been the natural consequence of the impressions I received in my earliest childhood; and that, so to say, the pickaxe and the spade for the excavation of Troy and the royal tombs of Mycenae were both forged and sharpened in the little German village in which I passed eight years of my earliest childhood.'[6] In other words Schliemann wanted to show an early interest not only in Homer and in the sites associated with the Homeric heroes but in actually *excavating Troy*. As we have seen, the groundwork for this new version of his childhood had already been laid in 1875, apparently as a reaction to Calvert's letter to the *Guardian*. Now new details were added. For instance, he recounted how, when he spoke to his childhood friends of one day excavating Troy, he was laughed at by everyone except the Meincke sisters, Louise and Minna, who listened to his stories with rapt attention. He and Minna took dancing lessons together and developed a warm attachment to one another: 'It was agreed that as soon as we were grown up we would marry, and then at once set to work to explore all the mysteries of Ankershagen; excavating the golden cradle, the silver basin, the vast treasures hidden by Henning, then Henning's sepulchre, and lastly Troy.'[7] Smith suggested keeping the Minna section, as it showed an early interest in archae-ology, but omitting the dancing lessons and other extraneous material.[8] Virchow had reservations about the propriety of identifying a woman who was still alive and then appearing to fault her for not remaining true to her childhood promise to marry. He urged the omission of her last name and the information on her later life. Perhaps the tone of the Minna episode was modified in places but her full name and marital history remained in *Ilios*, as did the dancing lessons. John Murray himself wanted the entire autobio-graphical section omitted but this was unacceptable to Schliemann. The autobiography, he argued, 'is as interesting as [it is] instructive; nay, for ages to come the book will be bought by thousands merely for the lessons in the autobiography.'[9] Here Schliemann showed a keener grasp of what the public wanted to read than his publisher, for the autobiography proved by far the most successful part of book. Later updated and reprinted separately as Schliemann's *Selbstbiographie*, it was avidly read by generations of Germans, for it provided an inspiring example of a boy who grew up to achieve, by hard work and perseverance, his romantic childhood dream. Murray allowed the autobiography but, fearing the book's sales might be adversely affected, saw to it that all reference to Schliemann's first marriage and divorce was sup-pressed.[10]

In February Schliemann had an embarrassing misunderstanding with the Athenaeum Club in London. Ignoring the advice of James Fergusson, the noted architectural historian, he tried to buy his way to club membership. He wrote to the Secretary: 'I beg leave to remind you of your kind promise to endeavour to get me elected member of your celebrated Athenaeum club in May next. It is distinctly understood that your kind efforts for me shall be remunerated and I beg you will kindly stipulate the amount in your answer.'[11] The Secretary was deeply offended by this violation of club rules and proposed to bring the matter before the appropriate com-mittee. Fergusson outlined in detail how Schliemann should try to rectify his position:

> You must begin by expressing your surprise and regret that you had so misunder-stood what he had said to you. That his expressions were so vague that you must be excused – as a foreigner – that you put a wrong construction upon them, and fancied that there was some road for attaining your object that money would smooth. That had you for one moment fancied that there was anything improper or unusual in the proposal made in your letter of 14 February, you would never have made it so openly and without any attempt at concealment, and that your ignorance of English habits and customs must be your excuse for acting as you did.[12]

Schliemann's letter to the club Secretary followed Fergusson's recommendations precisely.

In 1880 Schliemann was also in frequent contact with Frank Calvert, who continued to excavate at Hanai Tepe with Schliemann's funds till mid-March. Schliemann had agreed to publish this excavation in *Ilios* and was now putting pressure on Calvert to come up with the report. In January Calvert sent Schliemann a cross-section of the mound (see Fig. 19). This is an exceptionally fine piece of archaeological drawing, far superior to Burnouf's sections of the two great (admittedly much more complex) trenches at Hisarlik published in the same volume. What distinguishes Calvert's section is its clear delineation of the stratification. Calvert noted three strata: a historic stratum at the top and two prehistoric strata below. The historic level contained graves of the archaic and classical Greek periods and later, the upper prehistoric level had Troy VI material, and the lowest level, pottery similar to that of Troy I. Archaeological strata are, of course, not of uniform depth. We can see at a glance that the top and bottom strata at Hanai Tepe are rather thin towards the eastern end of the mound and at their thickest just inside the innermost wall near the western end. This simple fact graphically illustrates the inadequacy of Schliemann's method of recording finds – by depth rather than by stratum. Calvert's section shows very clearly from which stratum and from where in that stratum each significant find came. Unfortunately, Schliemann did not appreciate the excellence of Calvert's section. He instructed Murray that the engraver should put it on one page rather than two. 'But let him do it roughly and cheaply, because it is most unimportant, and I merely do it to please Calvert.'[13] Calvert was disappointed: 'The fault I find with the engravings you have had made is they are too much reduced and the effect is in great part lost.'[14]

By late April Calvert had sent the cross-section, the plan and some drawings but still no report. On 23 April Schliemann wrote rather peremptorily: 'My book is now all printed in slips, and you cause me an enormous delay . . .'[15] Calvert had been busy with other tasks and very unlucky. At the end of March he had gone to the interior for two weeks to look after his mining interests there. When he returned, he lost his notes on Hanai Tepe for two weeks. In May and June his crops were ruined by a plague of locusts. He finally sent Schliemann his notes to work up himself. Schliemann later wrote to Sayce: 'If you can bring a little order in his dissertation, then I would add to it, in my name, a page of notes on the Hanai Tepeh pottery, which would render this appendix much more valuable. Because what scholars want to see are the analogies of the antiquities to those found in other places, and this, of course, our friend is unable to do. . . . I expected something better from Calvert. His

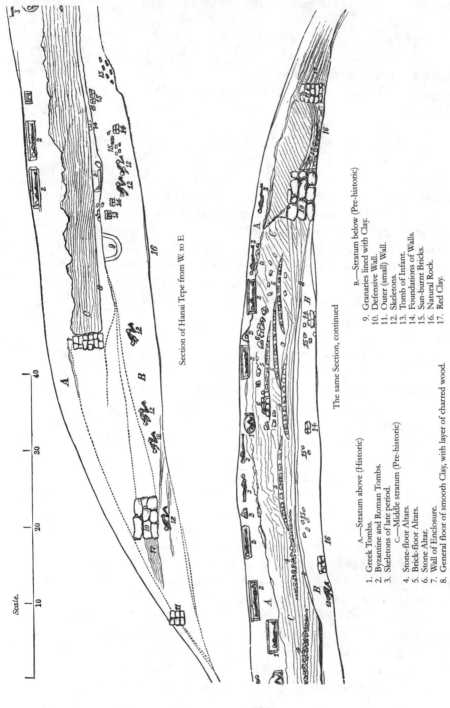

Scale.

Section of Hanai Tepe from W. to E

The same Section, continued

A.—Stratum above (Historic)
1. Greek Tombs.
2. Byzantine and Roman Tombs.
3. Skeletons of late period.
   c.—Middle stratum (Pre-historic)
4. Stone-floor Altars.
5. Brick-floor Altars.
6. Stone Altar.
7. Wall of Enclosure.
8. General floor of smooth Clay, with layer of charred wood.

B.—Stratum below (Pre-historic)
9. Granaries lined with Clay.
10. Defensive Wall.
11. Outer (small) Wall.
12. Skeletons.
13. Tomb of Infant.
14. Foundations of Walls.
15. Sun-burnt Bricks.
16. Natural Rock.
17. Red Clay.

Fig. 19 Calvert's cross-section of Hanai Tepe, 1880

paper hardly does honour to our book and it is a pity for the engraving, which cost me a heap of money.'[16] The finished version in *Ilios* is therefore a joint effort of Calvert, Schliemann and Sayce.

It was from Calvert that Schliemann first learned some disturbing news about Virchow. On 2 March Calvert wrote to Schliemann that he had just heard from Virchow: 'This friend writes he is preparing for publication a description of Hanai Tepe accompanied by plates of the most important objects found in the excavations. How far his intention conflicts with your forthcoming publication you are the best judge.'[17] Calvert was clearly annoyed at what seemed to him to be poaching on his territory. Schliemann was appalled. He had invited Virchow to Hisarlik on the understanding that whatever Virchow wanted to publish about Troy would be contributed to Schliemann's new book.[18] Since then they had exchanged almost a hundred letters without any indication from Virchow that he was planning to publish these results independently. Certainly, he had been working on a study of the skulls from Hanai Tepe and Hisarlik, but Schliemann understood that the findings were to be contributed to his book. Schliemann felt betrayed. On 8 March he sent a telegram (in French) to Virchow: 'Publish nothing Hanaitepe. Your publication would kill our friendship my love Germany.'

Virchow was astounded. He was planning to publish a scholarly monograph for the Berlin Academy on the skulls of Hanai Tepe together with the highlights of the excavation in general. He wrote: 'I believed that I had a definite obligation to introduce your and Mr. Calvert's gift to the scholarly public and make it known. For me it was an act of gratitude.'[19] Virchow argued, quite correctly, that the scholarly audience for which the monograph was destined was very different from the large general audience envisaged for *Ilios*. On the other hand, Virchow's failure to mention his intentions to Schliemann suggests that he knew Schliemann would disapprove of what he was doing.

Schliemann's thinly veiled threat to alter his will ('my love Germany') is significant. He clearly saw this as a way of exercising some control over Virchow. Though Virchow protested that he would 'do more out of friendship for you than out of regard for your will', it is clear that the threat to change the will carried weight.[20] On 1 April a compromise was reached. Virchow was permitted to publish the monograph but only after the appearance of *Ilios*.[21] Thereafter the correspondence resumed as before, though, presumably, there was now a certain guardedness that had not existed before. Two days later, almost as if to re-establish their former intimacy, Schliemann confessed to Virchow that he was troubled by impotence. He attributed it to his strenuous work on the book. 'When I am writing, I often feel a great need for a nap and at night, about once a week, I have a complete erection so that I can satisfy my wife, but since I have not produced a drop of semen for the past five months, I have absolutely no joy in the act.'[22] Virchow suggested Bavarian beer and cold showers, both in moderation.[23]

Virchow would have been very surprised to learn that despite Schliemann's declared intention to bequeath his Trojan collection to Germany, negotiations to sell it to the Hermitage in St Petersburg, which had begun in 1876, continued unabated in 1880. His chief contact was Baron N.K. Bogushevsky, a member of the Russian Archaeological Society and an enthusiastic collector of the autographs and letters of famous people. Bogushevsky had been educated at Eton and Cambridge and communicated with Schliemann in English. Ironically, it appears that Bogushevsky had no real prospect of being able to consummate the deal and seems really to have been more interested in adding more Schliemann letters to his collection.[24] He kept stringing Schliemann along with reports that the museum officials were very interested but needed more details before a concrete offer could be made. In his letter of 15 January 1880 Schliemann exclaimed in exasperation:

How is it possible to ask for the weight of Trojan jewels? . . . The whole collection is in the S. Kensington museum, where everyone can see it . . . It is of unique and immense value for the *whole* of Troy is brought to light and ransacked by me. In my letter of April last I have hardly asked one eighth part of what the collection is worth solely because I wished to make friends with Russia and hoped that by the cheap sale, and because they want a man like me to put up the collection and to find Troys in Russia, I might be recalled. I would have no objection to give the whole of my collection now in the above museum for the price ask ⟨ed⟩ and to give credit for five years in yearly instalments with only four per cent interest per annum under a London banker's guarantee for the payment to me.[25]

In March Schliemann wrote a long letter to a Russian official, describing his excavations and the desirability of his Trojan collection:

From England, France, Germany, Austria – from everywhere they make offers to acquire my beautiful collection; but I always reply that is not for sale. If, however, Russia wanted to acquire it, I would consent to yield it to her, for I love Russia above all other countries. I spent the 20 happiest years of my life there and the sweetest memories bind me to her; besides, I flatter myself with the hope that I will be needed to set up my collection for the Hermitage and to bring to light the ancient cities buried in south Russia.[26]

It is hard not to conclude from this correspondence that at this point Schliemann was just as serious about selling his collection to Russia as he was about bequeathing it to Germany. He was also clearly eager to undertake excavations in South Russia, whether in the Crimea, which had already shown itself rich in archaeological remains, or at Poti on the Black Sea near the Caucasus, thought to be the site of the legendary Colchis. Implicit in these negotiations was the condition that Schliemann be pardoned by the Emperor for some illegal act, whose precise nature is not known. It may well have had to do with his divorce and remarriage. It seems highly likely that under Russian law his divorce was not recognized and that his remarriage made him a bigamist. Without an imperial pardon therefore he would be subject to arrest on Russian soil.[27]

In March Schliemann's warm feelings for Russia were jolted by the publication in St Petersburg of a scholarly study by Ludolph Stephani, which argued that the finds in the Mycenaean tombs were about fifteen hundred years later than was generally assumed. Stephani argued that they had originated in South Russia and Persia and had been brought to Mycenae in the third century AD by the Heruli, a roving Teutonic tribe. He stated that the butterfly, found on the disks from Grave III, was a comparative latecomer as an artistic motif, not occurring before the Hellenistic period. On 1 April Schliemann sent a reply to Senator Polovtsoff, an influential figure in Russian political and intellectual life, asking him to have it printed in the *St Petersburg Herold* (*sic*), which had published excerpts from Stephani's study.[28] A scholarly debate ensued, with other scholars joining in.[29] Stephani's theory was no more plausible than the similar theories put forward in 1878 about Persian booty and marauding Goths but because of his stature as a scholar it attracted more attention. It was soon shown, however, to be without merit.

In April Schliemann wrote to his childhood friend Minna Meincke (now Richer), recalling the day in 1836 when he had to leave Neu Strelitz to begin work as a grocer's apprentice in Fürstenberg. 'You greeted me coldly and had for me only the four words: "*Was machen deine Schwestern?* [How are your sisters doing?]" . . . But for my work these four words were not suitable . . .'[30] Accordingly, he had altered the scene somewhat. Later, when *Ilios* was published, he sent Minna a complimentary copy and the following note: 'If you should find that I have exaggerated our friendship of fifty years ago, you must not take it amiss and simply attribute it to my old devotion to you. As circumstances have turned out, all my remarks can only redound to your high honour and all German women would wish to be so immortalized.'[31] One wonders, however, how she reacted when she read the farewell scene transformed as follows:

A few days before my departure from Neu Strelitz on Good Friday 1836, I accidentally met Minna Meincke, whom I had not seen for more than five years, at the house of Mr. C.E. Laué. I shall never forget that interview, the last I ever had with her. She had grown much, and was now fourteen years old. Being dressed in plain black, the simplicity of her attire seemed to enhance her fascinating beauty. When we looked at each other, we both burst into a flood of tears and fell speechless into each other's arms. Several times we attempted to speak, but our emotion was too great; neither of us could articulate a word. But soon Minna's parents entered the room, and we had to separate. It took me a long time to recover from my emotion. I was now sure that Minna still loved me, and this thought stimulated my ambition. Nay, from that moment I felt within me a boundless energy, and was sure that with unremitting zeal I could raise myself in the world and show that I was worthy of her.[32]

The entire English text of *Ilios*, apart from some of the appendices, was finished by mid-March. Proof-reading continued throughout the summer. In April Schliemann told Brockhaus to hire three German translators immediately and put them to work translating the English text. Brockhaus was anxious not to reveal that their edition was a translation. This concern dovetailed nicely with Schliemann's reluctance to acknowledge help with editing or translating on the title page. German readers were accordingly left to infer that Schliemann had written the work in German. Schliemann wanted to keep a close eye on the translation and now, of course, there was the proof-reading of the German edition as well. To speed up the process, Schliemann moved with his family to Leipzig in mid-May and remained there till 10 September. In early August he allowed himself two brief respites in Berlin from the endless work on the book. On 5 August he gave the opening scholarly paper, 'Ilios', at the German Anthropological Congress and four days later attended a gala dinner with five hundred guests given in joint honour of the Swedish explorer, Baron Nordenskjöld, and himself. About the same time, Schliemann's son by his first marriage, Serge, now a young man of twenty-five, came to see him in Leipzig. All that we know about this visit is Schliemann's terse remark in his letter of 15 August to Sophia: 'Sergei left this evening for Berlin.'[33] Schliemann set aside little or no time for his son, though it was he who had encouraged Serge to visit him in Leipzig. This was the first time that father and son had met in eleven years. They never saw one another again.

By mid-September work on both the German and English editions was completed and after three weeks of well-earned vacation in Paris and Biarritz Schliemann returned with Sophia to Athens in late October. After spending two weeks settling into their sumptuous new home, Iliou

Melathron, they set out for Orchomenos, where they began excavations on 16 November. Schliemann sank shafts at various locations in search of another grave circle or at least some Bronze Age graves. Most produced very little. A burial he came across close to the nearby monastery turned out to be Roman. Of the pottery resembling that found at Mycenae he noted that the painted variety, with spiral and other decoration, was always close to the surface, whereas monochrome (black or yellow) sherds analogous to pieces found in the shaft graves were found at lower depths.[34] It was Sophia, however, who made the most remarkable find, though we learn this not from Schliemann but from a report in a Greek newspaper by the engineer, G. Ioannides:

> The excavation of the Treasury of Orchomenos conducted by Mr. Heinrich Schliemann proceeds apace with 40–45 workers, half of whom are women. The women carry away the earth by means of dough-buckets. This is the idea of Mrs Schliemann, who returned to Athens last Tuesday. To date the excavations in the treasury have reached a depth of 9 metres below the surface on the west side and 7 metres on the other sides. . . .
>
> Last Monday (22 November) at 3 p.m., while I was standing near Mrs Schliemann, with my eyes on a different group of workmen from those that she was supervising and directing, Mrs Schliemann called out joyfully, 'Heinrich, Heinrich, look! the doorway!' It was the moment when the pick of Elias Kanouses, a workman from Petromagoulas, struck into the void of the sumptuous side-chamber that was coming to light. Soon the top part of the doorway was uncovered. It was beautifully worked. At the time of the discovery I officially summoned and notified the mayor and the head of the gendarmerie, Apostolos Andzolinos, who immediately placed the treasury under constant guard.[35]

Inclement weather forced Schliemann to postpone further excavation until March the following year. He returned to Athens on 8 December.

Waiting for him in Athens was a letter from the South Kensington Museum, politely asking him to remove the Trojan exhibit:

> When the Collection was received in December 1877, it was not thought likely that so large a space in such an important position of the museum could be given up for a longer time than two years, but their Lordships are pleased to have been able to retain a collection of so much antiquarian interest for a period of very nearly three years. It has however now become necessary to ask you to remove the collection at your early convenience, and I am to state, for your information, that Professor Archer, the Director of the Museum of Science and Art at Edinburgh, has expressed the hope that you may be willing to lend the collection

for exhibition at that museum. I am to add that arrangements have been made which render it necessary that the space now occupied by the collection should be made available by the end of January at the latest.[36]

Schliemann wrote at once to Virchow telling him that he was thinking of moving his Trojan collection immediately to Germany. He did not reveal, however, that he had been asked to remove it from the South Kensington Museum. Instead he said that he had become anxious about the number of officials that had keys to the cases where the collection was displayed and the fact that the museum assumed no liability for theft. He suggested that Virchow have two rooms cleared out in the Königliches Museum in Berlin to accommodate the Trojan collection until the new Anthropological Museum was completed. If this was not possible, then he would have to bring his collection back to Athens or else he might lend it to the Louvre, whose directors seemed very interested.[37] Virchow immediately leapt into action. He conferred with the appropriate museum and government officials. No space could be provided in the Königliches Museum. Less prestigious space was available, however, in the Kunstgewerbe Museum, adjacent to the site of the Anthropological Museum under construction. Virchow urged Schliemann, now in London, to come to Berlin himself to see if it was suitable.[38] On 26 December Schliemann arrived in Berlin, inspected the premises, grudgingly approved them, and returned immediately to London to supervise the packing of the collection and to see to its proper insurance.

The British seem to have made a last-ditch effort to buy the collection, for on 31 December Schliemann wrote with some satisfaction to Max Müller:

> Now the English people commence to perceive its great value, for Mr Newton, who 4 years ago refused to receive it on loan in the British Museum, requested me to name any price as he felt sure Mr Gladstone would persuade Parliament to buy it. I told him it had never been for sale, but that, had he shown the same interest 4 years ago, I might have donated it to the Br. Museum, as I was at that time overpowered by the libels of the German scholars. How strange it is that in England people always come too late.[39]

In his new book Schliemann sought above all to be comprehensive. He assured Murray, '*Ilios* exhausts forever the most interesting subject of Troy.'[40] This notion of exhaustiveness is reflected on the title page:

> Ilios: the City and Country of the Trojans; the Results of Researches and Discoveries on the Site of Troy and throughout the Troad in the years 1871–72–

73–78–79, including a Biography of the Author, by Dr. Henry Schliemann, F.S.A. F.R.I. British Architects, Author of 'Troy and its Remains,' 'Mycenae,' &c. With a Preface, Appendices and Notes by Professors Rudolf Virchow, Max Müller, A.H. Sayce, J.P. Mahaffy, H. Brugsch Bey, P. Ascherson, M.A. Postolaccas, M.E. Burnouf, Mr. F. Calvert, and Mr. A.J. Duffield. With Maps, Plans, and about 1,800 Illustrations.

In its attempt at comprehensiveness lie both the chief merit of *Ilios* and its chief fault. With its special studies on the topography, climate, drainage, flora and fauna of the Troad *Ilios* seems to anticipate the modern view that archaeological evidence must be seen in the context of a full understanding of the site's natural environment. In fact, this broad approach to archaeology was more common in the nineteenth than in the twentieth century, reflecting the discipline's origins in the physical sciences, particularly geology, paleontology, and physical anthropology. No one placed more emphasis on viewing prehistoric man within a full understanding of his physical environment than Rudolf Virchow, and it is undoubtedly to his influence that Schliemann's new vision of archaeology is to be attributed. However, with his eyes firmly fixed on comprehensiveness Schliemann lost sight of the need to keep to the point. Since he knew that Murray would be reluctant to assume the risk of publishing a lengthy book so lavishly illustrated, he had proposed at an early stage, and Murray had agreed, that the book should be published on commission. The normal constraints against wordiness were accordingly absent, for Philip Smith, though in many respects an astute and competent editor, was himself insufferably long-winded. As a result, the undoubted virtues of *Ilios* are smothered under a welter of unnecessary verbiage.

The German, British and American editions of *Ilios* were published on 10 November 1880. Sales were brisk. Murray sold 600 copies, half of its entire run, on the first day. The German edition was sold out before the end of the year. The reviews in the British press were, on the whole, unfavourable. One review began, 'The title page of Dr. Schliemann's new book is longer, more copious, more elaborate than any that has been printed, to our knowledge, since the sixteenth century', continued with a reference to the 'copious autobiography, in which he acknowledges his obligations to Heaven and Mr. Consul Quack', and ended with 'Dr. Schliemann's book seems to us to add little of value to his earlier account of his researches.'[41] Another began: '*Ilios* is perhaps the worst arranged book that ever came under our notice.'[42] Many criticized Schliemann for drawing on quotations from the *Iliad* to illustrate the artefacts and buildings of the 'burnt city' when he acknowledged that that stratum had been buried centuries before Homer was born. A particularly damning review appeared in the *Edinburgh Review*, whose author, it later transpired, was the noted classicist, Richard Claverhouse Jebb, then at the University of Glasgow. Jebb rightly excoriated Schliemann for the frequent illogicality of his reasoning and, perhaps carried away by his own eloquence, ventured a very different interpretation of the successive settlements at Ilion, which he must later have regretted. In Jebb's view, all the levels belonged to the Greek period: Troy I was Ilion *c.* 900–550 BC, Troy II, Ilion *c.* 550–334 BC, and Troy III–VI, the city as it was successively rebuilt by Alexander, Lysimachus, Sulla and Augustus.[43] Of course, if this were the case, Troy II would show the familiar pottery of classical Greece and not the strange, indubitably prehistoric, ware that is found in this and succeeding strata. That so distinguished a scholar should have committed this obvious blunder is symptomatic of the narrow training that classicists received in Britain at this time. Ironically, Jebb himself was a leading advocate of establishing British Schools of Archaeology in Athens and Rome so that the training of young classicists could be broadened through exposure to the monuments and material remains of antiquity.[44]

Schliemann quickly mobilized his troops against the enemy. To Max Müller he sent two engraved Trojan gems with the request that he write an answer to the hostile review in the *Saturday Review*: 'The libel is written by the *same* party whom you so admirably licked and silenced three years ago by a short article in the *Times* – I can't do it myself. But I send you enclosed an answer such as I would have made in a similar circumstance . . .'[45] Gems were also sent to Virchow, who was asked to respond to a pamphlet by E. Brentano critical of Schliemann's theories.[46] To Sayce he wrote: 'Should all reviews of *Ilios* have fallen into the hands of my libellers and should no periodicals be left to you or Prof. Mahaffy to review the work, then, pray, do me at least the justice to write an article to the *Academy*, in which you confound the *false* statements of Paley in the British Quarterly for April.'[47] And a few days later: 'If you refuse to answer, or to cause an answer to be given to Paley at least, then I cease to by your friend.'[48] Schliemann had arranged as early as July 1880 with William Smith, the editor of the *Quarterly Review*, that his brother Philip, Schliemann's copy-editor, should do the review of *Ilios* for that journal. In September 1880 Schliemann paid Philip Smith £250 (roughly £15,000 today) for his editorial work on *Ilios*.[49] When Smith's review did not appear in either the January or March issues of the *Quarterly Review*, Schliemann was quite indignant. Finally, in May 1881 Smith sent the draft of his review to Schliemann for his approval. Schliemann found it excellent but suggested that Smith might answer some of the specific charges brought by his critics. Smith agreed and the review appeared in the July 1881 issue.[50] The *Quarterly Review's* practice of leaving reviews unsigned made this breach of ethics possible.

After dispatching the Trojan collection from London to Berlin in forty chests, Schliemann headed back for Athens, stopping for a few days at Paris. From here he wrote an extraordinary letter to Virchow on 6 January 1881.

> As I told you orally, my wife insisted that I bring the Trojan collection back to Athens and decorate our *Palazzo* with it. The news of the gift to the German people has brought her to a state of despair, which she expresses to me in several telegrams a day. As she is very highly strung and unwell, I fear the worst. You know how meaningless worldly honours are for me but at this point the life of my dear wife and the happiness of my entire family are at stake and ways and means must be found to calm my wife and so prevent so great a misfortune. My wife, in common with all women, has a dark side – she is very ambitious. In the name of all the gods, seize her on this side and try to calm her with honours, for otherwise my house will fall to the ground and I will perish with it. Arrange that the City of Berlin grant honorary citizenship to my wife and myself and get whatever other honours are available. With many tears I direct this earnest entreaty to you; given my character, which you know, it is extremely hard for me to do this; but as it's a question of the life of my beloved wife, I don't hesitate. Also, please arrange that the honours that you can obtain for my poor wife are announced to her by telegram. We have handed over our finest possession to the German nation; try therefore to ensure that our gift receives the widest and highest recognition and so rescue my wife and my family's happiness. You can do it if you want to. I am counting on you. I will arrive in Athens on Wednesday evening, 12 January, and with shudders and horror I wonder how my poor wife will welcome me. Couldn't you meanwhile wire her something to comfort her? I will repay you the cost of your telegram one hundredfold.[51]

Virchow sent a comforting letter to Sophia and seems also to have prompted the Prince von Saxe-Meiningen to do the same. Sophia replied to Virchow on 29 January 1881.

> I wish to express my most sincere thanks for your considerate lines of the 10th of this month and for the good wishes for me and my family, but at the same time I cannot avoid confessing that the contents of the rest of the letter filled me with the greatest astonishment. I am the keenest and warmest friend and admirer of Germany and of the German people and I certainly do not deserve to be accused of looking unfavourably on my husband's handing over of the Trojan antiquities to the German state. It is absolutely inconceivable to me what can have caused you

to deliver this Philippic. I was the first to suggest that the collection be sent to your Fatherland, I was the one who from the first year of our marriage strove to convert my husband from his deep prejudice towards Germany, and I tried hard to fan to full flame the slumbering spark of patriotism and love for country in his heart. You must have misunderstood my husband, dear Professor. All the same, I did reproach him – though only after I got your letter, the contents of which I found so completely unexpected, so strange and so enigmatic. I hope that these words will suffice to clarify completely my attitude towards Germany and my view of the matter of the donation. I want to add, however, that your admonitions did not in any way offend me. I sensed the voice of a friend and I knew that you were writing in good faith and with the best of intentions under the influence of some misunderstanding![52]

It is not hard to discern what is going on here. From conversations with Virchow Schliemann learned that he set little store by medals and other such honours. Not wishing to appear bourgeois, Schliemann claimed to have similar views. In a letter to Virchow, dated 26 June 1879, he mocked the pretentiousness of Burnouf, who, after Virchow's departure, insisted on coming to the dinner table at Hisarlik wearing his medal of the Legion of Honour.[53] Naturally, Schliemann could not now tell Virchow that he wanted to be made an honorary citizen of Berlin. His letter about Sophia's despair was his remarkable solution to the problem.

Virchow, however, thought that honorary citizenship was a good idea and implied that it could be arranged. Two weeks later Schliemann told Virchow that he thought in addition he should be made a corresponding member of the Berlin Academy and be given the medal 'Pour le Mérite'.[54] Virchow ignored the former request and explained that no one could be awarded a medal 'Pour le Mérite' until a fellow specialist in that field, who already held one, had died. They were therefore very difficult to obtain. Virchow had long ago come to accept that he himself would go to the grave without one.[55] In reply, Schliemann pointed out that Max Müller had one and that his own achievements were as deserving as Max Müller's.[56]

By mid-January the Trojan collection had arrived in Berlin. Since Schliemann's gift was to the German people, Kaiser Wilhelm made a formal statement of acceptance on their behalf. The text was published in the official *Reichsanzeiger* of 7 February 1881. Given the still disputed legal status of Priam's Treasure, this document, addressed to Schliemann, is of more than historical interest.

From a report of the Chancellor and the Minister of Education and Health I have learned with satisfaction that you have designated your collection of Trojan antiquities, hitherto exhibited in London, as a gift to the German people for their permanent possession and inalienable safekeeping in the capital. In approving the conditions attached to this patriotic gift I have gladly signified my assent that the gift is accepted on behalf of the German people and that the collection will be subject to the administration of the Prussian State government. I have also consented that in future it will be kept in the Ethnological Museum in Berlin, presently under construction, in as many rooms as are appropriate for its proper exhibition and that the rooms where it will be kept will forever bear your name. Until the completion of the Ethnological Museum the collection will be kept in the exhibition hall of the new *Kunstgewerbe* Museum in Berlin and, for the duration of the temporary exhibition, this room will also be marked with your name. I would further like to express my profound appreciation of this gift of a collection of such importance for scholarship, which bespeaks a warm devotion to the fatherland, and I cherish the hope that in your unselfish pursuit of science, you will be allowed to achieve service, to the honour of the fatherland, of equal importance to your achievements hitherto.

Back in Athens by mid-January Schliemann explained his actions to his American friend John Francis: 'The U.S. government's refusal to give me the consulate for Athens and particularly Evart's letter to you, in which he speaks of me in such indifferent terms, has had two offsprings, first, that I struck out in my last will my donation of my Trojan collections, and, now lately, that I make the donation to the German nation. The collections are already at Berlin and provoke, you may imagine, immense enthusiasm.'[57] Anxious to resume excavations at Troy and confident now of German diplomatic support, he wrote to R. Schöne, Director General of the Berlin Museums, to have either the Crown Prince or Bismarck order the German Ambassador in Constantinople to secure him a liberal firman that would allow him to excavate anywhere in the Troad for a period of up to five years.[58]

The new house that the Schliemanns moved into in October 1880 is still located on Panepistimiou Street between the university and the former royal palace, now the parliament building. Designed in the German neo-classical style by Ernst Ziller, the façade is interrupted by a two-storey loggia, where dark Pompeian red contrasts with the white marble elsewhere. On the course of marble between the loggias is inscribed in large gilt lettering Iliou Melathron (Palace of Troy). From the terrace on the flat roof Schliemann could point out to his visitors the Parthenon and the sea off Salamis, where the Greek fleet defeated the Persians in 480 BC. The surrounding balustrade is decorated at intervals with statues of Greek gods and goddesses. It appears that some highly placed government officials were offended by the nudity of the statues and formally requested that Schliemann either remove or cover them. The next day Athenians were amused to see the statues draped in gaudy garments. The embarrassed officials backed down and begged Schliemann to restore them to their pristine nudity.[59]

The interior of the house was richly decorated with marble. The mosaic floors incorporated motifs from Schliemann's finds, such as the octopus, the butterfly, and an 'owl-faced' pot. The walls were decorated with paintings in the Pompeian style. Throughout the house were moralizing aphorisms from Hesiod and other writers, such as 'If you add a little to a little and keep on doing this, soon you'll have a lot'; 'Know the right moment'; 'Nothing to excess' and the like. The copies of Guido Reni's *Aurora* and *Beatrice Cenci*, bought in Rome in 1868, graced the upstairs rooms. The quality of material and workmanship was everywhere superior. The obtrusive presence of Schliemann's personality and achievements, still there today, while having the effect of turning art into high kitsch, has its own peculiar charm and makes the house as eloquent a monument to Schliemann's memory as his archaeo-logical collections and even the books he wrote. Few buildings anywhere reflect their owner's character with quite such intensity.

The German ambassador to Greece, J.M. von Radowitz, recalled an elabo-rate reception the Schliemanns gave to celebrate their new home:

> I must also mention a particular festivity that took place in the Schliemann house in the first week of March. To inaugurate his new residence officially, he had invited to dinner all the foreign ambassadors known to him and, in addition, a number of Greek politicians. From a culinary point of view, the meal appeared to be more suited to the tastes of those who once ruled ancient Troy than to the requirements of modern stomachs. During the meal Schliemann got up and gave a speech, in which he individually apostrophized each of the diplomats present. He spoke about the various countries they represented in remarkable French laced with even more remarkable comments, which frequently, though certainly unintentionally, bordered on insults, and which produced every variety of amazement and embar-rassment on the faces of my colleagues. Schliemann, nevertheless, sat down quite satisfied with his performance and signalled to his wife. Thereupon she rose and also read off a speech to the assembled diplomats but this time directed at Europe as a whole. It was a call to lend immediate assistance to the noble Hellenes, descen-dants of Pericles and Alexander, in their rightful claims to very extensive lands at the expense of the barbaric Turks.[60]

The German ambassador broke the tension of the moment by a speech in which he extolled the beauty of Greek women, as exemplified in particular by their charming hostess.

At this time, Schliemann was preparing to complete excavations at Orchomenos. Since Sayce was to join him but would not reach Athens until 27 March, Schliemann took a trip to Olympia with Sophia in early March. Wilhelm Dörpfeld, the twenty-eight-year-old architect heading the technical side of the excavation, recorded their visit in a letter to his father-in-law: 'Yesterday [16 March] Mr Schliemann was here with his wife; I took him around the excavations the whole day and convinced him of the thoroughness of our work. He was very enthusiastic about you, as the first to consider the graves in Mycenae older than the Lion Gate . . . Dr. Schliemann pressed us to come to Orchomenos. We'll see!'[61] Since Schliemann seems to have known Dörpfeld since 1879 or earlier, he probably went to Olympia with the express purpose of recruiting the talented young architect for Orchomenos.[62] It turned out that Dörpfeld had commitments to the German Archaeological Institute in Athens that prevented him from joining them there. However, Dörpfeld did help produce the drawings for the published report, including one of the elaborately carved ceiling of the side-chamber, from a cast that Schliemann brought back.[63]

The season at Orchomenos was short (30 March–13 April) and disappointing. Schliemann was joined by Sophia and Sayce and the work was supervised by P. Eustratiades. Both the main chamber and the 'thalamos' (side-chamber) were fully excavated but no burials were found. Above the thalamos they found mixed debris washed down from the hill behind, on which the ancient acropolis of Orchomenos was located. Shafts were sunk in various locations in the hope of finding another tholos tomb but without success. The excavators found for the first time a highly characteristic, smooth grey ware that has since become known as 'Minyan' after the legendary king Minyas of Orchomenos. It is characteristic of the Middle Helladic period and therefore pre-Mycenaean. Schliemann wrote up the report on the 1880–1 excavations in English for the *Journal of Hellenic Studies* and then translated it into German for publication as a short monograph.

On 11 May Schliemann set out for a ten-day excursion around the Troad on horseback. Starting from the Dardanelles, he spent the first night at Hisarlik. From there he headed south along the Aegean coast to the Gulf of Adramyttium (now Edremit), then east along the Gulf to Edremit itself, north and west through the range of Mount Ida, via Beiramitch, Ezine, Alexandria Troas, and Ujek Tepe back to the Trojan plain.[64] Highlights were his discovery at the summit of Cape Lectum of what he identified as the altar of the twelve gods, whose construction was attributed in Strabo's day to Agamemnon, and on the summit of Mount Gargarus an excrescence of mica-schist resembling a gigantic throne: 'It appears indeed that Homer had visited this summit, and that, precisely because of this throne-like excrescence, he assigned the top of Gargarus as the seat of Zeus.'[65] The point of the trip seems to have been to determine likely sites for excavation once he received the liberal firman he was hoping for.

Brockhaus published the account of this excursion but Murray thought it insufficiently interesting for the British market. When Gardner also turned it down for the *Journal of Hellenic Studies*, Schliemann asked him to send the manuscript to Harper in New York, adding: 'I am exceedingly sorry to see that, whilst in Germany my name and fame are on the ascendant and honours and distinctions are poured here on me, I am completely run down in England. Nay, my last work, "Ilios", which has cost me two years of labour, at the rate of 14 hours daily, is universally pronounced in England as a ridiculous humbug, whilst in Germany it is universally declared to be a masterpiece.'[66]

In June Schliemann went with Sophia to Berlin to arrange the display of the Trojan collection. On 7 July he was formally presented with the honorary citizenship of Berlin and, following the ceremony, was fêted at a gala dinner in his honour in the banqueting hall of the Berlin Rathaus. The menu was written in Greek and comically decorated with 'The Discoverer of Troy' sitting on the throne of Priam with a spade in his right hand and a miniature Victory in his left. While Victory reached forward to place a laurel wreath on his head, a bear, the emblem of Berlin, cowered at his feet. From Schliemann's mouth came the words: 'In spite of her former cold treatment, you see that Berlin has done me honour at last. She has three great citizens – Bismarck, von Moltke, and myself.'[67]

While in Berlin he received his Orchomenos manuscript with Sayce's corrections from Percy Gardner, the editor of the *Journal of Hellenic Studies*. Schliemann promptly responded to these corrections with indignation and unconscious irony: 'I am displeased with Prof. Sayce's corrections for they take away the charm of the originality without improving the text.' Gardner had reservations about the classical inscriptions that Sayce had copied from around the site. These had in fact already been published. Besides, comparison of Sayce's readings with those already published convinced Gardner that Sayce's were less reliable. This rather negative experience with the Orchomenos manuscript seems to have cooled Schliemann's enthusiasm for the editorial assistance of the genial Assyriologist.

After taking the treatment at Carlsbad with Sophia, Schliemann spent four days in Berlin arranging the Trojan collection for exhibition. In September he contracted with Firmin Didot in Paris to publish the French edition of *Ilios*, while Virchow attended the Anthropological Congress in Tiflis (Tbilisi), Georgia, and visited Poti, which Schliemann was now eager to excavate. In

October Schliemann negotiated in Constantinople for a firman to excavate in the Troad. His hopes of resuming excavations at Hisarlik in late October, however, accompanied by Virchow, were dashed by bureaucratic delays and by Virchow's decision to return to Berlin earlier than planned. In late 1881, with firman finally in hand, he was making plans for a spring campaign in Troy. He had hired a Viennese architect, Joseph Höfler, to accompany him. His hopes to recruit Dörpfeld had, however, failed. Dörpfeld, now married and looking for long-term employment in Greece, wanted a three-year engagement with Schliemann or, failing that, a commitment that he would be hired for three summer campaigns. Schliemann was not interested.[68]

13

Dörpfeld, Troja and Thermopylae

SCHLIEMANN WAS BY NOW almost as much of a tourist attraction in Athens as the Parthenon itself. He catered to the stream of visitors who wanted to see him by inviting all those who left their cards to the literary salon held at his house every Thursday evening during the winter. Otherwise he remained largely inaccessible. A fascinating picture of both the house and its owner in February 1882 is given by an American visitor:

We enter the basement, which is occupied chiefly by a museum stored with such of the Trojan antiquities as have not been sent to Berlin. These consist of a vast number of terra cotta drinking cups, 'whorls', and other objects, made familiar by the illustrations of the 'Ilios'. Over the entrance to the museum is a plaster cast of the beautiful metope of the Temple of Apollo, the only piece of the temple's sculptures which Dr. Schliemann recovered at Troy. From the basement we ascend by a winding staircase to the grand entrance hall . . . The decorations of the house depend for their subjects to a great extent on the excavations at Mycenae and Troy. Ideas of this kind are prominent in the two chief features of the interior – the mosaic pavement and the wall-paintings. The first floor is occupied by the reception rooms . . . The *salon* opens on the loggia, where the music is concealed on the occasion of parties . . . On the walls are inscriptions from Homer relating to dancing, and in the dining-room are other Homeric inscriptions on the subject of the banquet. Through the apartments of this floor 300 or 400 guests might move with ease . . . ⟨The library⟩ occupies the same place on the second floor as the *salon* does on the first, and consequently opens upon the upper loggia, which affords a pleasant promenade and a fine view of the acropolis. The Doctor's two private studies – one for Winter and one for Summer – are at the ends of the room. The library is well lighted by means of three large glass doors opening on the loggia. The walls are painted a light red and the ceiling is beautifully frescoed. A series of low book cases extends completely around the room. On top of these are placed many interesting specimens of Greek pottery . . . In the library are also a portrait of Dr. Schliemann as a young man, and portraits of some of the worthies of his native village, which he had painted out of gratitude to these gentlemen for inspiring him in his work. The walls are further adorned by Homeric texts in gilt letters, and above the doors are these Greek mottoes: 'Know thyself', 'Study is everything', 'The mean is best', 'A grievous thing is ignorance', and 'Let no-one enter who knows not geometry', the motto of the school of Pythagoras. An open fire-place with a mantel-piece of white marble, occupies one end of the room. On the mantel a few figurines, archaic marbles, and unique specimens of pottery and glass are grouped around an elegant black marble clock, which is set with bronze panels containing Homeric subjects in relief and surmounted by a bronze figure of Homer, on which is always kept a sprig of fresh olive. Above the mantel hangs a photograph of Mme. Schliemann, in native Greek costume, wearing on her head one of the gold diadems found at Mycenae. On the walls nearby are the many diplomas awarded to Doctor and Mme. Schliemann by the various archaeological and other scientific societies of Europe. The most recent of the Doctor's honors is his nomination as a member of the Academy of Belgium. The centre of the library is occupied by two cases of antique coins, and a long table covered with the leading pamphlets and magazines of all languages.

Dr. Schliemann is an omnivorous reader and is equally at home in German, French, English, Italian, modern Greek, Russian, and Dutch. His library is not, however, an extensive one. It has a multitude of scrap-books, magazines, and newspapers on file, and scientific pamphlets. But, with the exception of the classics, the literary works are confined to the Doctor's favorite authors – Leibnitz and Kant, Goethe and Schiller, Racine and Victor Hugo, Bulwer [Lytton] and Dickens. Books of travel and archaeological works form by far the greater part of the collection. In fact, it is the library of a specialist rather than that of a general scholar. We sit down to look at the latest numbers of the London *Times,* and presently a servant enters bringing us cups of the black Greek coffee. Then the door of the Winter study opens revealing the Doctor, pen in hand. He comes out to speak to us, and wants to know if we can advise him about the provisions which he is getting ready to take to Troy . . . We enter into a long discussion on the comparative merits of English and Vienna beer, at the close of which we are invited into the study.

The study is a remarkable room. Around the walls are glass cases of antiquities, over which hang the most valuable of the Doctor's diplomas, many framed letters and such other souvenirs as he particularly prizes. The room contains a number of desks, but the one most used seems to be a high desk in the centre, for the Doctor is accustomed to stand while working. . . . The Doctor entertained us by showing letters from Gladstone and the Emperor William and one from a merchant who offered to employ him when a young man at a salary of $45 a year for a period of 19 years. This last letter has suffered shipwreck, and is stained yellow with salt water but the Doctor has carefully preserved it, and shows it with pride, as a witness of the slender beginning out of which he built up the fortune that yields him an annual income of £10,000. Other of the Doctor's cherished mementoes are the naturalization papers which testify that he is a citizen of the United States of America, bird's-eye views of Indianopolis and New York, and photographs of his native village. Among the last he shows the house of Minna, the first love of his boyhood, with whom he dreamed of digging up Troy at the age of 6.[1]

217

As Schliemann was preparing to resume excavations at Hisarlik, Dörpfeld secured the position of excavation architect for the German Archaeological Institute at Athens. Though the salary was modest, the terms of appointment permitted him to seek temporary employment elsewhere. Accordingly, Dörpfeld informed Schliemann that he would be able to work for him at Troy on a short-term contract after all. Schliemann eagerly took him on at a monthly salary of £35 (roughly £2,100 today).[2] Schliemann was anxious to try the disciplined technique of excavation used at Olympia, that is, digging down slowly from the top and clearing across one stratum at a time instead of pushing a deep trench through the hill, excavating all layers simultaneously. To ensure that the workmen did their work properly he hired two foremen from the Olympia excavations. Though Schliemann had quarrelled with him in 1880 and vowed never to employ him again, the indispensable Nikolaos Yannakis was once again his paymaster and major-domo. Schliemann had about 150 labourers, mainly Greeks, but including about 25 Turks and a few Spanish Jews. The season lasted from 1 March till 21 July. There was little rain, but an unrelenting north-east wind, which blew dust in everyone's eyes until the end of April, was a constant reminder of the aptness of Homer's recurring phrase, 'windy Troy.' Schliemann's eyes became so inflamed that he could not see well enough to write and he had to dictate his correspondence to his architects.[3]

Schliemann's attention was primarily focused on the unexcavated block of earth, roughly triangular in shape, in the east-central segment of Hisarlik (Plan III, Appendix V). Across the great east–west trench of 1872–3 Schliemann had left a ramp of earth to allow access to and from the bottom of the trench. Where the city wall (b on Plan III) of Troy II met this ramp it seemed to take a sharp turn to the north-west and then became lost in the tangle of walls in the centre of the mound. Early in the 1882 season Dörpfeld discovered that the city wall of Troy II in fact continued after the ramp in a north-east direction. This was a very important discovery, for it virtually doubled the size of Troy II. What had seemed an angle in the wall eventually proved to be one of the sidewalls of the south-east city gate. This led to the decision to dig the 'great north-east trench' (from L to K on Plan III) to clarify the course of the city walls.[4] All of this trench, 80 metres long by 7 metres broad, lies outside the city wall of Troy II.[5] The main finding from this colossal effort was that all the area east of the Troy II wall was occupied only from the period of Troy IV onward.

It was at the centre of the site (D in Plan III) that the principal architectural discoveries were made. As the soil was cleared away and the trained eyes of Dörpfeld and Höfler sorted out the confusing jumble of walls, the plans of two substantial buildings of Troy II (A and B on Plan IV) became distinct.

These looked rather like temples in floor plan and were at first so identified. Only after the excavation of the Mycenaean palace at Tiryns did it become clear that these were early examples of the Homeric house, the megaron, and that the circle in the middle of A was a hearth.

Practically all the metal objects found in 1882 other than those in the 'Palladium' treasure discussed below were attributed by Schliemann (*Troja* 91–106) to 'Temple A'. These included many nails, a cup, flat axes, spearheads, daggers, bolts, a gimlet, knives, arrowheads, a surgical (?) instrument, and pins, all of bronze or copper, and a frontlet and sceptre knob of gold. Most of the other interesting objects he also said came from 'Temple A' – knife-handles, an arrowhead and a spoon, all of ivory, pieces of polished stone, some egg-shaped and some identified by Schliemann as sling-shots, and axes of diorite (*Troja* 115–19). The attribution of all these finds to one building may be genuine enough but it seems more likely that Schliemann enhanced the building's genuine finds with many pieces that had been brought to him clandestinely by the workers. 'Temple A' was by far the most impressive building in Troy II. It needed finds to match its architecture.

Schöne had expressed a desire for more pieces of classical and Hellenistic sculpture for the Berlin museums and, in particular, for more pieces like the Helios metope. This seems to have stimulated the sudden interest that Schliemann showed in 1882 for the remains from the classical, Hellenistic and Roman periods at Troy. He excavated at the north-east edge of the mound (V on Plan III), where the Helios metope had been found. He also started excavations at the theatre some 200 metres east of the main site, where he found a relief medallion of the wolf suckling Romulus and Remus and other pieces of Roman sculpture.[6] Sculpture from the great Hellenistic Temple of Athena was also sought and found in the surrounding Turkish cemeteries or purchased from Frank Calvert's collection.[7] Virchow, who had an insatiable appetite for bones and particularly for human skulls, asked that all the bones from the lowest levels be collected and sent to him.[8] Further activity in 1882 included the sinking of numerous shafts outside the acropolis itself but within the boundaries of Greco-Roman Ilion. These produced Troy I and II pottery at the lowest levels, demonstrating that prehistoric occupation had extended beyond the acropolis. Schliemann also was led to change his mind about the Scaean Gate, which he now thought must have been located not on the acropolis but where the lower city of Troy II debouched on to the plain.[9]

Dörpfeld and Höfler seem to have enjoyed working with Schliemann. 'We get along well with him,' Dörpfeld wrote to his parents, 'and I wouldn't know what to complain about. Before he starts any project, he always asks me if I am in agreement; and if I consider it impractical, then he doesn't do it.'[10]

Dörpfeld was soon able to convince Schliemann that the burnt stratum, which he had first seen as the top layer of Troy II but later, persuaded by Sayce and Calvert, had called Troy III in *Ilios*, should after all be seen as the top layer of Troy II. The Troy III 'walls' found in this stratum, he argued, were in fact merely the *foundations* of Troy III buildings, which, naturally, were sunk below the occupation level. The artefacts found in the burnt layer belonged to the destruction level of Troy II.[11]

In April Schliemann left his two architects in charge at Troy and began exploring a number of the heroic tumuli in and around the Troad. The results were again disappointing. No signs of burial were found and the pottery was mostly of the classical or later periods. By far the most interesting of these mounds was the so-called Tumulus of Protesilaos located across the Hellespont on the Gallipoli peninsula. Schliemann was well aware that his permit for excavation in the Troad did not extend to European Turkey. He moved quickly. After one and a half days of digging he was stopped by the authorities but not before he had found quantities of pottery and artefacts identical to what he was finding at Troy I and II levels at Hisarlik.[12] Excavations at Balli Dagh revealed two occupation levels. Schliemann dated the earlier to the pre-classical period (900–500 BC) and the later to the Classical and Hellenistic periods (500–200 BC).

Two incidents of this time, minor perhaps in themselves, are important for what they reveal about Schliemann's methods. Virchow had asked him if he could send half a dozen skulls from one of the older Turkish cemeteries. Schliemann pointed out that while he expected to be allowed to remove classical sculpture from these cemeteries, it would be quite impossible to get permission to remove skulls. Nothing daunted, however, he assured Virchow, 'I will have the one-eyed workman, Demos of Kalifatli, whom you know – he seems to me to be the wiliest of all my people – do it clandestinely and I hope to be able to secure for you the desired number of skulls.'[13] Given this behaviour in 1882, it is not hard to imagine Schliemann organizing clandestine excavations of tombs in the vicinity of Mycenae in 1876.

The second incident once again concerns a 'treasure'. In a letter dated 14 May Schliemann reported to Virchow:

In the 2nd city (the first burnt one) we found beautiful things: for example, a sling[shot] (or weight?) of haematite, weighing 1130 grammes, also a complete treasure of bronze objects, among them, a very remarkable ring, three inches broad – similar to our napkin rings – so skilfully worked that were it made of gold, it would do honour to a Berlin goldsmith. Since I got all these things secretly on the side, I cannot send you a drawing and I must also ask you to say nothing about them.[14]

Schliemann successfully kept these pieces concealed from the Turkish super-visor. This is clear from the fact that this treasure was not shared with Constantinople. The whole treasure went to Berlin, where it was catalogued in 1902 as Treasure K.[15] Among the items of the treasure was the prize find of the season – a bronze figurine, which he promptly identified as the 'Palladeum or a copy of it'.[16] The Palladium, according to Trojan legend, was an ancient image of Pallas Athena that had been sent down to Troy by Zeus. Troy would not fall as long as the Palladium was kept safely in the city. By breaking into Troy and carrying off the Palladium Diomedes and Odysseus ensured the city's ultimate downfall. Schliemann was particularly pleased with the piece, for he saw its head as 'owl-like' and therefore confirming his interpretation of the 'owl-like' vases. In *Troja* he explains why the Turks missed the figurine in the division of the finds: 'Fortunately, as may be seen in the engraving, it had broken into three fragments; I am indebted to this lucky circumstance for having obtained it in the division with the Turkish government; for the three pieces were covered with carbonate of copper and dirt, and altogether undiscernible to the inexperienced eye.'[17] Almost certainly, however, neither the figurine nor any of the other bronzes secretly brought to him were ever included in the pool of finds to be divided. It was not just bronze pieces, however, that Schliemann kept hidden from the Turks. Regarding pottery, he wrote to Virchow on 1 September: 'I note, however, that to avoid handing over any to the Turks, I put aside all the more characteristic pieces and sent them away secretly.'[18]

This behaviour provides us with a good model of how Schliemann might have assembled Priam's Treasure in 1873. In 1882, the Turks had good reason to watch Schliemann's workmen very closely, for they were well aware they had been cheated out of their proper share of the finds in 1873. Even so, it seems clear that the Turkish overseer was unable to prevent valuable finds making their way to Schliemann illicitly. One problem certainly lay in the scale of the excavations. One overseer could not possibly supervise 150 workmen properly even if they were working in one location, and Schliemann had his men working in several locations at once. Another difficulty was that the overseer received his pay from Schliemann. In early May the Turkish authorities appear to have become aware, or at least to have suspected, that valuable finds were being secretly passed to Schliemann, for around 20 May the Ministry of Public Instruction sent a second overseer, Beder Eddin. In June Schliemann told Virchow, who had asked about the Turkish supervision, how that situation had developed in 1882:

Through the intervention of the German embassy I succeeded in freeing myself from Kadri Bey and getting a simple Turk instead of him. I have to pay him £6 a month instead of the £20 I paid Kadri Bey. A fortnight ago a second Cerberos was imposed upon me by the Ministry, whose salary I don't have to pay, but who acted in such an arrogant and high-handed manner that I was compelled to humiliate him deeply, for otherwise it would have been difficult to continue working with him. I think that in future, however, things will go well.'[19]

Not surprisingly, things got worse – much worse. A few days later Schliemann and his architects were forbidden to take measurements, make plans, or even jot down notes at Hisarlik on the grounds that they might be spying on the Turkish military installations at Kum Kale. Despite repeated calls to the German diplomatic corps at Constantinople and the personal intervention of Bismarck, it was not until mid-November that permission was granted and Dörpfeld was sent back to Troy to make the principal site plan for *Troja,* Schliemann's next book (see Plan IV).[20] Schliemann exacted his revenge in *Troja,* describing Beder Eddin as a 'monster . . . whose arrogance and self-conceit were only equalled by his complete ignorance and who considered it his sole office to throw all possible obstacles in my way.'[21]

In May Schliemann heard good news from Sayce in Oxford: 'The Council today, by a special vote, has declared its intention of proposing that an Honorary Degree shall be conferred upon you, if you can come to take it. The honorary degrees this year will be conferred on June 14th.'[22] Since Schliemann did not plan to leave Troy until 1 August, he asked Max Müller to arrange that the degree be awarded on the same occasion the following year. The degree appears to have been granted by Oxford less in recognition of his achievements as an archaeologist than in acknowledgement of a significant gift to the university. An early stage of the story can be seen in a letter Schliemann wrote to Max Müller on 3 February 1881: 'But now regarding potsherds, I think you and Prof. Rolleston would not mind to receive also entire Trojan vases. I cannot give the latter from the 1st and 2nd cities, the number of entire specimens from them being too small, but I can give you same from the 3rd, the burnt, and the 2 subsequent cities. But plenty of potsherds you shall have from the 1st and 2nd. Shall I also send some stone hammers, an axe and a hand-mill?'[23] This gift to the University Museum was brought back to Oxford by Sayce in April 1881 after the excavations at Orchomenos. In March 1882 Sayce explained why the university had taken so long to express its thanks: 'I was unable to hand over the antiquities to the University Museum last year owing to the absence and death of Dr. Rolleston; & a successor to him was not appointed until last Christmas, when I was away. Immediately upon my return to Oxford I placed the antiquities in his charge and they are now exhibited in the Museum.'[24] The formal thanks of the university were given on 14 March

1882 and the decision about the honorary degree was made less than two months later. The degree was to be awarded at the Encaenia, the annual commemoration of the founders and benefactors of the university.

Though Dörpfeld was sensible enough not to quarrel openly with his employer, it soon became clear that they had very different views regarding the dating of the strata above level II. Their differences are summarized in Appendix III.[25] Schliemann avoided assigning even rough dates to his strata. One reason for this was the difficulty in explaining why so many occupation levels or 'cities', as he rather misleadingly called them, intervened between Priam's Troy, whose destruction date was traditionally given as 1184 BC, and the 'Lydian' level, only 180 years later. A date for the Trojan War significantly earlier than 1250 BC was implausible for several reasons. One consideration was that the earlier it was dated, the greater the interval between Homer, who probably lived around 750 BC, and the events about which he sang. The major difficulty with Dörpfeld's chronology, which was based primarily on the architectural remains, was the same as with Jebb's: the pottery associated with Troy IV in no way resembled that of classical Greece and in fact looked much the same as in the prehistoric levels. Dörpfeld's explanation for this, namely, that from the time of the Trojan War to the Hellenistic period the population of Troy was poor and backward, reveals an inadequate grasp of the significance of pottery type as a dating tool.

Dörpfeld knew that it was fruitless trying to discuss these topics with Schliemann.

> To talk about these matters seriously with Schliemann is quite impossible; he cuts off all discussion with a single sentence: 'From the primitive pottery and the construction tools it is certain that the fourth and fifth cities were still "prehistoric".' In my opinion, however, what follows from those finds is that in the posthomeric period an impoverished people lived here that had neither painted vases nor metal implements until the Macedonian period.[26]

Schliemann was quite right, of course, to insist that the pottery from Troy I–V made it clear that these levels were all prehistoric. The problem with both Schliemann's and Dörpfeld's schemes was that Troy II was a thousand years too early for Priam's Troy, as Calvert had seen ten years earlier. Since it had produced the richest finds, however, there was a natural reluctance to abandon the notion that it was Homeric Troy. The key to the correct understanding of the archaeological history of Troy lay in the outer fringes of the acropolis, where the stratigraphy was less disturbed, and these were not systematically tackled until 1890.

In Virchow's absence Schliemann again took on the role of physician for the nearby villagers. In many of his letters to Vichow he asks for information on the correct treatment of scurvy, haemorrhage in the mouth, swollen spleen, and so on. Regarding his own health and that of his family he was remarkably imprudent. Virchow was shocked to learn that Sophia and Andromache had joined him at Troy in mid-June and urged that they return to Athens as quickly as possible. June to September, as was well known, were the prime months for malaria in the Troad. Schliemann himself had a reason for taking a chance with his health, Virchow argued, but there was no reason to expose his wife and child to such danger.[27] Schliemann acted on the advice immediately. Sophia and Andromache returned to Athens about 4 July. Two weeks later Schliemann himself had a severe attack of malarial fever that forced him to abandon the excavations. Though he recovered fairly quickly, relapses, some serious, recurred intermittently for the rest of the year.

At the August conference of the German Anthropological Society in Frankfurt Schliemann delivered a report on the 1882 season at Troy. Here the fever returned. He wrote to Murray a few days later: 'I was tormented by it to death in the midst of the lectures, banquets and rejoicings.'[28] Schliemann was honoured by toast after toast. 'Nothing was more touching than a song in thirty-two verses, describing my life, which was sung in my honour at the great banquet on the 14th ist. I made a long reply but it completely exhausted me.' The occasion was somewhat marred by an unpleasant incident. Put into circulation at the conference 'with unenviable taste', as the classical scholar John Mahaffy wrote, was the latest pamphlet by one of Schliemann's detractors, Professor Brentano, who held that Troy was not at Hisarlik but a few miles further up the Dumbrek valley.[29] Brentano argued that the destruction of Troy II should be dated to 85 BC! After the conference Schliemann relaxed with Sophia for three weeks at Marienbad (now Marianske Lazne in the Czech Republic), then went to Paris to consult with Firmin Didot about how the new findings should be incorporated in the French edition of *Ilios.* In October Dörpfeld wrote to his father-in-law: 'Schliemann recently asked me to write a rebuttal to a pamphlet of a Dr. Brentano. I sent him one and to my astonishment I see it in print today in the *Allgemeine Zeitung.*'[30] While Dörpfeld dutifully excoriated Brentano for the absurdity of his views, he also indicated that he himself found architectural evidence for only six superimposed 'cities'. Moreover, though he clearly indicated that he held that Troy II must be Homer's Troy, his description of the upper levels was cast in such neutral terms that it was just as applicable to his own chronology as to Schliemann's. This modest article was to play a significant role in a heated debate that flared up at the end of the year.

Actually, the debate had begun a year earlier with the anonymous review of *Ilios* in the *Edinburgh Review*. Sayce, who was clearly just as much the target of the reviewer's scorn as Schliemann, responded with a short and acerbic letter in the *Academy*: 'It is a pity that the anonymous author, before writing it, did not either learn the elementary principles of archaeological science or examine Dr. Schliemann's excavations on the spot . . . So important a work as Schliemann's *Ilios* deserved to be placed in more competent hands.'[31] It soon emerged that the anonymous reviewer was none other than R.C. Jebb, Professor of Greek at Glasgow. Perhaps because of Sayce's jibe, Jebb visited the Troad in September 1882. He was accompanied by his friend, the American classicist W. W. Goodwin, a Mr Clarke of the American excavations at Assos, and Frank Calvert, acting as guide. The entire party seems to have agreed that while it was clear there were several superimposed strata at Troy and these strata together represented a very long period of occupation, there was no sure way of determining how long any given stratum lasted or indeed of assigning a date to any of them except the uppermost, which belonged to the Roman period. Jebb seems to have learned from Calvert not only that Dörpfeld dated the strata very differently from his employer but also how he dated them. When Jebb returned to London and read Dörpfeld's review of Brentano, he saw that the guarded interpretation of the strata given by Dörpfeld concealed a serious difference of opinion between Schliemann and his architect, such as Calvert had indicated to him.[32] In October Jebb delivered a paper at a meeting of the Hellenic Society, in which he put forward a substantially modified version of the chronology he had first outlined in the *Edinburgh Review*.[33] Jebb's new chronology was, in all essential points, identical to that of Dörpfeld. Jebb therefore had successfully driven a wedge between Dörpfeld and Schliemann.

In the winter of 1882–3 Schliemann lobbied energetically to obtain German medals for two friends at the Dardanelles, Emilio Vitalis, the Italian consul, and Nikolaos Didymos, the dragoman for the Turkish government. For many years Vitalis had seen to Schliemann's banking needs there and had received and dispatched packages for him. In 1882 Didymos, as Schliemann wrote to Virchow, 'saw to the purchasing of provisions every day'. But Didymos helped in other ways: 'At the risk of losing his position and livelihood, he managed to send 21 large baskets with wonderful antiquities to Athens. Some of the small pieces I brought with me to Frankfurt, where they were much admired.'[34] Here, incidentally, is clear proof that in 1882 Schliemann was successful not only in having many of the best pieces brought to him secretly at the site but also in smuggling them out of the country. As early as April 1882 Schliemann had virtually promised these two men their decorations and Schöne had agreed to take care of the matter. By the end of the year, however, no medals had reached the Dardanelles. Schliemann was furious. He directed his anger against Berlin. On 2 January 1883 he wrote a long, angry letter to Virchow, threatening to send the rest of his Trojan collection not to Berlin, where 'the Academy continually shows me its backside', but to Munich, where the Bavarian Academy had already appointed him a member. If the medals were not promptly forthcoming, he threatened, he would 'never again set foot in Berlin, even if I reach the age of Methuselah.'[35] Once again Virchow moved quickly. The requested medals were sent off before the end of January.

Schliemann had been working hard on his new book since his return to Athens in October 1882. By the end of the first week in 1883 he had finished the English version and was looking forward with gloomy satisfaction to the task of translating it into German. Then, too, there were the corrections to the French *Ilios* – a monstrous work that incorporated, and so had to be accommodated to, the 1882 findings. Nonetheless, Schliemann was already planning more excavations. Crete and Thermopylae offered intriguing possibilities.

The excavations of Minos Kalokairinos at Knossos in the winter of 1878–9 had revealed a very extensive building there. Almost immediately the 'scramble for Knossos' began.[36] The British consul in Crete urged Newton to continue Kalokairinos' excavations. A French scholar published some of the pottery in 1880 and the French School showed interest in excavating the site. The American consul, W.J. Stillman, made the most progress. He reached an agreement with the proprietor but was unsuccessful in procuring a firman. In two letters published in 1881 Stillman described what had been excavated so far and provided illustrations of what he thought might be hieroglyphics or some other early form of writing that he had found on those walls that had been exposed.[37] On 7 January Schliemann wrote to the governor of Crete, asking for a firman to excavate at Knossos. He agreed to comply with the terms prescribed by Turkish law – to give two thirds of the finds to the government and retain only one third for himself.[38] Photiades, once the governor himself, suggested that if he offered to surrender everything to the government, retaining only duplicates for himself, as in the contract between the Greek and German governments for the excavation of Olympia, he would have a better chance of success.[39] Schliemann quickly agreed to these terms. But his real difficulties lay not with the governor but with the patriotic sentiment of the Cretans themselves. At this time, though still under Turkish rule, Crete enjoyed a certain amount of autonomy and much of the government was conducted by a democratically elected parliament. Most Cretans were opposed to any excavations as long as Crete was subject to Turkish rule, for there could be no guarantee that any treasures unearthed would remain on Cretan soil. Schliemann realised that to get a firman he would have to invest several weeks personally lobbying the Cretan parliament when it met in Chania in April or May.[40] Meantime he wanted to excavate with Virchow and the latter's only free time was in March.

Given Virchow's passion for skeletal remains and Stamatakis' recent discovery of about 300 skeletons of the Theban dead at the battlefield of Chaironeia, it is not surprising that Schliemann's thoughts turned to the battle sites of Thermopylae and Marathon.[41] Though these sites were classical rather than Homeric, their names were every bit as evocative as Troy and Mycenae. Whoever discovered the dead heroes of these battles would command the attention of the world's press. Stamatakis' success at Chaironeia gave reason to believe that they could be found buried near the battlefields, just as Herodotus had reported. The question of course was exactly where.

On 28 January, three days after a grand ball at Iliou Melathron, to which 600 guests were invited, Schliemann set off to survey Thermopylae. He wanted to see if the prospects for success were sufficiently good for him to plan an excavation there with Virchow in March. The most important consideration was to see if there was a reasonable chance of determining the site where the Greeks had been buried. When Xerxes invaded Greece in 480 BC, the Greeks decided to make their stand against the invading army at Thermopylae, where there was only a narrow road between steep cliffs and the sea. Under the leadership of Leonidas and his three hundred Spartans, the allied Greek forces kept back the much larger Persian army for two days. Eventually, however, the Persians found their way round by a mountain pass, overcame the contingent posted to guard it, and outflanked the Greek position. Leonidas learned of this manoeuvre in time to save the main body of his troops but remained at his post with a small band of Spartans and Thespians. In the last desperate struggle, Leonidas himself was killed. The surviving Greeks retreated to a small hill, Kolonos. Here they fought to the death. They were buried where they fell.

Reconciling the facts on the ground with Herodotus' narrative of the battle is no easy matter. Schliemann outlined the problems in his letter to Virchow of 4 February:

The narrow defile of Thermopylae derives its name from the hot mineral springs, which flow from the steep eastern cliff of Mt Kallidromos, an outrunner of the Oetaean ridge, and are now used, as certainly also in antiquity, as medicinal springs. The heavy deposits made by these springs as well as the alluvia of the River Spercheios, that flows through the valley, have so completely altered the physiognomy of Thermopylae that the traveller needs time to orient himself and discover where the famous defile really was. According to Herodotus it was wide enough for only one wagon. It is known that it was formed on the south side by the steep cliff face of Kallidromos and on the north side by the sea immediately adjacent. However, in the course of 2363 years alluvium has caused the sea to retreat more than 10 km. It is easy enough to locate the defile exactly, for it could only have been on the narrow stretch where the cliff face is steepest and has no spur, but it is impossible now to determine precisely the location of the different phases of the struggle between the Spartans and the Persians described by Herodotus.[42]

Schliemann's analysis of the topography at Thermopylae is impressive for his quick grasp of the essentials and the independence of his views. He considered and rejected three possible candidates for Kolonos.[43] He excavated without success at the first two of these sites but not at the third. Ironically, subsequent excavation has shown the third to be Kolonos. Schliemann sent Virchow a telegram on 30 January with a suitably laconic message: 'unfindbar' (not discoverable). Virchow thereupon decided to go for a holiday in Italy instead.

On 7 February Sayce arrived in Athens to stay with the Schliemanns for a few weeks. He had come via Malta, where spiral decorations on the ancient temples on the northern island of Gozo reminded him of those on the Mycenaean tombstones. He concluded: 'The "treasuries" of Mykenae and Orchomenos, the tombs of Spata, and Menidi, and the Phoenician temples of Malta, are all constructed on the same principles. Truly, the Phoenicians were the architectural teachers of the early Greeks.'[44] Schliemann was busy working on the German translation of his new book. In his *Reminiscences* Sayce testifies to the extraordinary power of Schliemann's memory: 'What he once read seemed indelibly imprinted upon it.'[45] One evening, after a lecture at the American School, which had just opened that year, Sayce and W.W. Goodwin had different recollections of a passage in one of Lucian's *Dialogues*. A student was sent to fetch the relevant volume, 'whereupon Schliemann, who had been sitting silently in a corner of the room, remarked, "I do not think it is necessary that Mr. X should trouble himself; I think I remember the passage," and he repeated it to us.'

Schliemann was still casting around for a suitable place for his next excavation. He mentioned to Sayce his desire to excavate Knossos and, rather surprisingly, Hamadan, in present-day Iran. He was also checking out the tholos tombs in Greece. An early eighteenth-century traveller had come across one near Sparta that sounded promising. So Sayce was dispatched to find it and determine whether it was worth excavating. Though he soon identified the site of Amyclae, also near Sparta, for the Greek Archaeological

Society, he had less success in his search for the tholos tomb. On his last day, he was riding along the banks of the Eurotas with a local schoolmaster when he saw a good spot for their picnic lunch. When they climbed the adjoining hill to admire the view, they found at the summit

> a ruined tholos-tomb, the walls of which rose about six feet above the ground, and in the hollow within them there were sixteen wild-looking fellows, armed to the teeth, who made it their home; one or two of them, in fact, were at the time performing their toilet in it. There could be little doubt that I had discovered the object of my search, and the occupants of the tomb, interested like all Greeks in the antiquities of their country, helped me to measure and examine it.[46]

The schoolmaster later informed Sayce that it was lucky that they had left their escort of soldiers at the bottom of the hill for otherwise the brigands would have thought they were about to be arrested and would certainly have killed them. Sayce reported to Schliemann that the tomb was too much of a ruin to be worth excavating. Ironically, when C. Tsountas excavated the tomb in 1889, it produced the richest finds ever made in a tholos tomb – a fine collection of engraved gems and two exquisitely decorated gold cups with scenes of men trapping a bull. These famous cups, called Vapheio cups after the tomb where they were found, remain among the most beautiful works of Mycenaean or Minoan art.

Sayce and Sophia conducted modest excavations for Schliemann in Athens along the Academy road from the Dipylon Gate until they were halted by cold weather. Later they dug on the Kyrades islands in the bay of Salamis, which Schliemann identified with the Pharmakousai, where tradition located Circe's tomb. Though they did not find Circe's tomb or anything Mycenaean, they accidentally stumbled upon a monument set up to commemorate the battle of Salamis (480 BC).[47]

It was at this time that Sayce first met Dörpfeld. Schliemann wanted Dörpfeld to write a reply to a disturbing letter that had appeared in *The Times* of 29 January. An earlier report in *The Times* had been remarkably dismissive of Schliemann's 1882 excavations, stating that they had 'failed to develop anything confirmatory of his Ilian hypothesis' and that his system of stratification had been 'shown to be untenable'.[48] This had prompted an indignant rebuttal from Schliemann: 'The succession of five prehistoric and two later settlements, as given by me in "Ilios", is confirmed by my architects.' In support, he cited Dörpfeld's article on Brentano. Schliemann's letter had appeared in *The Times* of 29 January 1883. Just below it, however, was a letter signed 'One who has seen the excavations', unmistakably from Jebb. Referring to

Dörpfeld's article, Jebb stated categorically: 'Not a word in it tends to show that Dr. Dörpfeld believes in five prehistoric cities and two later settlements.' Jebb correctly pointed out that Dörpfeld recognized only six cities, of which the uppermost was Roman, the second lowest was the city of Priam, and the intervening three were undated. He suggested that at least two of them should be attributed to the Greek and Macedonian periods of the city and so historic rather than prehistoric. Dörpfeld agreed to write a response in German, which was to be sent to the *Augsburg Allgemeine Zeitung.* Sayce was to translate his letter for submission to *The Times.*

Dörpfeld's response is an equivocating document, ostensibly supporting Schliemann but clearly offering just as much comfort to Jebb. *The Times* version, moreover, contains a most peculiar sentence. After dismissing Brentano's views as absurd, Dörpfeld continues: 'It is otherwise with a hypothesis which has found supporters in *The Times,* and which maintains that the uppermost city is the Roman one, the fifth prehistoric city being Macedonian, the fourth Greek, and the third pre-Greek . . .' The phrase 'the fifth prehistoric city being Macedonian' makes no sense. When Jebb checked the German version in *Allgemeine Zeitung,* he noticed that the German version made excellent sense for it had no word corresponding to 'prehistoric'. Jebb naturally inferred that the word 'prehistoric' had been added in a clumsy attempt to make Dörpfeld's letter appear to support Schliemann's view that the first five cities were prehistoric. In an article published in the *Journal of Hellenic Studies* in the summer of 1883 he all but accused Schliemann of tampering with the translation of Dörpfeld's letter. Under pressure from Schliemann, Sayce, Smith, and perhaps also Virchow, Dörpfeld publicly acknowledged that he had signed the English translation of his letter, noting, however, that in doing so he had overlooked the insertion of the word 'prehistoric' in connection with the fifth city at Hisarlik.[49]

After finishing the German translation in early April, Schliemann took a week off his work in Athens to revisit Hisarlik with the surveyor I. Wolff to make a plan that would include the lower town around the acropolis. Just why he did not take Dörpfeld instead is unclear. Perhaps he needed Dörpfeld to stay in Athens to review the manuscript of the book – certainly, some of the rather technical discussions of the architecture look as if they must come from Dörpfeld's hand – or perhaps the equivocal nature of Dörpfeld's response had cooled their relations. The plan produced shows the course of the circuit wall of Hellenistic Ilion and the trenches that were dug in the lower town.

Schliemann's strenuous exertions on his three books over the winter and spring had worn him out. On 3 May he wrote to R. Cooke at John Murray's, indicating that he would stop by in mid-June on his way to Oxford: 'Do not be frightened at my present appearance, for this winter I have overworked myself, having written the English book, made the German translation and corrected the English, German and French proofs; so I am broken down.'[50] Five days later he had a riding accident. 'My riding horse became frightened and went backward into a deep ditch; I jumped off but fell on a heap of stones and the horse fell on me; the concussion was so tremendous that I was seized with a violent fever.'[51] Later in May he learned that Queen's College, Oxford, Sayce's college, had appointed him an honorary fellow. On 13 June, dressed in scarlet robes, he received his honorary doctorate from Oxford at the Encaenia ceremony. The *Morning Post* described Schliemann as 'the bright particular star of the Oxford commemoration.'[52] He brought a further gift for the University Museum: a bronze axe-head from 'Temple A' at Troy. He did not stay long in England. He returned to Ankershagen, where he had rented the house he had grown up in from mid-June to mid-July. Here he was joined by his wife and children. Just as at Athens and Troy, he went for a swim first thing every morning. This entailed riding the pastor's horse, which he renamed Bellerophontes, to Bornsee lake about two miles from the village. On the return trip he enjoyed talking in *Plattdeutsch* with the locals about old times. Most of the morning he devoted to work, for every mail brought more packages of proofs, or correspondence from one of his four publishers. In the afternoon he renewed acquaintance with his family and schoolday friends. Even Minna Meincke came to see him.

In 1883 Schliemann showed symptoms of suffering from an enlarged prostate. He decided to spend a month from mid-July to mid-August in Bad Wildungen, a German spa where the waters were thought to be beneficial for this ailment. Here, besides taking the water, he was put on a strict dietary regimen: no coffee, potatoes, vinegar, sugar or desserts and no riding. Sophia and the children divided the four weeks between Carlsbad and Franzensbad. The 'cure' at Wildungen was ineffective, for later Schliemann wrote to John Murray asking for the titles and addresses of two London specialists in bladder ailments.[53] From Paris he wrote: 'Ricord, the greatest authority here, declares it to be the natural consequences of overwork; he orders me to drink a wineglass of Vichy water early in the morning and not to work more than 6–8 hours daily.'[54]

Schliemann could not resist including in *Troja* attacks on his two principal critics, Brentano and Jebb. After refuting Brentano's theories, Schliemann tastelessly added: 'While these pages are in the press, he has died by his own hand in a fit of insanity, on the 25th of March, 1883.' Though Murray, Smith and even Mahaffy advised against responding to Jebb in the book, Schliemann attacked him with relish. Sayce egged him on: 'I suspected that Murray and

Philip Smith would, in the charity of their hearts, wish what you had said about Jebb to be softened down. You know my opinion about what you have written – that it is by no means too severe and does not imply that you are in a passion. Jebb is so encased in self-conceit that it is necessary to speak plainly to reach him.'[55] And again: 'We must "kick" him until he is never able to bark again.'[56]

Since Schliemann attributed the decline in his reputation in Britain to the poor reviews that *Ilios* had received in the British press, he took pains to ensure good reviews for *Troja.* In March Schliemann wrote to Murray: 'Please prevail on Dr. Smith to let his brother review the new book in the *Quarterly.'* Sayce, who had agreed to write the preface to *Troja,* gave Schliemann his thoughts on the allocation of reviews:

> If I write the Preface, I shall not be able to write a review of it for the *Academy* (where the articles are signed), & I do not know of any other person into whose hands it can safely be placed. Mahaffy will not be able to write the review for the same reason as myself, though he will review the book for the *Athenaeum* (where the articles are unsigned). Now I do not feel sure whether it is not of more importance that the work should be fully and properly reviewed in the *Academy* than that it should be provided with a preface. What do you think of the question?[57]

Mahaffy had contributed an appendix on 'The Site and Antiquity of the Hellenic Ilion', for which Schliemann paid him £40. Philip Smith received £200 for his editorial work on *Troja.* Neither should have reviewed the book.

There still remained the *Academy* review, which Sayce was in a position to place, thanks to his influence with its editor. Schliemann seems to have sounded out Philip Smith about doing it, for on 9 July Smith pointed out that he would be doing the *Quarterly* review and could not do one for the *Academy,* whose reviews were signed. He suggested instead Newton, Percy Gardner or the orientalist S. Poole. In July Schliemann wrote to Sayce: 'Not Dr. Blind, but *Tylor* must review the new book in the *Academy.* I wrote him that on my return to Athens I shall be too happy to send to his Museum a box full of Trojan antiquities, provided it could be done without the newspapers knowing anything about it.'[58] In the event, Edward Tylor, Keeper of the University Museum and famous Oxford anthropologist, arranged with the young Arthur Evans, the later excavator of Knossos, to write the *Academy* review.

On 9 August Schliemann gave Sayce some suggestions as to what the preface should contain. Here is an excerpt:

> Pray, therefore, immortalize the new book at your earliest convenience with a Preface by your pen. In doing so please consider what an enormous impulse my

excavations and discoveries at Troy and Mycenae have given, at least in Germany, to Homeric studies. Excuse me if I tell you frankly on this occasion, that with the pupils in the gymnasia and the students in the universities in Germany, I have become a half-god, on every occasion I am welcomed by them with an enthusiasm bordering on frenesey [*sic*] and the Trojan war has now become to them a complete reality. Please consider besides what a stir in archaeol. pursuits has been produced by my excavations and discoveries; nay, the excavations in Olympia, in Pergamon and in dozens of other places are only offsprings of those of Troy. Consider also that the number of foreigners who flock to Athens to see the immense treasures I have unearthed at Mycenae is so great that there are now at Athens 10 times more hotels than there were at the time I began those excavations . . .[59]

A more appealing side of Schliemann is seen in his reaction to the news of the death of Nikolaos Yannakis, which he learned from Frank Calvert's niece in September:

The poor fellow was drowned in the Scamander about a fortnight ago whilst going over from Yenischer to Renkoi. It seems that he was drunk and instead of crossing the river at the usual ford, he tried to make a short cut over a very deep & boggy place, into which he fell headforemost, & not being able to extricate himself, was drowned. His little son Hector was riding behind on the same horse; he warned his father of the dangerous place, but Nichola was too much intoxicated to heed the child's words, so pushed forwards. The little fellow jumped off just in time to save himself, whilst the father came to grief. His wife is in despair, Nichola has left her *nothing* but *debts* – & the poor woman is in a dreadful state.

Schliemann promptly sent the widow a cheque for £8 (about £480 today), the first of several such payments.

The new book, *Troja*, appeared in both its German and English editions in November in time for the Christmas market. The generally favourable reception accorded it by reviewers was spoiled for Schliemann by the publication of a radically different interpretation of the ruins at Hisarlik. It was proposed by a retired army captain, Ernst Bötticher, who was to prove Schliemann's most persistent critic. According to Bötticher, so far from uncovering Homer's Troy, Schliemann had not excavated a city at all. Hisarlik was simply one vast crematorium or *Feuernecropole* (fire-necropolis).

14

Marathon, Tiryns and the Break with Virchow

I N A LONG LETTER written in January 1884 Schliemann updated Virchow on his medical condition and informed him that he was buying from the Turks the colossal pitchers from Troy that Virchow had so much admired. Most of the letter, however, focused on Bötticher's recent article. He asked Virchow to write a strong response and gave him an extensive list of arguments that he could use. He warned Virchow that if Bötticher's views prevailed in Germany he would never return there and would certainly not send any more of his finds to the Berlin museums.[1] Virchow promised to answer Bötticher's article but said that Schliemann was taking the attack too seriously, assuring him that no one of any standing in Germany believed in the 'fire-necropolis' theory.[2] Meanwhile, Schliemann was looking for a project that would lure Virchow back to Greece as his collaborator. The situation was exactly the same as in 1883. If he was to get a firman for Knossos, the Cretan parliament had to be lobbied in April or May, but Virchow was free only in March and April. He had drawn a blank at Thermopylae in 1883. Why not Marathon in 1884?

Marathon is conveniently close to Athens. It made a popular day-trip for tourists long before 1884. The conspicuous mound, called Soros, near the south-west corner of the plain, was generally identified as the tomb of the 192 Athenians who died in the battle that occurred there in 490 BC. Visitors liked to climb it and enjoy the splendid view of the mountains, the grassy plain and the sea. Then, as now, they tried to visualize the battle that took place on the plain before them. A large Persian force, sent by Darius to punish the Athenians for assisting his Greek subjects in Asia Minor in their revolt of 499 BC, beached at the sandy shore of Marathon. About 10,000 Athenians were sent against them. They were joined by 1000 Plataeans. At dawn on 12 September, after several days of warily watching one another, the Greeks sud-

234

denly swooped on the Persians. The Persians stood their ground and even broke through the Greek centre, but the two wings of the Greek line closed in on them and they fled in a rout to their ships. A courier ran the twenty-six miles back to Athens with news of the victory – a run now honoured and commemorated all over the world. The Persians lost 6400 men, the Athenians 192. As a special honour the Greek dead were buried at the site, as they would be later at Thermopylae.

Schliemann was sceptical of the tradition that identified the mound with the tomb of the Athenians. His scepticism was based partly on his reading of the ancient sources, none of which indicated that a mound had been raised over the Athenian dead, and partly on his experience in the Troad, where similar mounds had proved to be cenotaphs and, for the most part, considerably older than the fifth century BC. Still, he acquired a permit to excavate and in early February set out for Marathon with Sophia and Demetrios Phlios, the government representative. He dug a vertical shaft down the centre of the mound and a horizontal tunnel along the ground to meet it. Attempts to dig below the level of the plain, where any burials were most likely to be located, were thwarted. At only one metre below the surface they encountered the water table. The pottery found in the mound seemed to Schliemann very ancient and rather similar to that of Troy. The early date suggested by the pottery was confirmed by finds of obsidian knives. What seemed to him the latest piece of pottery he dated to the 9th century BC.[3] Phlios had a different view. He considered most of the pottery undatable. Two or three sherds he assigned to a very remote period but at least one, he was sure, dated to the time of the Persian Wars.[4] Schliemann was unlucky in choosing to excavate the mound in winter when the water table was raised by the winter rains. When the mound was re-excavated by B. Stais in the summer of 1890, the bodies of the Athenians were found three metres below the level of the plain.

The reviews of *Troja* were largely favourable, though the results of the 1882 season of excavation could hardly be called exciting. In the *Academy* Arthur Evans rightly pointed out: 'Never before, in any part of the earth's surface, have so many successive stages of human habitation and culture been laid bare by the spade.' Jebb, predictably, exacted revenge for Schliemann's disparaging remarks in *Troja*. Sayce commented on his review in a letter to Schliemann:

> Meanwhile Jebb has been writing a furious attack on you, Mahaffy and myself in the April number of the *Fortnightly Review*. It is very cleverly written, but full of ignorance and misrepresentation. I thought at first of replying to it, but my friends

whom I consulted strongly advised me not to do so upon two grounds. First of all, Jebb is so angry that he has shown his readers that he is in a passion. Consequently those who know nothing about archaeology will be prejudiced against him, while archaeologists know that his arguments are futile. Secondly, he will be much more vexed at finding that his article is treated with silent contempt than he would be if it received the honour of a reply. Jebb claims to have the support of Ernst Curtius and Michaelis whose letters to himself he quotes, and he now declares that he always held Bunarbashi (which has been imperfectly examined!) and not Hissarlik to be the site of Homer's Ilion. The ignorant newspapers have been speaking of this article as the 'convincing criticism' of 'the greatest of living English Hellenic scholars'. What will Mahaffy say to this? We did not trample upon Jebb sufficiently in *Troja*: that was always my opinion, derived from a knowledge of the man.[5]

Philip Smith dutifully sent the draft of his review for the *Quarterly* for Schliemann's approval. Schliemann's initial reaction was to thank Smith 'for the very flattering review of *Troja* in the *Quarterly Review*, which is a masterpiece of learning and literary skill and it will command universal admiration' but expressed some reservations about Smith's attacks on Jebb.[6] Later he was considerably less tactful: 'I am very glad that your brother invited you to curtail it because your exceedingly long and altogether superfluous arguments against Jebb are tedious in the extreme.'[7]

Schliemann now turned his attention to Tiryns. He had acquired a permit and planned to begin excavations in mid-March. He told Virchow of the provisions he had ordered: 120 bottles of finest Bass Pale Ale, 50 tins of American peaches, 50 tins of corned beef and 10 of tongue.[8] Virchow replied that he could not be tempted by 'hecatombs of Pale Ale and corned beef', though he very much wanted to join Schliemann in Tiryns. Family reasons would keep him in Germany in March and later take him to London, where his son worked at Kew Gardens. Once again the hoped-for collaboration had failed to materialize.

Tiryns, like Mycenae, was a well-known site before Schliemann first visited it in 1868. Its fortification walls were regarded as the finest example of prehistoric walling in Greece. In mythology it had particularly close connections with Heracles. In 1832 F. Thiersch, excavating on the north-west side, 'discovered a level floor of a hard white substance, showing the bases of columns nine feet apart.' It was judged probable that these were the remains of the prehistoric palace.[9] Surprisingly, however, little interest had been shown in following up this discovery, perhaps because it had never been properly published.[10] Schliemann arrived at Tiryns on 15 March. Finding his accommodations there too dirty he soon moved to the Hotel des Etrangers in Nauplion. In *Tiryns* he described his morning routine as follows:

My habit was to rise at 3.45 a.m., swallow 4 grains of quinine as a preservative against fever, and then take a sea bath; a boatman, for 1 fr. daily, awaited me punctually at 4 o'clock, and took me from the quay to the open sea, where I swam for 5 or 10 minutes. I was obliged to climb into the boat again by the oar but long practice had made this somewhat difficult operation easy and safe. After bathing, I drank in the coffee-house *Agamemnon*, which was always open at that hour, a cup of black coffee without sugar, still to be had for the old sum of 10 Lepta (a penny) though everything had risen enormously in price. A good cob (at 6 frcs. daily) stood ready and took me easily in twenty-five minutes to Tiryns, where I always arrived before sunrise, and at once sent back the horse for Dr. Dörpfeld. Our breakfast was taken regularly at 8 a.m. during the first rest of the workmen, on the floor of the old palace at Tiryns. It consisted of Chicago corned beef . . . bread, fresh sheep-cheese, oranges, and white resined wine.[11]

Almost immediately Schliemann found himself at odds with the government supervisor, Demetrios Phlios. Phlios naturally wanted to establish a system for the orderly removal of the excavated earth and debris from the citadel. At Troy and Mycenae, however, Schliemann had simply dumped the earth down the nearest slope or over the nearest wall. He saw that Phlios' plans for removing the rubbish to some distance were going to delay his uncovering of the buildings at the centre of the citadel. Within a few days he complained in a telegram to the Minister of Culture in ancient Greek:

Ephor Phlios and I disagree about the method of excavation. As I began to dig out a building on the west side, Phlios highhandedly forbade me, compelling me to excavate from the south end, where he thinks the main gate is. He is forcing me to build a broad path there for the transport of rubbish. I complied, wishing to show Phlios' mistake and injustice. A great wall whose top is visible above the ground precludes the possibility that the entrance is there. In addition it is absolutely impossible to build a path there because of the height and the steepness of the slope. I have spent an entire week of my precious time utterly in vain. Excavation is learned not in schools or universities but by practical experience. The thirty shafts I dug in Tiryns in 1876 showed that Tiryns is full of wonderful cyclopean rooms, many of whose walls reach up to the present surface. Hence it is absolutely necessary to clear away the earth from the surface in search of the interconnecting rooms. It cannot be done any other way. If you allow me to excavate without the interference of Phlios, I will apply myself with religious zeal and complete the great task. I promise I will remove the rubbish again from the walls.[12]

He sent the telegram to Sophia with instructions to take it and read it to the Minister herself. Two days later another telegram to the Minister suggested that Phlios should stop his supervisory work and restrict himself to receiving the finds. Some sort of compromise seems to have been reached. But a few days later another telegram flew to Sophia to be read to the Minister. Schliemann claimed that he had built the paths for the removal of the soil and would now be making rapid progress but for Phlios, who insisted that they should be working only in two places at once. Schliemann said that because of the constricted nature of the site they needed two places for excavating and two places for loading the carts.[13]

Dörpfeld did not join the excavations until the first week in April. Soon after his arrival he wrote to his father-in-law:

> Schliemann had piddled about for 20 days before my arrival without finding anything out of the ordinary. He had excavated a few walls, which he took to be Byzantine. But these walls are certainly those of the ancient royal palace, which extends over almost the entire upper citadel. You will recall perhaps that we had already noted 3 column bases, 1 pillar, and a floor in all the holes that Schliemann dug. This floor is made of lime and is still well preserved everywhere and is an excellent guide for the excavations.[14]

The following day Schliemann reported to a friend in Paris some exciting discoveries:

> I have almost finished clearing the immense prehistoric palace of Tiryns, in which I have not found a sherd later than the 9th century B.C. It shows two different periods. The palace was fitted with numerous columns with Doric capitals – the earliest that have ever been discovered – the friezes with sculptured palmettes and rosettes and with marvellous mosaic ornamentation in glass paste are unique. The wall-paintings are marvellous. Among the motifs is the entire ceiling of the thalamos of Orchomenos. The representation of men and animals is even more primitive than in the tombs of Mycenae.[15]

That same day he sent a telegram to Sophia, telling her to arrange with the artist Emile Gilliéron to come at once to Tiryns to make full-colour reproductions of the paintings.[16] On 11 April Schliemann gave a more detailed account to John Murray:

> Three cheers to Pallas Athena! In fact I have succeeded here in a wonderful way, having brought to light an immense palace with innumerable columns, which occupies the entire upper acropolis of Tiryns and of which the floor and all the walls are well preserved. It denotes two different epochs, of which the oldest is that of the Mycenaean tombs, whilst the second and *latest* must be earlier than the 9th

century B.C. Of paramount interest are the wall-paintings, which my architect and assistant, Dr. Dörpfeld, is now copying with the same colours. Of the very highest interest are also the vase paintings with the most primitive representations of men and animals. The plan of the wonderful prehistoric palace can be made with great accuracy and it will excite universal amazement, for nothing like this has ever turned up.[17]

Excerpts from this letter were published in the *Athenaeum*, prompting Percy Gardner to ask Schliemann if he would consider publishing a full report in the *Journal of Hellenic Studies*. Schliemann, however, did not want to abandon his long-standing association with Murray. Murray, on the other hand, who had found the sales of *Ilios* and *Troja* disappointing, was alarmed by the cost of the large number of coloured plates needed to show the wall-paintings and the most interesting of the vase-paintings, and proposed that the book be published on commission. This did not please Schliemann. So he sent a sketch of the palace plan to the noted architectural historian James Fergusson, a friend and adviser of John Murray, who from the beginning had responded enthusiastically to the news of the discovery. He was even more enthusiastic when he saw the sketch of Dörpfeld's plan. He was influential in convincing Murray to take the book on the usual terms. Cost-sharing arrangements were eventually worked out between the various publishers to reduce Murray's risk.

Gilliéron came to Tiryns in response to Schliemann's urgent request but after three days returned to Athens. Schliemann then insisted that the wall-paintings be sent to Athens so that Gilliéron could copy them there. The largest fragment of wall-painting showed 'a man dancing on a bull', as it was then interpreted. The discovery of a number of similar scenes has since shown that the man is not dancing but engaged in 'bull-leaping'. The question is often asked whether this was a sport or a religious ritual, but it is most unlikely that the Minoans and Mycenaeans would have distinguished clearly between these two activities. The Olympic and other Greek games after all were held as part of a religious festival. Other fragments showed ornamental motifs virtually identical to those on the ceiling of the side-chamber at Orchomenos or on small objects of ivory and gold found in some of the tholos tombs. Surprisingly, however, in contemplating these fragments of wall-painting Schliemann does not seem to have recalled that he had found similar fresco fragments at Mycenae but had assumed that they must date from the classical period or later.[18]

In mid-April Schliemann went off to Athens for three weeks, leaving Dörpfeld in charge of the excavations. He had arranged to receive Prince

Bernhard von Saxe-Meiningen as a guest in Iliou Melathron and to act as his guide around Athens and Greece. Meanwhile in London, as Fergusson studied the plan of Tiryns, he noticed that the central structural elements of the palace complex resembled 'Temples A and B' at Troy: 'The two temples are so nearly identical, in both cities, that they must be of the same age, and belong to the same civilization.'[19] Dörpfeld had formed a similar opinion. When he came to write up his description of the architecture of the palace in *Tiryns*, Dörpfeld called the building a 'megaron', Homer's great hall. The name has stuck. Increasingly, he came to believe that 'Temples A and B' at Troy must be megara and not temples. The inference, however, made by both Dörpfeld and Fergusson and adopted by Schliemann, that the similarity between the megara of Troy II and Tiryns proved that they were contemporary, was mistaken. The megaron was a long-lived architectural form. Troy II and the palace at Tiryns were separated by about 700 years.

The palace at Tiryns dates to the Lower Helladic IIIA period (1400–1300 BC) and later. The crude obsidian knives and arrowheads, which Schliemann adduced to prove the prehistoric nature of the palace, insisting that they were found in its destruction level, can hardly be of this date.[20] More likely they came from an Early Helladic level below the palace or from the lower acropolis. Unfortunately, the Tiryns diary, along with all the other excavation diaries that Schliemann presumably kept for the period 1877–89, is lost. We have therefore no primary source to use as a check against Schliemann's statements in *Tiryns*. One forms the impression, however, that, as at Mycenae, he seldom knew where individual items were found. Whether Phlios himself kept a day-book of the excavations is unclear. What is clear is that information on the exact provenance of the finds is unsatisfactory. Yet Tiryns, far more than Troy and Mycenae, was a site where accurate reporting on stratification was a comparatively straightforward task. At Tiryns the stratification was not disturbed by large-scale remodelling and is therefore more regular. Moreover, the lime floor throughout the palace provided a very obvious line of demarcation between different strata. It would have been simple and very helpful to record whether objects were found above or below this floor. Also, even if one accepts the basic assumption that the depth at which an object was found is an adequate indication of its stratum – an assumption which Schliemann knew from his own observation to be fallacious – it is clear that the stratum at a depth of 2 metres in the lower citadel, outside the palace area, may well be rather different from the stratum at a depth of 2 metres on the upper citadel, where the palace was located. Generally speaking, however, we are told only the depth at which a given object was found, without any further indication of where the find was made. A section giving even a rough indication of stratification, such as Calvert offered for Hanai Tepe in *Ilios* (see Fig. 19), would have been most useful. Instead, Dörpfeld's sections (Plate III of *Tiryns*) show only the location of the architectural features. The soil is presented as an undifferentiated mass. Probably Schliemann's excessive haste is to be blamed.

The arrows on Plan V (see Appendix V) show the approach to the centre of the palace up the ramp marked △, through the gate in the northern circuit-wall, through the interior gate (⊖), on to the large propylaeum or gateway (H), which opens into the great forecourt (F). From here a smaller propylaeum (K) leads into the colonnaded courtyard (L) before the large (or 'men's') megaron (M). In the megaron itself a porch and an anteroom precede the main hall, where four columns surround the central hearth. Here, presumably, the king sat with his courtiers. Adjacent to this but connected to it only circuitously is a smaller (or 'women's') megaron (O) with its own forecourt (N).[21]

On 31 May 1884 Schliemann wrote to Mahaffy:

> It is now decided that Dr. Dörpfeld writes *himself* the whole text on the architecture of Tiryns, that Dr Fabricius writes himself a couple of pages on the wallpaintings and that I give the text on all the other antiquities. As those friends write their part in German, I shall do the same. Since I am overworked I shall not make myself the English translation but let it translate by somebody else. As you offered me last year at Oxford your literary assistance, I would ask you whether it would suit you to make the English translation and help editing it *without* any mention being made of this service either on the titlepage or in the text, for my N. York and London publishers would absolutely be opposed to it. Thus your only reward would be in pounds Stlg.

In July Schliemann consulted Sir Henry Thompson, the leading London urologist. Thompson found no sign of an enlarged prostate and attributed Schliemann's urinary difficulties to stress brought on by overwork. He prescribed limited doses of strychnine and abstinence from sweets, fatty foods and alcohol. Pepper, vinegar and curry, strictly forbidden at Wildungen, were allowed by Thompson.[22] After relaxing for a couple of weeks at Marienbad, where Sophia enjoyed the mud baths, he gave a report on his excavations at Tiryns at the 1884 congress of the German Anthropological Society in Breslau (now Wroclaw in Poland). Both Virchow and Dörpfeld were present. Schliemann was very pleased with his reception:

> If an old benefactor of Breslau could arise from the dead and appear suddenly in the streets of the city, he could hardly be received with greater enthusiasm than that

with which I was hailed there at every step. The fireworks on both sides <of> the river, producing in the most beautiful colours Virchow's name and mine, was grand beyond description.[23]

It was almost an equal triumph for Dörpfeld. His splendid plans were the centre of attention. A few days later in Berlin, Dörpfeld's father-in-law gave a party to show off his son-in-law's talent to potential employers:

All his drawings and plans were exhibited on Friday evening to a party of the most eminent Berlin architects Adler had invited to meet me. I can assure you that they excited universal applause and that no-one looked on them without the most lively admiration.[24]

Schliemann spent the last week of August in London and settled the contract for *Tiryns* with Murray. Brockhaus was once again to do the German edition while Scribner took the American and Reinwald the French. To Virchow he confided: 'The key thing was Murray, for everyone wants what he takes on.'[25]

In the closing months of 1884 Schliemann concerned himself with Virchow's suggestion that the next International Conference on Prehistory be held in Athens. Much of the discussion centered on who would be chosen as president and secretary of the conference. In an interesting letter, Schliemann ran through the leading figures of the Greek Archaeological Society, pointing out why none was suitable for presiding at the conference. The Society's President, Kontostavlos, 'has not the remotest idea about archaeology'; Koumanoudis (General Secretary) became jealous of Schliemann because of his success at Mycenae 'and Tiryns has made him so furious with me that he could roast me alive'; Phinticles (Vice-President) was also hostile because of jealousy; Kaphtandjoglou (Architect) had written a long letter to the Society of British Architects when it had made Schliemann an honorary member, attacking him 'with outrageous insults'; Nicolaides had conceived a profound hatred for Schliemann, calling his work 'the most awful fraud and villainy', because his excavations had disproved Nicolaides' theory about the location of Troy. The only Greek Schliemann thought worthy of the honour of presiding at the proposed convention was Stephanos Dragoumis, the Greek Foreign Minister, and *he* refused absolutely to have anything to do with it.[26] Clearly, Schliemann's stock had fallen among the Greek archaeological establishment. At least one reason for this lay in his manner of conducting the excavations at Tiryns. Michael Deffner, Librarian of the National and University Library in Athens, expressed current resentment in a letter to *The Nation*:

If I am now called upon to express myself openly concerning the mode in which the excavations have been conducted, my judgment is by no means favourable. Friend Schliemann has dug over the whole upper and middle Acropolis, which, as I have already said, was covered with a débris nearly a metre in thickness. He made it very easy for himself, however, by merely dumping the rubbish on the cyclopean walls. To be sure, the Cultus-Minister, with excessive compliance, finally permitted the stuff to be temporarily thrown down over the walls, after Dr. Schliemann had pledged himself by telegraph to remove it from the citadel at the conclusion of the excavations. . . . And yet he terminates his excavations, lets the rubbish lie, and assures the Ministry that it has been removed. I am greatly distressed by this impiety, which borders on vandalism, and God knows that it rendered my stay and walks in Tiryns disagreeable. . . . And if the Cultus-Ministry intends, as I am informed, to prosecute Schliemann on account of <his excavations>, it will only be doing its duty.[27]

Late in 1884 Schliemann and Dörpfeld began writing *Tiryns*. Since Dörpfeld could not write in English, they both wrote in German. By the beginning of February 1885, it was virtually finished and Schliemann was compiling the index.[28] The English translation, however, was lagging far behind. Schliemann was already in a dispute with Murray over the plans, which had been reproduced by photolithography – defectively, in Schliemann's view – rather than by lithography. Dörpfeld threatened to withhold his name from them unless they were improved. Schliemann now blamed Murray for being slow at sending out the English proofs. In fact, the problem seems to have lain with Mahaffy, as Murray made clear in a stiff letter to Schliemann:

Mr Fergusson has just sent to me your letter of 5 February and I can only express my amazement at the accusations which you bring against me. You appear to be under a complete misapprehension of the circumstances of the case and I will endeavour to explain them. In the first place you appear to have forgotten that the translation rests with Professor Mahaffy and not with me. In October one or two of your German sheets reached me, and these I forwarded by the next post to Prof. Mahaffy. From that day to this I have never seen another German sheet of the work. In due time Prof. Mahaffy's translation of these sheets reached us, and was immediately (11 November) sent to Messrs. Clowes [the printer]. It made 28 slips and in due course proofs were sent out, and there have been several revises but neither we nor Messrs. Clowes have received any more copy. We suppose that Prof. Mahaffy, who is in direct communication with yourself, has received the remaining German sheets; if he has not, it is no fault of mine.[28]

In mid-January a sad event occurred in Schliemann's house. With his usual dramatic flair he described it in a letter to Virchow:

The day before yesterday was my wife's birthday and we had invited all her relatives for dinner. But when my mother-in-law stepped over the threshold of the front door, she had a stabbing pain in her chest and collapsed. I was immediately called to her side and found her lying on a mattress at the front door in fearful convulsions. She recognized me, however, among those standing around her and called out in modern Greek: 'My good son-in-law, come, let me kiss you. I am dying.' Then she kissed me six times very affectionately. I still had no notion that she could be dangerously ill. But Zochios, the doctor, who had been hastily summoned, indicated that she already had one collapsed lung and that her condition was very critical. On his orders a mustard poultice was prepared but before this could be applied, we laid her on the bed, unconscious and in the throes of the death rattle. She passed away one or two minutes later. Her entire illness had lasted scarcely twenty minutes. It is impossible to give you an idea of the heart-rending scenes that followed, impossible to describe the despair of my poor wife. By giving her two eggs with her early morning coffee, their yolks and whites whipped up to a foam, and a small glass of tonic wine before every meal, and even stopping her from taking injections once a day, I have with great tenderness, now put her on the road to recovery.[30]

Schliemann recalled that twelve years earlier his father-in-law had died of a stroke and remarked on the coincidence that both of his parents-in-law had died in his house.[31] He also remarked: 'They both loved me much more than I deserved.' At the funeral he noticed that many learned men were buried in simple graves. To Virchow he confessed: 'I felt ashamed at the thought that I had set aside 70,000 fr. for my family tomb. What do you think of the idea of reducing the sum to 10,000 fr. and with the remainder setting up a scholarship for Homeric research with the pickaxe and the spade?'

On 26 January 1885 Khartoum fell to Muslim forces led by Muhammad Ahmed after a siege of ten months. General Gordon was killed in the ensuing slaughter. The expeditionary force sent by Gladstone to relieve Gordon arrived two days later. Word of the fall of Khartoum reached European capitals on 3 February and of Gordon's death on 11 February. Opprobrium was heaped on Gladstone for his months of indecisiveness and inaction. On 11 February Virchow remarked to Schliemann: 'Gladstone is completely incomprehensible to me. How can a man of his life experience practise such a childish foreign policy? It is truly pitiful.'[32] Schliemann echoed his sentiments: 'Gladstone's politics are profoundly hateful to me. I hope that before you read this he is no longer at the helm.'[33]

In March Schliemann received some very good news. The Royal Institute of Architects in London had nominated him to receive the Royal Gold Medal for 1885 and Queen Victoria had approved the nomination. The

Queen had instituted the award in 1847. It was awarded annually, on the recommendation of the Institute, to an architect who had designed a building of high merit or to someone who had made an outstanding contribution to architecture. The Institute had recommended Schliemann because of the light his excavations had thrown on the early history of architecture. The award was to be made in London on 8 June. Naturally, Schliemann wanted to attend the ceremony but this would interfere with his plans for lobbying the Cretan parliament. Work on the proofs of *Tiryns* was going to keep him in Athens until the end of April. If he now had to be in London before 8 June, there simply would not be enough time to lobby effectively in Crete. Reluctantly, he reached the decision in April that he would not excavate in Crete in 1885.

In the spring Schliemann was kept very busy, as he wrote to Murray:

> I have had *very hard* times of late being inundated by German, French and English proofs, the French even of two books simultaneously (*Ilios* and *Tiryns*). The French *Tiryns* has given me an immense trouble to correct, but still more so the English, for Mahaffy's translation abounds with omissions, false translation and wrong numbers, so that slips 105–149, which I returned the day before yesterday to Clowes have taken me not less than 4 days.[34]

Mahaffy, who had been sent a letter detailing his shortcomings with similar candour, wrote back in protest that he had undertaken the task of translating *Tiryns* as a favour for a friend:

> But when you urged and urged in such a way that we were killing ourselves to please you, now this is our thanks. But now I am disheartened at your last very unfriendly note, and but for my sincere regard for your other kindness and your splendid work should be disposed to quarrel with you. But I will regard this letter of yours as not written, and hope that you will think seriously before you offend one of your best friends.

Mahaffy ended the letter with a touch of humour: 'I am very sincerely, indeed most truly, your packmule, J. Mahaffy.'[35]

Meanwhile Dörpfeld had been sent back to finish the work at Tiryns. This was explained as follows in the *Revue Archéologique*: 'Following the complaints that have been made against M. Schliemann, who is accused of having buried the circuit wall at Tiryns under the soil from his diggings in the course of his recent excavations there, M. Dörpfeld had been sent to Tiryns to attend to the complete clearing of this circuit wall.'[36] Schliemann also wanted Dörpfeld to excavate all the inner passageways.[37]

Regarding the walls of Tiryns, Schliemann assumed, 'with great probability', that they were built by Phoenician colonists.[38] Sayce, as we have seen, saw strong Phoenician influence on early Greece. He believed that there was a Phoenician settlement at Athens itself but admitted that this could not be proved.[39] In Phoenician colonies in Africa, notably Carthage and Thapsos, Dörpfeld found close parallels for the gallery and room arrangement in the fortification wall at Tiryns and he too became an ardent supporter of the Phoenician theory. Though fashionable in 1885 and recently revived by Martin Bernal in *Black Athena*, the theory that the Phoenicians were early colonizers of Greece has practically no adherents among archaeologists today; no archaeological evidence for any Phoenician settlement in Greece has so far been discovered.

Despite Fergusson's advice that Schliemann should not give a speech at the Royal Institute of Architects, Schliemann had prepared one anyway. Fergusson managed to persuade him to read the speech to him individually rather than at the Institute.[40] After two weeks at Boulogne, Schliemann took Sophia and the children to St Moritz-Bad in Switzerland but went on himself to Abano in Italy to take the famous mudbath cure for rheumatism in his right arm.[41] On 6 August Schliemann went to Karlsruhe to give a paper on the 1885 excavations at Tiryns at the German Anthropological Congress. It was here that the rupture with Virchow occurred. By any account, the issue was extraordinarily petty. It is clear from a letter Virchow wrote a few days after the incident that he was completely unaware that he had in any way offended Schliemann, whose precipitous departure from the conference had caused much speculation. Schliemann gave his version of what happened in a letter addressed formally to 'Counsellor Virchow' instead of the usual 'Honoured friend'.

> I thought we had concluded a lifelong bond of friendship, not only for ourselves but also for our children, and nothing was further from my thoughts than the notion that it could suddenly be destroyed. But that is what happened. Twice Wagner invited me in your and your wife's presence to escort your wife to the table and to take my place beside her. If this was not what you wanted, a friendly word spoken to him or to me would have been enough to arrange matters in accordance with your wishes. You preferred, however, to direct me publicly, in an imperious tone, to another seat. I have had to endure many insults and slanders in my life but none of them – at least in the last 40 years – has hurt me so deeply as that which I suffered at your hands at the banquet in Karlsruhe. You have thereby deliberately and forcibly broken our friendship. All that remains for my wife and myself to do is to take our leave of you forever.

Not surprisingly, Virchow's view of the incident was very different:

Honoured friend:

I began my letter, in spite of yours, in the usual way and if it is to be the last I write to you, at least you should not have the impression that my feelings for you are other than they were. How is it possible for you to make such a mountain out of a molehill! Wagner is not very gifted socially. He had told me that all the places at the high table were reserved for the executive committee; we wanted to be free to do what we liked with them. Accordingly, Schaaffhausen engaged my wife as his dinner partner, I took the eldest Fräulein Schaaffhausen and Hans the younger. But before we could take our seats, the places were already partly occupied so that Hans had to go to a completely different section of the table. If you had sat next to my wife, who, as I said, had been spoken for by Schaaffhausen, I too would have been obliged, with the other Fräulein Schaaffhausen, to look for a place at the lower end of the table, for there were not two adjacent seats free on the high table either to the left or to the right. Unfortunately, I did not learn of Wagner's invitation to you to sit beside my wife in time. In any case, I considered it more a matter of courtesy when I asked you to take your seat beside the wife of the local representative, Herr Wagner.

If I had had any idea that you set store by such a triviality, I could, of course, have explained my reasons to you. I am certain that you would have agreed with me that on certain formal occasions friendship must yield to courtesy. However, I was so convinced that I was offering you the first place after the President that I considered further explanations unnecessary, especially since I had no time for them in view of the jostling for seats. I am very sorry if the few words I recall having said to you were spoken in an inappropriate manner. But I would like to add to my apology that just before that I had asked the President of the Museum, Herr Ulmann, if he would move one seat along so that Hans and Fräulein Schaaffhausen could have a seat opposite us. He had answered with a curt refusal; so I was in an irritable mood.

As I read your letter once again, I see that you say that Wagner had invited you *in the presence of my wife and myself* to take my wife to the dinner table and sit beside her. You appear to conclude from this that we heard this invitation. However, neither my wife nor myself recall having heard anything of the kind. Rather, Schaaffhausen had asked my wife to escort her to table and she had accepted, though she does not belong to the circle of his admirers. When you add to this that it all happened publicly, I am convinced that although the event took place in a public setting, no-one paid any heed to it. On the contrary, in most of the conversations about your sudden departure, not even the slightest suggestion was made in my presence that anyone thought I had hurt you. All conjectures were focused only on the Grossherzog von Baden.

You are a distrustful man and this is not the first time you have ascribed malice to me. This time, however, I am more upset because you have more or less taken me for a fool. It will not stop me from thinking with thankful heart on the many pleasant and instructive days that I have spent with you and you can count on it that

I will be happy to be of service to you again when necessary. But I find that you have less and less need for this assistance the more the world learns to appreciate you. In my own name and in the name of my wife I bid you a friendly farewell.

This incident marks a dramatic break in their relationship.[42] There were no further letters between Schliemann and Virchow until June 1886, when Schliemann wrote to Virchow and the correspondence slowly picked up again.[43] Unfortunately, by a strange twist of fate, all of Virchow's remaining letters to Schliemann are missing except for those written in 1889.

Schliemann spent the latter part of August in St Moritz-Bad with his family. Here he renewed his acquaintance with the ophthalmologist Dr H. Cohn of Breslau, whom he had met at the anthropological congress in 1884. Cohn was the father of Emil Ludwig, the first biographer of Schliemann. He published a brief account of his recollections of their meeting at St Moritz-Bad after Schliemann's death.[44] He considered the Schliemanns' marriage a happy one. Both husband and wife worked for seven or eight hours a day on the proofs for the different editions of *Tiryns*. They chose to stay in the old Kurhaus rather than in the expensive and fashionable Hotel du Lac. He likened them to a pair of modest academics. Cohn's conversations with Schliemann were largely about short-sightedness – Schliemann expressed scepticism about ophthalmology – and Homer, from whose poems Schliemann recited long passages, mostly in modern Greek. Cohn was most impressed by the ability of both Schliemanns to speak with practically all of the very diverse clientele of the spa, switching easily from one language to another. Sophia spoke North German so well that in his opinion she might well have been mistaken for a native of Pomerania.

A young girl, Helene Schelberg, who played tennis, croquet and 'Excavating Troy' with Andromache and Agamemnon that summer at St Moritz-Bad, had a rather different impression of the Schliemanns.[45] 'Here comes your grand-papa,' she said to Andromache one day. Andromache replied: 'That's my papa.' When Helene curtsied and said 'Good morning, Dr Schliemann,' he took no notice of her. After that she avoided contact with the 'grouch'. But Schliemann treated even distinguished visitors to the spa in a similarly offhand manner. When they introduced themselves, he said 'Ja, ja,' lifted his hat and moved on. Like Schliemann, Helene's father had been working too hard and was restless. He and Schliemann went for early morning walks together from four until breakfast. They had much in common. Schelberg was in the whole-sale business and had often been to America and England. Helene noticed that Sophia, the children and the governess were all in awe of Schliemann and reserved and unassuming in his presence.

Schliemann had offered to buy from the Turkish government the pottery that had fallen to their share of the finds from the 1878, 1879 and 1882 excavations in the Troad. When he learned that the offer had finally been accepted, Schliemann returned to Athens via Constantinople, where he had the pieces properly crated and sent off to Berlin.

On 10 November the German, French, British and American editions of *Tiryns* were published simultaneously. On the same day the long-delayed French edition of *Ilios* (incorporating *Troja*) also came out in Paris. This was truly a remarkable achievement. But more than ever Schliemann was anxious to ensure that the books were favourably reviewed. He wrote to Brockhaus:

> I will send you from Constantinople a list of copies of *Tiryns* to be sent out, charged to my account. There are other people, however, whose reviews will help your sales enormously, but I must also pay them enormously for the reviews. You must send copies to these individuals on your account and particularly to Dr. Karl Blind, whom I can pay not less than £50 for his dissertations. Please send him 1 copy so that he can write his article and publish it on your publication day, which he has been given.[46]

Schliemann was now exhausted. He needed a complete change. As early as April he had made up his mind that after the books came out he would go to Cuba.[47] Schliemann, like Sayce, liked to be in a warm climate during the winter months. A more important reason was that he had very substantial holdings (£35,000 or £2,100,000 today) in two Cuban railway companies and he was concerned about the economic situation there. The price of sugar, the staple of the Cuban economy, had been declining rapidly throughout the 1880s. It also looked as if slave labour would soon be completely abolished.[48] Schliemann decided to go there to size up for himself the prospects for his railway shares. He left from St Nazaire in late December and did not return until mid-February.

In September the Schliemanns had gone to Lausanne to find a suitable school for Andromache. The following month Sophia returned to Lausanne. She was very concerned to find that one of Andromache's classmates had fallen in love with the nephew of Madame Krafft, who ran the school, and that Andromache (now fourteen) was learning too much, too fast about sex, or what she thought of as romantic feelings: 'We all need instruction except about the expression of love.'[49] Since Sophia thought that Madame Krafft was far too liberal, she wanted Andromache back in Athens under the tutelage of a governess. Sophia returned with Agamemnon to Lausanne in late December

249

to spend Christmas with Andromache. She became ill and spent five days in her room in the Hotel Gibbon in front of a blazing fire. She hated the cold. After concluding that Andromache's morals were in even more acute danger, she scooped up the children and fled to Athens.[50]

I

15

Cuba, Cairo and Kythera

SCHLIEMANN ENJOYED HIS BRIEF stay in Cuba immensely. 'I have never,' he wrote to Brockhaus from Havana, 'since my Nile trip of 1858–59, spent such happy days as these in Cuba. Unfortunately, I am well known even here and the ovations are such that the two railroad companies in which I am interested have put extra trains at my disposal so that I can inspect everything at my convenience.'[1] That these courtesies were extended to Schliemann had, of course, nothing to do with his fame as an archaeologist. Rather, they reflected his status as a major shareholder, who could, at any moment, wreak financial havoc by selling off his shares. The tone of the letter, feigning weariness with his status as an international celebrity, is a nice touch. Schliemann rode back and forth on the lines of his railroad companies, questioned plantation owners about shipments of sugar, and generally made a careful assessment of the economic prospects. Immediately on his return to Paris in mid-February he sold £9000 worth of shares in the Havana Railroad Company and started negotiating to buy property in Berlin.[2] In March he purchased an apartment building at 5 Potsdamer Strasse. At the time of his death he owned it jointly with Sophia.[3]

Reinvigorated by his trip to Cuba, Schliemann's thoughts turned again to archaeology. The discovery of the prehistoric palace at Tiryns naturally prompted the expectation that there must be a similar palace at Mycenae.[4] Indeed Schliemann had found traces of just such a building at the summit of the acropolis there in 1874. Clearly, after having laid bare at Tiryns a palace that might with some plausibility be attributed to Diomedes, the prospect of revealing to the world the plan of Agamemnon's palace at Mycenae must have been irresistible. However, as he had explained to Virchow in November 1884, Schliemann now had few friends among the archaeological establishment in Athens. He was convinced that most of the Greek archaeologists were envious of his achievements. So the more he talked of making further glamorous discoveries in Greece, the less likely he would be to obtain permission to excavate. Accordingly, he tried to be more cautious. In April he told Schöne: 'I have now almost decided, instead of pursuing my researches in Crete, to excavate carefully the whole of the citadel of the Atridae in Mycenae. This will take perhaps four years and be the last work of my life.'⁵ But to another correspondent in Berlin he was less cautious, adding: 'But even now I venture to promise that I shall there unearth a palace, the plan of which has most resemblance to that of Troy or that of Tiryns.' Not surprisingly, these remarks found their way into the press.⁶ Presumably, Schliemann had applied for permission to resume excavations at Mycenae. Two other projects he mentions in the letter to Schöne were further advanced:

> In 9 days I am going with Dr. Dörpfeld to Levadia to look for and to excavate the oracle of Trophonios; and then to Orchomenos to continue excavating out from the secret thalamos. Besides the remarkable ceiling, there was an empty room, and in one of its walls there was an entranceway walled with crude bricks. I disregarded it, as I then thought that the bricks dated from the Middle Ages, while I now suspect that they may be as old as the thalamos itself.

The search for the oracle at Levadia proved fruitless. At Orchomenos, only a few miles distant from Levadia, the main purpose for resuming excavations was almost certainly to find a palace. But this may not have been stated in the application for a permit. As it turned out, the main outcome of the excavations was a group of excellent plans by Dörpfeld. They found no royal graves or further 'treasuries', as Schliemann still persisted in calling what nearly everyone now saw as tholos tombs. They dug some exploratory shafts and found 'many individual housewalls of sun-dried bricks or undressed stone, similar to those in Troy or Tiryns, but no interconnected building whose excavation would have been desirable.'⁷ In the phrase 'no interconnected building' we get a clear indication of what Schliemann and Dörpfeld were really looking for: a prehistoric palace similar to that at Tiryns.

After a brief stop in Athens Schliemann and Dörpfeld hurried on to Crete:

> Next we visited Crete, where the sites of Gortyn and Knossos particularly attracted our attention. Both are covered with Roman ruins and potsherds, but on a hill at Knossos, which seems to us for the most part to be man-made, two remarkable, hewn blocks jutted out. Minos Kalokairinos of Herakleion, who dug 5 holes there, found in them parts of walls of a large prehistoric building with several corridors, which vividly reminded us of our learned and sensitive discoverer of the fire necropolises, Captain Bötticher – all the more so as one cor-

ridor had, standing upright next to one another, 12 large pitchers, decorated with geometrical patterns in relief, all of which, unfortunately for him, contained lentils or beans. Samples of both enclosed. It is a most remarkable fact that in the building there was otherwise found only pottery with Tirynthian or Mycenaean shapes and patterns. It is an interesting question what might be found in the lowest strata of this hill, when such ancient terracottas are found here lying on the surface.[8]

From Knossos itself Schliemann wrote to Max Müller:

I have therefore resolved to excavate this hillock systematically and to put off the Acropolis of Mycenae until Knossos is done. Dr. Dörpfeld will serve me in both works as architect. As I work from pure love for science and give up my finds to the Museum at Heracleion, I have not the slightest difficulty to get the permission to excavate at Knossos or wherever I like in Crete. On the contrary, my arrival in Crete produced a storm of enthusiasm in the better classes of the Greek population, and as soon as the Cretan parliament meets (say at the end of July) a law will be made for the expropriation of lands for scientific explorations, so that the hillock in Knossos may be had at a low price, for otherwise the proprietors think their lands are goldmines and ask monstrous prices. So f<or> i<nstance> a miller on the site of Gortyn asked me £2000 for a piece of ground which is not larger than your house . . . I hope to begin work in November . . .[9]

Schliemann's optimism about obtaining permission to excavate appears to derive from his acquaintance with Dr Iosif Hatzidakis, the leading figure in Cretan archaeology, who was highly influential in the Cretan parliament. An unexpected problem, however, seems to have arisen because of the high prices asked by the owners. Schliemann clearly hoped that the Cretan parliament would requisition the land for him. This did not happen. The owners at Knossos were not interested in selling merely the archaeological site. They would only sell all their land, which included arable fields and thousands of olive-trees, or nothing. The asking price was 100,000 francs.[10]

Meantime, controversy over Schliemann's excavations had erupted in the columns of *The Times*. W.J. Stillman, the former American consul in Crete, had recently become the Athens correspondent for *The Times*. A few years earlier he had taken it on himself to cast Luigi Palma di Cesnola, who had sold most of his collection of Cypriot antiquities to the Metropolitan Museum of New York, and then become its Director, as a free-wheeling tomb robber, collector and dealer. Stillman had a similarly low opinion of Schliemann and in a letter to *The Times* had referred to the recent successes in Cyprus and Mycenae as the 'fortunate groping of unskilled explorers'.[11]

In the spring of 1886 Stillman visited Tiryns and Mycenae in the company of F.C. Penrose, who subsequently became Director of the British School of Archaeology in Athens, and two members of the American School. The unanimous findings of the group were that the grave circle and the burials within it should be dated after the destruction of the city in 468 BC and that the palace at Tiryns was probably of Byzantine date.[12] These startling conclusions were based for the most part on rather technical judgements about walling and the use of certain instruments in the cutting of stones. But it was not so much the arguments that carried weight as the fact they were made by F. C. Penrose, the leading historian of architecture in Athens. At Mycenae, the city walls, the Lion Gate and the 'Treasury of Atreus', the party unanimously agreed, were unquestionably of prehistoric date. With the grave circle, however, it was a different matter. 'After careful examination of every part of the structures, Mr. Penrose declared them, without hesitation, subsequent to classic Greek work, and even late in the period of decline of Greece.' Similarly, at Tiryns the architectural features were pronounced to be post-Macedonian. In short: 'Our party came unanimously to the conclusion that both these constructions – that of the tomb [i.e. grave circle] of Mycenae and the Palace – are the remains of some obscure barbarous tribe which re-occupied the ruins of the old cities, and established a temporary rule there during the decay of Greece.' In other words, another version of the theory first put forward independently by two scholars in 1878 and then reintroduced by Stephani in 1880 had once again reared its head. A week later Stillman returned to Mycenae and Tiryns with some friends from Oxford, including H.F. Pelham, the Oxford ancient historian. The second group confirmed the findings of the earlier group.[13]

Copies of the *Times* articles reached Schliemann in Levadia. He had Dörpfeld write a reply and asked Murray to persuade Percy Gardner to write one too. Gardner called the articles by Stillman foolish but said that he personally was not competent to reply to them as he had never been to Tiryns. He went on: 'The Hellenic Society is thinking of having a special meeting about 1st July to fully discuss the question. I will do what I can on the right side, but I am afraid that the adversaries will say that they have been to Tiryns and I have not. How I wish that you or Dr. Dörpfeld could be present on the occasion. It would be a great opportunity for silencing these unpleasant attacks.'[14] Schliemann took up the challenge. He and Dörpfeld hurried to London to attend the meeting. Stillman had gone off to Italy. His paper, which essentially repeated the arguments put forward in *The Times*, was read by Pelham. Penrose's arguments were also largely based on construction techniques. In addition, he pointed out, reasonably enough, that the swords found by Schliemann at Mycenae were rather similar to the much later Celtic swords of northern Europe and suggested a parallel for the gold masks in a lead mask found at Bath in the Roman period. Schliemann's response was particularly effective. The opposition had made much of the apparently later character of the retaining wall on the south side of the grave circle. He made the startling revelation that it was in fact only ten years old. 'Wishing to consolidate the terrace of the tombs, the Greek Archaeological Society has reconstructed this enclosure wall in 1876. It has also restored approximately, in the shape in which I had found them, the internal walls of the tombs of which I had been obliged to take out every stone in order to save the gold.'[15] Newton read a translation of Dörpfeld's paper. Though in its account of the session *The Times* tried valiantly to give the impression that the result was inconclusive, there can be little doubt that it was perceived as a clear-cut victory for Schliemann and Dörpfeld. George Macmillan, the Honorary Secretary of the Hellenic Society, wrote to Schliemann two days after the debate: 'I am sure that the universal opinion here among all who are really competent to judge, was that, so far as the high antiquity of the palace at Tiryns is concerned, the case of your opponents utterly and completely broke down.'[16]

The summer was spent as usual in northern Europe in quest of a cure for Sophia's mysterious, apparently largely psychological, ailments. They tried Dr Mezger's famous massage cure in Amsterdam, then the baths at Burtsheid, just outside Aachen. The new museum in Berlin was finally ready and Schliemann was able to supervise the arrangement of the finds to his satisfaction. The ceiling of one of the rooms devoted to his finds was, in accordance with his instructions, decorated in the style of the ceiling of the side-chamber at Orchomenos.

When Schliemann learned that the Cretan parliament had dissolved without requisitioning the site at Knossos, he decided to abandon his plans to excavate there in October. He seems to have continued to negotiate with the owners through Hatzidakis, presumably with the intention of excavating there in the spring of 1887. This summer the spa treatments had had little beneficial effect on the Schliemanns, for in Paris in September they both felt far from well. In view of their state of health Schliemann wrote to Sayce, telling him that following his oft-repeated suggestion they proposed to join him on his annual winter Nile cruise. Sayce replied: 'I cannot express my vexation at learning that the winter you propose to pass in Egypt is precisely the winter I shall have to remain at home.'[17] Sayce's mother had died that summer and he was staying to clear up her estate.

In October or November Schliemann visited the new excavations at

Mycenae that were being conducted by the Greek Archaeological Society under the direction of Chrestos Tsountas. He wrote about his impressions to a friend in London:

> A fortnight ago I was at Mykene, and I have convinced myself that, on the summit of the rock, the foundations of the prehistoric edifice have really been found. But they have afterwards been altered, and evidently been used for a Doric structure – evidently a temple. The prehistoric building seems to have been the old palace.

In October Schliemann held out an olive branch to Virchow:

> I am therefore in a position this winter to make the long-planned Nile-trip as far as the second cataract, Wadi Halfa. Since you earlier showed an interest in such a trip, I cordially invite you to accompany me. Naturally, I pay for all your costs from and to Berlin, hire a fine Nile boat (dahabeeyah) from Thomas Cook & Son, and we shall lack for nothing. To my great sorrow my wife will not travel with me, as she is afraid of being continually seasick even on the Nile boat. So I am taking only Pelops[18] with me, as he seems to me to be consumptive and the air of Upper Egypt will soon heal him. Otherwise there will be no-one with me except you.[19]

To please Virchow Schliemann enclosed with the letter a copy of his economic report on Cuba for J.H. Schröder of London, which included data on the population. Virchow declined the invitation and Schliemann sailed for Alexandria on 27 November. He kept a detailed diary of his trip in ancient Greek.

Shortly after his arrival in Cairo Schliemann made inquiries at the Bulak Museum. Emil Brugsch, who worked in the museum's conservation department, was prepared to sell him three or four skulls of the Early Dynastic period. Schliemann informed Virchow that though they were not cheap, he would willingly buy them if Virchow assured him 'that they would be welcome in Berlin and that Emil Brugsch's information could be relied upon.'[20] Clearly, Schliemann was trying to insinuate himself into Virchow's good graces and inveigle him into resuming their correspondence. But Virchow would have none of it. In declining the Nile trip Virchow had raised the matter of the incident at Karlsruhe but in his letter from Cairo Schliemann avoided the issue entirely. Later he explained his silence on the grounds that the topic was too painful for him. He vowed, however, that 'in no way would the Berlin Anthropological Society suffer because of your hostility to me' and sent a comprehensive report on his Egyptian trip, which Virchow duly read at the meeting on 10 March 1887.[21]

In Cairo, where he stayed at Shepheard's Hotel, Schliemann was surprised to find that he was a well-known figure to the British, German and French tourists. After seeing the standard sights in and around the city, including the pyramids and sphinx at Gizeh, he rented a dahabeeyah and prepared to leave: 'I contracted with Halil Chanliri from Beirut to take me in his fine boat, 'New Star', for £4 stg. per day, including the hire of the boat, the fare, meals, baksheesh, and the outlay for the mules. We have 8 sailors, 1 helmsman, 1 captain, 1 servant and 1 cook.'[22] He embarked on 8 December.

Schliemann had brought plenty of reading material with him and planned to read all of Euripides before reaching Wadi Halfa. In one diary entry he describes a typical day:

Truly, time has never passed so quickly as it does for me now – and alone at that. The variety of my activities amounts to this, it seems. At 7 a.m. I get up and wash; I walk around for half an hour on the deck; I drink tea, eat 3 eggs, and walk around another hour, smoking. Immediately after this I study an Arabic book for an hour and Euripides for 2 hours. Then I have lunch. Immediately after, I walk around for an hour, and again study scholarly books till four-thirty. After this I walk around until I dine at 6. After this I again walk around for an hour and a half, breathing in the invigorating desert air. Before going to bed I write up my diary.[23]

Murray's *Handbook for Travellers in Egypt*, which Schliemann took along as his bible, had a lengthy section on ailments for which the climate of Upper Egypt was thought to be particularly beneficial. The following excerpt, which Schliemann quoted to Virchow as applicable to him, was even more applicable to his own case:

To the overworked teacher and student, the care-burdened merchant and man of business, and those subjected to a hard daily routine, which has broken down their stamina, and induced a highly-excited state of nervous system; the confirmed dyspeptic and hypochondriacal invalid; the nervous and hysterical female; – to all these the Egyptian climate may be beneficial.[24]

Certainly, the leisurely pace of life on the dahabeeyah seems to have soothed Schliemann's nerves. He had been overworking for far too long. The strain had precipitated the break in his friendship with Virchow, which he now clearly regretted and sought to mend. It seems also to have created more tension in his relations with Sophia. Although devoted to her husband, Sophia clearly did not relish spending several months alone with him, far from her children, siblings, friends and her beloved Athens. The fear of seasickness was just an excuse. Up to the last minute she seems to have considered going with him after all, provided they went on the steamer, thereby considerably shortening the trip, but in the end she did not. In the early entries we can see the emotional effect of this on Schliemann. In one entry he actually addresses her: 'Oh, heartless Sophidion! What happened that you did not come with me? For then we would have gone on the steamer and would already be enjoying ourselves in Thebes. As it is, although we have been sailing for six days, we are still struggling along near Cairo.'[25] A few days later he was glad, given all the bad luck they had been having with the winds, that Sophia had not come with him. She would only have grieved at being separated so long from the children.[26] As time passed and the Nile worked its magic, he adjusted very well to his own company.

At Asyiut, the terminus of the railway line from Cairo, Schliemann put Pelops ashore. 'I had the good fortune to find for Pelops, at the cost of 30 fr. a month, a clean room in the house of an honourable Turk. I paid the rent for his room for one month in advance, promising to pay the rest when I return from Wadi Halfa.' Schliemann also gave him enough money to live on till his return.

Since the dahabeeyah was powered only by sails, the general plan was to sail on upstream whenever the north wind was blowing and to utilize calm periods for visiting temples and tombs in the vicinity and other forms of amusement. If this meant sailing past interesting sites, then they could always be seen on the return trip. Schliemann had brought his rifle and sometimes amused himself shooting pigeons and other birds along the banks of the Nile. One day he shot fifteen pigeons. On one occasion Schliemann had a minor accident. 'When shooting a pigeon in Tuch I brought my mouth too near the gun so that I received a severe shock in the mouth. One of my four remaining teeth was knocked out. My false teeth were also damaged.'[27]

Schliemann also took a lively interest in the economy of the villages he passed. He noticed that most of the thousand homes in the village of Negada incorporated a round dovecot housing 500 to 1000 pigeons. These were kept primarily for the pigeon dung they produced, which fetched high prices in Alexandria and Cairo. Reckoning the pigeon population of the village to be 700,000, Schliemann wondered whether the crop losses from the adjoining fields, where the pigeons fed, did not outweigh the profits from selling the dung. He also thought that the Egyptian Copts would be well advised to grow vines for wine instead of merely for table grapes.

Schliemann occasionally had the opportunity to visit ancient monuments on his way up the Nile. Armed with Murray's *Handbook* Schliemann visited the Middle Kingdom tombs at Beni Hassan, making extensive notes on them in his diary. But he seems to have been just as interested in ordinary village life, asking about marriage customs, watching funerals, exploring the open-air markets. At Suhako he saw 'many prostitutes – one street was filled with them. I was amazed at the brazenness with which these Moslem women called out to me (in Arabic): "I am a prostitute; do you want me?" But I was not tempted.'

As he drew nearer to Thebes, where the most interesting temples and tombs were concentrated, he was frustrated by a spell of calm weather. But the closing line of his 31 December entry reads: 'But nonetheless I am confident that tomorrow I will finally reach Thebes.'

The Thomas Cook hotel at Luxor, where Schliemann picked up his mail on 1 January, was virtually empty. He met the British and German consuls, both of whom he had seen in the same posts on his trip up the Nile almost thirty years earlier. Now old and lame, they remained extremely important figures in Luxor. Enjoying diplomatic immunity and ready access to the wealthy European tourists, they formed a natural conduit for the thriving black market trade in antiquities. Schliemann paid a quick visit to Karnak. Since there was a favourable wind, he decided to postpone a careful study of the sites until the return trip and sailed on. At Esneh he noticed a riverside café, which instead of a sign had hung out a stuffed crocodile. Two prostitutes sat on the balcony overlooking the Nile, playing dominoes. E.A. Wallis Budge, the British Egyptologist and avid collector for the British Museum, who had been excavating tombs in the neighbourhood of Aswan, recalls Schliemann's arrival there.[28]

As soon as he arrived his secretary, or companion, landed and sent some of the crew to announce to the native officials that his great master had arrived, but with what object he did this no one understood. The British military authorities had not been instructed from Cairo to give Dr. Schliemann a public reception, and they did nothing. Mr Henry Wallis, the artist, who very kindly made for me many drawings of the Aswan tombs, was very anxious that some one should show civility to Dr. Schliemann, and offer to act as a guide for him over the tombs. Therefore he, Major Plunkett, and I were rowed over to the dhahabiyah, and announced ourselves. The butler received us civilly, and led us into the large reception room in the stern of the vessel, and after the usual salutations and coffee and cigarettes, Major Plunkett acted as spokesman, and said that we had called to offer him our boat and crew if he wished to go over to the tombs, and that we were ready to accompany him at any time, and show him what we had done. Dr. Schliemann replied very stiffly, 'It is very kind of you to be so amiable. I should like to place my archaeological science at your disposal by showing and explaining to you the tombs, but I have not the time as I am going up to Halfa.' He then reached out one hand, and lifted up a paper-bound volume of the Greek text of Homer's "Iliad," in the Teubner series, which he was holding in his hand when we entered (it was then lying face downwards on the cushion), and went on with his reading. Major Plunkett, lighting up another cigarette, asked in a sweetly soft voice if we had his permission to withdraw, and we did so with as much dignity as was possible under the circumstances.[29]

At Aswan Schliemann made the customary arrangement with a local sheikh for towing the dahabeeyah safely up the first cataract. Thereafter he visited the Temple of Isis (third century BC), stunningly located on the island of Philae. Schliemann reached Wadi Halfa on 23 January. Like most Nile travellers he ventured beyond the town to the rock of Abusir for the famous view of the second cataract. Here on his first trip up the Nile, like countless others before him, he had inscribed his name at the farthest point of his journey. He and his crew now looked for his name on the rock without success.

On the return trip he spent two full days at Abu Simbel. He was tremendously impressed. His diary notes on the temple there extend to twenty pages. They conclude with these sentiments: 'I leave Abu Simbel with great reluctance; I would like throughout my entire life to gaze every day at its gigantic wonders. The visit to Abu Simbel is a critical moment in one's life. It is the happiest moment and at the end of our lives we remember it with joy.'[30] He elaborated on these thoughts in a letter to his old schoolfriend Wilhelm Rust:

Above all, I have to tell you that this is the most wonderful trip that one can take anywhere in the world. The wonderful, cloudless sky, the beautiful spring air, the golden peacefulness, the gorgeous scenery that is constantly changing, the immense temples of the most remote antiquity – all this has a most beneficial effect on body and soul, and I recommend a Nile trip most especially to all newly-weds. But speaking of newly-weds, I must add that the moment in which you step on to the strand of Abu Simbel is epoch-making in your life. Just as a happily married couple always thinks back on their wedding day with joy, so too the day in which the traveller visited Abu Simbel remains the most beautiful memory of his life. Here are the most tremendous works of art in the world. In comparison, the most massive works of the Greeks and Romans, even the Pyramids, are merely the work of dwarfs. Here in the desert King Ramses II, in the middle of the 14th century B.C., hewed two huge temples with all their columns, plain and decorated, out of the lonely cliff. One of the temples has 14 rooms, of which one is 17 metres long, 16 metres broad and 12 metres high. In front of the temple are four seated colossal statues of Ramses, each 19 metres high. The scenes and inscriptions that cover every chink of the walls and ceilings of all 14 rooms were chiselled in relief, covered with thin stucco, and painted. The freshness of the colours of these 3200 year old wall-paintings is amazing – they depict battles, sieges, peace treaties, sacrifice scenes and so on.[31]

While visiting Thebes on his way upriver Schliemann must have mentioned that he was interested in acquiring good examples of Egyptian pottery, for when he returned in mid-February, he was promptly met by the German consul who had about 300 well-preserved vases to sell him. Among them 'practically all the vases depicted on the granite gate of Thutmes III in Karnak, in the tomb of Rameses III and in the great temple at Abydos, as well as in the temple of Abu Simbel in Nubia were represented.'[32] Regarding antiquities for sale at Thebes the 1875 edition of Murray's *Handbook* had the following warning: 'a great portion of those sold by dealers are forgeries; and some are so cleverly imitated that it takes a practised eye to detect them.'[33] On the other hand, early in 1887 a large number of genuine antiquities did come on the market in Luxor. The orientalist E. A. Wallis Budge, who arrived just a few days after Schliemann, reports: 'When I arrived in Luxor I found that the dealers had indeed collected many valuable things from the tombs at Western Thebes, and that the prices were, when compared with prices in England, very moderate. Antiquities were plentiful, but money was not.'[34] In Nubia Schliemann had been able to acquire only a few complete vases but had accumulated a collection of characteristic sherds from the various sites. He wrote to Virchow from Thebes that he would be presenting the whole collection to the Museum for Ethnology in Berlin. He also sent him some notes on how pottery was still made by hand in certain parts of Nubia and inferred that some of the handmade ancient pottery in his collection had been made by a similar process.

When he visited the tombs in the valley of the Kings on 17 August, he was delighted to find his name in the tomb of Seti I. He had carved it in the first passageway of the tomb in 1859. He now added the date 1887. Of considerably greater significance was his discovery among the vases illustrated in the tomb of Rameses III the characteristic shape of the Mycenaean stirrup vase (see Fig. 20). This provided a fairly firm date for the stirrup vase. Rameses III ruled from 1182–1151 BC. It is rather surprising that scholars had not made this connection before, as the stirrup vase appears on a plate illustrating scenes from the tomb of Rameses III in the well-known *Description de l'Egypte.*[35]

On 22 February Schliemann took a short donkey ride to see the temple of Hathor at Denderah. It has the dual distinction of being one of the most complete temples in Egypt and also one of the better examples of a temple of the Roman period. Schliemann was particularly impressed by the huge figures of

Cleopatra VII and her son by Julius Caesar, Caesarion, on the rear wall of the temple. At Asyiut Schliemann learned that Pelops had not waited for his return. The climate had apparently failed to improve his lung condition. He had used the sum of money that Schliemann had sent him to pay the rent and had departed.

Schliemann had left himself with little more than two days altogether for Cairo and Alexandria. His complete Cairo entry reads:

> Today I sent the 6 chests of Egyptian vases to the Bulak Museum, where Emil Brugsch promised to send them on to Berlin. Brugsch has not acquired really old skulls. He hoped to find them in Sakkara, but the Director of the Museum forbids him to work there. He offers to excavate there in the summer and to give me all the ancient skulls he finds. In addition, for 100 franks he is offering me 150 examples of ancient Egyptian cloth dating from the 4th to the 12th Dynasties mounted on thick cardboard. After completing the account with Chalil at the consulate, I still had £205. I had lunch and visited once more the marvellous Bulak Museum. Then I bought a great many photographs of the monuments from the photographers and of the kings from E. Brugsch. I dined with him in the Shepheard Hotel.[36]

In Alexandria he made arrangements to take his Abyssinian servant, Telamon, with him back to Athens. He also met the German consul, Michaelis, who showed him a suitable place for excavation behind his garden. On his departure Schliemann hurried through customs at the last minute. The captain, whom he had happened to meet the previous evening, delayed the steamer's departure. Since the ship was full, Schliemann and Telamon were given quarters normally reserved for the captain.

Two weeks after his return to Athens Schliemann wrote to Virchow, planning a joint trip up the Nile with him and both their wives in October. He also asked Virchow for his advice about Sophia, 'who since her last childbirth nine years ago has been completely hysterical and is withering away more and more each day so that I have to fear that I may not see her much longer. Should some illness come, she will not have the strength to resist it.'[37] On the same day Sophia wrote to Virchow, explaining how deeply she had been hurt by the friends' quarrel. It had long been the Greek custom, she went on, to resolve disputes by quoting relevant passages from Homer. The one who had started the quarrel would quote *Odyssey* 8. 408–9: 'Farewell, respected stranger! If a harsh word has been spoken, may the winds at once catch it up and carry it off'; the other would quote *Iliad* 18.: 'Let us let the past be over and done with, though it grieves me deeply. I will force back the anger that rises in my heart.'[38] Whether Sophia wrote this on her own initiative or at Heinrich's behest is unknown. The fact that both letters were written on the same day (3 April) suggests prompting from Heinrich. Moreover, it is certain that Heinrich knew that Sophia's letter had been sent and was aware of its contents, for he began his next letter to Virchow by quoting both the Homeric passages referred to.

Naturally, it was difficult to resist Sophia's call for reconciliation and Heinrich's plea to help save the life of his dying wife. Virchow offered to accompany the Schliemanns to Egypt in October and appears to have suggested the St Moritz cure for Sophia, with warm but not hot baths and a restriction on drinking the spa water.[39] Schliemann was delighted and proceeded with plans for the trip to Egypt. On 1 May, uncertain how long Virchow could stay away from Berlin he proposed that they might take the steamer rather than a dahabeeyah to save time. He was anxious to excavate for Cleopatra's palace in Alexandria. He continued: 'I am particularly eager to find some statues of Cleopatra VII (Mark Antony's); according to Plutarch, Alexandria had several thousand columns with portraits of the beautiful woman, but by an irony of fate neither a statue nor a gold coin of her has ever been found.'[40] Schliemann seems to have become obsessed with this notion. On 12 June he wrote: 'How marvellous it would be if we found there a statue of Cleopatra!'[41]

Meanwhile, two intriguing reports had come from the Troad. According to the first, an ancient tomb on the Kaz Dagh, the mountain to the south-east of the Trojan plain, had yielded a rich belt, sheets of gold leaf, and a woman's gold headdress with imitation roses.[42] According to the second, a Turkish priest had dreamt that one of the mounds near Bunarbashi contained buried treasure and had persuaded a large number of workers to excavate the southernmost of the four mounds on and near the Balli Dagh – a mound which Schliemann had left unexcavated.[43] They discovered a burial with an impressive array of gold ornaments, including a gold oak wreath with thin oak leaves and acorns, three gold fillets with embossed pattern, and several other items of gold and bronze.[44] Whether prompted by this discovery or merely by coincidence, Schliemann arrived in the Dardanelles with the intention of escorting Carl Schuchhardt, one of the excavators of Pergamon, and later to write a book on Schliemann, and two other scholars round Hisarlik and the Troad. Because of the enormous excitement generated by the recent finds, foreign visitors were temporarily prohibited from visiting the Troad. As a result, Schliemann returned to Athens, though his companions stayed on in the Dardanelles, apparently in the hope of eventually making their way to the Troad.

Throughout 1887 Schliemann shows signs of having lost a sense of direction. From Wadi Halfa he had written to Calvert, expressing reservations about resuming excavations at Troy.[45] He was particularly concerned about finding someone suitable to replace Nikolaos. Back in Athens he wrote again to Calvert to say that '<Dörpfeld> is decidedly of opinion that Troy must wait until we have finished the projected excavations at Knossos in Crete.'[46] But in the same letter he spoke of visiting Ithaca with Dörpfeld, presumably with the intention of locating and ultimately excavating Odysseus' palace. In May he made formal application to the Greek Minister of Public Instruction for permission to excavate at Delphi. This was a long shot, made just as the Greek parliament was considering formal ratification of a contract with the French government for excavation of the site.[47] It had taken the French six years of negotiating to reach this point. Schliemann's timing recalls his last-minute attempt to wrest Olympia from the Prussian government in 1874. To some extent, of course, he was merely hedging his bets. Obtaining permission to excavate was not as easy as it had been a decade earlier. The more permits he applied for, he probably reckoned, the more likely it would be that one would come through. Nonetheless, the scattershot approach does suggest a certain loss of direction. No doubt he missed Virchow as counsellor and confidante.

In the end, he excavated at Kythera under the supervision of ephor V. Stais. Kythera was famous in antiquity for the cult of Aphrodite Ourania. In fact, in Homer and other Greek poets Aphrodite was often called simply 'The Kytheraean'. Herodotus (1.105) attributed the founding of the cult of Aphrodite to the Phoenicians.[48] It is this that seems to have stimulated Schliemann's interest. Now that he had excavated what he and Dörpfeld believed to have been a Phoenician settlement at Tiryns, it would be useful if points of comparison could be found in the artefacts or architecture of another site with Phoenician connections. In addition, there was the challenge of trying to locate the famous temple. Schliemann focused his attention on the church of Ayios Kosmas on what was clearly the acropolis of the ancient city. The church contained eight Doric columns with archaic capitals. Schliemann excavated at seven different spots within the church. He saw that two of these columns were actually set on the rock of the acropolis. He concluded that here, as often elsewhere, the Christian church had been built directly on the site of the pagan temple and that these two columns had not been moved from their original location. It seems more likely, however, as British and American archaeologists have suggested, that the temple was located 'on a terrace midway between Ayios Kosmas and the chapel of Ayios Georgios at the summit of the mountain.'[49]

Schliemann excavated near the church but found no sherds. He bought a fine bronze statuette of a deer of the classical period, which allegedly had been found near Ayios Kosmas. He thought that very probably the object was an offering to the goddess.[50] He was unsuccessful in finding any evidence that would suggest a Phoenician presence. In the classical period Kythera was famous for the production of purple dye from the murex shellfish and this may have given rise to the story of its Phoenician foundation, for this industry was a speciality of the Phoenicians. At the nearby port of Kastri clear signs have been found that the site was a Minoan colony and that the purple dye industry was already well established there in the Bronze Age.[51]

Shortly after returning from Egypt Schliemann sold his remaining stock in the Havana Railroad Company.[52] This provided him once again with a very substantial sum to invest. This time he decided to invest in property in Athens. He bought two houses and a plot of prime land. He planned to rent out one of the buildings to the Greek government but first he needed to make substantial additions. The other had to be refurbished. On the plot he decided to build a suitable home for the German Archaeological Institute in Athens. He made arrangements with the Institute for a twenty-five year lease. Ernst Ziller drew up the plans for the Institute, though Dörpfeld was much involved in supervising the actual construction, which began promptly in August.[53] The building, where the German Archaeological Institute is housed to this day, is located near the university, on Pheidias Street (Odos Fidiou), and remains one of the ornaments of Athens.

Because of all this building activity Schliemann was unable to leave Athens this summer. He sent Sophia and the children off to St Moritz. Later he was horrified to learn that she had gone to Baden Baden instead. He begged Virchow to intervene and urge her to go at once to St Moritz.[54] Sophia, who found that at Baden Baden she lost even more weight, went to St Moritz before the end of June.[55] In late August Heinrich picked her up there and took her to Wiesbaden, where they both took the cure for ten days. On the way back to Greece they spent a few days in Trieste, where they visited Sir Richard Burton, the explorer and linguist.[56] It was probably at this meeting that one of the most bizarre 'facts' about Schliemann was born. Emil Ludwig reports that, according to Schliemann's family, Schliemann visited Mecca in 1859 and 'that he secretly had himself circumcised in order to lessen the risk of detection.'[57] Ludwig notes that in his 1858–9 diary Schliemann passes over this visit in silence. He concludes that Schliemann dared not record the impiety out of fear for his life. In fact, the diary demonstrates clearly that the anecdote is a fiction. The closest that Schliemann came to Mecca in 1859 was Petra in Jordan, about 700 miles distant. Burton, however, *did* visit Mecca in disguise in 1853, having first had himself circumcised as a precaution. It seems not unlikely that Schliemann learned of this incident during a visit to the Burtons and subsequently appropriated it as a colourful detail for his own life.[58]

November brought another victory. In the summer of 1887 Penrose had accepted Dörpfeld's invitation to visit Mycenae and Tiryns with him so that he could see for himself that Stillman's views about the dating of the walling were impossible. Penrose was now convinced that Schliemann and Dörpfeld were right. He had a letter to that effect published in the *Athenaeum*. The year's end sweetened the victory. On 31 December Penrose's letter was reprinted in *The Times*.

16

Cleopatra's Head and the Feud with Bötticher

A T THE END OF January Schliemann sent Virchow an extensive list of clothes and other items to bring on their Nile trip. He recommended taking only a few books for reading but a large notebook for a journal; also, 'a packet of snuff so that I can have some too.'[1] Schliemann reached Alexandria at the end of January and promptly went to Cairo to obtain the necessary permit for excavation. Initially he sought, and was reasonably confident of obtaining, a general permit for excavations in Alexandria. In this, however, he was unsuccessful. He was also refused permission to excavate for the temple of Augustus, also known as the Caesareum. This was one of the few buildings of ancient Alexandria whose location was known with some degree of certainty, for it had been marked by Cleopatra's Needle and another obelisk, which remained *in situ* until late in the nineteenth century.[2] The grounds for refusal were that an Italian archaeologist had already spoken for the project. Schliemann was also interested in searching for the tomb of Alexander the Great. According to the view then prevailing, the most likely spot for the tomb was within the grounds of the Mosque of the Prophet Daniel. Like others before him, Schliemann was unable to win over the religious authorities, who remained adamantly opposed to archaeological excavation within the precincts of the mosque. This left him with the option of digging for the palace of the Ptolemies. Ancient authors indicate that it was located near the habour and the Caesareum but more precise information on its location is lacking. Schliemann was allowed to excavate at a site on the eastern edge of town, near the Ramleh station.[3] The station was adjacent to the site of Cleopatra's Needle, so there was a fair chance that he might uncover the ruins of the palace. The duration of Schliemann's excavations seems to have been from 6 February till Virchow's arrival on the 22nd.[4] An Egyptian official was designated to supervise the excavations and take possession of the finds.[5] Two reports later appeared in the *Academy*.

> Dr. Schliemann has begun his excavations at Ramleh near the railway station and close to the sea, in order to discover the remains of the palace of Cleopatra. He has already come upon three steps which he thinks belonged to the palace, but he intends to continue digging to a depth of fourteen metres. The work has been much hindered by the inflowing water.[6]

and later:

> Before the arrival of Dr. Virchow, having three weeks at his disposition, he drew in that part of the city two great trenches, in which he came upon many graves, and at last, at a depth of 12–14 metres, upon the foundations of a large building. In all probability they are the foundations of one of the palaces of the Ptolemies . . .[7]

These news items, both probably sent in by Schliemann himself, provide us with the most detailed information we have on this excavation, for Schliemann did not publish a formal report and his 1888 diary is missing, as are the copies of his outgoing correspondence.

The 1888 trip up the Nile was an accelerated version of the previous year's. As soon as Virchow arrived Schliemann closed his excavation and they travelled as quickly as possible to Upper Egypt, taking the train at once to Cairo and then on to Asyiut and the steamer from there. They arrived in Aswan on 28 February. From Aswan they proceeded by heavily guarded mail steamer, which was carrying the pay for the troops in Wadi Halfa. On 2 March the steamer was shot at by rebel forces 'but our black soldiers shot excellently, killed the leaders and wounded a number of the rebels. Finally, a gunboat came to our assistance. It bombarded the old mudbrick fortress, in which the Dervishes had established themselves.'[8] On 3 March Schliemann and Virchow disembarked at Ballanye and spent a week there studying the temple of Abu Simbel located nearby. It was here that Virchow was particularly impressed by Schliemann's knowledge of Arabic and the Koran:

> When we took a Nile trip together in the spring of 1888, it was not only myself he astonished with his knowledge of Arabic but also, and to a far greater extent, the native speakers. The evenings we spent then in Nubia will remain for me among my most agreeable memories. On 3 March we arrived at the Nubian village on the left bank of the Nile in order to examine more closely the gigantic cliff temple of Ramses the Great [Abu Simbel], which was located nearby. It was at the time when

the Dervishes had risen in revolt, making the entire right bank of the Upper Nile insecure. Two days earlier our ship had been fired upon by the rebels and only the coincidence of several fortunate circumstances kept our ship unharmed, out of reach of the attackers. River traffic had more or less ceased and for one week we were completely shut off, as there are no proper roads in that region. The Muslim inhabitants of Ballanye – that was the name of the village – had given us a friendly reception and each day bound us closer to them. It quickly became known that I was a doctor and my practice developed rapidly. They very soon recognized in Schliemann a learned scholar of Arabic. In all of Ballanye there was only one person who could read Arabic – the Imam. But Schliemann could not only read it, he could write it as well. Watching him, as the Arabic script flowed from his pen, was a spectacle of the greatest interest for the villagers, and when, towards the end of the week we spent in Ballanye, a message reached us from Wadi Halfa, brought by armed guards, and before the eyes of the whole village Schliemann wrote an answer in Arabic, they regarded him as a miracle worker. He had his greatest triumphs, however, in the evenings, when the night fell suddenly and the stars began to gleam above us, the Southern Cross shone far above the horizon and, apart from the soft murmur of the mighty river, not another sound could be heard. Then the neighbours came and Schliemann recited to them excerpts from the Koran.

The house of the old sheikh who had taken us in as guests lay right on the edge of the desert, which is there making rapid inroads. Every year the sand pushes further towards the Nile. Here along the bank there is still a narrow strip of fertile land. At that time it was filled with a ripening stand of wheat. On the landward side it was fringed with several rows of date palms, whose luxuriance indicates the richness of the underlying soil. But the desert sand already reaches to the feet of these palm trees. Then there is an open space in front of the secluded and rather spacious house, whose front section was turned over to us. This space is already desert, although on it stand two of those wonderful *Lebbachbaum* trees, whose splendid proliferation in Cairo surprises the arriving visitor.

Under the leafy spread of one of these trees all festive and solemn events took place. Here, on our arrival, we had been hospitably received by all the male members of the family. And here every evening after dinner Schliemann held a kind of prayer meeting.

A large lantern, similar to stall lanterns – a modern import to the village – was placed in the sand. Schliemann set himself in front of it on a small wooden bench; the Nubians squatted on the ground and formed a large circle round the lantern. In the centre there was an empty space, around which the beetles gathered; in great haste they scurried towards the unaccustomed light and with their hind legs inscribed peculiar markings in the sand. Everyone was listening in hushed expectancy for the beginning of the reading.

Then Schliemann began to recite from memory a sura from the Koran. Initially muffled, his voice rose higher and higher and when in his own ecstatic manner he pronounced the closing words, everyone lowered his head and touched the earth with his brow. After a while Schliemann would deliver a second sura, and so rich was his memory that he could give new excerpts practically every evening. Then in solemn mood our brown friends departed. The seriousness of the occasion was never broken by an unseemly remark or look.[9]

On the return trip Schliemann and Virchow visited most of the major sites, which they had hurried past on their way upriver. When they made a detour into the Fayoum district, they were joined by the German explorer and botanist Georg Schweinfurth. On 3 April they paid a call on Flinders Petrie, who was excavating at Hawara. Petrie's diary provides memorable sketches of the visitors:

Schliemann, short, round-headed, round-faced, round-hatted, great round-goggle-eyed, spectacled, cheeriest of beings; dogmatic, but always ready for facts. Virchow, a calm, sweet-faced man, with a beautiful grey beard, who nevertheless tried to make mischief in Cairo about my work. Schweinfurth, a bronzed bony, powerful fellow of uncertain age, an infatuated botanist. They were all three much interested in the work in different ways – the Iliad papyrus for Schliemann; the plant wreaths for Schweinfurth, and the skulls for Virchow . . .[10]

Shortly after his return to Athens, Schliemann wrote to Richard Schöne, the Director of the Museums in Berlin, who had expressed a desire for more classical sculpture. He described his excavations as follows:

The excavations were to the east of the city on what I believed to be the site of the palace of the Ptolemies. I could not bring myself to continue them after the arrival of Virchow (22 Febr.), as, according to Strabo, the palace with the gardens, the Museum etc., constituted a quarter or a third of the entire town (of at least 500,000 inhabitants). Consequently, only blind chance could guide my spade. To my greatest astonishment, luck was good to me this time too, for I found a female marble head there, of excellent workmanship, with very characteristic, wonderfully preserved hairstyle (similar to that of Mark Antony's Cleopatra), and well-preserved face, with the exception of the nose, which has only partly survivied. In spite of the many guards that watched me in the excavations with Argus eyes and even followed me wherever I went, I succeeded not only in making the head disappear before their eyes but also, even though it weighed some 80 pounds, in getting it through customs in Alexandria in a little chest as hand-luggage and bringing it here. On my arrival I left it at the customs in the Piraeus and on the same day submitted on the correct, stamped form a request to the Ministry, in which I sought to record the head as a foreign import so that at any time I could export it again.

This letter, dated 17 May 1888, contains the first mention of this extraordinary discovery. By 24 August, however, Schliemann had abandoned the notion that the bust might portray Cleopatra.[11] No doubt following the view expressed by experts in Berlin, to whom he had sent a photograph, he referred to it from now on as a work of the third or fourth century BC. Today the standard view is that the bust is a Roman copy, probably of the first century AD, of a fourth-century BC original.[12] Since Cleopatra lived in the first century BC she could not have been the subject of the original. There is, of course, always the possibility that it is a modern forgery.[13] To this view, however, there are two major objections: why would a forger give his 'Cleopatra' a fourth-century BC appearance? And why would Schliemann have so readily accepted the view that it was not a bust of Cleopatra at all but of some nameless woman of the third or fourth century BC?

Schliemann's report of the discovery of the bust in his excavations invites scepticism. In his 1986 study the German art historian Wolfgang Schindler declared that he did not believe that Schliemann excavated to a depth of twelve to sixteen metres and found the 'Cleopatra' head in his trench.[14] Schindler's scepticism was founded on Schliemann's prior announcement of the hope of finding a portrait of Cleopatra; the brief duration of the excavations; the great depth allegedly reached, considerably below the normal water table;[15] and Schliemann's apparent failure to mention the discovery to Virchow or any of his correspondents until three months later.

Schliemann's anticipatory hope of finding a portrait of Cleopatra is certainly suspicious. It suggests that the bust was already in his possession in May 1887. If so, and if the bust actually came from Egypt, it was brought back to Athens when Schliemann returned in March 1887. Schliemann's boast about bringing the 80-bound bust through customs as hand-luggage has a ring of authenticity to it. Schindler points out that it is hard to imagine the sixty-six-year-old Schliemann doing this himself in 1888.[16] In 1887, however, Schliemann was accompanied by a more likely candidate for the task – his Abyssinian servant, 'Telamon'. The Homeric nickname Schliemann chose for him suggests that he was big and strong. Moreover, in 1887 Schliemann was hurried through customs, being the last to board the ship. The entire episode seems to have been carefully planned, for the evening before his departure he met with the ship's captain, the Director of Customs at Alexandria, A. Schmidt, and the German consul, Michaelis. Following Schmidt's advice Schliemann did not open his luggage in customs.[17]

If Schliemann did not find the bust in his excavations in 1888, how did he acquire it? We know that in 1887 he bought antiquities from Emil Brugsch of the Bulak Museum in Cairo. Brugsch was deeply involved in the antiquities market and it was widely believed that he supplemented his income by selling off pieces that belonged to the museum.[18] Schliemann certainly met with Brugsch in December 1886 and indicated that he was looking to buy choice antiquities, for Brugsch offered to sell him a number of skulls dating from the first six Egyptian dynasties and a bust of Herodotus.[19] At this point Schliemann might well have expressed his interest in acquiring a bust of Cleopatra, agreeing to look over what Brugsch was able to find when they met again at the end of his trip in March. This, of course, is only one of many possible scenarios.

In the summer of 1888 work on the building that was to become the German Archaeological Institute in Athens was nearing completion. Just as he had done for Iliou Melathron Schliemann chose moralizing aphorisms from classical Greek authors to adorn the walls of all the rooms. He imagined them filling future generations of scholars with appropriate sentiments.[20] He was also working on a house he owned on Mouson (now Karageorges tes Serbias) Street, which runs westwards out of the north-west corner of Syntagma Square. In the course of excavations at this house, he discovered twelve tomb inscriptions, which he published in the prestigious *Mitteilungen* of the German Archaeological Institute.[21] Subsequent excavation in the area has confirmed that there was a cemetery here in the classical period.[22] In 1974 George Korres of the University of Athens made the astonishing discovery that four of these twelve inscriptions had in fact already been found, published and housed in private collections before 1888![23] There is some confusion as to exactly where these four inscriptions were housed immediately prior to their 'discovery' in 1888 but three of them seem to have belonged to the previous owner of the house in Mouson Street. Korres does not rule out the possibility that they had become buried in the garden and were then uncovered by Schliemann.[24] However, even if we grant this possibility, it is hard to imagine how an experienced archaeologist would have failed to recognize this. Korres was not convinced by this explanation. He called Schliemann's claim to have discovered the four previously excavated inscriptions 'unconscionable'.[25] In fact, it looks like another example of a familiar pattern of behaviour of Schliemann's: supplementing genuine finds with related objects that he had purchased or found elsewhere.

On 17 June Schliemann informed Schöne that he had obtained from the Greek government the re-export permit for the 'Cleopatra' head and that he was ready to bequeath it in his will to the German people. All he needed now was a letter from Bismarck promising that the head would be displayed in the Trojan collection in the Ethnological Museum and kept there forever! The required letter, signed by Bismarck, duly arrived. Schliemann added a codicil to his will, specifying the bequest of the head to the Ethnological Museum.[26] Neither Schliemann nor Bismarck, of course, could foresee the Second World War and its consequences. In recent years the bust has been languishing in a storage room in Berlin.[27]

Meanwhile, Sophia's health was causing considerable concern. She had become very thin. In July she went to St Moritz with the children, where she renewed her acquaintance with Mrs Leland Stanford. Since their last meeting in 1884, Mrs Stanford and her husband had founded Stanford University in memory of their son. Schliemann stayed in Athens to supervise the construction of his houses. While Sophia complained of snow in St Moritz, Schliemann slept under a mosquito net on the roof of Iliou Melathron in July and August to escape the heat of the house.[28] Sophia failed to put on weight in St Mortiz, so in September she went to Paris to take a *douche* cure. There she was joined by Heinrich. Though the Paris treatment seemed to be having a beneficial effect, in October they went to Heidelberg, where, on Virchow's recommendation, Sophia tried the fattening regimen of Professor Kuhsmaul: milk, porridge and lots of bedrest. Schliemann himself had a small growth on his lower lip removed. Sophia disliked her diet and the weather of Heidelberg and was bored with the bedrest. Besides, she argued, she could follow the regimen just as easily in Athens. When they got home, Schliemann saw to it that she continued the diet and, to his relief, she gained weight.

For two weeks in November and December Schliemann went on a trip to the Peloponnese. He was looking for promising Homeric sites to excavate, in particular sites that might have palaces, like those at Tiryns and Mycenae. Besides the palace of Odysseus in Ithaca the *Odyssey* gives prominence to those of Nestor in Pylos and Menelaos in Sparta. Schliemann decided to make trial excavations at both these sites and also at Pherai (modern Kalamata), where Telemachos and Peisistratos stayed overnight when travelling from Pylos to Sparta.[29]

The location of Nestor's Pylos, like that of Troy, was disputed even in antiquity. Strabo proposes three very different sites on the west coast of the Peloponnese, of which that on the Bay of Pylos is the southernmost. Though Strabo himself (subsequently followed by Dörpfeld) inclined to the central site, most authorities, both ancient and modern, have favoured a location on or near the Bay of Pylos. The bay is about five miles long. It is protected on the west side by a peninsula and the long narrow island of Sphacteria. Until 1939, when Carl Blegen discovered an impressive Mycenaean palace on a ridge overlooking the bay, about four miles to the north-east of it, Nestor's palace was generally expected to be found at

Paleocastro. This is the acropolis site at the south of the peninsula facing Sphacteria. It is a natural place for a stronghold, for it commands one of the entrances (now largely silted up) to the bay. On the summit the Venetians built a castle (*c.* 1500), whose impressive ruins dominate the site today. Here, among the ruins sloping southwards from the summit, Murray's *Handbook* confidently located Nestor's Pylos and here in 1888 Schliemann sank 'count-less' trial shafts looking for signs of a Mycenaean palace.[30] Though he dug down to the rock, he found, to his surprise, neither classical nor Mycenaean pottery. Nonetheless, he remained convinced that this was where 'Nestor's palace' had been located, reasoning that all traces of Mycenaean occupation had been washed away by the winter rains. The Mycenaean pottery he had found in 1874 and again this year in the 'Cave of Nestor' on the precipitous northern slope only strengthened this conviction. Schliemann explored the uninhabited island of Sphacteria and was happy to find stretches of the fortification wall built by the Spartans in 425 BC, when they were besieged by the Athenians: 'This fortification wall consists of well-fitted polygonal masonry; three rows of it are *in situ*; it is ca. 50 metres long, but has been seen by no visitor to Greece before me because nobody has made the effort to climb the steep cliffs, 270 metres high.'[31]

Since his search for Mycenaean remains in Kalamata and Sparta also proved negative, Schliemann's thoughts began to turn once again to Crete. When Virchow wrote to him suggesting, apparently, that he might think about further excavations in Egypt, Schliemann outlined his plans as follows:

> I would rather round off my life's work with a great undertaking in the field of scholarship with which I am familiar – Homeric geography specifically with the excavation of the prehistoric palace of the kings of Knossos in Crete. I am once again in negotiation with the owner and I hope to find a buyer for the rest of the land so that only the ownership of the palace hill, which is roughly the size of Hissarlik, rests with me. Unfortunately, however, it will not be possible without great sacrifice and I will have to give all the finds to the museum in Heraklion. Scholarship, however, would benefit more from this undertaking than from the greatest works I could achieve in Egypt in a hundred years.[32]

Not wanting, however, to discourage Virchow's interest in excavating with him in Egypt, he added: 'But this work in Crete would not prevent us, in the course of a Nile trip, from sinking shafts in one of the hills in Memphis, if, as seems likely, I could get the permission for this from General Grenfell.'

Since his search on the mainland for a Mycenaean palace had failed, Schliemann resumed negotiations, through Hatzidakis, with the owner of

Knossos. This time he seemed to be getting somewhere. In January both parties were nearly ready to settle for the sum of 40,000 francs, but something aroused Schliemann's suspicions. He went to Crete to see what was going on. From there he wrote to the art historian Georges Perrot in Paris:

> I had finally almost reached agreement on the sum of frcs. 40,000. But, astonished to see that they wanted at all costs to prevent me from coming in person before the purchase price was paid, and having grave suspicions regarding the honesty of my intermediary at Heraklion, I went to verify the description that had been made of the property two years ago. It did not take me long to find large discrepancies: thus, for example, the land had diminished to about one third and instead of 2500 olive trees there are at present only 888. Never having believed that the property would give me a revenue, I would have passed over these discrepancies or at least settled things by means of a small decrease in the price. But at this point there arose a new and formidable difficulty. There are in Crete two political parties, of which the more powerful, which includes practically all the educated Greeks of the island and commands a large majority, is profoundly opposed to any sort of archaeological research in Crete as long as the island is under Turkish domination, for they say: 'In the first place, we would run the risk of allowing the director of the museum in Constantinople to exercise his right to remove all the important finds; in the second place we can be perfectly certain that the first thing that the Cretan Turks would do in the first revolution that breaks out would be to destroy the object we hold most dear – our museum of antiquities.' So it is now clear to me why they considered my visit to Crete before the site of Knossos was paid for inopportune and inappropriate![33]

Schliemann's indignant rejection of the new terms did not have the effect he hoped for. Instead of lowering the price the owner raised it substantially. In March Schliemann plaintively described the developments to Virchow:

> The owner, who accompanied me, refuses to give permission to excavate under any condition but offers to sell me the hill for 100,000 francs, while three years ago he desired this sum for his entire property, with 2,500 olive trees, and in January of this year he asked only 40,000 francs for a part of it, including the hill and 888 olive trees. But not only is 100,000 francs (80,000 marks) too much for me to throw away on excavations that will be completed in a week and whose finds, to the last potsherd, go to the benefit of the museum in Heraklion, but the same holds true for even 40,000 francs (32,00 marks).[34]

Abandoning all hope of work in Crete, Schliemann again decided to look for opportunities for excavation on the mainland. He set off on a tour of a number of sites in the south and west of Greece.[35] He was particularly struck by the citadel of Argos, called Larissa, where he saw in the walls a variety of styles of masonry, which he attributed to widely different periods: Mycenaean, sixth or seventh as well as fourth century BC, and medieval. Tegea, near Tripolis, was an extensive site, but, apart from the ruins of the theatre and the temple of Athena Alea, there were no signs of the ancient city, even its walls having disappeared. Moreover, excavation would be extremely difficult, for the water table was encountered at a depth of only 1 metre. At Mantineia he climbed the hill Gurzuli, where the acropolis was located. From here he had a marvellous view.

> The view from there over the lower town, whose circular site is precisely indicated by the walls with their 100 towers, is beautiful beyond all description and is especially interesting if one calls to mind the events that happened in or near the town – for example, the battle in July 362 BC, when Epaminondas with his army of approximately 30,000 Thebans, Arcadians and Euboeans defeated the combined might of the forces of the Spartans, Mantineians, Eleans and Achaeans, but in so doing lost his own life.[36]

In writing up his visit to Mantineia, however, Schliemann attacked the French archaeologists, who had been excavating there, with surprising venom.

> There is the same trouble at the site of Mantineia, where the French Archaeological Institute in Athens have been excavating for two years, but with such a complete lack of method that the excavations are of no use for science and nothing has been found. Yet nowhere is it easier to excavate than at Mantineia, where the ruins of the old buildings lie directly under the surface and one needs scarcely dig 0.5 to 1 metre deep. But as the French continuously move from one spot to another and never have the patience to complete even the eighth part of a building, they have dug here, as at Delos, in more than a hundred different places.[37]

This attack was ill-informed, as Schliemann later admitted.[38] The motive for it is unclear but the French, as we shall see, were not slow to counter-attack.

At Megalopolis, which was founded only after the battle of Leuktra (371 BC), there was nothing to see except bits of walls and the outlines of the stadium and theatre. Excavations at the nearby tomb of Aristodemos might be productive, Schliemann thought, 'but not particularly interesting for me, as I am too much attached to Homeric geography.'[39] His real goal in this part of the Peloponnese was Lykosura, said by Pausanias to be the oldest town in Greece. On its acropolis, however, he could see no sign whatsoever of old walls. Since most of the town was built directly on the rock, he concluded that excavations here were out of the question.

Returning to Argos, he took the train to Patras and the steamer from there to the island of Leukas. In Homer's day Leukas was a peninsula of the mainland. According to Strabo, it was made into an island about 600 BC by the Corinthians, who drove a canal through the isthmus. Schliemann's chief interest was the town of Nerikos, mentioned in the *Odyssey* (24. 377). He identified Nerikos with Palaiopolis, where there was fine polygonal masonry but almost no sign of anything prehistoric. Since the depth of accumulated debris nowhere exceeded 1 metre, he saw no point in excavating. At the south end of the island he found the temple of Apollo Leucatas mentioned by Strabo, and the adjacent cliff, from which Sappho was said to have leaped to her death to assuage her love. But since the cliff was not actually overhanging, as Strabo reports, he concluded that 'the physiognomy of the high cliffs has been altered by earthquakes.'[40]

Following the recommendation of Murray's *Handbook*, Schliemann crossed over to the mainland and visited Prevesa and the nearby sites of Nikopolis and Cassope. Prevesa is close to the headland of Actium, where the great sea battle of Actium took place in 31 BC, in which Octavian, later Augustus, defeated Mark Antony and Cleopatra. Nikopolis was the town Augustus established nearby to commemorate his victory. Both Nikopolis and Cassope, which lies some ten miles further north and was founded in the fourth century BC, have extensive and impressive ruins. But both were too late for Schliemann to be seriously interested in excavating them. Unlike Thermopylae, Marathon or Cleopatra's palace they had no glamorous historical associations to compensate for their lateness.

In March Schliemann learned from his daughter Nadeshda that she had become engaged to Nikolai Andrussow, Director of the Geological Museum at the University of Odessa. The marriage was to take place in late July or early August. Schliemann planned to meet Nadeshda in Florence in early June and apparently did so. He did not attend the wedding, which was held in St Petersburg. On 17 July he wrote to her:

I have just received your letter of 27 June, from which I see with joy that you will celebrate your wedding on the 26th inst. In congratulating you – both you and your fiancé – on the occasion of your marriage from the bottom of my heart, I wish to tell you that I have just written to Mr. J.E. Günzberg of St Petersburg to hold at your disposal an additional R3000. At the same time I have asked him to take note that I am not making any changes in my recrediting of R4000 per annum in your favour and in that of your mother; but that I insist that each of you withdraw half in your name, on the receipt. Thus each quarter you receive R500 and you give your receipt for it, and the same holds for your mother.[41]

Schliemann's methodical arrangements to honour his obligations to his daughter and former wife arouse both respect and disquiet. On the one hand, the payments appear regular and generous enough; on the other, he seems to react to his daughter's wedding plans much as he would to news affecting a business venture.

Relations with Sophia in the summer of 1889 were strained. Schliemann sent her a strange letter from Rome that could only have been intended to cause her pain.

> I have twice invited Helbig to dinner, for I am much diverted by his talk of antiquities and the women here. A great many *principessas* are absolutely obsessed with archaeology, to the point that they attach themselves, body and soul, to those who practise it. It is impossible for us to live in Rome, for you would be very jealous of them. This evening Helbig came to me in a carriage with a young *principessa*. I was much struck by her beauty. Thrice blessed is archaeology! Say 'hello' to the children for me. Tomorrow, Thursday, I have decided to depart for Paris, having tasted all too little – alas! – of the beauty of the women here.[42]

A similar note is struck in a letter Schliemann wrote to her from Paris about his plans for his son Serge, now thirty-four, who was apparently ill at this point. Schliemann wanted to send him, when he recovered, to the Crimea, where he could pass his time riding and practising horticulture, 'for when he was a child he was a famous botanist, and whatever one has loved in childhood will be adored throughout one's life, for old loves don't tarnish, as you can see from my love for Minna.'[43]

Schliemann's main reason for going to Paris appears to have been to visit the Paris Exhibition of 1889. He wrote to Virchow that he was surprised that Sir John Lubbock had no wish to see it:

> When I first visited it, it seemed to me that he was quite correct to pass it by contemptuously. But the Exhibition has this in common with the Niagara Falls, that it seems to grow in grandeur the longer one looks at it, and today on my fifth visit it seems to me so superior to all other earthly delights, so marvellous, wonderful, etc. that I could spend my entire life in it and never be bored for a moment. The great attraction is, of course, Eiffel's Tower; in a few days you will be able to climb all the way to the top of it by means of a lift. At the moment steps lead only up to the second terrace (115 metres high). Compared with the top, the second terrace is so very low and yet, amazing to say, four times higher than the church tower in Ankershagen, which as a child I regarded as the highest point in the world.[44]

In July Schliemann spent time in Berlin arranging and labelling the exhibits in the Trojan collection in the Ethnological Museum. This led to an unfortunate incident: 'On Sunday I had a bad experience, for the gallery attendant locked me in and forgot about me and only after shouting in vain for a long time did I manage to get hold of a woman to rescue me.'[45] Much more troubling for Schliemann was the astonishing news he learned the following day: the *Correspondenzblatt* of the German Anthropological Society had just published an article by Ernst Bötticher. It was potentially damaging, for Bötticher claimed that his theory that Hisarlik was merely a 'fire-necropolis' had been confirmed by the excavations of Robert Koldewey, who had recently found similar sites in Babylonia. Since the Anthropological Society, dominated by Virchow and his friends, had always been sympathetic to Schliemann, the publication of Bötticher's article came as a shock. Schliemann felt betrayed. He indignantly asked Virchow if he and the editor of the *Correspondenzblatt* had had a falling-out. Virchow was embarrassed and promised that nothing of the sort would happen again.[46]

Carl Schuchhardt, one of the excavators of Pergamon, had agreed to write a synthesis of all Schliemann's excavations. In July he explained to Schliemann that the book had evolved considerably from its original conception: 'I thought I would serve you and your reputation much more successfully if I did not make myself your mouthpiece, but introduced the great results of your excavations with a judgment which the public would recognize as independent.'[47] Schliemann, however, was anxious to see just how independent Schuchhardt's views were and visited him in Hanover to examine the manuscript before it was sent to press. In his autobiography Schuchhardt recalled their July meeting.

> When I met him, I found him in high dudgeon. He was outraged that I had rejected his interpretation of the Trojan face-vases as representations of the 'owl-headed Athena' and had explained them as attributable to mere playfulness, like today's monk-jugs. He was also angry that I had refused to consider the remains with the bearded mask in Mycenae to be Agamemnon, and on many other points. I explained that these were trivial details compared with the great truths of his work, which I thought I had brought to a wider circle of readers. Scholars would never really believe in the owl-headed Athena, I pointed out, and now even with scholars, who had for so long feuded bitterly with him, peace would finally be made.[48]

This argument seemed to make an impression on Schliemann and he calmed down somewhat. Lunch with Schuchhardt and Ferdinand Werry, an enthusiastic admirer of Schliemann, improved relations considerably. In the afternoon Schuchhardt accompanied Schliemann on a visit to his old employer of Amsterdam days, Heinrich Schröder, who now lived in Hanover. Schuchhardt found Schröder cooler than he expected but attributed this to the frailty of the old merchant and to Schliemann's bold enterprise 'which might always have been rather alarming to his staid firm.'[49] Schuchhardt had invited about ten distinguished people to join them for dinner, at which he gave a speech praising Schliemann's outstanding achievements. He recalled:

> At 11 o'clock he stood up silently to go home. As this was an early hour for Hanover, I was afraid that he had not been pleased with the company. But as soon as we were outside, he took my arm and said: 'You are all awfully nice people here and everything in the book can stay as is!' . . . This explains the independent tone of my book, which met with confident acceptance and was soon widely circulated.[50]

Schliemann had agreed to attend and give a paper at the tenth International Congress of Anthropology and Prehistory in Paris at the end of August. Here he was horrified to find Salomon Reinach, a knowledgeable French archaeologist, giving a résumé of yet another paper by Bötticher. Schliemann responded in a long and emotional speech, in which he defended his interpretation of Hisarlik and offered to pay Bötticher's travel expenses if he would go there and examine the ruins with Dörpfeld. In a report of the session that appeared in *Le Soleil*, victory was attributed to Schliemann. To show his gratitude Schliemann sent the author of the report a cheque. It was promptly returned with an indignant note:

> Sir, you are certainly mistaken about me, about my character and about that of the newspaper at which I have the honour of writing. That is the explanation that I choose to see for the gift you wish to make me. Allow me to return the cheque that you sent me.[51]

It seems very likely that the conference incident was staged by French scholars seeking revenge for Schliemann's attack on the French excavations at Mantineia. Reinach, who later said he was 'charged' with giving a résumé of Bötticher's article, was probably not the real enemy. Shortly afterwards he wrote a conciliatory letter to Schliemann:

> I am sorry that my paper, which I made as *objective* as possible, provoked you so profoundly. If I were Mr. Schliemann and had acquired such brilliant claims to immortality, I would be less severe towards my critics. I understood your perspicacity fifteen years ago, when you found yourself caught in a prism of stubborn and systematic incredulity, but today no-one contests the magnificence of your discoveries.[52]

The challenge that Schliemann had thrown down in Paris was reiterated more formally by Dörpfeld in a German newspaper on 23 August: 'To show all the world that Schliemann and I have no need to shrink from the criticisms of Herr Bötticher, I hereby challenge him publicly either to withdraw his false assertions or to travel with me to Hissarlik so that we can examine the ruins together.'[53] As Schliemann thought things over, he made the decision to resume excavations at Troy. While the Paris conference had brought matters to a head, events over the past few months had been pushing him in this direction. He clearly wanted to excavate again, but Knossos had proved elusive and outbreaks of revolutionary violence in Crete in the summer of 1889 had made the prospect of excavating there even more remote. In his trips to the Peloponnese and western Greece in late 1888 and early 1889 he had found no site that seemed to him worth excavating. But life in Athens was not sufficiently stimulating and relations with Sophia were prickly at best. The appearance of Bötticher's article in the *Correspondenzblatt* seemed to him, despite reassuring words from his friends, proof that his rival's theories were gaining scholarly acceptance. Reinach's talk at the Paris conference was an alarming confirmation of Schliemann's worst fears. But surely here at last was an opportunity to dig again! Bötticher's theories would be shown to be groundless by a new campaign of excavations at Troy and Bötticher himself would be compelled to admit his error.

Schliemann lost no time in applying for permission to resume excavations. On 13 September he wrote to Hamdy Bey, Director of the Imperial Museum in Constantinople:

> I take leave to remind you of your kind promise to grant me permission to continue the excavations at Troy and to send you herewith the plan of the site which I desire to explore. At the same time I promise to submit to the new regulation, whereby the explorer has no right to any of his finds.[54]

It is clear, however, that Schliemann had no intention of giving up all his finds. In a letter to Herbert von Bismarck, the Chancellor's son, requesting his help in gaining the necessary permission, he indicated that Berlin would be the beneficiary of whatever he acquired.[55]

It also became clear that there would need to be impartial witnesses. Schliemann wanted the Academies of Germany, France and Austria each to send a delegate. Virchow was charged with bringing the proposal before the Berlin Academy, while Schliemann himself made the approaches to Vienna and Paris. Vienna proved the most amenable, allowing Schliemann to choose between two distinguished architects. Schliemann chose George Niemann.

Berlin proved more difficult. There was a general reluctance to become involved. It was felt that an Academy delegate would inevitably be seen as speaking on behalf of the Academy and thereby committing it to a certain view. Anticipating this reaction, Virchow suggested that the Academy should merely endorse someone as a suitable person to send without actually designating him as a delegate. Virchow's choice, Major Bernhard Steffen, who had made a highly regarded map of Mycenae, was selected on these conditions. Georges Perrot, who assisted Schliemann in his dealings with the French Academy, was under the impression that the 'Hisarlik Conference', as it came to be called, would not take place until the spring of 1890. He reported on 9 December that Charles Babin, a specialist in Near Eastern archaeology, had been selected by the French Academy. But by that time the first Hisarlik conference was over.

In September, October and November Schliemann threw himself into the daunting array of tasks that needed to be completed before a new campaign of excavation could begin: obtaining permits, shipping the excavation tools, and constructing a range of huts for the accommodation of workmen and guests, and the storage of finds. Timber was cut on Mount Ida and transported to the site. The complex was variously dubbed 'Schliemannopolis' and 'Schliemannburg' by visitors. Though Schliemann covered the huts with waterproof felt, the temperature inside was only 5°C on 19 November. Equipment for removing the rubbish by rail had been ordered from France but had not yet arrived. So the earth was carried off in baskets. Excavations closed on 8 December, by which time two Greek inscriptions had been found.[56] Schliemann described the conference in a letter to Virchow:

Major Steffen and Prof. Niemann reached Hissarlik on Saturday 30 November with Captain Bötticher and everything was done to make their stay there agreeable. For six days of fine weather the first two kept very busy trying to prove to Bötticher that all your data conformed with the truth . . . furthermore, that all the ruins of buildings, gates, towers, and walls described in my book are accurately depicted in the plans and that nothing in them has been falsified. As Bötticher had maintained the opposite for six years and thought he had made a great discovery, it was only with indescribable effort that the gentlemen succeeded in convincing him of the truth. But he acknowledged the protocol and so it was more or less all over. But since he expressed his regret for having portrayed us for so many years as frauds and liars, at the moment of our departure for Hanay Tepe I requested that he should make a public apology and ask for our forgiveness. When he replied that he could not do this, I informed him that further communication between us was impossible and that two horses stood ready for him for his departure for the Dardanelles. So he left on Friday 6 December. But

Niemann and Steffen say that the protocol is completely valid, since he acknowledged it (though did not sign it), and will have 250 copies printed at once, along with Burnouf's Plan I and Dörpfeld's Plan VII and their own explanation of the facts of the case.[57]

17

Troy, Halle and Naples

IN JANUARY AND FEBRUARY Schliemann busied himself making plans for a second Hisarlik conference and the resumption of excavations. His method of drumming up interest in sending delegates to the conference is both instructive and amusing. On 7 January he wrote to Charles Waldstein, Director of the American School of Classical Studies in Athens, inviting him to represent the American School at the conference. He pointed out that the French Academy was sending Charles Babin and the Society for the Promotion of Hellenic Studies and the British School at Athens were jointly sending Ernest Gardner, Director of the British School. On the same day he urged George Macmillan of the Society for the Promotion of Hellenic Studies to persuade the Society and the British School in Athens to appoint Gardner as their representative, pointing out that Babin and Waldstein had already been selected by the French and Americans.[1] Schliemann was also anxious to secure Virchow's participation and sent him an advance of 1000 marks to cover travel expenses. Virchow returned the money. He felt that accepting any payment from Schliemann would compromise his role as an impartial witness.[2]

Since the 1882 season at Troy, a much stricter antiquities law had been passed in Turkey.[3] All excavated antiquities now belonged to the state. Schliemann tried to enlist the support of a number of correspondents to have this provision waived. He asked Karl Humann, the excavator of Pergamon, to plead his case for him at Constantinople, arguing that the coming excavations would be very expensive and that he would need to be recompensed by a half share of the finds. Humann replied that the Turks could not waive their law to accommodate Schliemann because of the precedent it would set.[4]

Excavations resumed at the beginning of March. In 1882 Schliemann had found ceramic evidence that Troy II extended beyond the city walls in a southerly direction. A major goal this year was to trace the streets leading from the acropolis to this lower town. Much effort was spent on clearing the areas in front of the two main gates and the adjacent stretches of the city walls. Rails were set up on the east and west sides of the mound. Wagons were filled by the workmen and then pushed to the dumping areas at the ends of the lines. This greatly speeded up the excavation process, though it was slowed by other factors, as Schliemann explained to King George of Greece:

> We encounter great difficulties in this work, for there are huge masses of debris, 16 meters high, to cope with. Also much time and money are lost on the houses of the four or five settlements following the second (the burnt) city, for we cannot destroy these buildings before they have been cleaned and photographed.[5]

For the first time Schliemann was taking the time to make a photographic record of structures before removing them. The ambivalent tone shows him torn between wanting to take credit for proceeding so carefully and exasperation at the delays and the expense. This innovation, which reflects the increasing awareness of the value of photography in archaeology, was almost certainly due to Dörpfeld.

Towards the end of March the scholars began arriving for the second conference. First came Charles Babin and his wife and Karl Humann on 25 March, accompanied by Wilhelm Grempler of Breslau, who, like Virchow, was both physician and anthropologist, and Friedrich von Duhn, the Professor of Classical Archaeology at Heidelberg University. Two days later Waldstein arrived and on 28 March Virchow and Hamdy Bey. Frank Calvert and his sister Edith and the Turkish overseer Halil Edhem also attended. Bötticher was not invited. After examining the excavations the scholars confirmed that the texts and plans in Schliemann's books accurately represented the facts on the ground and that there was no sign that any of the structures had been used for the burning of corpses. A protocol was drawn up and signed by the eight official participants at the conference and copies were sent off to *The Times* and Brockhaus.[6] It was a complete victory for Schliemann (see Plate 24).

In April excavations were suspended for a week to celebrate Greek Easter and Schliemann and Virchow took this opportunity to go on a trip to Mount Ida. They visited the source of the Scamander, where according to a local legend Paris made his fateful judgement that Aphrodite was more beautiful than Hera or Athena.[7] It was on this trip, as Virchow later recalled, that Schliemann's deafness returned.

> On 13 April we were climbing Sarikis, one of the peaks of Mt. Ida. The temperature was 17.5°C when we arrived at the foot of the hill. Higher up we encountered

a powerful storm from the southwest, which lowered the temperature to 5.5°C and brought some rain at times. The force of the wind was such that we could not stand upright and the raindrops driven against our faces felt like little pebbles. Half-frozen, we started on our way back. We reached our quarters for the night, Evjilar, late in the evening. The next day we rode over the eastern pass to visit the south side of the mountain. Our guide took us by a narrow ridge-path, which ran high above the valley floor along a steep slope. Our caravan, which included six horses carrying riders and two pack animals, extended in a long line along the ridge. It was here that Schliemann's loss of hearing reached the point that even with shouting it was almost impossible for me to make myself understood. He then began to complain about the pain in his ear. We reached Zeitünlü rather late in the evening. Next morning I examined his ear and found a swelling in it so massive that the auditory canal appeared completely blocked. Unfortunately, I did not have my set of surgical instruments with me so that closer inspection was not possible. We made do therefore with cleaning the ear passage and warm syringes, which in the event brought relief. We did not reach Hissarlik until 18 April. Here it became clear that the swelling consisted for the most part of a bony extrusion and that there was a similar extrusion in the other ear too, where a scar from an earlier operation was still noticeable.

There could be no doubt that it was a case of bone extrusion or exostosis ... It was a condition of long standing, which had merely been aggravated to the point of producing catarrh. The catarrh had blocked the auditory canal, which was normally still functional. I could not conceal from Schliemann that removal of the exostosis could only be effected by means of a serious operation. He decided therefore to wait for the catarrh to recede under appropriate treatment and to have the operation only if it became unavoidable.[8]

Hearing soon returned to the right ear but the deafness, often accompanied by buzzing, continued in the left until mid-June. In general, though, Schliemann's condition improved with the warmer weather.

The major weakness in Schliemann's case against Bötticher, as Virchow had pointed out, was his failure to find a cemetery, particularly one for the prehistoric period. Schliemann was now determined to plug this gap. Since the grave circle at Mycenae was located in a flat area below the acropolis, he reasoned that the prehistoric cemetery at Hisarlik should be similarly placed. Unfortunately, in his earlier campaigns he had used the edges of the mound as the dumping-ground for excavated spoil. This was particularly true of the northern and southern edges. Accordingly, Schliemann decided to concentrate his search for the cemetery on the east and west sides.[9]

May was a critical month. During the first week there were a number of visitors, including Georges Perrot, Alfred Brückner, future editor of Schliemann's autobiography, and Carl Schuchhardt.[10] To Schliemann's chagrin

Fig. 20   Stirrup vase (¾ actual size)

he was finding no sign of Troy II buildings outside the walls. Mycenaean sherds are first mentioned in the 3 May diary entry. These came from the same levels as the 'Lydian' ware (now generally referred to as Grey Minyan ware), namely Troy VI and VII. It will be remembered that in 1882 Dörpfeld had refused to accept Schliemann's view that the 'Lydian' pottery represented a distinct habitation level. This was because no architectural remains had been found that could be assigned to it. Now that they were excavating outside of the central part of Hisarlik, where levelling for the Hellenistic and Roman rebuilding had shaved off the top of the mound, deep strata of Troy VI and VII were found, rich in pottery, buildings and, eventually, a very impressive fortification wall, as Schuchhardt recalled:

> I witnessed only the beginning of work on the sixth city; but it was already appar-
> ent that its impressive stone buildings contained good Mycenaean pottery. Since
> this sixth stratum was contemporary with Mycenae, Dörpfeld regarded it as the
> Troy destroyed by Agamemnon. Schliemann was annoyed. He did not want to
> abandon the 'Palace of Priam' and the 'Treasure of Helen' [*sic*] from the second city
> and looked with displeasure at each stirrup jar that emerged from the earth.[11]

As more and more Mycenaean sherds and sometimes whole pots appeared in the Troy VI level, Schliemann was forced to think the unthinkable. Could it be that Troy II was not the Homeric Troy after all? He toyed with this idea in his letter of 16 May to King George of Greece:

I hasten to inform Your Majesty that we are finding here quite near the surface the remains of the culture of Mycenae and Tiryns, which was once spread over the whole of Greece but suddenly ceased with the Dorian invasion (ca. 1100 B.C.). The pottery of Mycenaean and Tirynthian type, which is characteristically represented by the stirrup jar, seems to us to have been imported from the Greek mainland, for it occurs contemporaneously with the grey monochrome pottery, which was once in general use throughout the whole Troad for many centuries and must be of local manufacture. The date of this stirrup jar can be determined, as it first appears in Egypt in graves of the time of Ramses II (ca. 1350 B.C.). It can therefore serve as a guide fossil for the chronology of the upper strata of debris in Troy and give us at least an idea of the enormous age of the five Trojan settlements preceding this Greek Ilion. These settlements have a cumulative depth of 14 meters, of which the second is rich in gold, has only large parallel buildings exactly like those of the plan of the palace in Tiryns, and was destroyed in a frightful catastrophe. It must be the Pergamos of Homeric Troy.[12]

That Troy II houses were all of the same plan he saw as proof that only the leading families lived on the acropolis. Ordinary people lived in the lower town, which he still believed must have existed in the Troy II period. But after the sack of Troy, he reasoned, the surviving inhabitants moved to the acropolis. The lower town lay abandoned and desolate for centuries and its walls and buildings eventually disappeared. For the moment then Schliemann was able to convince himself and others that he had been right all along. But a major difficulty remained unaddressed. If Troy VI was to be dated to the fourteenth century BC, Troy II could hardly be later than 2000 BC, as Frank Calvert had estimated in 1873, and this seemed far too early for the Trojan War.[13]

On 12 May Schliemann started sending baskets of sherds to A. de Caravel, who served as consul at the Dardanelles for both Spain and Italy, with the request that he keep them safe for him. He assured the consul that the sherds were his property, as Hamdy Bey had given them to him.[14] On 30 May there was a slight change. Along with the usual basket of pottery he sent 'a small chest containing rocks'.[15] He asked de Caravel to send the chest 'under the utmost security' (meaning, presumably, under diplomatic seal) to Schliemann's brother-in-law, Alexandros Castromenos, in Athens. On the same day, however, he wrote to his brother-in-law telling him to expect delivery of a chest containing a marble female bust. This was clearly one of the marble heads that were found in the Bouleuterion or council chamber (initially identified by Schliemann as an odeon or small, covered theatre) towards the end of May. In yet another letter dated 30 May, this time to Virchow, Schliemann described his discoveries there.

> Furthermore, in the Greek lower town, right at the SE end of the Pergamos, <we found> a beautifully preserved odeon with marble heads of Caligula, Claudius I, and the younger Faustina, all well-preserved and skilfully worked, as well as a marvellously sculpted lion. I will have to give the lion and the Claudius to the Turkish museum, although the Turkish overseer has been ill in the Dardanelles for a long time now. The two others, however, I hope to rescue for science and for the benefit of the fatherland, but no word about this must get out; otherwise Hamdy will learn of it right away and not only cancel our *firman* at once but hang a suit on us too.[16]

On 15 June Schliemann sent two chests to de Caravel for immediate shipment to his brother-in-law. Once again he told the consul that they contained rock but informed his brother-in-law that they contained marble heads.[17] It appears that he changed his mind about handing over the lion and the Claudius to the Turkish authorities, for all three marble heads and the lion were smuggled out to Athens.[18] In all he sent de Caravel nineteen baskets and nine chests.[19] Throughout the rest of the year he urged Virchow and others to do what they could to see that the consul be given a minor German medal for his services in 'saving' the antiquities for science and Germany.[20]

In May came the important discovery of a silver vase. Schliemann gives details in his 17 May diary entry:

> While the workmen were cleaning the foundations of houses of the second city, a tomb made of unhewn slabs was found with the remains of a skeleton. Near it was a silver vase 17 cm in height; on both sides of the body and the lid are tubes for suspension. The exterior is decorated with excellent horizontal lines.[21]

Very few burials have been found from any of the prehistoric levels at Troy. Two features make this one particularly interesting: firstly, the tomb's description recalls Yannakis' account of the enclosure where Priam's Treasure was found; secondly, the silver vessel is clearly a close relative of the lidded silver vases found in Priam's Treasure. One can infer that silver vases of this type were appropriate tomb offerings and that Priam's Treasure, or at least part of it, was probably found in a tomb, as Yannakis' account suggests. Moreover, the modest tomb found in 1890, which boasts a vessel of the same kind and quality as those in Priam's Treasure (still widely regarded as a royal hoard), lends support to the hypothesis that Priam's Treasure was assembled by Schliemann from a number of small finds of this kind made over a period of weeks or months.

Presumably, the workman who found the silver vase was appropriately rewarded for bringing it to Schliemann. This was Schliemann's standard practice in 1890.[22] The workman ought, of course, to have taken it to the Turkish overseer but then there would have been no reward. No mention of the tomb or vase was made in the report on the season's excavations.

The next day Schliemann went to Constantinople to consult Dr van Mellingen about the continuing deafness in his left ear. He wrote to Virchow from Constantinople on 19 May about the interview.[23] Van Mellingen, also diagnosing exostosis, had advised that the bony growths be removed from both ears in two operations. The operations and convalescence would take three months. Schliemann decided to wait until after the excavations were over and then, if an operation still seemed necessary, have it done in Germany.

Hearing finally returned to Schliemann's left ear when his wife and family were visiting him in June. He met Sophia with the children and their governess at the Dardanelles on 12 June. He was pleased to see that Sophia had colour in her cheeks but thought she was very thin. He had already decided to send her to the Christiana Baths near Oslo for treatment of her condition, which he was now calling 'hysterical'. But in the end Sophia seems to have put her foot down. She chose the baths at Kaltenleutgeben near Vienna. During her stay at Hisarlik, and no doubt in her honour, the mound of Pasha Tepe which she had excavated in 1873 was explored again. This time a staircase and a skeleton were found but no accompanying grave goods. Towards the end of June Schliemann accompanied his family to Constantinople, where they caught the train for Vienna. He returned to Hisarlik.

July brought the most important discovery of the season. Here is the diary entry for 8 July:

> While digging among the foundations of the houses of the 2nd city near the eastern wall, Demos found today many objects together, filling a space 50 cm. in length and breadth; in particular, four bright new axes of nephrite, of which three are green and one bluish-gray – so polished and smooth that at first I thought them to be made of glass. At the one end there is a blade and at the other a hammer. All have a hole bored through the middle and on either side of the hole can be seen a herring-bone decoration and wonderful semi-circles. The biggest is 32.5 cm in length. In addition, he found four sceptre knobs of crystal with a hole on either side; approximately 50 pieces of crystal in the shape of large semi-circles; two round plaques of crystal resembling watch glasses; one sceptre knob of iron but

much corroded; sticking to it were some small gold objects and a large number of small gold pins and nails and two clumps of bronze fragments with numerous small gold trinkets. In one of them I see a precious stone, whose one end is fastened with a gold pin and judging from its weight, I imagine that the other lump contains much gold. This is an extremely valuable find – not for publishing, unfortunately – I can't tell anybody about this.

A week later, however, he told Virchow. He confided that since he had already made some interesting finds this season, notably the marble heads, he had resigned himself to the fact that he could expect no further favours from the goddess Fortuna. To his astonishment, however, he had then found a treasure 'of immeasurable value':

Filled with deep emotion I threw myself on my face and humbly kissed the heels of the goddess, imploring her fervently for her future favour and thanking her with all my heart for her blessings hitherto. Even the manner in which the treasure was found – in a remote spot where only a single workman, Demos, was working – showed the sweet goddess's great benevolence.[24]

There are grounds for scepticism. Once again, we have the major find occurring close to the end of the season. In later versions Demos disappears and Dörpfeld takes his place, sometimes cited as merely 'present' and sometimes as sole witness, though Dörpfeld's own diary makes no mention of the discovery in the entry for 8 July or anywhere else.[25] Moreover, the four gorgeous axes are reckoned by Carl Blegen to have a 'distinctly non-Trojan appearance'.[26] They are thought to be imports from near the mouth of the Danube on the Black Sea. Close parallels suggest, however, that the axes are about 700 years too late for Troy II and would be more at home in Troy VI or VII.[27] The entire find, known to scholars as Treasure L, was smuggled to Athens, where Schliemann boldly put the axes in one of his showcases, labelling them 'from Egypt'.[28] After his death they went to Berlin. It is to be hoped that they will be found among the many valuable pieces from Germany that have recently surfaced in Moscow, where they were taken after the fall of Berlin in April 1945.

Schliemann closed the excavations at the end of July and returned to Athens, where he immersed himself in further building projects. He had tried to persuade the German government to build its embassy on his land, but since they showed little interest, he decided to construct four apartment buildings there instead. In the process of digging the foundations, he found eleven graves from the classical period, one with four skeletons in it.[29] He sent the skulls to Virchow. Meanwhile he wrote up his section of the report on the season's work at Troy. He had assigned himself the general overview and the pottery. It was ready by 11 September. Dörpfeld was to prepare the plans and the section on the architecture.

Meanwhile, John Murray had declined to take the English translation of Schuchhardt's book. Schliemann was offended and wrote to him in October:

> You have done wrong not to publish Schuchhardt's book, 'Schliemann's Excavations', which will have a very large sale both in England and America, for I gave to Macmillan gratuitously the permission to add to it as an Appendix, the English version of our present opusculum with the new plans.[30]

In the same letter he promised to send Gladstone a copy of the report on the 1890 excavations and expressed the hope

> that it may assist him in making new discoveries in Homer, and that it may divert him a little from politics, with which he ought never to have meddled. His greatest exertions to humiliate England in the Egyptian question, and his shameless blunder not to take possession of Egypt after the battle of Tel el Kebir gave me such a profound disgust, that I cannot conceive how it was only possible that the nation tolerated all the mischief and did not *lynch* him. What a glorious country, what a grand pearl in the English crown would have become Egypt if that fickle-minded, weak man had never come to power!

Relations between Heinrich and Sophia were decidedly mixed in 1890. They saw little of one another. Between 26 February and Christmas they were together for only two weeks at Troy and two days in Athens. Both had a tendency to idealize their relationship when they were apart but they quickly became irritated with each other when they were together. On the eve of their wedding anniversary Heinrich was at his most charming when he wrote to Sophia his thoughts about their twenty-one years of married life. She was still at the baths at Kaltenleutgeben, trying to gain enough weight to please him. After regretting that they could not celebrate their anniversary together and praying that they might share another twenty-one years in good health and happiness, he continued:

> Today, as I look back at the long time I have spent with you, I see that the Fates have spun us many sorrows and many joys. We are accustomed to look at the past through rose-coloured spectacles, forgetting the past woes and remembering only the pleasant things. I cannot praise our marriage enough. You have never ceased being a loving wife to me, a good comrade, and an unfailing guide in difficulties, as

well as a loving companion and a mother like no other. I am so delighted with the virtues with which I see you adorned that I have already agreed to marry you in the coming life.[31]

Yet it was Heinrich's insistence that she not return to Athens until she weighed 11½ stone that was keeping them apart.[32] Two days after writing the above he was scolding her for withdrawing 2000 marks from his German bank. He suspected that she was planning to leave Kaltenleutgeben and return to Athens:

> But since you solemnly promised to remain there until mid-October and then, if your weight was less than 75 kg., you would go to Heidelberg to spend the winter there, it is impossible to believe that you can spurn the good fortune and safety that have presented themselves. But if you intended to stay, why did you send for such a large sum of money? In the name of the gods I implore you to reduce your expenditures to a more reasonable level and not to waste money . . . If you reach the weight of 75 kilos at Kaltenleutgeben and wish to return from there to Athens write to Messrs Emile Erlanger & Co in Paris: 'Please send me fcs. 2000 from the account which M. Heinrich Schliemann, my husband, established with you in my favour on 25 September.' . . . 1000 francs is enough for the trip back but it is better to ask for 2000 so that you have plenty if you happen to stay some time in Brindisi and Corfu. But see that you don't return here until you reach the weight of 75 kilos, for you would very much regret it.[33]

When Sophia and the children reached Corfu in late October, Schliemann recommended that they spend the winter there. But his left ear had gone deaf again and he soon decided he would have the operation after all. He wrote to Sophia that if she wanted to stay in Corfu, he would see them there on his way to Germany via Trieste but if she returned to Athens, then he would head north by the Thessaloniki route shortly after she arrived.[34] Sophia and the children seem to have reached Athens about 3 November. Schliemann left on the 5th. This was the last he saw of his family.

Dr Schwartze of Halle was the leading ear specialist in Germany and had been recommended to Schliemann by Virchow. He examined Schliemann on 12 November and operated on both ears the next day. The bony growths were removed under chloroform by mastoidectomy – essentially a chiselling process. Schliemann reported to Virchow:

> Of the operation I saw and felt nothing except the small table on which I had to lie down and which is very like the tables on which bones are set; so it made an alarming impression. Prof. Schwartze says that the operation lasted 1¾ hours. He could operate through the auditory canal on the right ear without difficulty but not on

the left. Its whole muscle had to be removed and later put back. Prof. Schwartze says that he has two matchboxes of excised bone fragments that he wants to give me as a souvenir.[35]

The difficult part for Schliemann was the convalescence. He had been told to expect deafness in both ears for three weeks. This made it rather impractical for him to have visitors, as he explained to Virchow:

It is extremely kind and considerate of you to think of me and to want to visit me. Naturally, I would very much like to see you but I am quite incapable of receiving you, as I am deaf in both ears and my head is bound with thick bandages. But I won't be long in this condition; today I already feel well enough that I have been able to get up and as soon as Prof. Schwartze allows me, I will come and greet you and your family.[36]

To while away the hours Schliemann read the *Arabian Nights* in Arabic, probably in conjunction with Burton's English translation.[37] He had also time to make plans. Though he had not yet received the firman for the renewal of excavations in March, the signs were favourable and he was optimistic. For the following winter he looked forward to going somewhere tropical with Virchow. He suggested Mexico or the Canaries. The anthropological and archaeological appeal of Mexico is obvious, but why the Canaries? The answer provokes a smile but the irony is moving nonetheless. Some scholars identified the Canaries with the Isles of the Blest, where specially favoured heroes like Menelaos went after death.[38]

Schliemann also had time to work up some anger. This was primarily directed against Dörpfeld, who, he was shocked to learn from Brockhaus, had still not submitted his section of the report on the 1890 Troy excavations. In asking for an explanation, however, he tempered forcefulness with tact:

I can only explain your behaviour on the grounds that there is a misunderstanding between us and that you must have taken serious offence at something. But such things must not come between us, for we have already done important work together and much important work remains to be done, which only the two of us can achieve in unison and which cannot be done without us.[39]

To Sophia, however, who was sending him reading material, he was considerably less sensitive:

Your mockery of me doubles my pain. You make me extremely angry when you proudly keep sending me the worthless Greek newspapers, while retaining the

Athenaeum and the Academy, which you promised to send me regularly. Are you deliberately making me the butt of one of your jokes? Your jokes are absurd, just too absurd. Now it's too late. Don't send me any more.[40]

Post-operative complications seem to have developed while Schliemann was still in the clinic. In a letter to Sophia on 23 November he mentioned that his ear passages gave off an odour. Schwartze was irrigating the ears daily with a carbolic acid solution to remove the discharge.[41] On 28 November Schliemann complained to Virchow about a persistent pain in his left ear, the cause of which Schwartze had not yet diagnosed. Schwartze apparently suspected infection of the periosteum in the middle ear and warned Schliemann of the dangers of leaving the clinic before the pain had gone.[42] By 3 December the pain was considerably worse. 'How can I excavate at Troy like this?' he wrote to Virchow in despair.[43] On 6 December he wrote to Sophia in a more positive vein:

Yesterday having severe pain in my ear I had already made up my mind that I would never get out of Halle alive. But late in the evening, as I was stretched out in my bed, it occurred to me that there is a drug for me, whose prescription shines out above the entrance to our library: 'Know thyself'. I persuaded myself that the pains are nonsense, an illusion, and that I am not in danger. For if there were irritation and inflammation of the periosteum, it is clear that I would have uninterrupted fever and be enduring ceaseless pain. But since I have had no fever and am not constantly in pain, it is very clear that the pains derive from the surgery; so I should pay no attention to them.

Schliemann left the clinic on 12 December. Virchow states that he did so with Schwartze's permission but the medical record seems to have indicated otherwise.[44] Schliemann's letter to Sophia on 10 December settles the matter and reveals Schliemann's state of mind when he made his fateful decision:

I have not recovered yet completely from the trouble. I continue to feel pain in my left ear at intervals. Moreover, not only is it difficult for me to talk but also I am beginning to have stabbing pains in my ear. Hence I cannot receive or visit friends or participate in social intercourse. Somehow or other I have to put an end to this distressing way of life. But their orders are that I should stay here till they stop the burning and pain in my ear. But I can't bear the loneliness any longer. So I have decided to go on Friday, the day after tomorrow, to Leipzig and on the following day to Berlin. From there I hope to proceed to Paris on Sunday 14 December. I don't think it will do me any harm, for I will . . . see to it that I don't catch cold.[45]

295

Schliemann arrived in Berlin in the evening of 13 December and saw Virchow the next day, when he presented him with the boxes of bone fragments from his ears. Virchow later recalled the final meeting with his old friend:

He came to Berlin via Leipzig, where he consulted with his publisher, Mr. Brockhaus. He had blown a great quantity of iodoform powder into the auditory canal and it was apparent that a dried mass was blocking the rear part of it. Only a small part could be easily removed. As he wanted to depart at midday on 14 December, I advised him to content himself with mild palliatives. His condition in general appeared to be quite satisfactory. He had no pains worth mentioning and no fever. Together we visited on foot his collection in the Museum für Völkerkunde [Ethnological Museum]. Its new arrangement met with his highest approval. Then he ate breakfast at my house with a good appetite, was as cheerful, interested, and alert, as he ever was in his best periods, and when we parted, he called out to me: 'Our next trip – the Canaries!'[46]

Schliemann caught a cold in his right ear on the way to Paris. He had forgotten to protect it with cotton wool.[47] In Paris he went to see the ear specialist Jules Ladreit de la Charrière, who found too much iodoform powder in the right ear. In addition he removed a 'mass of bone fragments'. Schliemann was shocked that Schwartze had not seen them. He assumed that the powder must have concealed them. He gave Virchow the details of Ladreit de la Charrière's prescription which he was supposed to take for six months but said that he would not follow it as he would get bored.[48] He pressed on to Naples, where he planned to take the steamer to Piraeus. On 22 December he sent a telegram to Sophia: 'Cable Grand Hotel how you are. Will arrive Saturday.' He planned to arrive in Athens on 27 December. By the Greek calendar that would be 15 December, still in good time for Christmas. A day or two later a second telegram arrived: 'Having begun ear treatment here will not arrive till Tuesday.' This was his last communication with his wife.

Virchow gave the following sketch of Schliemann's final days in Naples:

Reports from Naples inform me that in spite of all warnings and without regard for the chilly weather, he constantly concerned himself in his usual manner with taking note of what was new. On the 24th he was in the German zoological station, apparently untroubled, full of interest in the arrangement of the station and the life of the inhabitants of the sea. He complained of nothing except the feeling that there was still something forming a blockage in his ear . . . Nonetheless, he remained fully active in Naples. On the 25th, when at 9 a.m. gentlemen from the zoological station wished to visit him in his hotel, he had already gone out. But on the same day he was found unconscious at the end of the Toledo and the doctor to whom he was finally brought, diagnosed hemiplegia [paralysis on one side of the body] and, in addition, severe bronchitis.[49]

A contemporary newspaper report fills in other details.[50] Schliemann first consulted Dr Cozzolino, of Naples University, who called in his colleague, Professor von Schroen, for assistance. Until the 25th he was in fairly good spirits. On Christmas morning he went for his usual walk. He collapsed about midday and was taken back unconscious to the Grand Hotel. He recovered consciousness for a while and was able to take some bouillon, though he could not speak. It was clear that the situation was very dangerous. The infection in the left ear had spread and formed an abscess on the brain. By the morning of 26 December his condition had deteriorated further. In the afternoon a group of eight doctors convened in a room adjoining Schliemann's. They were discussing the advisability of trepanning when at 3.30 a nurse emerged from the patient's room to announce that Schliemann had died.

Sophia sent Dörpfeld and her brother Panagiotis to Naples to accompany the body back to Athens for burial. The casket was placed in the salon of Iliou Melathron on 3 January. A bust of Homer was set up nearby and copies of the *Iliad* and the *Odyssey* were placed beside the body.[51] Wreaths were sent by the King of Greece, the Minister of Public Instruction and learned societies from around the world. The funeral took place on 4 January 1891. After a ceremony in Iliou Melathron attended by the King and Crown Prince of Greece, government ministers, members of the foreign diplomatic corps and other notables of Athenian society, the coffin was escorted to the First Cemetery of Athens. There, at a predetermined spot at the highest point of the cemetery, he was buried. Above the grave was set a simple cross bearing Schliemann's name in its English form, 'Henry Schliemann', the way he preferred it.[52] Speeches were given both in Iliou Melathron and at the graveside honouring this exceptional man and his extraordinary achievements. Most apt and moving were the words of his colleague Wilhelm Dörpfeld: 'Rest in peace. You have done enough.'

18

The Schliemann Legacy

THROUGHOUT HIS ADULT LIFE Schliemann was conscientious about updating his will. Before he set out on his world tour in 1864, he wrote out a will and lodged it with J.H. Schröder of London with instructions to open it if they did not hear from him for six months.[1] Thereafter, whenever he went on long trips or was about to start excavating in a remote area like Troy, he would adjust his will to suit his altered circumstances. He composed his last will in his own hand on 10 January 1889 with two short codicils added on 14 and 20 January.[2] The entire estate was evaluated at fifteen million francs.[3] He left to Serge his houses at 7 rue Aubriot and 33 rue de l'Arcade in Paris and a hundred thousand francs; to Nadeshda, his house at 6 rue de Calais, Paris and his property at 161 Buchanan Street, Indianapolis, and a hundred thousand francs.[4] The principal beneficiaries were Andromache and Agamemnon, to whom he left the balance of his estate, with the exception of Iliou Melathron and its contents and a number of bequests to individuals and institutions. Andromache and Agamemnon thus inherited the rest of his property in Athens and Paris as well as very substantial holdings of shares, bonds and other securities. To Sophia, by a special deed of gift, he gave Iliou Melathron and its contents with the exception of the Trojan antiquities, which were bequeathed to the Ethnological Museum in Berlin.[5] To his first wife, Katerina, he left one hundred thousand francs. There were smaller bequests to his surviving sisters and brother, Minna Richers (née Meincke), Wilhelm Dörpfeld, two daughters of Rudolf Virchow, A. H. Sayce,[6] the Berlin Anthropological Society, the Archaeological Society of Athens, and a number of charitable institutions in Athens.

The surprising omission in the will is the lack of a source of income for Sophia. Heinrich had already given her an apartment building in Berlin in 1887 or 1888, which at the time of his death was valued at 1,500,000 francs. The rents would provide Sophia with a very comfortable income for the rest of her life. Heinrich considered her naïve and irresponsible in financial matters. Until his children came of age he appointed the executors (the Director and Vice-Director of the National Bank of Greece and Professor von Streit) as trustees for their inheritance, severely restricting Sophia's role.

> On account of the inexperience of my wife in financial matters I associate with her for the guardianship of my children, who are under age, the said executors or advisers, and I ordain that without the consent of the executors my wife will not have the right of selling or encumbering by mortgage any of the property which I leave to my children or of disposing of this property in any way whatsoever.[7]

Until they came of age the executors were to provide for the upbringing and education of Agamemnon and Andromache the sum of 7000 drachmas each.

Schliemann's will also included plans for a mausoleum that was to be built after his death.[8] It was to be a burial place for himself, Sophia, his children and their descendants. The plans were drawn up by Ernst Ziller and approved by Schliemann himself. The mausoleum was built in 1893–4 at a cost of 50,000 drachmas. Besides Heinrich (1822–90) and Sophia (1852–1932), Andromache (1871–1962) and her husband Leon Melas (1872–1905) and their three sons, Michael (1895–1924), Alexandros (1897–1969) and Lenos (1899–1964) were buried there. Agamemnon (1878–1954) chose to be buried where he died, in Paris. Since Agamemnon and all of Andromache's children died childless, there are no direct living descendants of Sophia and Heinrich.[9]

The mausoleum is the gem of the First Cemetery of Athens and a remarkable work of art. Like Iliou Melathron the tomb is an expression of Schliemann's character and life's work. It consists of a small Greek temple of white marble set upon the roof of the burial chamber which takes the form of, and also functions as, a high pedestal. Around the base of the temple is a frieze, beautifully sculpted in the classical style. The scene on the front (west) segment depicts King Proetus directing the Cyclopes, as they are shaping massive stones for the walls of Tiryns. On the south side are four scenes from the Trojan cycle: Agamemnon sacrificing a bull to Artemis at Aulis; the fighting at the ships at Troy; the fighting over the body of Patroclus; and Electra, accompanied by Orestes and Pylades, making an offering at the tomb of Agamemnon. The four scenes neatly represent the whole Trojan War from its beginning at Aulis through the fighting at Troy to the death of Agamemnon at Mycenae. On the east side three scenes represent the *Odyssey*: Nausikaa setting off on her chariot with Odysseus following; Eumaeus sitting on a rock; and Odysseus slaying the suitors. The scenes on the south and east sides are closely modelled on John Flaxman's famous illustrations for the *Iliad* and the *Odyssey*. On the north side the references to Schliemann's excavations are more explicit, with scenes of workmen at Mycenae, Tiryns, Orchomenos and Troy. In the centre, next to Sophia, stands Schliemann himself, holding a copy of Homer in his hand.

On the steps in front of the temple stands a bust of Schliemann, its gaze directed towards the Parthenon. Below the Tiryns frieze is the epitaph, which takes the traditional form of an elegiac couplet in Greek: 'I cover Heinrich Schliemann of great renown. You should imitate him; he laboured hard for mortals.'[10] These lines were approved by Schliemann before his death. On the architrave above the columns a Greek inscription reads: 'To Schliemann the Hero'.

Sophia provided funding to support the continuation of the excavations at Troy under Dörpfeld. The major result of this campaign was to recognize Troy VI as the Homeric stratum. It would appear, however, that Heinrich's view of Sophia's financial capabilities was correct. In 1906 she sold the property in Berlin. She could not have used the proceeds wisely, for her financial circumstances in 1926 forced her to sell Iliou Melathron to the state and move to a modest house in Phaleron, a coastal suburb of Athens. The latter part of her life she devoted to working for various charities, particularly hospitals and sanatoriums. When she died at the age of eighty in 1932, she was given a state funeral and buried in the mausoleum beside her husband.

From 1934 to 1981 Iliou Melathron was used as the seat of the Areopagos, the Supreme Court of Greece. In this period the interior decoration suffered significant damage. At present the building is in the process of being restored. When it is reopened, it will house the numismatic collection of the National Museum.

In accordance with Schliemann's will, the substantial collection of Trojan antiquities in his possession at the time of his death was transferred to Berlin. Towards the end of the Second World War, the most valuable pieces from the Museum for Prehistory and Protohistory in Berlin, where the Schliemann collection was then housed, were sent in crates to a heavily fortified 'flak tower' that had been constructed in the Zoological Gardens in the heart of the city. Included were all of the gold and silver pieces from the smaller Trojan finds and Priam's Treasure itself. When Soviet troops captured Berlin in 1945, Wilhelm Unversagt, the director of the museum, handed over the crates to the Soviet authorities. They were then taken to Moscow. For almost fifty years the Soviets denied that they had ever reached their destination. In 1993 the Russian government officially acknowledged that the Trojan treasures were indeed in Moscow, stored in the Pushkin Museum. In 1994 it was indicated that they would go on display to the general public in late 1995.

The question of repatriation of the objects to Berlin is bound up with the resolution of a number of issues and conflicting claims. The Trojan treasures are only a small part of a huge collection of art works removed from Germany to the Soviet Union in the weeks following the end of the Second World War. Before returning these pieces to Germany, the Russian government seeks restoration of, or reasonable compensation for, the many thousands of works of art removed from Russian museums by German troops. The present whereabouts of most of these objects is unknown. Regarding the Trojan treasures, Turkish authorities are claiming the return of pieces illegally removed from Turkish soil. This would appear to include not only the stone axes and other items of Treasure L, now presumably in Moscow, but also the marble Julio-Claudian heads in Berlin. Priam's Treasure itself would appear to belong to Germany, since Turkey surrendered its rights to the find in the financial settlement reached with Schliemann in 1875. Adding to the legal complexities is the fact that the Soviet Union, which removed the art works from Germany, no longer exists, having been replaced by a number of sovereign states.

'I have opened up a new world for archaeology,' said Schliemann in 1873 after his successful campaign at Hisarlik. Indeed he had. Three years later he opened up another world for archaeology, of even greater significance for our understanding of the evolution of European civilization, when he uncovered the spectacular wealth and sophistication of the shaft graves at Mycenae. For these reasons he has been called the 'Father of Mediterranean Archaeology'. Even if we conclude that he substantially manipulated the facts of his excavations and included purchased and forged pieces among his 'finds', these achievements will nonetheless abide as landmarks in the history of archaeology.

When Schliemann began excavating at Hisarlik in 1870, probably about half of the scholars who had thought seriously about the problem would have said that Homer's Troy was a figment of his poetic imagination and that to seek for its location on terra firma was folly. Most of the rest would have placed it at Bunarbashi. By the time of his death twenty years later Schliemann had convinced the world that Homeric Troy had once existed, that the second stratum at Hisarlik held the ruins of that city and that the Homeric poems contained at least a kernel of truth. He had also demonstrated that Greek civilization was about one thousand years earlier than anyone had imagined. He had filled museums in Athens, Constantinople and Berlin with marvellous finds of gold, silver, bronze, pottery and stone. His excavations, phenomenally successful and skilfully promoted, had given a great boost to archaeology and inspired many others to go out and do likewise. A century after his death his discoveries remain central to our understanding of Aegean civilization in the Bronze

Age. Only the excavations of Sir Arthur Evans and Carl Blegen can stand comparison to Schliemann's in overall significance. These two scholars certainly excavated and recorded with greater care than Schliemann but their work is more limited in scope. They also had the advantage of excavating later, when more exacting standards had become the norm.

One of the keys to understanding Schliemann's life and achievements is to be found in his remarkable ability to master foreign languages. Besides his native German, Schliemann had a good to excellent command of Dutch, English, Danish, Swedish, French, Italian, Spanish, Portuguese, Russian, Polish, ancient and modern Greek, Latin, Arabic, Turkish and Hebrew, though his knowledge of the last two was imperfect.[11] In the last decade of his life he increasingly used ancient Greek as though it were a living language, writing letters and keeping diaries in it and even conversing with any scholar daring enough to respond. What is the explanation for this extraordinary ability? Schliemann's self-discipline and perseverance and his enormous capacity for hard work are a major part of the answer. Schliemann himself certainly believed so: 'Talent means energy and persistence and nothing more.'[12] I believe also that to a remarkable degree Schliemann retained a child's ability to pick up languages through imitation well into his adult life. Hard work and a knack for imitation lie at the heart of Schliemann's achievements. Significantly, they are enshrined in his epitaph.

According to the terms of the contract under which Heinrich served as an apprentice grocer, Theodor Hückstaedt was to look after his young charge like a father.[13] It seems most likely that Hückstaedt provided an important model for Heinrich in his adolescent years. Heinrich learned a great deal from him: the importance of keeping adequate stock on a wide variety of items, writing to suppliers in good time, keeping careful records of outgoing and incoming correspondence, and all the skills and practices that are necessary for a well-run business.[14] More generally, he learned the importance of approaching tasks methodically, working hard, and persisting even when difficulties arose. These qualities characterized Schliemann for the rest of his life.[15] In short, Hückstaedt taught Heinrich how to become the ideal grocer. To a remarkable degree Schliemann assimilated himself to that ideal.

His rapid advancement in the firm of B.H. Schröder is no doubt attributable to his willingness to work hard and his ability to observe carefully the principals of the firm and copy their methods. He quickly saw the importance of accurate and detailed information and developed an insatiable appetite for facts. Among the other talents that emerged at this time are an extraordinary ability to grasp the essentials of a complicated situation and a brash self-confidence that enabled him to reach decisions quickly and act on them. He was naturally impulsive, but this was controlled by a firm grasp of all the relevant facts. His natural charm, affability and gift for telling stories in a colourful way worked well for him in his transactions.

One of the most attractive aspects of Schliemann's character is the care which he took to send money to his father and sisters in Mecklenburg. Sums were sent regularly at Christmas and quite often at other times too. Moreover, after his divorce he was conscientious about sending money for the raising and education of Serge and Nadeshda. He also frequently helped out old Mecklenburg friends such as Carl Andress and Minna and her brother and sister. He was generous too in helping others with small courtesies such as writing letters of recommendation for them. By all accounts, he was extremely hospitable.

In Schliemann's formative years he would naturally have modelled himself on his father. It is likely that this is the source of most of his unattractive traits: his short temper, lying, wiliness, unscrupulousness, readiness to resort to fraud to achieve his ends, and the callous way he sometimes had of dealing with people who had gone out of their way to help him. There are signs too that like his father Schliemann made sexual advances to female servants employed in his household. It is clear, at any rate, that Sophia accused him of this and that Katerina called him a 'debauchee'. When he was seeking his divorce in Indianapolis in 1869, his inability to keep female servants for more than a day or two was probably due to his unwanted sexual advances.[16] While most of these disturbing traits persisted throughout his life, as he grew older they showed themselves less frequently.

It is of course his lying and penchant for fraud that are of greatest importance when we consider Schliemann's career as an archaeologist. The prevalence of lies in Schliemann's writings and the peculiar quality of many of them suggest that his lying was pathological.[17] Consider, for instance, his 'eyewitness' account of the fire of San Francisco or his interview with President Fillmore, both in his 1851–2 diary. There is also the bizarre entry in the 1869 diary, in which he insists that he will have nothing to do with the 'horrors' of 'false certificates and perjury' to obtain a New York divorce on the very day on which he obtained his American citizenship by these means. Here too Schliemann's behaviour improved as he grew older. The influence of Virchow from 1879 onwards and Schliemann's efforts to please and emulate him were no doubt factors in this improvement.

Schliemann almost certainly fabricated the story concerning his original impetus toward archaeology. The evidence points overwhelmingly to the conclusion that Schliemann had no childhood dream of excavating Troy. What was it then that prompted him to devote the last twenty years of his life to

Homeric archaeology? The answer may surprise and disappoint, but it is quite clear. He fell into it. In the spring of 1868 he planned to return to St Petersburg to see his children. His route was to take him via Italy, Greece, and the Black Sea. Ithaca and Troy were to be stops on the way, since he had missed them on his previous Grand Tour. Discussions at the learned societies in Paris had stimulated his interest in Homeric sites but the thought of actually excavating them seems not to have even occurred to him at this stage. The news that he would face renewed litigation in St Petersburg forced him to abandon his visit to Russia. This allowed him to take a much more leisurely trip than he had originally planned. In Rome and Pompeii he saw excavations in progress. On Capri he met some English visitors who sought to excavate the ruins of Tiberius' villa, hoping to find the imperial bedrooms. Accordingly, when he visited the supposed site of Odysseus' palace in Ithaca and wondered about the layout of the rooms, it was a natural step for him to return later to seek an answer with the spade. He was sure that his friends in the learned societies in Paris would be interested in his findings.

Naturally, the influences that had prompted him to excavate at the summit of Mount Aetos affected him in the Troad too. But there was an additional factor. This was his meeting in Athens with Ernst Ziller, who had excavated at Bunarbashi. Not surprisingly then, Schliemann went to the Troad convinced that Bunarbashi was the site of Troy. When his excavations there proved negative, he left disappointed. It was not until he met Frank Calvert at the Dardanelles on 15 August that he learned that Hisarlik was a good contender for the site of Homeric Troy. He had visited the mound cursorily before excavating at Bunarbashi without, apparently, according it serious consideration. The interview with Calvert focused his attention on Hisarlik and changed his life.

How then are we to assess Schliemann's excavations? The greatness of his achievements and their enduring significance are beyond dispute. But given his propensities, the question naturally arises, how much can we believe? His archaeological reports clearly provide, *for the most part*, a reliable record of his excavations. That is not in dispute. On the other hand, the comforting formula that he told lies in his private life but not in his archaeology is no longer tenable.[18] Neither can we say that he told lies in his published work but not in his diaries. There are a great many lies in the diaries. We need to be sceptical at all times, but especially when it comes to the most dramatic finds.

Consider Priam's Treasure. Sophia did not witness the discovery in May 1873 as Schliemann reports. She was in Athens at the time. Schliemann's earliest account placed the findspot in a room in the so-called Priam's Palace. Later the findspot was moved to the city wall 'directly next to Priam's Palace'.

But all the plans place it just *outside* the city wall. This coincides with the testimony of Yannakis. The earliest accounts imply a discovery date of 31 May. Later this was changed to 7 June. Several pieces that appear in photographs of Priam's Treasure also appear in photographs taken in 1872 of the previous two years' finds. The gold jewellery is not mentioned in the earliest accounts of the discovery. Should we accept Schliemann's account as essentially true with a few honest mistakes, or was Priam's Treasure actually a more modest find of bronze and silver pieces enhanced by the season's unreported gold pieces and even some earlier finds? The building just within the Scaean Gate, which he identified as Priam's Palace, was not very impressive. Was the treasure a dramatic attempt to authenticate it?

In 1882 very few of the season's more valuable finds ever reached the museum in Constantinople. It is clear from Schliemann's correspondence with Virchow that he was carefully keeping his best finds hidden from the Turks. Accordingly, when he came to write up his report, he could assign his finds to whatever part he wanted. He reported that the overwhelming bulk of the more interesting pieces came from what was now the most impressive building in Troy II: 'Temple (later Megaron) A'. This looks like another instance of Schliemann 'bundling' his best finds in much the same way he seems to have done in 1873 and for similar reasons.

In his later excavations, Schliemann resorted less frequently to dishonesty. It is hard to imagine, for instance, that there are many serious distortions in his reports on Orchomenos and Tiryns. On the other hand, in 1890 he smuggled all the best finds – the stone axes, the silver vase, and the marble heads – past the Turkish supervisors and off to Athens. He thereby deceived Hamdy Bey, who courteously allowed him to take the pottery, which legally belonged to the Turkish government. Even at the end of his life he could act in an unprincipled manner towards those who helped him and he had no qualms about paying the workmen who brought him finds clandestinely. His success and the ineffectiveness of the supervision are all the more remarkable in that the Turks knew from 1873 onwards that Schliemann was a wily and unscrupulous manipulator, who needed to be watched very carefully.

What then of Mycenae? The extraordinary wealth of Shaft Graves III, IV and V has never been adequately explained. A noted expert on the finds comments on the 'startling discrepancies in quality and organization of design.' May not the great wealth and 'startling discrepancies' of these tombs be attributable to more 'bundling' by Schliemann? It is clear that Schliemann came across quite a few tombs and burials long before he reached the shaft graves. There were rich finds of bronzes in some of these tombs. There may well have also been gold pieces, smuggled past Stamatakis to Schliemann by the workmen for payment and then saved for the grand finale: Shaft Graves III IV and V. At Troy in 1882 Schliemann paid local villagers to make clandestine excavations in the surrounding area. In 1876 he was well aware that there were rich tholos and chamber tombs in the vicinity of Mycenae. Some of the pieces that seem too late for the shaft graves, like Nestor's Cup, may come from clandestine excavations commissioned by Schliemann. A simple microscopic examination should be able to determine whether there are any modern forgeries among the pieces that occur in multiple copies or, like some of the gold masks, are suspicious for other reasons. If, however, Schliemann added to Shaft Graves III, IV or V authentic objects that had in fact been found elsewhere it is hard to see how this can now be proved conclusively. Stylistically, a number of pieces seem too late for these graves. Should we trust Schliemann's account of them because it cannot be disproved? Or should we be sceptical because it is hard to reconcile their attribution to these graves with evidence from other excavations?

Schliemann was an extraordinary individual. In his life and character there is much to admire and much to deplore. It is hard, and probably misguided, to develop a consistent attitude towards him. His egotism, mendacity and often cynical behaviour inevitably alienate our sympathy. In light of his difficult childhood, however, his flaws become more understandable and one can only admire the unquenchable resolution to improve himself by sheer hard work. A picture emerges of a profoundly contradictory and elusive personality. He strove to become a hero. Although questions remain, and indeed are becoming more insistent, Heinrich Schliemann, thanks to his astonishing success, is likely to remain the emblematic archaeologist of all time.

APPENDIX I

Mycenae and Troy: Chronology

Mycenae

Traditional Dating[1]

Early Helladic (EH)	3000–2000 BC
Middle Helladic (MH)	2000–1550
Late Helladic (LH) I	1550–1500
LH II	1500–1400
LH IIIA	1400–1300
LH IIIB	1300–1200
LH IIIC	1200–1050

[1]Ceramic evidence from Thera makes it clear that the cataclysmic eruption of Thera occurred in LH I. Until recently the eruption was dated to *c.* 1525 BC. In recent years different types of scientific evidence (from carbon testing, tree-rings, and ice cores) have combined to point to a firm date of *c.* 1630 BC for the eruption. This means that the traditional chronology for LH I and adjacent periods needs to be adjusted. Since there is as yet no general agreement on a new chronology, the traditional chronology is followed in this book.

Troy

Blegen's Dating[1]

Troy I	3000–2500 BC
Troy II	2500–2200
Troy III	2200–2050
Troy IV	2050–1900
Troy V	1900–1800
Troy VI	1800–1300
Troy VII	1300–1100
Troy unoccupied[2]	1100–700
Troy VIII	700–325 BC
Troy IX	325 BC–AD 600

[1]Blegen classified Troy I–V as Early Bronze Age (EBA), Troy VI as spanning the Middle Bronze Age (MBA) to the end of the first phase of the Late Bronze Age (LBA I), Troy VII as the later phases of the Late Bronze Age, Troy VIII as the Greek Archaic and Classical periods, and Troy IX as the Hellenistic and Roman periods. Since the eruption of Thera falls in the middle of Troy VI, no new chronology is needed. The Trojan War (if historical) is attributed to Troy VIIA by Blegen, to late Troy VI by Dörpfeld and many modern scholars.
[2]Some scholars believe that Troy was occupied continuously between Troy VII and Troy VIII.

APPENDIX II

Chronology of Schliemann's Visit to the Troad in 1868

Aug	Diary	Ithaque
6	Dep. Piraeus 1 a.m. Pass Dardanelles 10.30 p.m.	Dep. Piraeus 1 a.m.
7	Arr. Constantinople 10 a.m. Dep. Constantinople 5 p.m.	Pass Dardanelles 10 p.m.
8	Arr. Dardanelles 6.30 a.m. Arr. Bunarbashi 7 p.m.	Arr. Constantinople 10 a.m. Dep. Constantinople 5 p.m.
9	Bunarbashi–Ezine–(Bunarbashi?)	Arr. Dardanelles 7 a.m. Arr. Bunarbashi 6 p.m. Visit to springs
10	(?Bunarbashi)–Hisarlik–Tomb of Ajax–Yenishehir	Bunarbashi: survey of whole site. Attempt to run around it
11	Yenishehir–Ujek Tepe–Bunarbashi Survey and excavation	Excavations on lower slope
12	Bunarbashi. Excavations on lower slope and at Balli Dagh	Excavations on lower slope
13	Bunarbashi–Alexandria Troas–Ujek	Excavations on Balli Dagh
14	Ujek–Neochorion–Renkoi–Dardanelles	Bunarbashi–Thymbra–Hisarlik–Tomb of Ajax–Yenishehir
15	Dardanelles. Meeting with Frank Calvert	Yenishehir–Neochorion–Ujek Tepe–Bunarbashi.
16	Depart Dardanelles for Constantinople	Bunarbashi–Hisarlik–Paleo Castro–Bunarbashi
17	Constantinople	Bunarbashi–Alexandra Troas–Ujek
18	Constantinople	Ujek–Neochorion–Renkoi–Dardanelles
19	Constantinople	Dardanelles
20	Constantinople	Dardanelles
21	Constantinople	Dardanelles–Constantinople

APPENDIX III

Dating of Strata at Troy in 1882

	Schliemann	Dörpfeld	Dörpfeld's dates
Troy I	Prehistoric	Prehistoric	
Troy II	Priam's Troy	Priam's Troy	(?)–1100 BC
Troy III	Prehistoric	Aeneas' Troy	1100–700
Troy IV	Prehistoric	Archaic & Class.	700–356
Troy V	Prehistoric	non-existent[1]	
Troy VI	Lydian c.1000 BC	non-existent	
Troy VII	Greek Ilion	(V) Hellenistic	356–150
Troy VIII[2]	Roman Ilion	(VI) Roman	150–
Troy IX			

[1] In the central part of Hisarlik the Troy V, VI, VII and VIII strata had been largely eliminated by the levelling of the mound for rebuilding in the Hellenistic and Roman periods (Troy IX). Dörpfeld was therefore correct in observing that he could find no occupation level between Troy IV and the Hellenistic stratum.

[2] At *Troja* 195–218 Schliemann refers to Greek and Roman Ilion together as the 'seventh city', though he does distinguish between Greek and Roman ruins. Dörpfeld, however, in his letter of 18 June to Adler states that Schliemann distinguished nine cities at this time: 'While he recognizes 5 "prehistoric" cities, 1 Lydian (from the year 1000), and then the Aeolic, Macedonian and Roman cities, and so 9 in all, from the ruins and particularly from the city walls I can recognize only 6.' In this table, accordingly, I have split the difference and separated the Greek and Roman levels.

309

APPENDIX IV

Schliemann's Movements 1868–90

1868

10–11 Jan	New York
25 Jan–11 Mar	Paris
11–18 Mar	Bonn
18 Mar–29 Apr	Paris
1 May	Susa
2 May	Milan
3–4 May	Bologna
5 May–7 Jun	Rome
7–12 Jun	Naples
13–14 Jun	Ischia
15–17 Jun	Naples
18 Jun	Sorrento
19 Jun	Capri
20–21 Jun	Sorrento
22–30 Jun	Naples
1 Jul	Messina
2 Jul	Nicolosi
5 Jul	Gallipoli (Italy)
6–7 Jul	Corfu
8–17 Jul	Vathy (Ithaca)
18 Jul	Corinth
19 Jul	Piraeus
20–29 Jul	Athens
30 Jul	Corinth
31 Jul	Mycenae
31 Jul–3 Aug	Nauplion
4–6 Aug	Athens
7 Aug	Constantinople
8–10 Aug	Bunarbashi
11 Aug	Yenishehir
12–13 Aug	Bunarbashi
14–16 Aug	Dardanelles
17–26 Aug	Constantinople
28 Aug	Piraeus
30 Aug	Messina
4 Sep–31 Dec	Paris

1869

5–9 Jan	St Petersburg
10 Feb	Paris
18 Feb	Paris
?–? Feb	St Petersburg
2–12 Mar	Paris
13 Mar	Brest
27–31 Mar	New York
1 Apr–20 May	Indianapolis
23–24 May	Memphis
26 May–1 Jun	Indianapolis
2–4 Jun	Fort Wayne
5 Jun–16 Jul	Indianapolis
18–24 Jul	New York
6–22 Aug	Paris
3–23 Sep	Athens
4 Oct	Naples
9 Oct	Rome
14 Oct	Florence
23 Oct–31 Dec	Paris

1870

1 Jan–8 Feb	Paris
11–12 Feb	Marseille
19–26 Feb	Athens
26 Feb–20 Mar	Cyclades
21–30 Mar	Athens
31 Mar	Itea
1 April	Delphi
2 April	Itea
3–5 April	Athens
6 Apr	Piraeus
8–9 Apr	Renkoi
10–19 Apr	Chiplak
20 Apr	Dardanelles

22–27 Apr	Athens	**1872**	
29 Apr–2 May	Constantinople		
3 May	Black Sea	1 Jan–26 Mar	Athens
4 May	Bulgaria	2 Apr–13 Aug	Troy
5 May	Turnu-Severin	13–15 Aug	Dardanelles
7–8 May	Vienna	16 Aug	Smyrna
10–19 May	Schweizermühle	20 Aug–11 Sep	Athens
19 May	Paris	15–16 Sep	Troy
20 May	Schweizermühle	22 Sep–31 Dec	Athens
21 May	Dresden		
23 May	Zurich	**1873**	
24 May	Lucerne		
25–26 May	Geneva	1–29 Jan	Athens
27–28 May	Marseille	4 Feb–14 Jun	Troy
2 Jun	Athens	19 Jun	Thessaloniki
7 Jun	Marseille	25 Jun–31 Dec	Athens
8–29 Jun	Paris		
30 Jun–2 Jul	Marseille	**1874**	
10–13 Jul	Athens		
20 Jul–7 Aug	Paris	1 Jan–22 Feb	Athens
18 Aug–9 Sep	Boulogne	24–28 Feb	Mycenae
21–23 Sep	Edinburgh	1–2 Mar	Nauplion
29 Sep–28 Oct	Arcachon	8 Mar–20 Jul	Athens
6 Nov	Marseille	20 Jul–3 Aug	Tour of Northern
21 Nov–13 Dec	Athens		Greece
14 Dec	Syra	3–16 Aug	Athens
15–16 Dec	Smyrna	17 Aug–5 Sep	Tour of
18–20 Dec	Dardanelles		Peloponnese
	and Chiplak	5 Sep–31 Dec	Athens
1871		**1875**	
1–13 Jan	Constantinople	1 Jan–25 Apr	Athens
24 Jan–4 Feb	Athens	14 May	Marseille
17 Feb–26 Mar	Paris	31 May–3 Jun	Paris
13 Apr–13 Jun	Athens	9 Jun	Boulogne
17–26 Jun	Constantinople	10–15 Jun	London
1–11 Jul	Athens	20–25 Jun	London
	via Trieste, Berlin and	26–27 Jun	Brighton
	Paris to	1 Jul	Brighton
12 Aug	London	8 Jul	Brighton and
9–19 Sep	Athens		London
26 Sep	Constantinople	19–20 July	London
27 Sep	Dardanelles	24 July	Brighton
28 Sep–4 Oct	Troy	27 July	London
4–10 Oct	Dardanelles	1–2 Aug	Paris
11 Oct–24 Nov	Troy	3–4 Aug	Hague
3–14 Dec	Salamis	? Aug	Copenhagen
16–31 Dec	Athens	13 Aug	Stockholm
		20 Aug	Rostock and
			Roebel

311

25 Aug	Danzig
27 Aug	Budapest
1–3 Sep	Mainz
8–11 Sep	Paris
27–29 Sep	Rome
1–7 Oct	Albano
8–10 Oct	Rome
13–14 Oct	Palermo
19–25 Oct	Motya
29 Oct–4 Nov	Palermo
20 Nov	Castellammare
27 Nov	Florence
1–17 Dec	Naples
25–31 Dec	Athens

1876

1 Jan–19 Feb	Athens and latterly in Constantinople
19 Feb–12 Mar	Athens
17 Mar–27 Apr	Constantinople
28–30 Apr	Cyzicus
3–5 May	Constantinople
7–10 May	Troy
14–16 May	Athens
19 May–7 Jun	Troy and Dardanelles
9–27 Jun	Constantinople
27–29 Jun	Dardanelles
30 Jun	Thessaloniki
2–27 Jul	Athens
31 Jul–6 Aug	Tiryns and Nauplion
7 Aug–9 Oct	Mycenae
13–16 Oct	Dardanelles and Troad
21 Oct	Athens
23 Oct–4 Dec	Mycenae
5–31 Dec	Athens

1877

1 Jan–15 Mar	Athens
22 Mar–22 Jun	London
(17–18 May	Paris)
24 Jun–8 Aug	Boulogne
11–21 Aug	Paris
22 Aug–10 Sep	London
12–21 Sep	Paris
22 Sep	Marseille
27 Sep–25 Oct	Athens

1 Nov	Marseille
3–6 Nov	Paris
7–12 Nov	Würzburg
20 Nov–17 Dec	London
21–31 Dec	Würzburg

1878

1–11 Jan	Würzburg
14–16 Jan	Paris
2–23 Feb	Athens
7 Mar–6 Apr	Paris
7–8 Apr	London
10 Apr–8 May	Paris
Late May and early June	Athens
12 Jun–14 Jul	Paris
30 Jul–3 Aug	Constantinople
17 Aug	Athens
Late Aug and early Sep	Ithaca
10–18 Sep	Athens
9 Oct–27 Nov	Troy
9 Dec	London
17–19 Dec	Paris

1879

11 Jan–23 Feb	Athens
27 Feb	Syra
19 Mar	Dardanelles
27 Mar–4 Jun	Troy
7–19 Jun	Athens
26 Jun–4 Jul	Paris
6 Jul–1 Aug	Kissingen
3 Aug	Würzburg
6 Aug	Dillenburg
11 Aug	Roebel
17 Aug	Paris
19 Aug	Boulogne
20 Aug–5 Sep	London
6–11 Sep	Boulogne
12–20 Sep	London
21 Sep	Boulogne
24–30 Sep	London
7–9 Oct	Paris
11 Oct	Marseille
16 Oct–31 Dec	Athens

1880

1 Jan–13 May	Athens

19 May	Munich
21 May–25 Jun	Leipzig
26 Jun	Berlin
27 Jun–3 Aug	Leipzig
4–5 Aug	Berlin
6 Aug–10 Sep	Leipzig
12–14 Sep	Carlsbad
17 Sep	Vienna
21–29 Sep	Paris
30 Sep–14 Oct	Biarritz
22–23 Oct	Marseille
25 Oct	Naples
28 Oct–13 Nov	Athens
Late Nov and early Dec	Orchomenos
8–16 Dec	Athens
20 Dec	Berlin
22–24 Dec	London
25 Dec	Aachen
26 Dec	Berlin
27–31 Dec	London

1881

1 Jan	London
2–6 Jan	Paris
13 Jan–12 Mar	Athens
16 Mar	Olympia
18–29 Mar	Athens
Early April	Orchomenos
14 Apr–12 May	Athens
13–23 May	Troad
29 May–9 Jun	Athens
12 Jun	Brindisi
15 Jun	Schwandorf
16–30 Jun	Berlin
6 Jul	Leipzig
6–18 Jul	Berlin
19 Jul	Leipzig
20 Jul–16 Aug	Carlsbad
19–23 Aug	Berlin
23 Aug	Stuttgart
24–26 Aug	Basel
28 Aug–5 Sep	Thun
7–21 Sep	Paris
7–14 Oct	Constantinople
16–25 Oct	Athens
28–29 Oct	Dardanelles
1 Nov	Troy
2–3 Nov	Dardanelles
6 Nov–31 Dec	Athens

1882

1 Jan–1 Mar	Athens
6 Mar–21 Jul	Troy
22–26 Jul	Dardanelles
6–7 Aug	Vienna
9 Aug	Marienbad
13–18 Aug	Frankfurt
20 Aug–5 Sep	Marienbad
7–10 Sep	Dresden
11–23 Sep	Paris
1–4 Oct	Rome
4–9 Oct	Naples
12 Oct–31 Dec	Athens

1883

1–28 Jan	Athens
29 Jan–4 Feb	Thermopylae
4 Feb–18 Apr	Athens
19–28 Apr	Trip to Troy
29 Apr–30 May	Athens
1 Jun	Brindisi
2–4 Jun	Lugano
5–6 Jun	Kassel
6–7 Jun	Berlin
12–13 Jun	Oxford
15 Jun	Neustrelitz
16 Jun–12 Jul	Ankershagen
15–16 Jul	Berlin
18 Jul–16 Aug	Wildungen
23 Aug–1 Sep	Leipzig
2–3 Sep	Hanover
5 Sep	Sandown, IOW
6–12 Sep	London
12 Sep	Sandown
14–15 Sep	London
15–17 Sep	Sandown
18–19 Sep	London
19 Sep	Sandown
20 Sep	London
21 Sep–3 Oct	Boulogne
4–21 Oct	Paris
22 Oct	Turin
26 Oct	Brindisi
30 Oct–31 Dec	Athens

1884

1 Jan–3 Feb	Athens
4–9 Feb	Marathon
10 Feb–13 Mar	Athens

18 Mar–16 Apr	Nauplion and Tiryns	**1886**	
19 Apr–6 May	Athens	1–10 Jan	Sails to Cuba
15–24 May	Tiryns	10–21 Jan	Havana
3 Jun–1 Jul	Athens	13–14 Feb	Paris
5–6 Jul	Munich	17–20 Feb	London
10–15 Jul	London	23 Feb–5 Mar	Berlin
20 Jul	Paris		via Rome to
23–31 Jul	Marienbad	15–18 March	Naples
2–8 Aug	Breslau	23 Mar–25 Apr	Athens
9–13 Aug	Marienbad	Early May	Levadia (6) and
14–15 Aug	Berlin		Orchomenos (9)
17–21 Aug	Warnemünde	15–17 May	Athens
24–30 Aug	London	18–22 May	Crete
31 Aug–1 Sep	Lübeck	25 May–23 Jun	Athens
2 Sep	Rostock	30 Jun–3 Jul	London
2–11 Sep	Warnemünde	5 Jul	Paris
12 Sep	Schwerin	5–7 Jul	Brussels
15 Sep	Leipzig	11–24 Jul	Amsterdam
16–19 Sep	Vienna	28 Jul–15 Aug	Burtscheid
(17? Sep	Berlin)	(14 Aug	Aachen)
27 Sep–31 Dec	Athens	17 Aug	Berlin
		23 Aug	Doberan
1885		24–29 Aug	Heligendam
		30 Aug–2 Sep	Ostende
1 Jan–26 May	Athens	4–16 Sep	Paris
1–8 Jun	London	17–18 Sep	Marseille
10–23 Jun	Boulogne	23 Sep–27 Nov	Athens
25 Jun	Paris	29–30 Nov	Alexandria
28 Jun	St Moritz	30 Nov–8 Dec	Cairo
29 Jun–13 Jul	Abano (Padua)	14 Dec	Rigga
20 Jul–2 Aug	St Moritz	16–18 Dec	Beni Hassan
4–7 Aug	Karlsruhe	20 Dec	Asyiut
8–9 Aug	Geneva	28 Dec	Denderah
9–10 Aug	Lausanne	30 Dec	Negadeh
13–25 Aug	St Moritz	31 Dec	Gemola
26–27 Aug	Chur		
29–30 Aug	Berlin	**1887**	
31 Aug–21 Sep	Lausanne		
(9 Sep	Paris)	1 Jan	Thebes
22 Sep–14 Oct	Paris	2–3 Jan	Esneh
18 Oct	Bosporus	23–27 Jan	Wadi Halfa
21–23 Oct	Constantinople	29–30 Jan	Abu Simbel
25 Oct–2(?) Dec	Athens	7 Feb	Philae
3 Dec	Lausanne	15–19 Feb	Thebes
8–20 Dec	Paris	3 Mar	Asyiut
(10 Dec	Leipzig)	15–16 Mar	Alexandria
20 Dec	St Nazaire	18 Mar–23 Apr	Athens
20–31 Dec	Sails to Cuba	24–29 Apr	Dardanelles
		30 Apr–21 Aug	Athens
		5 Sep	Neuhausen
		7–17 Sep	Wiesbaden

3–6 Oct	Paris	17–27 Jun	Athens
9–10 Oct	Milan	1 Jul	Verona
13–19 Oct	Trieste	3 Jul	Munich
22–29 Oct	Corfu	9–18 Jul	Berlin
3–29 Nov	Athens	21 Jul	Hanover
Early December	Kythera	23 Jul	Roebel
11–31 Dec	Athens	26–27 Jul	Hamburg
		29 Jul–17 Aug	Boulogne
1888		17 Aug–17 Sep	Paris
		24 Sep–1 Nov	Athens
1–26 Jan	Athens	6 Nov	Dardanelles
30 Jan–1 Feb	Alexandria	8 Nov–8 Dec	Troy
1–3 Feb	Cairo	13–31 Dec	Athens
3–15 Feb	Alexandria		
15–18 Feb	Cairo	**1890**	
18–22 Feb	Alexandria		
22–24 Feb	Cairo	1 Jan–26 Feb	Athens
24 Feb	Asyiut	28 Feb–17 May	Troy
27 Feb	Edfu	19–20 May	Constantinople
28 Feb	Aswan	20 May–28 Jul	Troy
2–9 Mar	Abu Simbel	30 Jul	Thessaloniki
10 Mar	Wadi Halfa	4 Aug–5 Nov	Athens
15–22 Mar	Luxor	9 Nov–12 Dec	Halle
23 Mar	Denderah	13–14 Dec	Berlin
25 Mar	Abydos	15–18 Dec	Paris
3 Apr	Hawara	21–26 Dec	Naples
6–13 Apr	Cairo		
16 Apr	Alexandria		
22 Apr–17 May	Athens		
22–26 May	Paris		
29 May–4 Jun	Naples		
9 Jun–7 Sep	Athens		
13 Sep–3 Oct	Paris		
9–28 Oct	Heidelberg		
31 Oct	Brindisi		
4–21 Nov	Athens		
21 Nov–6 Dec	Tour of Peloponnese		
6–31 Dec	Athens		
1889			
1 Jan–13 Feb	Athens		
18–20 Feb	Crete		
23 Feb–30 Apr	Athens		
(29–30 Mar	Troy)		
5–9 May	Rome		
11 May	Paris		
12–19 May	London		
20 May–1 Jun	Paris		
5 Jun	Florence		
10 Jun	Brindisi		

APPENDIX V

Plans of Excavations

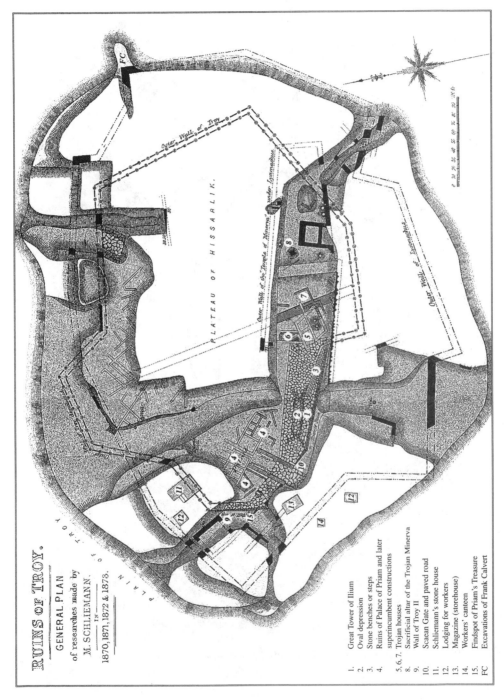

RUINS OF TROY.

GENERAL PLAN
of researches made by
M. SCHLIEMANN.
IN
1870, 1871, 1872 & 1873.

1.   Great Tower of Ilium
2.   Oval depression
3.   Stone benches or steps
4.   Ruins of Palace of Priam and later
     superincumbent constructions
5. 6. 7. Trojan houses
8.   Sacrificial altar of the Trojan Minerva
9.   Wall of Troy II
10. Scaean Gate and paved road
11. Schliemann's stone house
12. Lodging for workers
13. Magazine (storehouse)
14. Workers' canteen
15. Findspot of Priam's Treasure
FC   Excavations of Frank Calvert

Plan I: General plan of excavations made in 1870–3

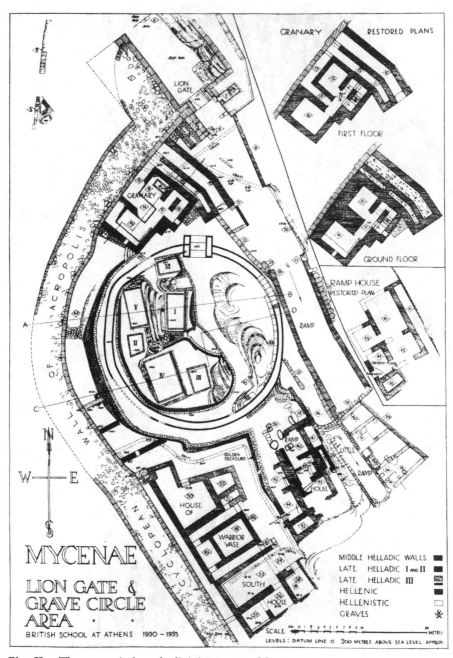

Plan II: The grave circle and adjoining areas at Mycenae

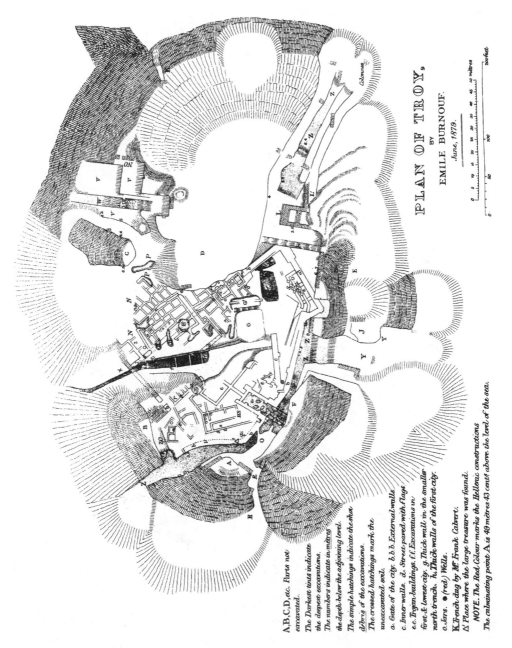

Plan III: Plan of excavations at Troy, June 1879

Unexcavated parts, as f.i., F, G.

Walls of the first city, as f.i., f.f., fa, fb, fc.

Walls of the second city of its first period, as f.i., OZ, O, xg, va.

Walls of the second city of its second period, as f.i.b. A, B, W, NN,

Walls of the third city, as f.i., H.S., σ m.

Roman Propylaeum L.

f, fa, fb, fc   House and fortification walls of the first city.

pw, p, o, ow.   Towers of the wall of defence of the Acropolis of the first period–second city.

RC. and NF.   Two gates of the Acropolis of the first period–second city.

E.D. and va.   Housewalls of the first period–second city.

B. C   Wall of the second lower city.

FM. and OX.   The two gates of the Acropolis of the second period–second city.

GM.   Tower of the wall of the Acropolis of the second period–second city.

A., B., C., W., rx., and rb.   The edifices of the Acropolis of the second city at the time of its total destruction.

xm.   The wall of defence of the third settlement. HS. and HT. edifices of the same time; the other buildings of the third settlement, which filled the whole Acropolis, are left out in order not to crowd the plan; but they may be seen on Plan I. in *Ilios*.

tz.   Hellenic well.

L.   Roman Propylaeum.

R.   Shaft sunk.

SS.   The great north eastern trench.

ST.   The great south eastern trench.

X–Z.   The great north trench.

Q.   The great south trench.

mz.   Western trench.

nz.   North western trench.

q and WV.   Deep trenches.

PLAN OF
THE ACROPOLIS
of the
SECOND CITY.

Scale of Metres

W. Dörpfeld. J.Häfler, fec.

Vincent Brooks Day & Son Lith.

Plan IV: Plan of excavations of acropolis of Troy II, 1882

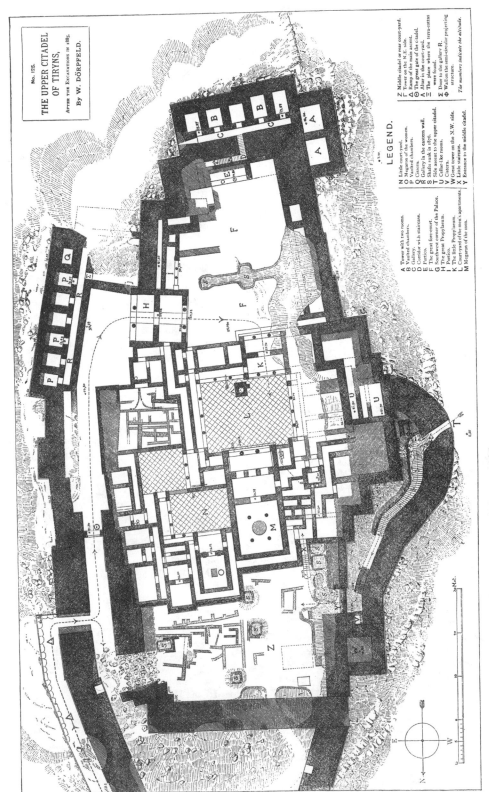

Plan V: Plan of excavations at the palace of Tiryns, 1885

Notes

ABBREVIATIONS AND SHORT TITLES

AA	*Archäologischer Anzeiger*
AAZ	*Augsburg Allgemeine Zeitung*
AJ	*Archaeological Journal*
AJA	*American Journal of Archaeology*
AM	*Deutsches Archäologisches Institut. Athenische Abteilung. Mitteilungen*
B	Schliemann Archive, Gennadius Library, American School of Classical Studies, Athens. Letters received by Schliemann
BB	Schliemann Archive. Original letters by Schliemann
BBB	Schliemann Archive. Copybooks of Schliemann's outgoing correspondence
Briefe	H. Schliemann, *Briefe*, ed. Ernst Meyer, Berlin, 1937
BSA	*Annual of the British School at Athens*
BSG	*Bulletin de la Société géographique*
Bw	H. Schliemann, *Briefwechsel*, ed. Ernst Meyer, 2 vols., Berlin 1953–8
Calvert file	Schliemann Archive (see B above)
CJ	*Classical Journal*
C-Blatt	Deutsche Gesellschaft für Anthropologie, Ethnologie und Urgeschichte. *Correspondenz-Blatt*
CR	*Classical Review*
CW	*Classical World*
DAI	Deutsches Archäologisches Institut
EdR	Edinburgh Review
ES	David A. Traill, *Excavating Schliemann*, Atlanta, 1993
FAZ	*Frankfurter Allgemeine Zeitung*
HSGrundlagen	*Heinrich Schliemann: Grundlagen und Ergebnisse moderner Archäologie 100 Jahre nach Schliemanns Tod*, ed. Joachim Herrmann, Berlin, 1992
HS+100	*Henrich Schliemann nach hundert Jahren*, ed. W.M. Calder III and Justus Cobet, Frankfurt, 1990
IG	*Inscriptiones Graecae*
Ilios	H. Schliemannn, *Ilios*, London, 1881
ILN	*Illustrated London News*
Ithaque	H. Schliemann, *Ithaque, le Péloponnèse et Troie*, Paris, 1869
JHS	*Journal of Hellenic Studies*
Kleopatra	*Kleopatra: Ägypten um die Zeitenwende*, Mainz, 1989
MittAnkershagen	*Mitteilungen aus dem Heinrich-Schliemann-Museum Ankershagen*
MS&H	*Myth, Scandal and History*, ed, W.M. Calder III and David A. Traill, Detroit, 1986
Mycenae	H. Schliemann, *Mycenae*, London, 1878
PAE	*Praktika tes Archaiologikes Hetairias*
RA	*Revue Archéologique*

SA	Schliemann Archive
Tiryns	H. Schliemann, *Tiryns*, London, 1885
Troja	H. Schliemann, *Troja*, London, 1884
TroyR	H. Schliemann, *Troy and its Remains*, London, 1875
ZfE	*Zeitschrift für Ethnologie*

CHAPTER 1: THE CURRENT CONTROVERSY

1. Most of these misunderstandings will be dealt with later. Here it may be noted that the most famous of the gold masks was not found on the mummy but with one of the other skeletons. Who first dubbed it the 'Mask of Agamemnon' is unclear. It seems not to have been Schliemann.
2. Daniel (1981) 8 observes: 'In 1976, at the Nice Conference of Prehistoric and Protohistoric Sciences, there was passed a resolution saying that the history of archaeology was not being properly studied or recognised.' In this respect they are not unlike their colleagues in other fields, for research on the history of a discipline is widely held to be of only peripheral importance to that discipline. In the last few years, however, there has been an encouraging growth of interest in the history of archaeology.
3. See Mellink (1982) 561 and (1985) 553.
4. MacDonald (1987) 258. This view of history would force us to regard as mean-spirited those twentieth-century historians who draw attention to the pogroms or the holocaust, since Stalin and Hitler are no longer around to defend themselves. Though clearly offended by the scepticism of the new view of Schliemann, McDonald poses as a champion of scepticism elsewhere (1967) 10–11: 'a healthy skepticism is one of the qualities that education is supposed to plant and nourish. We all know that unquestioning public acceptance of the judgment of "the expert" can be dangerous.'
5. Hooker (1988) 259.
6. B 98 268.
7. Gay (1988) 172.
8. *Ilios* 3.
9. *Ilios* 17.
10. *Ithaque le Péloponnèse et Troie* xv.
11. *Ithaque* v. When it is recalled that the subject matter of *Ithaque le Péloponnèse et Troie* is an account of Schliemann's 1868 visits to Troy and to the homelands of Ulysses and Agamemnon and that the book was submitted to the University of Rostock as his doctoral dissertation, it will be seen that once again the childhood incident is a precise foreshadowing of the adult achievement.
12. For instance, the autobiographies of Sir Richard Burton, Karl May and Richard Wagner are notoriously unreliable.
13. The story is still presented as factual in the article on Schliemann in the *Encyclopedia Britannica* (1991) and in Boorstin (1985) 588.
14. Traill (1979) 353–5=*ES* 47.
15. *Ilios* 17 and Ludwig (1931) 116.
16. Traill (1982)=*ES* 65–72.
17. Döhl (1981) 77 and Easton (1983) 287.
18. Korres (1975).
19. For this analysis of Ludwig I am indebted to Calder (1990) 362–69.
20. *Briefe* 25: 'Dem Verfasser fehlt das Organ für das Deutsch in Schliemann.'
21. *Briefe* 22: '. . . galt es auszuschneiden, was allzu transitorisch ist und dem Wesen des Schreibers widerspricht . . .'
22. Reported in the *Landeszeitung für Mecklenburg* (Monday 31 May 1937, Beilage to Nr. 123).

23. For a fuller discussion of Meyer as editor and biographer, see Calder (1990) 370–3.
24. Calder (1972).
25. Weber (1942) 25–6 and Calder (1972) 338–9.
26. Calder (1972) 339.
27. Calder (1972) 343.
28. Calder (1972) 350.
29. Weber (1942) 63–5.
30. For a more detailed discussion of this passage, see Traill (1979) 348–51.
31. Korres (1975) 54–62 and 492.
32. Schindler (1976).

CHAPTER 2: THE MAKING OF A SELF-MADE MAN

1. Ankershagen, though tiny, had one of the most richly endowed parishes in the Grand Duchy. For this and much other information on the early years of Schliemann's life I am indebted to the recent research of Wilfried Bölke, Director of the Schliemann Museum in Ankershagen; see, in particular, Bölke (1988) 34–62 and Crepon and Bölke (1990) 5–62.
2. *Ilios* 1–2.
3. *Ilios* 5.
4. Bölke (1988) 39.
5. Crepon and Bölke (1990) 30–1. Two of the nine children died in infancy.
6. Crepon and Bölke (1990) 33–5.
7. *Ilios* 5.
8. *Ilios* 6.
9. *Ilios* 6–7; an earlier version occurs in *Ithaque* vi–vii.
10. Ironically perhaps, it was the real-life Schliemann who succeeded in achieving his goal, whereas the fictional Jude failed.
11. BBB 27 354. Turner (1990) 40 cites a letter to Andress written in 1858, in which Andress's recitation of Homer is alleged to have had a similar effect.
12. *Ithaque* xiii.
13. Turner (1990) 40 mentions the story cropping up in letters to Andress and his father. Unfortunately, he does not give a date for these letters, though the context implies *c.* 1858. Turner appears to suggest that this comparatively early appearance of the story proves its authenticity. But we need to be cautious. Just as the childhood dream of excavating Troy comes into being only after he has in fact excavated it, so the boyhood dream of learning Greek appears only after he has learned it.
14. The report card shows little sign that Schliemann worked hard at school.
15. The major source for the period 1841 till early 1842 is Schliemann's long letter to his sisters dated 20 February 1842; see excerpts published in *Bw* 9–33 and translated in Deuel (1977) 37–52. In Rostock Schliemann stayed at a friend of Hückstaedt's.
16. *Bw* I 10; cf. Deuel (1977) 37.
17. Weber (1942) 5.
18. Weber (1942) 5.
19. *Ilios* 8.
20. *Bw* I 27; cf. Deuel (1977) 50.
21. *Ilios* 9.
22. On this point too there are discrepancies. *Bw* I 29 describes how he was hired by Hoyack. According to the 1851 life his first position was with B.H. Schröder. According to *Ilios* his first employer was F.C. Quien.
23. *Ilios* 9; cf. also *Bw* I 113.
24. Ibid.

25. *Ilios* 9–10.
26. The indigo plant was in great demand for the dyeing of military uniforms.
27. Weber (1942) 12; *Ilios* 12.
28. Cf. *Bw* I 34–5.
29. Ludwig (1931) 80–1.
30. *Bw* I 37–8.
31. Later, Schliemann's attitude to his Greek wife Sophia is similar.
32. Ludwig (1931) 96–7.
33. *Bw* I 38.
34. *Ilios* 12.
35. Besides the inaccuracies discussed, one might also point out that California became a state on 9 September 1850.
36. *Bw* I 47.
37. Weber (1942) 53–4.
38. Weber (1942) 45. For a sceptical view of this, see Calder (1972) 342.
39. Even if we assume only a 1% profit, this would amount to £162,000 in today's values.
40. For a more detailed discussion see Traill (1979) 351–5=*ES* 45–9.
41. See letter by Dr. W. Hasselblatt in *FAZ* 4 June 1984.
42. Weber (1942) 80–2.
43. *Ilios* 14.
44. In *Ilios* 14 he states that he began Greek in 1856 but Turner (1990) 40 says that he began Greek in 1855.
45. See Meyer (1969) 227.
46. *Ilios* 14.
47. *Bw* I 80–81.
48. Exactly when he began to study ancient Greek is not entirely clear. In *Ilios* 14 Schliemann implies that he began it about March 1856 but a letter cited by Turner (1990) 40 indicates that he had not yet started it by October 1857.
49. *Ilios* 17. Diary 2 notes his illness (p. 243) but gives no indication of plans to visit Ithaca.
50. Diary 2 245. He also noted, incorrectly: 'This morning we passed Tenedos, where, according to Homer, the Greek fleet assembled before the siege of Troy.' Homer does not say or imply that the Greek fleet assembled at Tenedos.
51. Meyer (1969) 176.
52. *Bw* I 95.
53. *Bw* I 99.
54. *Bw* I 111.
55. According to *Ilios* 17–18, he wanted to stay in St Petersburg until Solovieff had made his last payment in December 1863. This may also have been a motive.
56. He had just bought Tunisian bonds.
57. *Bw* I 124.
58. *Ilios* 18. For a continuous summary of the trip around the world see Meyer (1969) 183–226. On the five diaries covering it, see Easton (1982) 101–2. On the Asian section, see Carvalho (1992) and Keyser (1990). On the visit to California (Yosemite and Big Trees) see *ES* 51–9.
59. Meyer (1969) 185.
60. *Ilios* 18.
61. Letter from H. van Kempen, dated 26 Jan. 1866. B 60. Either Dumas *père* or *fils* could be intended. The father was 64, the son 42 in 1866.
62. Meyer (1969) 226.
63. Turner (1990) 41.
64. Letter dated 20 November 1866; BBB 27 1. On the way he appears to have visited an

archaeological excavation in the Crimea near Kerch. So David Turner, in a paper on the subject at the 1990 Schliemann conference in Berlin.

65. See Turner (1990) 41.
66. BBB 27 2. The equivalent in today's values would be approximately £6,000,000.
67. BBB 27 39.
68. Letter dated 6 February 1867; BBB 27 10–18.
69. BBB 27 25.
70. Letter to Katerina dated 10 July 1867; BBB 27 188.
71. *BSG* ser. 5, vol. 14 (1967) 296–314. The minutes of the meeting indicate that Schliemann was present; *BSG*, ser. 5, vol. 13 (1967) 523–24. I am grateful to Mark Lehrer of the University of Denver for bringing this information to my attention and providing me with the relevant photocopies. Turner (1990) 41 adduces the meeting of the Société Géographique on 20 March 1857, at which observations were made about J. von Hahn's recent explorations in Turkey as proof that Schliemann learned at this time about von Hahn's excavations at Bunarbashi, but the minutes of the meeting specify that the explorations in question were in *European* Turkey; see *BSG* ser. 5, vol. 15, 409.
72. On this and some other aspects of this diary see Calder (1992) 24–7.
73. Cf. *Bw* I 131 and 134.
74. *Bw* I 129.
75. See Calder (1992) 26–7.
76. *Bw* I 129.
77. For a detailed discussion of this entry see Traill (1991) 105–6=*ES* 61–3.

CHAPTER 3: FROM GRAND TOUR TO ARCHAEOLOGICAL SURVEY

1. Letter to Schröders of London, 11 February 1868 (BBB 27 259).
2. Letter in French addressed to Monsieur Schröder (no address), dated 11 January (in error for February); BBB 27 261f.
3. BBB 27 368.
4. This emerges from Schliemann's letter to Kucherzynski, 13 April 1868 (BBB 27 384).
5. Details of Schliemann's trip to Italy, Greece and the Troad are taken from Schliemann's 1868 diary (A12).
6. Lehrer and Turner (1989) 225.
7. For a lively discussion of Cleopatra's enduring hold on the imagination of the west, see Hughes-Hallett (1990); for a photograph of the Trevisani painting, see ibid. pl. 15.
8. Schindler (1986). The bust is now in the Pergamon Museum, Berlin.
9. The Desubleo *Cleopatra* appears to be a painting he saw in the Palazzo Colonna but I have been unable to find it in the gallery catalogue.
10. Schliemann means *Aeneid* 8, which describes Aeneas' visit to the Palatine.
11. The comic and tragic theatres are now identified simply as the large and small theatres.
12. *Odyssey* 6.
13. *Odyssey* 13.102–12 and 366–71.
14. Wace and Stubbings (1962) 418–19; one of the tripods is illustrated on p. 420. For more detail, see Benton's reports in *BSA* 35 (1934–5) 45ff. and *BSA* 39 (1938–9) 1ff.
15. *Odyssey* 13.13. For the number of Phaeacian nobles, see *Odyssey* 8.387–8.
16. *Odyssey* 13.366–71.
17. If the tripods are of the ninth or early eighth century, then they predate Homer and the latter possibility, which otherwise seems inherently the more likely, must be excluded.
18. Ancient spearheads, daggers and knives are often very difficult to distinguish. Compare, for instance, the shifting identification of the bronze weapons of 'Priam's Treasure'.
19. Hahn (1865) 36.
20. Pausanias 2.16.

21. *Ithaque* 97.
22. *Ithaque* 102–3.
23. *AAZ* (6 Jan. 1877) 79.
24. *Ithaque* 100.
25. Diary entry for 3 August 1868.
26. For a more detailed study of this trip, see Traill (1984a) = *ES* 73–95.
27. *Iliad* 22.147–56.
28. *Ithaque* 137.
29. *Ithaque* 161–2.
30. *Ithaque* 162.
31. *Ithaque* 169–70. For arguments against the Bunarbashi-Balli Dagh site, see the preceding pages 162–8.
32. On the debate see Lascarides (1977) *passim* and Cook (1973) 14–44.
33. *Ithaque* 175–6.
34. *Ithaque* 201.
35. *Ithaque* 214.
36. *Ithaque* 214.
37. *Ithaque* 225–6.
38. The entry for 9 August, under the heading 'Bunarbashi' describes a visit to a town which Schliemann identifies only by its Turkish name in Arabic script. In Traill (1984a) I took this town to be Renkoi, as later did Lehrer and Turner (1989) 241–54. I am indebted to Dr James Reid of the Vryonis Center for the Study of Hellenism in Sacramento for the information that the town is not Renkoi but Ezine. I hope to discuss the problem of the missing page at length in a future article.
39. The suspicion, repeatedly expressed by Lehrer and Turner (1989) 250–4, 260, 262, that Schliemann did not visit Hisarlik is thus unfounded.
40. See *Troja* 27 and Cook (1973) 107. The fact that Schliemann sees these columns before reaching Chiplak shows that he was coming from the south. If he had been coming from Renkoi he would not have seen them at all.
41. Calvert (1875) 1024.
42. Calvert (1875) and (1873).
43. *Briefe* 112. cf. *Bw* II 31.
44. Calvert (1875) 1024.
45. Lehrer and Turner (1989) 259.
46. See Lehrer and Turner (1989) 232.
47. *Bw* I 141.

CHAPTER 4: DIVORCE, DOCTORATE AND REMARRIAGE

1. *Bw* I 128.
2. BBB 28 195–6.
3. Lilly (1961) 12.
4. Traill (1982) 336 = *ES* 65–6.
5. Lilly (1961) 35.
6. Lilly (1961) 17 n.11.
7. Lilly (1961) 18–19.
8. The text of the bill of divorce is found in Scott (1931) 21.
9. See for further details Traill (1982) 338–9 = *ES* 68.
10. Lilly (1961) 49.
11. Lilly (1961) 50.
12. The English versions of these letters are published in Lilly (1961) 65–8.
13. Lilly (1961) 57–8.

14. BBB 28 31–5.
15. *Briefe* 112.
16. Letter of 1 (not 8, as Meyer indicates) May, *Bw* I 47 and BBB 28 53.
17. For a reproduction of the diploma, see Crepon-Bölke (1990) 182.
18. *Ilios* 20.
19. Calder (1972) 337.
20. Richter (1980) 670.
21. BBB 28 13.
22. BBB 28 12–14. Only a small part of this letter is published in Lilly (1961) 25.
23. BBB 28 45–6; cf. Lilly (1961) 30–1.
24. BBB 28 52.
25. BBB 28 51.
26. BBB 28 85.
27. BBB 28 235.
28. B 64; letter from Sophia, dated 26 August (=7 September) 1869.
29. B 64; letter from Sophia, dated 3/15 September 1869.
30. BBB 28 262.
31. BBB 28 269.
32. Letter of 12 December 1869 (BBB 28 307).
33. BBB 28 328.

CHAPTER 5: TRIAL TRENCHES AND TRIBULATIONS

1. BBB 29 20–1.
2. BBB 29 32.
3. *IG* xii.3.390. The pancration was a boxing and wrestling contest.
4. Error for southern.
5. C^{14} analysis, ice cores from Greenland, tree rings from California bristlecone pines and oaks from Irish bogs, all point to *c.* 1625 BC. See McDonald and Thomas (1990) 373–5.
6. BBB 29 47.
7. Diary 13 61.
8. *Bw* I. 164; cf. *AAZ* (24 May 1870) 2301.
9. The precise dimensions of the oblong area excavated cannot be determined as it was encompassed by Schliemann's 1871 excavations shown on Fig. 2.
10. Diary 13 70.
11. See *Troy and its Remains* 322–3 and Plan 2, where it is marked 36.
12. Diary 13, 70 and 75. The latter reads: '*J'ai acheté ici assez de monnaies d'Ilium, ce dont je suis charmé.*'
13. *Bw* I, 165–6.
14. Jenkins (1961).
15. Letter to Calvert; BBB 29 60–1.
16. BBB 29 90–3.
17. Letter of 23 June; BBB 29 122–5.
18. BBB 29 127.
19. Letter of 23 June 1870; BBB 29 126–7.
20. For the insults, see Diary 13 80; for the ruining of the land see *AAZ* (24 May 1870) 2302 and *Bw* I 168.

Notes

1. Letter of 22 February 1871; BBB 28 413–4.
2. Letter of 19 February 1871; BBB 28 410. Schliemann was misinformed. Under Greek law all antiquities found in Greece belonged to the state.
3. BBB 29 288.
4. Letter of 17 June; BBB 29 308–11.
5. Letter of 19 June 1871; BBB 29 312
6. Letter of 8 July; BBB 29 329.
7. Calvert File.
8. *TroyR* 62.
9. BBB 30 8; copies of the other letters to Sophia are also in this copybook.
10. Diary 13 242.
11. See Plan I, Appendix V.
12. Easton (1990) 436 with fig. 8.
13. It is often possible to distinguish copper from bronze only after chemical analysis. Schliemann tends to identify most of these objects as copper, though many of them were no doubt bronze.
14. The draft versions of these reports usually appear in the diaries and the final versions in the copybooks.
15. *Troy R* 220 and Diary 13 361.
16. Diary 13 348; cf. *Troy R* 132, where Schliemann has written 'western terrace' in error.
17. Blegen (1964) 91.
18. Letter dated 8 May 1873; *Bw* 1 209.
19. Diary 13 379.
20. Ibidem.
21. She and Heinrich apparently left Hisarlik on 26 June for the Dardanelles, where she caught the boat the next day; so Schliemann's letter of 24 June to Frank Calvert.
22. Diary 13 379.
23. *Troy R* 203 and *Iliad* 6.386–7.
24. When Schliemann wrote *Ilios* the burnt stratum 7–10 metres deep, which he had formerly identified as the second city (or Troy II), became the third city (Troy III). In *Troja* Schliemann reverted to his original arrangement.
25. See note 21.
26. Easton (1984b) 200–201 mistakenly assumes that Schliemann's large house is Megaron IIA, whereas the depths show that it is the house above it.
27. Easton (1984b) 201, perhaps correctly, believes that the lump of 'wire' is one of the lumps that Schliemann broke off from the layer of molten material (slag) that he found at 9 metres depth in early June. No mention of the jewellery is to be found in any of the early records: the regular diary entries, the diary drafts or copybook versions of the periodic reports. These finds make their first appearance in the published book. Perhaps it was only later in Athens that the lump fell off the table. More probably, I suspect that we have here another instance of Schliemann hoarding glamorous finds for later deployment.

1. Troy VI and VII levels, as has been already indicated, survived only around the perimeter of the acropolis. Though Schliemann's trenches occasionally encountered these levels, it was not until 1890 that significant finds from them began to appear.
2. *Troy R* 224–5.
3. Diary 14 2.

4. The precise date is unclear. Schliemann's correspondence suggests that Sophia probably arrived after 2 April but before 16 April.
5. Modern scholars consider the temple near the north slope to be that of Athena.
6. Letter of 18 March 1873, SA, Calvert File.
7. Letter of 19 March 1873, *MS&H* 56.
8. *Troy R* 244.
9. Letter of 29 March 1873, part of which is published in *Bw* I 223–6.
10. For Calvert's relief, see Holden (1964) pl. xx and on his discovery of the building, see *Ithaque* 175.
11. These laws are relevant because if the matter had gone further, since it was a dispute between two foreign nationals, it would probably have been dealt with by the British or American legations in Constantinople.
12. Diary 14 163.
13. Diary 14 163 (4 April).
14. BBB 32 226.
15. Though Schliemann does not mention this fact in the text of *Troy and its Remains* (or *Trojanische Alterthümer*), Sophia is clearly shown supervising the work at Pasha Tepe on Plate 179 of the *Atlas* and Schliemann acknowledges her role in the notes to the plate.
16. Recorded in the diary entry for that day (Diary 14 223).
17. BBB 32 236.
18. *Troy R* 287.
19. Diary 14 208.
20. Cf. Figs. 8 and 12 (where 'a' marks the findspot).
21. Easton (1984a) 145.
22. Easton (1984a) 145–7 with plan on p. 147; Diary 14 288, 290.
23. The letter, dated 27 December [1873], is preserved in the Department of Greek and Roman Antiquities of the British Museum and published in full in *MS&H* 110 and 117 (where it is misdated 23 December) and in Fitton (1991) 24. In the last sentence 'and servant' was added as an afterthought. Schliemann meant that the labourers struck the treasure and his servant (Yannakis) helped get it off.
24. Easton (1992) 196 argues that Schliemann did not identify the object (actually a chisel) as a key until his return to Athens and that the only key Yannakis could have known about was one found in 1872. The text of the early draft proves that this view is mistaken.
25. Schliemann reports in *Troy R* that it was discovered before breakfast. In a letter to Frank Calvert dated 11 July 1872 (Calvert file) he gave his schedule. Work began at five in the morning. The workmen were allowed an hour's break for breakfast at 9.30 and another hour for lunch at 2.30, after which they worked till sunset.
26. For the bonus, cf. the entry of 24 April of the 1873 diary: 'Unfortunately I observe that we throw away most significant objects without noticing them, for one workman, Constantine of Yenishehir, who is very observant, earns daily an average of 2½ gr extra, while all the rest together scarcely earn double that.' Letter from John Brown dated 19 March 1872 (B 72): 'When you find any small objects put them in your pocket . . . Money is the first question of the day in this. You must not find any large amount of Gold or Silver in your diggings.'
27. See Schliemann's description of the find in *Ilios* 485–8.
28. The article in *Levant Herald* (28 January 1874), written apparently by Frank Calvert, places the findspot 150 yards from where Priam's Treasure was discovered. This can only mean the east end of the east–west trench.
29. *Troy R* 267–8, no. 186.
30. It is also quite possible that more finds of gold and silver were made in 1872 than Schliemann reported.
31. Traill (1992) 183–9=*ES* 199–203.

32. The text of the annotations to the plates appears in BBB 32 interspersed with letters. Notes to plates 168–70 appear on pp. 269–70 immediately before a letter dated 14 May.
33. Schmidt (1902) no. 5826 and no. 6146. See also Traill (1992) 186–7.
34. The sword fragments are nos. 3054c (pl. 190) and 3155 (pl. 163). On pl. 163 the sword fragment still has the tanged dagger 3501 attached to it.
35. For further details, see Traill (1988b)=*ES* 167–72.
36. *AAZ* (14 June 1873) 2528 c. 1.
37. This constitutes version *B* in Traill (1984b).
38. BBB 32 369.
39. BBB 32 374–88. The date is still given as '7th of this month' (under a dateline of 'Troy, 17 June'). In the version actually published in the 5 August issue of *AAZ* the dateline has been mistakenly printed as 'Troy, 17 July' and the date generalized to 'at the beginning of this month'.
40. BBB 32 396.
41. Letter of 28 June to P. Beaurain; BBB 32 372. For the complete text of this letter and Beaurain's reply, see *MS&H* 110–21.
42. BBB 32 399.
43. Many items of jewellery found in Schliemann's later excavations at Troy, however, are identical to pieces in Priam's Treasure. A simple microscopic examination could determine whether any of them are nineteenth-century fakes.
44. Some 25,000 were rejected; so the total created was 125,000.
45. Letter of 26 July 1873; BBB 32 447.
46. Letter to Déthier; BBB 32 456.
47. Letter to C.T. Newton, 4 September 1873; BBB 33 55.
48. Letter to E. Burnouf, 18 October 1873; BBB 33 185.
49. The original of this letter is preserved in the British Museum. There is no copy of the letter in Schliemann's copybook.
50. *Bw* I 244.

CHAPTER 8: TRIAL AND MUSEUM TOUR

1. The French edition followed about a month later.
2. *Academy* 5 (14 Feb. 1874) 173.
3. *Academy* 5 (10 Jan. 1874) 41.
4. *Academy* 5 (Feb. 14. 1874) 175.
5. *Academy* 5 (10 Jan. 1874) 41.
6. Letter to Max Müller of 12 March 1874, BBB 33 442.
7. Ludwig (1931) 193.
8. Diary 15 5.
9. Letter of 16 April 1874, BBB 33 488.
10. Letter from E. Burnouf, dated 3 May 1874.
11. BBB 34 5.
12. The words in braces are no longer legible in the copybook. They have been restored from the similarly worded letter written on 16 May.
13. Presumably, it was still in the French School unless Schliemann had moved it to some other hiding-place.
14. *AAZ* (15 July 1874) 3065.
15. BBB 34 (1874) 55.
16. BB 34 55 (5 July 1874, addressee unclear).
17. Diary 15 8 and 11.

18. Diary 15 19–20.
19. Diary 15 25.
20. Diary 15 38.
21. See *Academy* (3 Oct. 1874) 381 (Stymphalian Birds) and (5 Sept. 1874) 263–4 (Thermopylae, Parnassus, Delphi) and (10 Oct. 1874) 408 (the Styx). For further publication details see Korres (1974) 12.
22. Letter by S. Comnos in the *Athenaeum* (8 Aug. 1874) 178–9.
23. *Athenaeum* (7 and 14 Nov. 1874) 610–11 and 643–4.
24. Calvert had the French edition, to which he refers. The English edition, *Troy and its Remains*, appeared in late 1874 though dated 1875.
25. *The Guardian* (31 March 1875), supp.
26. *TroyR* 257.
27. *The Guardian* (11 August 1875) 1024.
28. Priam's Treasure has recently come to light in Moscow and its ownership is now disputed. The precise terms of this settlement between Schliemann and the Turkish government are therefore of great importance. My summary here is based solely on what Schliemann wrote about the settlement to his correspondents. I have not seen the document that constituted the agreement.
29. Letter to John Murray, 4 March, 1875 (Murray archive).
30. *Academy* (3 July 1875) 20.
31. Letter to Gauthiot, *c.* 27 June 1875. BBB 35 14.
32. Letter to Boker of 16 March 1875. BBB 34 306.
33. See the 28 August and 4 and 18 September 1875 issues of the *Academy*.
34. *Academy* (28 August 1875) 222.
35. Fitton (1991) 33–4.
36. Letter of 20 November 1875; *Bw* I 297–8.
37. The first doubts were raised by Calder (1972); see also Traill (1985)=*ES* 29–40.
38. For Schliemann's report of these excavations, see *Academy* of 16 October 1875.
39. He excavated on the south-east side of the island (probably at D on Whitaker's plan), at the north gateway (J), somewhere on the west coast, and probably at or near the site of the modern village.
40. See Tusa (1964) 14n. A full account of Schliemann's activities in Sicily in 1875 is a desideratum. The scanty evidence in the Schliemann Archive needs to be supplemented by official records in Palermo.
41. Letter of 3 December 1875; BBB 35 105.
42. Letter of 20 November 1875; BBB 35 88.
43. Deuel (1977) 4; Michaelis (1908) 217.

CHAPTER 9: THE LIONS OF MYCENAE

N.B. In referring to the shaft graves I have used the standard numbering system. Thus Grave I=Schliemann's II; II=Schliemann's V; III=Schliemann's III; IV=Schliemann's IV; and V=Schliemann's I.

1. BBB 35 (1876) 277.
2. Letter dated 18 July; BBB 35 279.
3. E. Kastorches, *Historikê Ekthesis tôn Praxôn tês en Athenais Archaiologikês Hetairías* (Athens 1879) records that Schliemann donated 9015 drachmas in the period 1875–6; the next highest donor gave 2300 drachmas.
4. Besides *Mycenae*, see Schliemann's Mycenae diary, now published in *MS&H* 124–260.
5. To avoid needless confusion all Julian dates have been changed to the corresponding Gregorian dates.

6. BB Müller. When Schliemann wrote this up in *Mycenae* (p. 111), he added 'an inexplicable object with a ring', which is also absent from the 25 August entry.
7. Cf. *Mycenae* 131 and 144.
8. 'Mycenae VI' (dated 30 October) in *The Times* 14 December 1876.
9. Compare *Mycenae* 97 (no. 151) with the reconstruction of the façade of the 'Treasury of Atreus' in Wace (1949), pl. 51.
10. Letter of 8 October; BB Müller.
11. Stamatakis' report of 4 October mentions her return.
12. Cf. Wace (1949) 61 and 63 for probable tombs in this area.
13. J. Arthur de Gobineau was the author of *Essai sur l'Inégalité des Races Humaines* (Paris 1854), which later supplied a philosophical basis for the racist views of National Socialism.
14. Buenzod (1961) 185–7.
15. *Mycenae*, 112–13, no. 174 or 178.
16. Buenzod (1961) 193–5. The Tomb of Agamemnon and the Treasury of Atreus are different names for the same tholos tomb.
17. The diary entry for that date refers to the site of the tomb that 'was marked by the sculptured tombstones', the first use of the past tense in this context.
18. *MS&H* 189. The most likely dates, because of the number of the workmen shown, are 8, 9 or 10 November. The two tombstones above Grave III (to the right of the cart) were removed on 13 November (*MS&H* 192).
19. Diary entry for 10 November, *MS&H* 188.
20. *MS&H* 191.
21. *MS&H* 191.
22. *Mycenae* 319, no. 481; on the attribution of these disks to Grave V, see *MS&H* 221 n. 199.
23. Later reports of Grave I make no mention of these buttons of bone.
24. Similarly, Schliemann appears to have added to Grave I some obsidian knives found in Middle Helladic burials encountered on the slope of the rock east of the Grave III stelae and two Late Helladic III B figurines; see *MS&H* 195 and 222 n.212.
25. *Mycenae* 158–9.
26. Milchhöfer (1891) 281–2.
27. Unfortunately, Milchhöfer did not disclose what these grounds were.
28. The vertical cutting into the rock below the figures seems to suggest that between Shaft Grave III (to the right of the ledge below the figures) and Grave I (to the left of the figures) there was yet another Shaft Grave, largely obliterated by what Schliemann called 'dislocated' rock (the ledge): 'The now dislocated & incumbent large blocks of rock have evidently once been straight [i.e. upright], the rock having been cut into from above.' 18 November entry, *MS&H* 198.
29. Diary entry for 18 November, *MS&H* 197: 'I guess there is still another tomb hidden below the dislocated piece of rock.'
30. The best modern estimate for the weight of all the gold in Grave III is slightly less than 4 kg.
31. He means Grave IV.
32. Originally, Schliemann believed that there were six bodies, two of which were female.
33. Karo (1930–33) no. 254.
34. See *MS&H* 229–239.
35. This was pointed out by Dickinson (1976) 164 and again in *MS&H* 238 n. 26.
36. *MS&H* 232.
37. Full text in *MS&H* 234.
38. As late as December 1993 a notice beside the 'Mask of Agamemnon' in the National Museum, Athens, indicated that the king under the mask was 'believed by Schliemann to be Agamemnon.'
39. The weekly steamer from Athens reached Nauplion on Monday evening and started on the return trip early on Tuesday morning; see *ILN* (14 April 1877) 388. The 'Argolis',

reported that Professor Phinticles arrived from Athens on 27 November and Sophia returned by the same steamer, see *MS&H* 236.

40. Letter of Lenormant, dated 23 Dec, 1876; B 72.

CHAPTER 10: THE LION OF LONDON

1. Letter to W. Rust, dated 31 December 1876; Stoll (1953) 209–10.
2. Letter to John Murray, dated 11 March 1877.
3. *Times* (30 May 1877) 8 and (6 June 1877) 5.
4. Herrmann and Maaß (1990) 83.
5. Bülow (1931) 424.
6. Newton, *Times* (20 April 1877) 4; Gardner, *Academy* (21 and 28 April 1877) 346–47 and 366–67.
7. *Times* (4 June 1877) 5–6; *Times* (12 June 1877) 4.
8. Gardner (1891) 479.
9. Gardner (1933) 34.
10. *Athenaeum* (January 1877) 57.
11. He also found four other graves 'of the usual sort,' whose contents are not recorded. Presumably, these were modest Middle Helladic burials.
12. Vermeule (1964) viii.
13. Vermeule (1975) 1.
14. See Kopcke (1976).
15. To this group also belongs the very similar electrum mask of Grave Gamma (Circle B).
16. So most recently Mylonas (1983) 34.
17. So Dickinson (1977) 51 and Graziadio (1988) 372.
18. This distribution cannot be explained by the sex of the burials. It is generally believed that Graves I and III each contained the bodies of three women (Grave III also had two children), Grave II one man, Grave IV three men and two women, Grave V three men, and Grave VI two men. Accordingly, if the disks are feminine ornaments, it is strange that none were found in Grave IV, particularly when Graves III and IV both have cutouts, presumably also feminine ornaments, and in some cases identical cutouts.
19. Similar problems arise with the cutouts, some of which have holes and some do not.
20. *MS&H* 194–5 and *Mycenae* 162–3. Some, perhaps all, of these were probably Middle Helladic tombs.
21. *BSA* 50 (1955) 191–92. At least one of these tombs is datable to LH II.
22. *MS&H* 182, entry for 30 October.
23. Wace (1949) fig. 21 has inserted these slabs into his sections of Grave Circle A. The general view of the Grave Circle shown in *Mycenae* pl. VI shows a similar slab that appears to have been removed from Grave V.
24. *Mycenae* 351–52.
25. See these diary entries in *MS&H* 148, 149, 157, 179–80 and accompanying notes.
26. *MS&H* 183. The position of the 'cyclopean building' on plan D in *Mycenae* corresponds to the location of Kato Phournos.
27. The permit seems only to have applied to the Lion Gate, the Grave Circle area and the Tomb of Clytemnestra.
28. *PAE* (1878) 17.
29. Hope Simpson (1981)
30. Marinatos (1967) 24f. The thin 'moustache' (if it is one) on one of the masks from Grave IV (*SG* 259) can hardly be considered a parallel.
31. For a similar drooping moustache and beard compare the Minoan shell plaque from Ayios Onoufrios, conveniently illustrated in Hood (1978) 116.

32. *MS&H* 140 n. 47.
33. Though Circle B came into use earlier than Circle A, there is a considerable amount of overlap between the two circles. Circle B has no less than ten tombs with burials datable to Late Helladic I and therefore more or less contemporary with the Graves II–V of Circle A; see Dickinson (1977) 51 and Graziadio (1988) 372. The latest tomb in Circle A (Grave I) is no later than Grave Rho in Circle B, which, however, is not a shaft grave; both contained vases attributable to Late Helladic IIA.
34. For fuller discussion see Traill (1984b) 312–16=*ES* 91–5.
35. Cf. *Mycenae* 13, where Schliemann notes that all these figurines 'were found at a depth of 3 to 11½ feet below the surface and none at a greater depth.'
36. *Mycenae* 159.
37. See further *MS&H* 258–59, n. 11.
38. Cf. Furumark (1941) fig. 17, shape 274 and pp. 13 and 424–25.
39. Higgins (1981) 139; cf. Dickinson (1977) 82.
40. Dickinson (1977) 82.
41. Gregor-Dellin and Mack (1978) I 963.
42. The session is reported with the text of Sophia's speech in *Archaeological Journal* (1877) 453–59; for textual similarities, cf. *Times* (22 Dec. 1876) 4.
43. Letter to John Murray dated 29 September 1877. The trip from Marseille to Athens took about five days. Surprisingly, Schliemann emphasised the differences rather than the similarities between the finds at Spata and those in the Mycenae shaft graves. He concluded (*Mycenae* xlv), rightly, that the Spata tomb was later in date.
44. Letter to John Murray dated 15 August 1877. This sum translates to about $18,000 in today's terms.
45. Letter to John Murray, dated 30 August 1877.
46. Letter to Gladstone, 20 September 1877; British Library, Add. 44, 455.85
47. Letter to Gladstone, 20 November 1877; British Library, Add. 44, 455.269
48. Letters to Gladstone, dated 27 November and 3 December 1877.
49. The American and German editions were dedicated to Dom Pedro of Brazil and the King of Greece respectively.
50. This list is taken from the report published in the *Palingenesia* of 24 November (=6 December) 1877=*MS&H* 237.

CHAPTER 11: ITHACA, TROY AND RECONCILIATION WITH GERMANY

1. Newton (1878) 251 [=(1880) 294]. He pointed to similar pottery found at Ialysos in Rhodes. A scarab of Amenoph III (*c.* 1400 BC) found in one of the Ialysos graves gave a date for this pottery. He also drew attention to a mural of Thutmose III (15th century BC) that showed a vase in the shape of a bull's head much resembling the silver bull's head of Grave IV.
2. Newton (1878) 255 [=(1880) 300]; cf. Sayce (1878).
3. Murray (1877) 559.
4. Newton (1878) 241 [=(1880) 278].
5. *Academy* (2 March 1878) 195–97.
6. Letter to Sayce, 23 April 1878, BBB 36 25.
7. *Bw* II 72.
8. Borlase (1878) 235–6.
9. Meyer (1962) 98. At this time the Turkish countryside was unsafe because of the Russo-Turkish War (1877–8).
10. *Times* (6 March 1878) 10.
11. Letter of 19 July 1878; William Simpson Collection, Mitchell Library, Glasgow.

12. Letter to P. Dendopoulos, 12 June 1878, BBB 36 41.
13. Letter to P. Dendopoulos, 10 July 1878, BBB 36 79.
14. P.W. Forchhammer, *Times* (4 June 1878) 4.
15. H. Westropp, *Athenaeum* (17 August 1878) 217–18.
16. *Academy* (20 July) 63.
17. Stamatakis (1878) 277–8.
18. Letter of 14 August 1878; William Simpson Collection, Mitchell Library, Glasgow.
19. *Ilios* 47.
20. *Ilios* 50.
21. *Athenaeum* (14 December 1878).
22. *TroyR* Pl. XIII; *Ilios* 35.
23. Letter of 12 Nov. 1878 to J. Murray.
24. *The Guardian* (31 March 1875) Supplem. p. 1.
25. *Ilios* 488. Note that in *Ilios* the Third City is Troy II.
26. On the voyage back to Athens Schliemann met a Dr M.P. Kossonis from Smyrna, who sold antiquities. It seems that Schliemann expressed interest in acquiring some pieces that resembled the Mycenae finds and that Kossonis promised to see what he could do. On 27 December Kossonis wrote from Smyrna. He had seen the Mycenaean objects in Athens and was now sending him photographs 'of some ornaments of gold found in a tomb in Lydia, which resemble those of Mycenae . . . The proprietor of this Lydian thesaurus negotiate to sell them . . .' Schliemann expressed interest in seeing the actual objects; so he was given them for a week. Whether he acquired them or not is unknown.
27. Letter to J. Murray, dated 17 December 1878.
28. Burnouf and Lenormant were paid to write articles and reviews for Schliemann. On Schliemann's academic employees, see Traill (1990a)=*ES* 215–31.
29. Herrmann and Maaß (1990) 23.
30. Schliemann offered Sayce a salary of £200 (=£12,000 in today's terms) for staying two months at Troy; see letter to Sayce of 13 February 1879, Sayce Papers.
31. Herrmann and Maaß (1990) 85–6.
32. Herrmann and Maaß (1990) 86–7.
33. Herrmann and Maaß (1990) 87.
34. His participation in the Berlin revolution of 1848 brought about his suspension from his position at the Charité Hospital, Berlin, though he was later reinstated.
35. Virchow (1891) 299–300.
36. Virchow (1891) 67–8.
37. Treasures H and J at 'na' and 'v' on *Ilios* plan 1 respectively.
38. Virchow expresses reservations about attributing this treasure (H), found at a depth of only 2 metres, to Troy II in his letter to Schliemann of 14 July 1879; see Herrmann and Maaß (1990) 120. Schmidt (1902) 240 attributes the disks to Troy VI.
39. Given their own particular preoccupations, it seems most unlikely that one or other would actually be present when the workmen uncovered both 'treasures'. Virchow says he was present when the first (H) was uncovered, but makes no such claim about the second (J), allegedly found at a depth of 10 metres. If they were merely summoned to witness the findspot after the find had been made, then both the find and findspot may have been staged.
40. See Rapp and Gifford (1982).
41. See *Ilios* 648–71. The four that yielded nothing were the Tombs of Ajax and Ilius, 2½ miles north and 1 mile north-west of Hisarlik respectively, the tumulus on the south slopes of Ilium Novum, and Demetrios-Tepe, close to the Aegean coast due west of Hisarlik.
42. In the 1930s a British archaeologist, W. Lamb, who examined the pottery in Berlin, thought that it might even predate the Early Bronze Age; see *Praehistorisches Zeitschrift* 33 (1932) 124ff. For a report on the 1982 excavations, see *AA* (1984) 165–95.

43. Herrmann and Maaß (1990) 93.
44. *Architectural Review* N.S.I. (1912) 88.
45. Herrmann and Maaß (1990) 115–125 *passim.*
46. Virchow (1891) 107.
47. Herrmann and Maaß (1990) 137–143. Herrmann and Maaß assume that 'Briseis' must have left shortly after accepting the position and that the 'bonne' (maid) was a replacement for her. But Briseis was an 'Erzieherin' (governess), whose duties were restricted to Andromache. The 'bonne' was to look after Agamemnon; cf. end of letter Nr. 68, Hermann and Maaß (1990) 143.
48. Letter of 25 September, 1879; Herrmann and Maaß (1990) 143.
49. *Ilios* 676: 'This plain is an old fiord, which has been filled by river-deposit . . .'
50. The finds were shipped to Germany late in 1879.
51. Letter of 19 June 1879; Herrmann and Maaß (1990) 109.
52. Letter of 27 July 1879 to Bismarck; BBB 36 107.
53. *Ilios* 279.
54. Letter to Field of 28 March 1878; Arndt (1981) 2.
55. Whether this move was influenced by the US decision not to appoint him as its consul in Greece is unclear. The decision was sent to Francis on 15 August but on 21 August Francis wrote to ask the Secretary of State to reconsider; see Arndt (1981) 6. Francis reported the bad news to Schliemann in a letter dated 1 October. Whether Schliemann learned of the negative decision earlier is unclear.
56. Hermann and Maaß (1990) 139.
57. *ZfE* (1891) 55. The story that the decisive moment came when Virchow picked some flowers native to Mecklenburg and presented them to Schliemann with the words 'Greetings from your homeland!' is found in Ludwig (1931) 275 and Meyer (1969) 308 but I have not found confirmation of this in Virchow's accounts.
58. Virchow (1891) 108.
59. Letter of 26 August 1879 to John Murray.
60. Hermann and Maaß (1990) 136.
61. Hermann and Maaß (1990) 143.
62. Hermann and Maaß (1990) 145.
63. Hermann and Maaß (1990) 231.
64. *Athenaeum* (4 October 1879) 440–1.
65. See Schliemann's explanation at *Troja* 52–53. Troy II, however, continued to include the upper section of the original Troy I. From this point on therefore we shall follow the terminology of *Troja* and later publications. Troy I=lower section of former Troy I; Troy II=upper section of former Troy I and former Troy II. Levels above Troy II remain unchanged.
66. Hermann and Maaß (1990) 156.
67. Hermann and Maaß (1990) 158.

CHAPTER 12: *ILIOS*, ORCHOMENOS AND GERMAN HONOURS

1. Letter to John Murray of 30 June 1879.
2. BBB 36 123.
3. Letter to Sayce dated 10 January 1880; BBB 37 12.
4. B 81 865.
5. Letter of 18 March 1880; *Bw* II 96. Schliemann soon agreed with Murray that most of Sayce's changes were superfluous and 'take away all the bloom and originality of my work' and told him to concentrate on matters of more substance.
6. *Ilios* 1.

7. *Ilios* 5.
8. Letter to Schliemann dated 29 January 1879 (error for 1880); B 79 92.
9. Letter of 7 February 1880 to Smith; BBB 37 48.
10. Flickinger (1931–32) 24–25.
11. BBB 37 51.
12. Letter of Fergusson, dated 11 March 1880; B 82 162.
13. Letter to John Murray dated 28 February 1880=BBB 37 74.
14. Letter of Calvert, 27 March 1880; B 82 201.
15. BBB 37 185.
16. Letter to Sayce, 29 July 1880; BBB 37 292.
17. Letter of Calvert, 2/3 March 1880; B 82 133.
18. Letter of 26 January 1879; Herrmann and Maaß (1990) 87.
19. Letter of 13 March 1880, Herrmann and Maaß (1990) 171.
20. For the quote, see Herrmann and Maaß (1990) 173. For the importance attached to the threat, cf. 'Aber ich bitte Sie, daß Sie das Mißverständnis wenigstens nicht Deutschland zurechnen'; Herrmann and Maaß (1990) 171.
21. Herrmann and Maaß (1990) 176.
22. Herrmann and Maaß (1990) 177.
23. Herrmann and Maaß (1990) 180–81.
24. Gavrilow (1990) 379–87.
25. BBB 37 15.
26. Letter to Zotoff, dated ? March 1880; BBB 37 101.
27. For a discussion of Schliemann's illegal act see Meyer (1969) 154–5 and Gavrilow (1990) 390–2.
28. BBB 37 140–41. It seems likely that this was written with substantial help from A. Rhusopoulos, the Professor of Greek Archaeology at Athens.
29. Sayce, Virchow, and A. Milchhöfer on Schliemann's side, in response to specific requests from Schliemann, and E. Schulze on behalf of Stephani. For bibliography, see Korres (1974) 73–5.
30. BBB 37 158.
31. *Bw* II 114. For earlier suspicions that the farewell scene was to some extent fictionalized, see Meyer *Briefe* 34 and Calder (1972) 344–5.
32. *Ilios* 6.
33. BBB 37 308. Sophia had meanwhile gone to take the cure at Carlsbad.
34. *Athenaeum* (1 January 1881) 26.
35. *Palingenesia* 26 Nov. (=8 Dec. Gregorian) 1880.
36. Letter of 23 November 1880; B 84 955.
37. Herrmann and Maaß (1990) 234.
38. Letter of 20 December; Herrmann and Maaß (1990) 237–38.
39. Meyer (1962) 101.
40. Letter to John Murray dated 12 October 1880.
41. *Pall Mall Gazette* (3 December 1880) 11.
42. *Saturday Review* (8 January 1881) 55.
43. Jebb (1881) 538.
44. See his article in *Contemporary Review* 33 (November 1878) 776–91.
45. Letter to Müller dated 22 January 1881; BBB 37 456–57.
46. Letters to Virchow dated 9 and 12 March 1881; Herrmann and Maaß (1990) 252–3.
47. Letter to Sayce dated 7 May 1881; BBB 38 104.
48. Letter to Sayce of 11 May 1881; BBB 38 107.
49. Letter to John Murray, 6 September 1880.
50. Letter to Smith of 29 May 1881, BBB 38 114, and Smith's reply of 19 May 1881, B 85 258.
51. Herrmann and Maaß (1990) 241–2.

52. Herrmann and Maaß (1990) 246–7.
53. Herrmann and Maaß (1990) 112.
54. Herrmann and Maaß (1990) 244.
55. Herrmann and Maaß (1990) 250.
56. Herrmann and Maaß (1990) 251.
57. Letter of 15 January 1881; BBB 37 445. See further Arndt (1981) 8.
58. Letter to Schöne dated 3 March 1881; *Briefe* 180–2.
59. The story is reported in Poole (1967) 193–4.
60. Radowitz (1925) II 168–9.
61. Letter dated 17 March 1881; Adler papers, DAI Berlin.
62. A letter from Dörpfeld to Schliemann dated 10 November 1879 implies that they were already well acquainted by that date. See Traill (1990a) 238=*ES* 217.
63. Schliemann (1881) 163. He avoided the use of photographs in his publications after his unfortunate experience with them in *Trojanische Alterthümer*.
64. For details of this trip see *Troja* 303–47.
65. *Troja* 335.
66. Letter to Gardner of 5 August 1881; BBB 38 198.
67. *New York Times* (23 April 1882) 6.
68. Herrmann and Maaß (1990) 290.

CHAPTER 13: DÖRPFELD, *TROJA* AND THERMOPYLAE

1. *New York Times* (23 April 1882) 6.
2. *Troja* 5. Schliemann paid Dörpfeld thirteen times what he paid each of his guards.
3. Herrmann and Maaß (1990) 296–7.
4. *Troja* 19. At point K (Plan III) Calvert had come across part of the city wall of Troy VI but had thought it of Hellenistic or Roman date, as did Schliemann.
5. Unfortunately, only a short stretch of the trench is shown on Plan IV (Appendix V). The full course is shown on Plan VIII of *Troja* but the scale is too small to be of much practical value.
6. *Troja* 211–13.
7. *Troja* nos. 106–109.
8. Herrmann and Maaß (1990) 300.
9. *Troja* 65, 75 and plate. VIII.
10. Letter to his father, dated 23 March 1882; Goessler (1951) 69.
11. *Troja* 52–53.
12. *Troja* 254–62.
13. Letter of 24 April 1882; Herrmann and Maaß (1990) 303.
14. Herrmann and Maaß (1990) 306.
15. Schmidt (1902) 241–2. All the pieces illustrated by Schliemann in *Troja* (nos. 80–4) went to Berlin. Some minor items, not illustrated in *Troja* (six bracelets, two nails, two knives, etc.), are too vaguely described for certain identification.
16. Herrmann and Maaß (1990) 308.
17. *Troja* 169.
18. Herrmann and Maaß (1990) 374.
19. Herrmann and Maaß (1990) 315. It is noteworthy that in 1878 Schliemann considered Kadry Bey very civilized and reasonable and in fact insisted that he should represent the Turkish government when the finds were divided.
20. *Troja* 14.
21. *Troja* 12.
22. Meyer (1962) 102.

23. Letter to Max Müller dated 3 February 1881; BB Müller.
24. Letter of Sayce dated 18 March 1882; B 88 186.
25. Dörpfeld outlined his differences with Schliemann on these points in a letter to Adler dated 18 June 1882; DAI, Berlin.
26. Letter from Dörpfeld to Adler, dated 18 June 1882; DAI, Berlin. Goessler (1951) 72, who was anxious to gloss over any differences between Schliemann and Dörpfeld, quotes the words of Schliemann in this passage as representing Dörpfeld's own view!
27. Herrmann and Maaß (1990) 319.
28. Letter to J. Murray, dated 20 August 1882.
29. *Academy* 22 (21 October 1882) 301.
30. Letter from Dörpfeld to Adler, dated 7 October 1882; DAI, Berlin.
31. *Academy* (12 November 1881) 366.
32. It should be stressed that I am merely assuming Calvert's role here. However, it can hardly be a coincidence that Jebb's new version of the chronology corresponds so exactly with Dörpfeld's. Jebb could not have inferred Dörpfeld's chronology from the Brentano review, which is unspecific about dating. Calvert seems the most likely source for good information on Dörpfeld's views.
33. The main points of the paper are summarized in *Academy* 22 (2 December 1882) 398–99 and given in extended form in *JHS* 3 (1882) 185–217.
34. Herrmann and Maaß (1990) 335.
35. Herrmann and Maaß (1990) 345.
36. Hood (1992) 223.
37. Stillman (1881) 41–49.
38. *Bw* II 150–51.
39. *Bw* II 154.
40. Hood (1992) 225.
41. On Stamatakis' excavations at Chaironeia, see Hermann and Maaß (1990) 236 and Petrakos (1987) 49–53.
42. Herrmann and Maaß (1990) 349.
43. These candidates were the steep-sided spur at the east end of the central part of the defile, the so-called 'Polyandreion' at the south–west end of the Phocian wall, and the hillock excavated by Marinatos in the 1930s and now identified as the 'Kolonos'.
44. Letter of Sayce, dated 15 January 1883. Recently, radiocarbon testing has dated these temples to *c*. 3000 BC, making them the world's oldest stone buildings; see Renfrew (1976) 161–6.
45. Sayce (1923) 218.
46. Sayce (1923) 222.
47. Sayce (1923) 222–23.
48. *Times* (10 January 1883) 10.
49. *JHS* 4 (1883) 436.
50. Letter to R. Cooke (Murray Archive) dated 3 May 1883.
51. Letter to R. Cooke (Murray Archive) dated 8 May 1883. For more details on this episode see Traill (1990) 240–3.
52. Quoted in letter of A.H. Sayce, dated 4 July 1883.
53. Letter to J. Murray dated 21 September 1883.
54. Letter to J. Murray dated 21 October 1883.
55. Letter of Sayce dated 26 April 1883; B 91 391.
56. Letter of Sayce dated 9 May 1883; B 92.
57. Letter of Sayce dated 4 July 1883; B 92.
58. Letter to Sayce dated 26 July 1883, Bodleian Library, Eng. lett. d. 65, Fol. 198r.
59. Letter to Sayce, dated 9 August 1883, Bodleian Library, Eng. lett. d. 65, Fol. 211r–12r.
60. Letter of Edith Calvert, dated 19 September 1883; B 93.

CHAPTER 14: MARATHON, *TIRYNS* AND THE BREAK WITH VIRCHOW

1. Letter to Virchow, Herrmann and Maaß (1990) 391–5.
2. Letter of Virchow, Herrmann and Maaß (1990) 395–6.
3. For Schliemann's account of his excavations at Marathon, see *Academy* (23 February 1884) 138–9.
4. Philios (1890) 1–13.
5. Letter of Sayce, dated 14 April 1884; B 94 201.
6. Letter to Smith, dated 26 January 1884; BBB 40 53.
7. Letter to Smith, dated 8 March 1884; BBB 40 101.
8. Letter to Virchow, dated 10 February 1884; Hermann and Maaß (1990) 397 where, however, the editors misread 'Bass Pale Ale' as 'Bahs Pali ab'!
9. *The Nation* (1884) 351.
10. In his report of his 1876 excavations at Tiryns Schliemann shows no knowledge of Thiersch's findings.
11. *Tiryns* 4.
12. Telegram to Vulpiotes dated either 21 or 22 March 1884; BBB 40 117.
13. Telegram to Vulpiotes dated between 25 and 31 March 1884; BBB 40 123.
14. Letter to Adler, dated 9 April, 1884; DAI, Berlin.
15. Letter to Mme. E. Egger, dated 10 April, 1884; BBB 38 131.
16. Telegram to Sophia (undated); BBB 40 131.
17. Letter to John Murray, dated 11 April 1884; BBB 40 134.
18. See for instance the diary entries for 27 and 30 September 1876, *MS&H* 170–1.
19. Letter of Fergusson, dated 5 June 1884; B 94 286.
20. *Tiryns* 173.
21. *Troja* 231. Little pottery was found for the periods of Late Helladic I and II and much more than at Mycenae for LH IIIC. Schliemann shows some understandable confusion between sherds of the Geometric period, which was then just becoming known, and those of Late Helladic IIIC. Both exhibit rather crudely drawn human and animal figures. Here again there is regrettably little evidence as to where individual pieces were found. Perhaps the most interesting feature of the palace besides the megara and the wall-paintings was the bathroom. Its floor consisted of one huge block of limestone (3 by 4 metres and 70 centimetres thick).
22. Letter to Virchow, 14 July 1884; Herrmann and Maaß (1990) 411.
23. Letter to John Murray, 9 August 1884.
24. Letter to John Murray, 17 August 1884.
25. Letter to Virchow, dated 29 August 1884; Herrmann and Maaß (1990) 414.
26. Letter to Virchow, dated 26 November 1884; Herrmann and Maaß (1990) 429.
27. Letter dated 25 September 1884 in *The Nation* (23 October 1884) 351–2.
28. Letter to Fergusson, dated *c.* 4 February 1885; BBB 40 408.
29. Letter of Murray, dated 11 February 1885; B 96 98.
30. Letter to Virchow dated 15 January 1885; Herrmann and Maaß (1990) 443–4.
31. Sophia's father had died in May 1873, when both she and Heinrich were in Troy; see Chapter 7 above. If it is true that he died in Schliemann's house, then that house was not Iliou Melathron.
32. Letter of Virchow, dated 11 February 1885; Herrmann and Maaß (1990) 445.
33. Letter to Virchow, dated 22 February 1885; Herrmann and Maaß (1990) 446.
34. Letter to Murray, dated 31 March 1885; BBB 40 490.
35. Letter of Mahaffy, dated 9 April 1885; B 96 222.
36. *Revue Archéologique*, series 3, 6 (1885) 87. At the south end Dörpfeld, now assisted by another architect, G. Kawerau, cleared out the two galleries with the pointed arches (E and C on the plan). It was discovered that they were linked to one another and to the upper

acropolis by stairway (D) and that the lower gallery (C) opened into five rooms (B). Similarly, gallery (R) on the north side was now found to open out into six similar rooms (P). In the semi-circular bulge in the circuit-wall on the west side they found a long staircase leading to the gate (Y) into the middle acropolis and continuing (X) from there into the upper acropolis.

37. Letter to Virchow, dated 22 February, 1885; Herrmann and Maaß (1990) 447.
38. *Tiryns* 28.
39. Letter of Sayce, dated 10 November 1884; B 95 570.
40. Letter of Fergusson, dated 8 June 1885; B 96 375.
41. Letter to Virchow, dated 2 July 1885; Herrmann and Maaß (1990) 452.
42. Just how determined Ernst Meyer was to whitewash his hero can be inferred from the fact that he published only the first part of Schliemann's letter (to 'that is what happened') and suppressed Virchow's entirely, remarking 'the cause of the disagreement cannot be determined'! See *Briefe* 249 with n.1.
43. The break may have been less complete than the extant correspondence suggests. For instance, in Sophia's letter to Heinrich of 10 February 1886 (B 98) she speaks of a recent letter from Virchow. But as late as April 1887 Sophia was still trying to get them to forgive and forget; *Briefe* 262–3.
44. *Berliner Börser Courier* (11 January 1891).
45. Her letter to H.A. Stoll recalling her experiences in 1885 is printed in Stoll (1953) 258–59.
46. Letter to Brockhaus, dated 14 October 1885; *Briefe* 249–50. On this letter Meyer remarks: 'for paid reviews there is otherwise no evidence.'
47. Letter to Virchow, dated 7 April 1885; Herrmann and Maaß (1990) 449.
48. Slavery was finally abolished in Cuba in 1886.
49. Letter of Sophia, dated 4 November, 1885; B 97.
50. Letter of Sophia, dated 28 December, 1885; B 97.

CHAPTER 15: CUBA, CAIRO AND KYTHERA

1. Letter dated 20 January; *Bw* II 231.
2. In a letter dated 15 February, J.H. Schröder of London confirm that they have sold £9000 worth of Schliemann's Havanna Railway shares; B 98 44.
3. Witte (1990) 136.
4. In 1885 and 1886 Schliemann was urged by a number of scholars to look for a similar palace at Mycenae.
5. *Briefe* 253.
6. *Times* (3 May 1886) 5.
7. *ZfE*, 18 (1886) 379.
8. Ibid. 379–80.
9. Meyer (1962) 104–5.
10. Letter from (not to) Hatzidakis, dated 25 November 1886; *Bw* II 256.
11. *Times* (30 November 1876) 8.
12. *Times* (24 April 1886) 10.
13. *Times* (29 April 1886)
14. *Bw* II 249.
15. *Academy* (10 July 1886) 31.
16. *Bw* II 250.
17. Letter of Sayce, dated 17 September 1886; B 99 507.
18. One of Schliemann's servants.
19. Letter to Virchow, dated 31 October 1886; Herrmann and Maaß (1990) 461–2.
20. Letter to Virchow, dated 6 December 1886; Herrmann and Maaß (1990) 463.

21. Letter to Virchow, dated 19 February 1887; Herrmann and Maaß (1990) 463–4.
22. Diary 17 4.
23. Diary 17 31–32.
24. Murray, *Egypt* (1875) 5.
25. Diary 17 9.
26. Diary 17 13.
27. Diary 17 33.
28. For a lively and rather unflattering picture of Budge, see Fagan (1992) 295–304.
29. Budge (1920) I 108–9.
30. Diary 17 115–16.
31. *Briefe* 260.
32. *ZfE* 19 (1887) 210=*Bw* II 260.
33. Murray, *Egypt* (1875) 396.
34. Budge (1920) I 111.
35. This is the great study of Egypt undertaken by a team of French scholars and published in Paris between 1809 and 1822. The stirrup-jar is illustrated on Pl. 87 of vol. II.
36. Diary 17 254–5 (14 March).
37. Herrmann and Maaß (1990) 464.
38. Herrmann and Maaß (1990) 465.
39. The letter is not in the Schliemann Archive. Its contents have to be inferred from Schliemann's letter of 1 May 1887; Herrmann and Maaß (1990) 466–7.
40. Herrmann and Maaß (1990) 466–7.
41. Herrmann and Maaß (1990) 469.
42. *RA* ser. 3, 10 (1887) 95.
43. Ibid. and Herrmann and Maaß (1990) 467.
44. *JHS* 17 (1897) 319–20.
45. Letter to Calvert dated 24 January 1887; *Bw* II 259.
46. Letter to Calvert dated 5 April 1887; *Briefe* 263.
47. Amandry (1992) 99–100.
48. Herodotus 1.105. Murray's *Handbook* draws attention to this passage.
49. Coldstream and Huxley (1973) 35.
50. *ZfE* 20 (1888) 22.
51. Coldstream and Huxley (1973) 36.
52. Letter of 24 May to J. Ealo; *Bw* II 270–1.
53. *Bw* II 276; Korres (1990) 45.
54. Herrmann and Maaß (1990) 470.
55. Herrmann and Maaß (1990) 473.
56. Burton (1893) II 352.
57. Ludwig (1931) 115–16.
58. The common-sense objection that Sophia presumably knew that her husband was not circumcised assumes, perhaps rashly, that Sophia had a clear idea of what the term meant. Moreover, this objection applies to any interpretation of Ludwig's evidence. Perhaps Burton told the story in Sophia's presence and forty years later Sophia herself mistakenly transferred the story to her husband. Some of the information she gave Ludwig was wildly inaccurate. For instance, she said that she personally excavated the bull's head at Mycenae and that it took five days in July; see *Querschnitt* 13 (1933) 158. In fact it was excavated in less than one day on 25 November; see *MS&H* 201.

Notes

CHAPTER 16: CLEOPATRA'S HEAD AND THE FEUD WITH BÖTTICHER

1. Herrmann and Maaß (1990) 483.
2. One of the obelisks was removed to London in 1877 (Cleopatra's Needle) and the other to New York in 1879.
3. *Bw* II 286-87.
4. Herrmann and Maaß (1990) 487 and *Bw* II 287.
5. B 102 85.
6. *Academy* (10 March 1888) 315.
7. *Academy* (28 April 1888) 297–98.
8. Letter of Virchow to A. Woldt, dated 21 March 1888; *Bw* II 281. Schliemann (*Briefe* 277) dates the incident to 1 March.
9. Virchow (1891) 106–107.
10. Petrie (1932) 89.
11. In a letter of that date to G. Perrot (BBB 41 99) he attributed the head to the third century BC, regretting that it could not be his beloved Cleopatra.
12. Schindler (1986) 90.
13. A surprising amount of circumstantial evidence points in this direction. In the spring of 1886 Schliemann commissioned a Greek sculptor to make a bust of Emile Egger, his former professor, who had just died. Presumably, he provided the sculptor with a photograph. This may have suggested to Schliemann how easy it would be to produce an 'authentic' ancient bust. About the same time he requested A. Postolaccas, the numismatist of the National Museum in Athens, to send him casts of coins with portraits of Cleopatra. In May 1886 Postolaccas complied, sending him five casts. In his account of Schliemann's 1886–7 trip to Egypt, Ludwig (1931) 308 makes the following tantalizing observation: 'He fell in love on this journey: Cleopatra was the object of his passion; he had a marble mask of her made from a coin and hung it up at home over his writing table.' Ludwig unfortunately does not cite his sources, so it is unclear on what evidence this statement is based. I have found nothing in the diary to support it, but I have not read every word of its 257 pages of classical Greek. More probably Ludwig's source was a letter in the 1886–7 copybook, which is now lost. Comparison between Ludwig's remarks and Schliemann's own words about the bust in his letter to Schöne of 17 June 1888 (*Bw* 285: 'I have fallen so much in love with the head that I would like to have it sit on my desk till the end of my days so that at every moment I can look at it') suggest that 'mask' might be a mistranslation and that 'mask' and bust are identical.
14. Schindler (1986) 91.
15. Breccia (1914) 55–6: 'In order to reach ruins of the Roman period it was very often necessary to go down to six or seven metres though strata of fill. It follows that the ruins of the Ptolemaic city must exist at a greater depth, and, I think that they are almost all in the strata below the water table.'
16. Schindler (1986) 88.
17. Diary 17 255–56.
18. Cf. the remarks of A. Erman in Krauss (1985) 174.
19. *Briefe* 259 and Diary 17 255. Adolf Erman, the Director of the Egyptian Section of the Museum für Völkerkunde, considered the Herodotus bust 'crude stone-mason's work'; cf. letter cited in Krauss (1985) 174.
20. Stoll (1953) 285.
21. *AM* 13 (1888) 207–210 and 428.
22. Korres (1975) 57 n.1.
23. Korres (1975) 58–62.
24. Korres (1975) 58.

25. Korres (1975) 492: 'contre toute conscience scientifique.'
26. *Bw* II 452, n. 299.
27. Schindler (1986) 85.
28. Herrmann and Maaß (1990) 489.
29. Their trip is described in the closing lines of *Odyssey* 3. For the identification with Kalamata, compare Murray, *Greece* 283.
30. *Bw* II 293–94.
31. *Bw* II 295.
32. Letter to Virchow dated 9 December 1888; Herrmann and Maaß (1990) 493; Virchow's letter, to which this is a response, is lost.
33. Letter dated 18 February 1889; *Bw* 297–8.
34. Letter dated 17 March 1889; Herrmann and Maaß (1990) 498–9.
35. The following version of his trip is a summary of his published account in *ZfE* (1889) 414–19.
36. *ZfE* (1889) 415.
37. Ibid.
38. In a letter (in classical Greek) to S. Reinach dated 11 February 1890, of which see excerpts at *RA* (ser. 3) 15 (1890) 271–2.
39. *ZfE* (1889) 416.
40. *ZfE* (1889) 417.
41. BBB 41 325.
42. Letter to Sophia, dated 7 May 1889; Sophia Schliemann Archive.
43. Letter to Sophia, dated 24 May 1889; Sophia Schliemann Archive.
44. Letter of 24 May 1889; Herrmann and Maaß (1990) 502–503.
45. Letter of 16 July to Virchow; Herrmann and Maaß (1990) 507.
46. Herrmann and Maaß (1990) 511.
47. Letter of Schuchhardt dated 19 May 1889; *Bw* II 313.
48. Schuchhardt (1944) 177.
49. Schuchhardt (1944) 178.
50. Ibid.
51. Letter dated 31 August 1889; for full text of letter see *HS+100* 253–54=*ES* 233.
52. *Bw* II 321.
53. Reprinted from the *Nationalzeitung* in *C-Blatt* (1889) 84.
54. Letter to Hamdy Bey, dated 13 September 1889; BBB 41 387.
55. Letter to H. von Bismarck, dated 11 October 1889; *Briefe* 293.
56. *AM* 14 (1889) 409–10.
57. Letter to Virchow, dated 13 December 1889; Herrmann and Maaß (1990) 531.

CHAPTER 17: TROY, HALLE AND NAPLES

1. Both letters at BBB 42 89.
2. Virchow's letter is lost but its contents can be inferred from Schliemann's letter of 28 February 1890; Herrmann and Maaß 538–40.
3. The text of the new law on antiquities (in French) is published in *RA* ser. 3, vol. 3 (1884) 336–43.
4. Letters to and from Humann; *Bw* II 348–50.
5. Letter dated 24 March 1890; *Bw* II 356.
6. The full text of the protocol is printed in Schuchhardt (1891) 325–26.
7. *Bw* II 361.
8. Virchow (1891) 66.
9. Letter to von Radowitz dated 22 January 1890; *Bw* II 345.

10. Dörpfeld, Perrot and Brückner arrived with Josef Durm, architect, and Dr Lissauer, a physician from Danzig, on 1 May; Schuchhardt arrived a day or two later. All the visitors except Brückner had gone by 7 May; see Diary 18.
11. Schuchhardt (1944) 181.
12. *Bw* II 359–60.
13. In his report of 2 June 1890 (*ZfE*, 22, 1890, 350–51) Schliemann suggested that the Mycenaean pottery of Troy VI might in fact have been made locally by mainland potters who emigrated to the Troad after the Dorian invasian at the beginning of the twelfth century BC. The argument is ingenious but implausible.
14. BBB 42 288. It does seem true that Hamdy and Halil allowed him to take the sherds; cf. *Bw* II 378 and Korfmann (1993) 261.
15. BBB 42 315.
16. Herrmann and Maaß (1990) 545–6.
17. BBB 42 352.
18. The three heads are now in the Museum für Ur- und Frühgeschichte, Berlin. They all clearly represent members of the Julio-Claudian imperial family though there is debate over precise identification. More recently scholars have seen in them portraits of Tiberius, Lucius Caesar and, perhaps, Livia; see the exhibition catalogue *Troy, Mycenae, Tiryns, Orchomenos: Heinrich Schliemann the 100th Anniversary of his Death* (Athens 1990) 256–9. What happened to the lion is unclear. I cannot find it in Schmidt's (1902) catalogue but it was certainly shipped to Athens, as is clear from Schliemann's letter to his brother-in-law dated 14 July (BBB 42 400).
19. BBB 42 431.
20. Letter to Virchow dated 17 June 1890; Herrmann and Maaß (1990) 548.
21. Diary 18, 17 May entry. The silver vase is Schmidt (1902) 6254.
22. *National Zeitung* 30 January 1891.
23. Herrmann and Maaß (1990) 543–44.
24. Letter to Virchow dated 15 July 1890; Herrmann and Maaß (1990) 552.
25. For a later version see *Bw* II 379. Dörpfeld's 1890 diary is preserved among the Adler papers in the DAI, Berlin. It is even more sketchy than Schliemann's, but it has entries for 3, 5, 8, 15, 16, 17 and 22 July, none of which mentions the treasure.
26. Blegen (1950–8) I 208.
27. Gimbutas (1965) 226 dates the Borodino hoard (ibid. pl. 12), which contains similar, though plainer, axes, to 1500–1450 BC.
28. Letter to Virchow dated 12 August 1890; Herrmann and Maaß (1990) 557.
29. Letter to Virchow dated 27 September 1890; Herrmann and Maaß (1990) 563.
30. Letter to John Murray, 28 October 1890.
31. Letter to Sophia dated 23 September 1890; *Bw* II 381–2 (misdated 28 Sep.).
32. The weight of 75 kilos (165 lbs.) seems unreasonably high but is repeated again and again in the correspondence.
33. Letter to Sophia dated 25 September 1890; BBB 43 23.
34. Letter to Sophia dated 25 October 1890; BBB 43 64.
35. Letter to Virchow dated 15 November 1890; Herrmann and Maaß (1990) 568–9.
36. Ibid.
37. Herrmann and Maaß (1990) 570–1. Schliemann owned a copy of Burton's translation and shortly before Burton's death (in October 1890) had written to ask him what edition of the Arabic text he had used because he wanted to compare the English with the Arabic. On learning that Burton had used MacNaghton's edition Schliemann had ordered it from Brockhaus. He received it during his stay in Halle.
38. Hesiod, *Works and Days* 171; cf. Homer's Elysium at *Od.* 561–4.
39. *Bw* II 385.
40. Letter to Sophia dated 30 November 1890; Sophia Schliemann Archive.

41. Some of these details come from the notes of Professor Jacobi of the Department of Otolaryngology at the University of Halle, who saw the medical record of Schliemann's operation before it was lost. A letter containing his recollection of the record is included in McGovern (1977) 1729–30. Jacobi believed that there had been a cholesteatoma.
42. Meyer (1969) 383.
43. Herrmann and Maaß (1990) 571.
44. Cf. Virchow (1891) 66 and McGovern (1977) 1729–30. Virchow may simply have assumed that Schliemann would not have left the clinic without the doctor's approval. On the other hand, Schliemann may have told him that Schwartze had allowed him to leave.
45. BBB 43 137; a few words are illegible.
46. Virchow (1891) 66.
47. Letter to Sophia quoted in Ludwig (1931) 326–27.
48. Letter to Virchow date 17 December 1890; Herrmann and Maaß (1990) 573.
49. *ZfE* 23 (1891) 21–2. Virchow has Schliemann visiting the Zoological Station on the 25th but since this seems to be contradicted by the following account of the 25th and the fact that Schliemann collapsed on the 25th about midday, I have assumed a misprint. Other sources say Schliemann collapsed at Piazza della Carità, which is half-way along Via Toledo (also known as Via Roma) between the Palazzo Reale and the National Museum, or on a side-street just off Via Toledo.
50. Most of the following details are taken from the report in *Neustrelitzer Zeitung* no. 201 as reprinted in Stoll (1953) 304.
51. Meyer (1969) 385.
52. This preference goes back at least to 1843. The long letter to his sisters of 20 February 1843 is signed 'Henry Schliemann' (in full). Throughout his life Schliemann habitually signed his letters 'Hy Schliemann'.

CHAPTER 18: THE SCHLIEMANN LEGACY

1. *Bw* I 124.
2. I am grateful to my friend G. Korres, for kindly providing me with a copy of the will. Extracts from the will were published by Lilly (1961) 69–71. A good summary is to be found in *The Times* (9 Jan 1891) 3.
3. Witte (1990) 136. Approximately £45 million today.
4. To the 50,000 francs he gave each of them in paragraphs 2 and 3 of the will, he added another 50,000 francs each in paragraph 42.
5. One of the codicils specified that the 'splendid female head in marble' (the 'Cleopatra' bust) should also go to the Ethnological Museum in Berlin.
6. The bequest to Sayce was revoked in the codicil dated 20 January 1889. Sayce reports that this was at his own request; Sayce (1923) 276.
7. Schliemann's will, paragraph 37.
8. For most of the details in the description of the tomb I am indebted to the excellent articles of Korres (1981) and (1984).
9. There are, however, direct descendants of Nadeshda, the daughter of Schliemann and Katerina, living in Paris and the Czech Republic.
10. The couplet contains two metrical irregularities; see Arnott (1978) 93.
11. His fluency in French, English, Russian, Italian, Spanish, ancient and modern Greek is obvious from his frequent use of these languages in his correspondence and diaries. There are occasional letters in Dutch. There are extensive diary entries in Arabic. His use of the other languages was very rare, but I do not doubt his competence in them.
12. *Bw* I 121.
13. *Deutsche Revue* 16.4 (Oct–Dec 1891) 59.

14. Probably he learned the elements of book-keeping from Hückstaedt too. This would explain why he was able to complete the course in Rostock so quickly.
15. Since there is little sign of these qualities in his 1835 school report card, it is reasonable to attribute them to Hückstaedt's influence.
16. See Schliemann's diary entries in Lilly (1961) 14–20. He finally had to settle for a male servant.
17. In his standard reference work on human behaviour Goldenson (1970) 710 makes the following observation on pathological lying: 'Among adults (and occasionally adolescents), the proverbial "pathological liar" is usually classed as an antisocial, or psychopathic, personality. This category includes individuals characterized by extreme egocentrism, irresponsibility, impulsiveness, absence of moral standards, and inability to form deep emotional attachments. Typically, they are opportunists, 'conmen', impostors – and typically also, they are consummate and convincing liars . . .' I have argued at length elsewhere that Schliemann's character was tinged with psychopathy; see *MS&H* 62–80=*ES* 113–25. The fuller picture that we now have of his early background and of his father's behaviour in particular tends to confirm this analysis. Schliemann was not, however, a 'full-blown psychopath'. This is shown partly by his responsible behaviour over many years to his family, as evidenced by the regular gifts of money, and partly by his success. The classic psychopath almost never works consistently towards a long-term goal.
18. This has been disproved just as thoroughly by the work of Easton and Korres, generally thought of as supporters of Schliemann, as by my own studies.

Bibliography

Amandry, Pierre, 'Fouilles de Delphes et Raisins de Corinthe' *La redécouverte de Delphes*, ed., Ecole française d'Athènes, Paris, 1992

Arndt, K., 'Schliemann's Excavation of Troy and American Politics' *Yearbook of German-American Studies* 16, 1–8, 1981

Arnott, W.G., 'Schliemann's Epitaph' *Liverpool Classical Monthly* 3, 93, 1978

Bernal, Martin, *Black Athena*, New Brunswick, 1987 (vol. I) and 1991 (vol. II)

Blegen, Carl, *Troy: Excavations Conducted by the University of Cincinnati, 1932–38*, 4 vols, Princeton, 1950–8

——*Troy and the Trojans*, Cambridge, 1964

Bölke, Wilfried, *Heinrich Schliemann und Ankershagen: Heimat, Kindheit und Elternhaus* =*MittAnkershagen* 2, 1988

——and Crepon, *see* Crepon

Boorstin, Daniel J., *The Great Explorers*, New York, 1985

Borlase, William C., 'A Visit to Dr. Schliemann's Troy', *Fraser's Magazine*, N.S. 17 (February 1878), 228–39, 1878

Breccia, E., *Alexandrea ad Aegyptum*, Bergamo, 1914

Budge, E.A. Wallis, *By Nile and Tigris*, 2 vols, London, 1920

Buenzod, J. (ed.), Arthur de Gobineau, *Lettres d'un voyage en Russie, en Asie Mineur et en Grèce. Etudes de lettres*, Ser. 2. Vol. 4, 1961

Bülow, Bernhard von, *Denkwürdigkeiten*, IV, Berlin, 1931

Burton, Isabel, *The Life of Captain Sir Richard F. Burton*, (2 vols) London, 1893

Calder, William M. III, 'Schliemann on Schliemann: A Study in the Use of Sources' *GRBS* 13, 335–53, 1972

——'Apocolocyntosis: the Biographers and the Archaeologists' *HS+100*, 360–78, 1990

—— 'The unpublished American Diaries of Heinrich Schliemann' *HSGrundlagen*, 15–21, 1992

Calvert, Frank, 'Excavations in the Troad' *The Levant Herald*, 4 February, 1873

——'Mr. Calvert and Dr. Schliemann on Troy', *The Guardian*, 11 August (1024) 1875

Carvalho, Elizabeth, 'Schliemann in Asia 1864/65' *HSGrundlagen* 29–35, 1992

Coldstream, J.N. and Huxley, G.L., (ed.) *Kythera*, Park Ridge, NJ, 1973

Cook, J.M., *The Troad*, Oxford, 1973

Crepon, Tom and Wilfried Bölke, *Heinrich Schliemann: Odyssee seines Lebens*, Berlin, 1990

Daniel, Glyn, *Towards a History of Archaeology*, London, 1981

Deuel, Leo, *Memoirs of Heinrich Schliemann*, New York, 1977

Dickinson, O.T.P.K., 'Schliemann and the Shaft Graves' *Greece and Rome* 23, 159–68, 1976

——*The Origins of Mycenaean Civilization*, Göteborg, 1977

Döhl, Hartmut, *Heinrich Schliemann: Mythos and Ärgernis*, Munich, 1981

Easton, Donald, 'The Schliemann Papers' *BSA* 77, 93–110, 1982

——review of Döhl, *Heinrich Schliemann* in *CR* 33, 286–7, 1983

——'Priam's Treasure' *Anatolian Studies* 34, 141–69, 1984a

——'Schliemann's mendacity – a false trail?' *Antiquity* 58, 197–204, 1984b

——'Reconstructing Schliemann's Troy' *HS+100* 431–47, 1990

Bibliography

——'Was Schliemann a Liar?' *HSGrundlagen* 191–98, 1992
Eckenbrecher, Gustav von, 'Über die Lage des homerischen Ilion', *RhM* New Series 2, 1–49, 1843
Fagan, Brian, *The Rape of the Nile*, Wakefield, R.I., 1992
Fitton, Lesley, *Heinrich Schliemann and the British Museum*, London, 1991
Flickinger, Roy C., 'Sayce and Schliemann.' *CJ* 27, 23–5, 1931–2
Furumark, Arne, *Mycenaean Pottery*, Vol. I, Stockholm, 1941
Gardner, Percy, 'Henry Schliemann', *Macmillan's Magazine*, April 1891 (No. 3781), 474–80
——*Autobiographica*, Oxford, 1933
Gavrilow, Alexander, 'Schliemann und Russland', *HS+100*, 379–96, 1990
Gay, Peter, *Freud: A Life for our Time*, New York/London, 1988
Gimbutas, Marija, *Bronze Age Cultures in Central and Eastern Europe*, The Hague, 1965
Goessler, Peter, *Wilhelm Dörpfeld: ein Leben im Dienst der Antike*, Stuttgart, 1951
Goldenson, Robert M., *The Encyclopedia of Human Behavior*, Garden City, N.Y., 1970
Graziadio, Giampaolo, 'The Chronology of the Graves of Circle B at Mycenae: A New Hypothesis,' *AJA* 92, 343–72, 1988
Gregor-Dellin, Martin and Dietrich Mack, *Cosima Wagner's Diaries*, I, New York, 1978
Grote, George, *A History of Greece*, London, 1846
Hahn, J.G. von, *Die Ausgrabungen auf der homerischen Pergamos*, Leipzig, 1865
Hermann, J. and Evelin Maaß, *Die Korrespondenz zwischen Heinrich Schliemann und Rudolf Virchow*, Berlin, 1990
Higgins, Reginald, *Minoan and Mycenean Art*, London, 1981
Holden, Beatrice M., *The Metopes of the Temple of Athena at Ilion*, Northampton, Mass., 1964
Hood, Sinclair, *The Arts in Prehistoric Greece*, London, 1978
——'Schliemann and Crete' *Grundlagen* 223–9, 1992
Hooker, J.T., review of *MS&H* in *JHS* 108, 258–9, 1988
Hope Simpson, Richard, *Mycenaean Greece*, Park Ridge, NJ, 1981
Hughes-Hallett, Lucy, *Cleopatra: Histories, Dreams and Distortions*, New York, 1990
Jebb, R.C., review of Schliemann's *Ilios*, *Edinburgh Review* 153, (April 1881) 514–47
Jenkins, Romilly, *The Dilessi Murders*, London, 1961
Karo, Georg, *Die Schachtgräber von Mykenai*, 2 vols, Munich, 1930–33
Kastorches, E., *Historike Ekthesis ton Praxon tes en Athenais Archaiologikes Hetairias*, Athens, 1879
Keyser, Paul, 'The Composition of "La Chine et Le Japon": An Introduction to Tendentious Editing' *HS+100* 225–36, 1990
Kopcke, G., 'Zum Styl der Schachtgräbermasken' *AM* 91 3, 1976
Korfmann, Manfred, 'Die Forschungsplanung von Heinrich Schliemann in Hisarlik-Troja und die Rolle Wilhelm Dörpfelds' *Studia Troica*, 3 247–64, 1993
Korres, G.S., *Bibliographia Herrikou Sleman*, Athens, 1974
——'Epigraphai ex Attikes eis Katochen Herrikou Sleman' *Athena* 75 54–67 and 492 (French résumé), 1975
——'Das Mausoleum Heinrich Schliemanns auf dem Zentralfriedhof von Athen' *Boreas* 4, 133–73, 1981
——'Neues zum Mausoleum Heinrich Schliemanns in Athen' *Boreas* 7, 317–25, 1984
——'Heinrich Schliemann auf den Spuren Nestors und die heutige Forschung in Messenien' *HSGrundlagen* 231–2, 1992
Krauss, Rolf, 'Schliemanns "altester Quecksiberfund" und seine Sammlung ägyptischer Altertümer' *Jahrbuch Preußischer Kulturbesitz* 22 171–83, 1985
Lascarides, A.C., *The Search for Troy, 1553–1874*, Bloomington, Indiana, 1977
Lehrer, Mark and Turner, David, 'The Making of an Homeric Archaeologist: Schliemann's Diary of 1868' *BSA* 84, 221–68, 1989
Lilly, Eli (ed.), *Schliemann in Indianapolis*, Indianapolis, 1961
Ludwig, Emil, *Schliemann of Troy: the Story of a Goldseeker*, London, 1931

Bibliography

Maclaren, Charles, *A Dissertation on the Topography of the Plain of Troy*, Edinburgh, 1822
——*The Plain of Troy Described*, Edinburgh, 1863
Marinatos, S., *Kleidung- Haar- und Barttracht. Archaeologia Homerica*, I B. Göttingen, 1967
McDonald, William A., *Progress into the Past*. N.Y., 1967
——review of *MS&H* in *Religious Studies* 13, 258–9, 1987
——and Carol G. Thomas, *Progress into the Past*, Bloomington, Ind., 1990
McGovern, Francis H., 'The Operation and Death of Henry Schliemann' *The Laryngoscope* 87, 1726–30, 1977
Mellink, M., 'Archaeology in Asia Minor' *AJA* 86, 557–76, 1982
——'Archaeology In Anatolia' *AJA* 89, 1985
Meyer, Ernst, 'Schliemann's Letters to Max Müller in Oxford', *Journal of Hellenic Studies* 82, 75–105, 1962
——'Schliemann's erste Briefe aus Troja.' *Ruperto-Carola* 17 77–80, 1965
——*Heinrich Schliemann: Kaufmann und Forscher*, Göttingen, 1969
Michaelis, Adolf, *A Century of Archaeological Discoveries*, London, 1908
Milchhöfer, Arthur, 'Erinnerungen an Heinrich Schliemann' *Deutsche Rundschau* 17 278–89, 1891
Murray, A.S., review of *Mycenae*, *Academy* (15 December), 558–60, 1877
Murray, John, (Publisher) *Handbook for Travellers in Greece*, London 1854
——*Handbook for Travellers in Egypt*, 1875
Mylonas, George E., *Mycenae and the Mycenaean Age*, Princeton, 1966
——*Mycenae Rich in Gold*, Athens, 1983
Newton, C.T. review of *Mycenae*, *Edinburgh Review*, January, 220–56, 1878
——*Essays on Art and Archaeology*, London, 1880
Owgam, Henry, *Miscellanea Homerica*, Dublin, 1843
Persson, Axel W., *New Tombs at Dendra Near Midea*, Lund, 1942
Petrakos, B., He en Athenais Archaiologike Hetaireia: He Historia ton 150 Chronon tes 1837–1987, Athens, 1987
Petrie, W.M. Flinders, *Seventy Years in Archaeology*, New York, 1932
Phlios, Demetrios, *Duo lexeis peri pos graphontai ta ton anaskaphon en to Archaiologiko Deltio*, Athens, 1890
Radowitz, J.M. von, *Aufzeichnungen und Erinnerungen aus dem Leben des Botschafters Joseph Maria von Radowitz*, ed. Hajo Holborn, Vols. 1–2=*Deutsche Geschichtsquellen des 19. Jahr hunderts*, Vols. 15–16, 1925
Rapp, George, Jr. and Gifford, John A., *Troy: The Archaeological Geology*, Princeton, 1982
Renfrew, Colin, *Before Civilization*, Harmondsworth, 1976
Richter, Wolfgang, '*Ithaque, le Péloponnèse et Troie* und das Promotionsverfahren Heinrich Schliemanns' *Ethnographisch-Archäologisches Zeitschrift* 21 667–78, 1980
Sayce, A.H. 'The Art of Prehistoric Greece' *Academy* (2 March), 195–7, 1878
——*Reminiscences*, London, 1923
Schindler, W., 'Heinrich Schliemann: Leben und Werk im Spiegel der neuen biographischen Forschungen', *Philologus* 120, 271–89, 1976
——'Schliemann's Cleopatra', *MS&H* 81–94, 1986
Schliemann, H., 'Exploration of the Boeotian Orchomenus', *JHS* 2, 122–163, 1881
Schmidt, Hubert, *Heinrich Schliemann's Sammlung trojanischer Altertümer*, Berlin, 1902
Schuchhardt, C., *Schliemann's Excavations: An Archaeological and Historical Study*, London, 1891
——*Aus Leben und Arbeit*, Berlin, 1944
Scott, John A., 'Ludwig and Schliemann' *CJ* 27 15–22, 1931
Stamatakis, P., 'The Clearing of the Tomb near the Heraeum' (in Greek), *AM* 3, 270–86, 1878
Stillman, W.J., 'Extracts of Letters of W.J. Stillman Respecting Ancient Sites in Crete', *Archaeological Institute of America, Annual Report* 41–49, 1881
Stoll, H.A. *Abenteuer meines Lebens: Heinrich Schliemann erzählt*, Leipzig, 1953 (rep. 1982)

Toynbee, J.M.C., *Roman Historical Portraits*, London, 1978

Traill, David A., 'Schliemann's Mendacity: Fire and Fever in California' *CJ* 74, 348–55(=*ES* 41–9), 1979

——'Schliemann's American Citizenship and Divorce', *CJ* 77, 336–42(=*ES* 65–71), 1982

——'Further Evidence of Fraudulent Reporting in Schliemann's Archaeological Works' *Boreas* 7 295–316(=*ES* 73–95), 1984a

——'Schliemann's Discovery of "Priam's Treasure": A Re-examination of the Evidence' *JHS* 104 96–115(=*ES* 127–53), 1984b

——'Schliemann's Dream of Troy: The Making of a Legend' *CJ* 81 13–24(=*ES* 29=40), 1985

——'Schliemann's Mendacity: A Question of Methodology' *Anatolian Studies* 36 91–98(=*ES* 183–92), 1986

——'Hisarlik, 31 May, 1873, and the Discovery of "Priam's Treasure" *Boreas* 11 227–34(=*ES* 155–66), 1988a

——'How Schliemann Smuggled "Priam's Treasure" from the Troad to Athens' *Hesperia* 57 273–77(=*ES* 167–72), 1988b

——'The Archaeological Career of Sophia Schliemann' *Antichthon* 23 99–107=(*ES* 235–43), 1989

——'Schliemann and his Academic Employees' *HS+100*, 237–55(=*ES* 215–34), 1990

——'Schliemann's Visit to Yosemite Valley and the Big Trees in 1865' *Das Altertum* (in German) 36, 209–16(=*ES* (in English) 51–9), 1990b

——'Schliemann on Dickens' *CW* 85, 105–106(=*ES* 61–3), 1991

——'"Priam's Treasure": Further Problems' *HSGrundlagen* 183–9(=*ES* 199–203), 1992

——*Excavating Schliemann*, Atlanta, 1993

Turner, David, 'Heinrich Schliemann: The man behind the masks' *Archaeology* 43, no. 6 (Nov–Dec) 36–42, 1990

Tusa, V., 'Introduzione' *Mozia* I, Rome, 1964

Vaio, John, 'Gladstone and the Early Reception of Schliemann in England' *HS+100*, 237–55, 1990

Vermeule, Emily, *Greece in the Bronze Age*, Chicago, 1964

——*The Art of the Shaft Graves*, Norman, Oklahoma, 1975

Virchow, Rudolf, 'Erinnerungen an Schliemann' *Gartenlaube* 39: 66–8 (pt. 1), 104–106 (pt. 2), 299–303 (pt. 3), 1891

Wace, A.J.B., *Mycenae*, Princeton, 1949

——and Stubbings, F., *A Companion to Homer*, London, 1962

Weber, Shirley H., *Schliemann's First Visit to America 1850–51*, Cambridge, Mass., 1942

Witte, Reinhard, 'Schliemann und Berlin' *Das Altertum* 36, 133–43, 1990

Index

Virchow, Rudolf, 191–2, 207–8, 241–4, 261–2, 264, 279, 289, 291, 293, 297, 303; HS meets, 137; HS writes to, 166, 187 and *passim*; HS plans to excavate with, 186, 215, 227–8, 234, 236, 274; in Troad, 187–90; and geology, 189–92; and flora, 188, 196; and governess for Schliemanns, 191; and medals, 192, 210, 225, 289; and Trojan collection, 193, 195, 201, 206, 209–10, 226; as medical consultant for Schliemanns, 194, 201–2, 224, 234, 265, 285–6, 290, 293; frictions with HS, 194, 201, 246–8, 256–7, 262–3; assists HS editorially, 197–8; and bones, 219–20, 227, 291–2; Nile trip with HS, 262–3, 268–70; and Hisarlik Conference, 282–4; on last days of HS, 296–7
Vitalis, Emilio, 225
Voss, J. H., 138

Wadi Halfa, 256–7, 260, 264, 268–9
Waldstein, Charles, 284–5
Wallis, Henry, 259
Waren, 15

Washington, D.C., 9, 24, 33
Webster, Daniel, US Secretary of State, 10
Wiesbaden, 265
Wolff, I., 230
Worcester, Massachusetts, 191
World War II, 273, 300–1
Würzburg, 29

Xerxes, 227

Yannakis, Nikolaos Zaphyros, 178, 284; as paymaster and major-domo, 89, 92, 218; and Priam's Treasure, 116–19, 121, 178–9, 289, 305; death of, 233
Yenishehir, 54, 233
Yokohama, 30
York, 82
Yosemite Valley, 1

Zeitünlü, 286
Zeus, 214, 221
Ziller, Ernst, 47–8, 211, 265, 299, 304
Zurich, 136